STONES TELL STORIES AT OSU

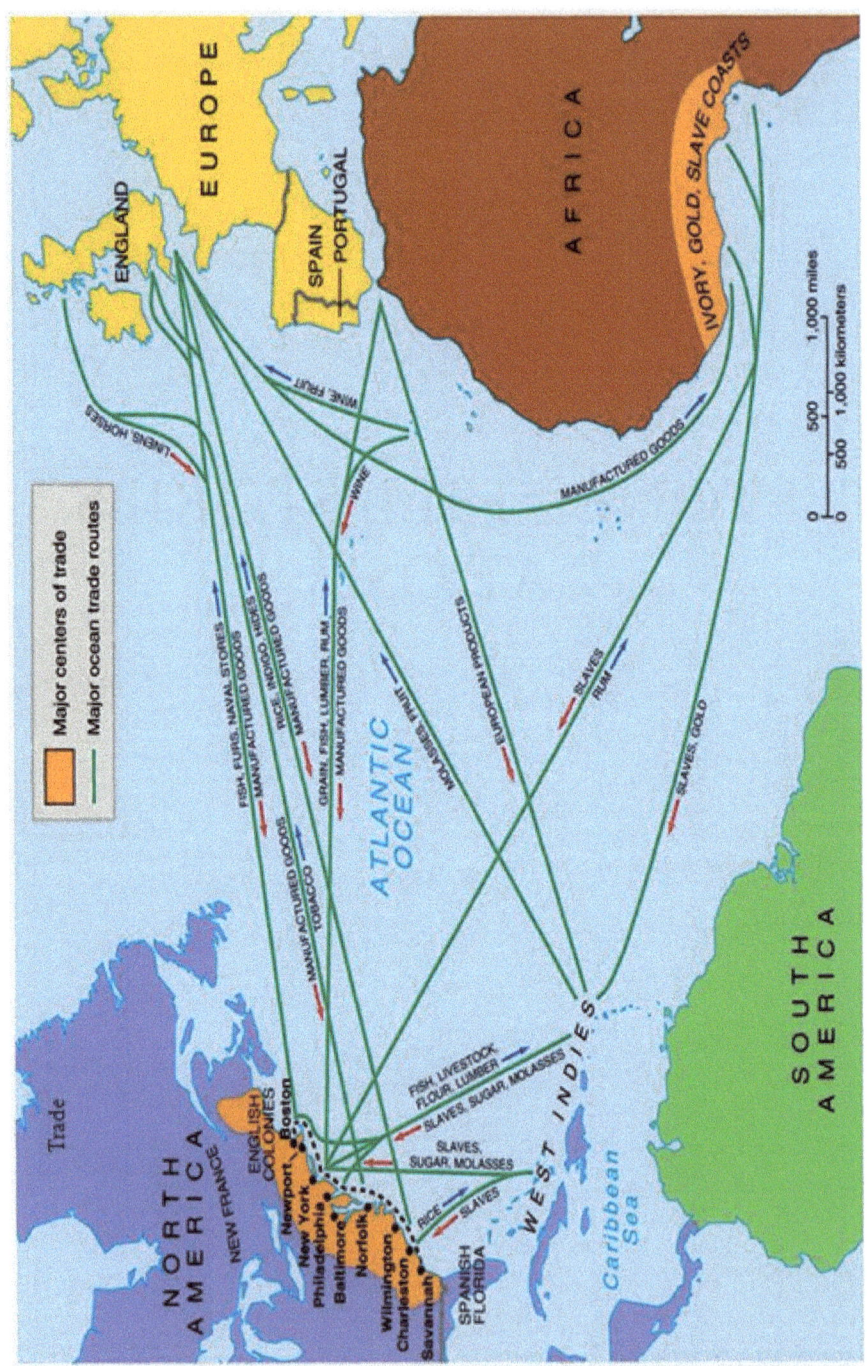

Figure 1: A map of the Transatlantic Slave Trade
© http://slideplayer.com/slide/9859866/

Praise for *Stones Tell Stories at Osu*

"This book gives us an entirely new insight into the history and memory of the people in Osu. There have been studies written and read for years, with scholarly, academic base. Here, now, is the firelight tale, told by a son of the soil who has grown up and lived in the milieu. His love of, and respect for the past of his people, as they remember it, pulsates through the text – drawing the reader in to join them. A truly singular and fine experience."
— Selena Axelrod Winsnes, Raelingen, Norway

"It would have been nearly impossible for Nii-Adziri Wellington to have captured the one time colonial community in its entire historical feel and form as he does in this book were it not for the fact that he has his roots there. Certainly, the culture and the spiritual contents of Osu, this mixed community of settlers, the indigenous and the European, have been brought together in a nice package of a story called *Stones Tell Stories at Osu*. And Ataa Forkoyi, the surrogate storyteller and a likable character of apparent good repute, will not be forgotten, even long after the reading is done."
— E. Ablorh-Odjidja
Executive Director, Emerging Media Institute

"Henry Nii-Adziri Wellington's book, *Stones Tell Stories at Osu: Memories of a Host Community of the Danish Trans-Atlantic Slave Trade,* a multipart biography of the slave trade at the Osu Coast, captures the kaleidoscopic notoriety and footprint on the landscape and culture of Osu. A professor of architecture and heritage studies (University of Ghana), Wellington succeeds in telling the story with "the rounded texture of the architect." His creative nonfiction narrative is rooted in the perspective of writing for the contemporary average African, who through no fault of his or hers has embraced institutional forgetfulness when it comes to the slave trade."
— Flora Trebi-Ollennu
Author of *Unquenchable Fire Unequivocal Call*

"Wellington's peculiar literary approach intriguingly wrestles the telling of history away from its conventional academic forms, making the life of Osu a vivacious one. In addition, the volume courageously confronts the grim slavery years, defying the Danes' tendency to gloss over their unseemly participation, and the habits of the Ghanaian people to avoid speaking of that era entirely: 'Adopting a position of honest confrontation of the horrors of the past will make the lessons to be learnt from this dark period in our common history authentic and proactive.' A refreshingly unconventional and bold account of a culturally complex place in Africa."
— *Kirkus Reviews*

"*Stones Tell Stories at Osu* is both uncommon and essential. The book is uncommon because it is both scholarly and readily accessible to non-specialists. The book is essential because it deals with a history that is thoroughly consequential to a geographical area of Ghana, to Denmark and, indeed, to the world. Having moved out of my African birthplace to live in North America about forty years ago, I see this book as a great tool in grounding both myself and my North American-born progeny in my African heritage."
— Efa E. Etoroma, PhD
Concordia University of Edmonton, Canada

H. Nii-Adziri Wellington

Stones Tell Stories at Osu
Memories of a Host Community of the Danish Trans-Atlantic Slave Trade

Foreword by
Philip Laryea

Second Edition

AMERLEY TREB BOOKS CANADA

Copyright©2017 by H. Nii-Adziri Wellington
All rights reserved
Distributed in US and Canada by Bookmasters Inc. (Atlas)

This second edition published by Amerley Treb Books 2017
First published in hardcover by Amerley Treb Books 2017
P. O. Box 3009, Beaumont, AB, T4X 1K8, CANADA

First published in 2011 by Sub-Sahara Publishers, Ghana

No part of this book may be reproduced or utilized in any form or by any means, electronic or mechanical, including photocopying and recording, or by any information storage and retrieval system, without permission in writing from the publisher.

Library and Archives Canada Cataloguing in Publication

Wellington, H. Nii-Adziri, author
Stones tell stories at Osu : memories of a host community of the Danish trans-Atlantic slave trade / H. Nii-Adziri Wellington ; foreword by Philip Laryea. -- Second edition.
Includes bibliographical references and index.
Issued in print and electronic formats.
ISBN 978-1-894718-15-8 (hardcover).--ISBN 978-1-894718-14-1 (softcover).--ISBN 978-1-894718-16-5 (ebook)
1. Osu (Accra, Ghana)--History. 2. Osu (Accra, Ghana)--Genealogy.
3. Gã (African people)--Ghana--Accra--History. 4. Slave trade--Ghana--Accra--History. 5. Ghana--History--Danish settlements, 1659-1850.
6. Denmark--Colonies--Africa--History. I. Laryea, Philip T., writer of foreword II. Title.
DT512.9.A3W45 2017   966.7'01   C2017-905606-9   C2017-9056077

Printed and bound in China
Book Cover Design by John Deheer-Adjaye
Cover concept by H. Nii-Adziri Wellington

This book has been published with the help of a grant from Queen Margrethe II & Prince Henrik Fund

Dronning Margrethes og Prins Henriks Fond

This book is dedicated to the memory of four individuals who occupied an important place in my heart and mind: my parents, Archibald Mensah Wellington and MaryAnne Ohenewa Opoku, who provided a loving and a caring environment and a wonderful childhood; next the late Reverend Constant Kwaku Sackey who touched my life deeply by showing a genuine interest in me when I was in elementary school; fourth is the late Vice Chancellor of the Kwame Nkrumah University of Science and Technology, Professor Kwesi Andam, who inspired me greatly and helped me discover the challenge of writing this book.

"….Let the winds breeze through and renew
the gossips of yesterday –
The stones will stand the test of truth!"

Philip B. D. Oyinka, *Lazy Breezes*, 2010

Contents

Dedication		vii
List of Figures		xi
Foreword		xv
Preface		xxi
Introduction		xxix
One	Long Time Ago at Osu	1
	Osu Kadigbɔi	3
	Osu-Doku Becomes Kinkawe and Ashinte	17
	'Allada' Becomes 'Alata' at Osu	23
	Osu Anahor	26
Two	The Making of Danish Osu	31
	Portuguese Lingua Franca at Osu	33
	Coming of Christiansborg to Osu	37
	Tarnishing of Osu with Danish Markings	42
	In the Shadow of Christiansborg	53
Three	Danish-Osu in Paths of Pain and Poise	65
	High Tide at Danish-Osu	67
	Turbulence, Turmoil and Travails at High Tide	81
	Low Tide at Danish-Osu	97
	The Emergence of a Cosmopolitan Community	99
Four	Danish-Osu Sprouting Seedlings	115
	Between the High and Low Tides	117

	Witt, a Danish-Osu Ancestor with a Withered Presence	122
	Svane, Obliterated Danish-Osu Ancestor	124
	Protten, an Elusive Danish-Osu Ancestor	134
Five	Blossoming of Danish-Osu Family Trees	173
	Beginnings	175
	Early Graftings	180
	Latter-Day Graftings	205
Six	Sung and Unsung Heroes of Danish-Osu	219
	Assembling for a Durbar	221
	Durbar to Celebrate the Sung Heroes	227
	The Unsung Heroes	250
Seven	Sites of Significance at Danish-Osu	255
	Discovering an Out-Of-Sight Architectural Heritage	257
	Stories of the Stones in Construction	258
	Stone House with a Living Memory	259
	More Than an Alma Mater	272
	A Monument and an Alma Mater	282
	An Incredible Community History	283

Epilogue	287
Acknowledgments	292
Appendix I	296
Appendix II	298
Appendix III	300
Notes and Bibliography	308
Index	313

List of Figures

Figure 1	A map of the transatlantic slave trade	ii
Figure 2	Map of Africa delineating Ghana	xx
Figure 3	A map composed by the author to show the extent of the geographical space of Danish-Osu as seen today	xxxii
Figure 4	Archival photograph of the Danish Slave-Ship "Fredensborg" loading slaves in the road of Christiansborg, 1768.	13
Figure 5	Showing the old cistern cover built by C. G. Engmann	15
Figure 6	Christiansborg Castle, Osu	46
Figure 7	A scene at the Governor's Parlour with dark-skinned nude Osu women serving white-clad European men at table	49
Figure 8	European Forts on the Gold Coast.	64
Figure 9	Osu Slave Market	76
Figure 10	A photograph of one of the drums on display in the National Museum in Copenhagen, Denmark.	88
Figure 11	A picture of a drawing of the two prisoners as they spent their prison time in Christianshaven in Denmark	88
Figure 12	A family portrait of the unknown ancestor with his wife, Rebecca, and their three-year-old daughter Anna, who died in 1754 and was buried in the world-famous Moravian cemetery known as "Gottesacker" in Herrnhut, Germany.	143

Figure 13	Manuscript of a formal speech written by Protten in both the Gã language ('Acraisch') and in German (Tauscht as an old version of the word "Deustch") on the occasion of bidding farewell to the Moravian Missionary Johann Bech going to the Inuits (Eskimos) in Greenland (C. 1746)	144
Figure 14	A portrait of the unknown ancestor, Jacobus Christian "Africanus" Protten, AKA Teiko Sacki, Blofonyo Bi Drawn by the famous portrait Artist, J.V. Haidt of the Moravian Brethren ca. 1735	146
Figure 15	Manuscript of an attempted translation of the Lord's Prayer from German into the Gã language ('Acraisch' as written by Protten) by Protten c. 1754	148
Figure 16	A section of Gottesacker, the world famous cemetery of the Moravian Brethren in which Anna, the infant daughter of the Prottens and historic persons such as the Baron Nicholas Von Zinzendorf, the originator of the Moravian Brethren, were buried	148
Figure 17	Part of the ruins of the castle belonging to the grandmother of the baron, Nicholas Von Zinzendorf, located at Grosshennendorf, Germany. Protten and his wife were banished here from Herrnhut, 15 kilometers away, due to a bitter misunderstanding between Protten and his fellow brethren in c.1756.	149
Figure 18	An eighteenth century map of Central Europe with an indication of the route which Protten traversed by hitch-hiking from Gross Hennersdorf, Germany, to Copenhagen, Denmark (C.1756)	150
Figure 19	The world famous Moravian Archives-Archivum Unittis Fratrum, Herrnhut, Germany, where Christian Jakobus Protten's portraits, his diary and some of his over three hundred manuscripts written between 1746 and 1761, are kept.	150

Figure 20	Engmann Family Tree	186
Figure 21	Malm Family Tree	190
Figure 22	Portrait of H. H. Malm (MBE/OBE)	195
Figure 23	Briandt Family Tree	202
Figure 24	Richter Family Tree	208
Figure 25	A three-dimensional projection representing a reconstruction of Richter Fort at Osu Alata	212
Figure 26	A picture of the dilapidated bastion on the South-West of the Richter Fort	217
Figure 27	A wall in ruins at Briandt's house at Osu	218
Figure 28	Danish architectural conservator, Nik Hallestad looking at a disused canon in front of Osu Anahor Chief's House	218
Figure 29	A picture of two Danish-Osu warriors in their battle accoutrements with "Terkleh" hanging between their thighs	225
Figure 30	Computerized image of the ground floor plan of Nii-Okantey Shikatse We	262
Figure 31	Computerized image of the first floor plan of Nii Okantey Shikatse We	262
Figure 32	Picture of baroque-style stone cover for a water cistern in the courtyard of Nii Okantey Shikatse We	265
Figure 33	Picture of courtyard showing residential block on the north and slave holding longroom on the east of Nii Okantey Shikatse We	265

Figure 34	Computerized image of roof plan of Nii Okantey Shikatse We	267
Figure 35	Computerized image of east and west elevations of Nii Okantey Shikatse We	267
Figure 36	Computerized image of north and south elevations of Nii Okantey Shikatse We	268
Figure 37	Picture of the masonry wall on the north side of the Nii Okantey Shikatse We	270
Figure 38	Picture of Osu Salem with Old Boys of 1958 Year Group	271
Figure 39	Contemporary photograph of Osu Salem from the west, showing some students of the school	271
Figure 40	Architectural drawing of the ground floor plan of the school complex, showing the main block on the south, staff residential units on the east and west with another dormitory block on the north	278
Figure 41	Detailed drawing of first floor plan showing classrooms and the headmaster's office	279
Figure 42	Showing timber floor on timber-framed and adobe-infilled wall construction of Osu Salem building	279
Figure 43	Showing various details of timber-framed and adobe infilled wall construction of Osu Salem building	280
Figure 44	Ruins of the Danish Country House at Osu Kuku Hill	286
Figure 45	A wall of ruins at Osu Amangfong bombarded by the British in 1854	286
Figure 46	Historical Chart of the Gold Coast	326

Foreword

Foreword to the Second Edition

As stated in my foreword to the first edition of *Stones Tell Stories at Osu*, the attempt to write history in a new key is not unprecedented. Indeed, as the author acknowledges in the preface to the book, others, like Danish novelist Thorkild Hansen, have blazed a trail in their use of fact and fiction to write history in the most creative and imaginative of ways.

What is unique about *Stones Tell Stories at Osu* is the way in which the author employs the skills and tools of his profession as an architect, to vividly bring home to his readers, the forgotten history of Osu, and the Danish settlement in Ghana. What is also interesting and remarkable is how the author manages to weave contemporary settings into the fabric of the stories, against a background of some typical cultural features and landmarks that appear to be vanishing from Gã society, the ethnic community indigenous to this area.

These features made the original book become so popular that within a short period of its appearance, its readership, both within and outside Ghana, grew so extensively to necessitate a reprint. Thus this second edition.

The central features, around which the story is woven, are Danish architecture and ancestry: stones left over from monumental architectural structures, provide the metaphorical archival sources for the author. The protagonist, Ataa Forkoyi, is a mythical figure, a legendary scholar of Danish Osu history. He is used by the author as a tourist guide of sorts, a mouthpiece for the Stones.

The chapters in *Stones Tell Stories at Osu* are replete with fascinating narratives about spaces and places that were hitherto of little or no significance, but which are of utmost importance to the author, a professor of some standing in the field of architecture.

In this book he tells us of the origins of the people of Osu, centuries before their association with the Danes. Whereas place names such as Kinkawe, Ashinte Blohum, Klottey Lagoon and Salem are well known, others such as Awusai Atso, Tolon, Ogbaame Naa, Agblanshie, Agbadza Dzoohe and Blogodo, are hardly mentioned in official documents, and this makes the information the author has offered his readers, rich and refreshing.

Many who read this second edition not having read the original, will, for the first time, begin to associate the founding of Osu not only with the migrant Osu-Doku people but also with a certain royal hunter by the name of Kadi.

The history of Osu, however, is not only about the indigenous people who first settled there; it is also about their socio-cultural and economic integration and interaction with other people over centuries, particularly their neighbours from La, Gã-Mashie, Akwamu, and more importantly, their flirtations with the empire builders, the Portuguese, the Swedes and the Danes.

It is the powerful influence of these latter people in the unequal trade partnership they brokered with the indigenous inhabitants, that eventually transformed Osu into a place aptly described by the author as a "hub of the Danish transatlantic slave trade with all its attendant perpetuation of inhumanity and demonstration of the depravity of human behavior." Details of the deplorable conditions in which the slaves toiled and the horrors of the trade are well documented in Thorkild Hansen's trilogy, *Coast of Slaves, Ships of Slaves, Islands of Slaves*.

Hansen's *Coast of Slaves*, it must be mentioned, inspired the author to write *Stones Tell Stories at Osu* in the first place. The author, though working in a similar genre as Hansen, adds a further dimension of passion and literary aesthetics, employing Ataa Forkoyi's style of narration as an effective tool to this effect, and writing with a passionate style all his own.

But the tale of Danish-Osu is not only about pain, suffering, untold hardships and turmoil; the dark side of its history is sharply contrasted with the bright side, which tells the stories of noble Danish governors, merchants, traders and chaplains who lay the foundations for the arrival of the first evangelical missionary society, the Basel Mission in 1828, which, incidentally, "marked the painful beginning of the successful attempt to plant the Christian Church in Ghana."

With this new branding and the fact that by 1850 it had become an important colonial centre of the British administration in the

Gold Coast, Danish-Osu began to attract important people of high repute. Among those mentioned in the original work is Johannes Zimmerman, who is credited with the translation of the Bible into the Gã language. The author's account of Zimmerman's admirable work will hopefully draw the attention of scholars and missionary historians to that bit of missionary history, to the indigenous Danish-Osu who played an active part in the translation and who have yet to be acknowledged. This is important because, with the exception of Rev. C. C. Reindorf, himself, a student of Zimmerman, the rest is lost to us.

Fortunately, one individual, Frederick Noi Dowuona, is mentioned by the author as the first of "ten high profile achievers" among Danish-Osu citizens. Dowuona arrived with the first four Basel Missionaries in 1828 and contributed immensely, in his capacity as an interpreter, to the success of the initial stages of the Basel Mission enterprise on the Gold Coast. For reasons unknown to us, the name of this indigenous pioneer missionary hardly features in the history of the Presbyterian Church of Ghana. It is also not known that Noi Dowuona assisted Rasmus Rask in producing a grammar book in Gã, *Introduction to the Accra Language on the Coast of Guinea,* published in 1828.

I wonder whether Ghanaians in general and citizens of Danish-Osu in particular, have sufficiently acknowledged the contributions of the nine others mentioned by the author in his hall-of-fame list. This book offers us the opportunity to reflect on the lives of others who may have contributed to the history of Danish-Osu.

Stones Tell Stories at Osu in its second edition, is a must-read for everyone, especially those who love history and have a passion for the treasured heritage of Danish-Osu and those who missed the opportunity to acquire copies of the original book.

Rev. Professor Philip Laryea
Scholar & Research Fellow
Akrofi Christaller Institute
Akropong-Akwapim

Figure 2: Map of Africa delineating Ghana
Reproduced by Henry Boafo

Preface

Preface

The Story Behind the Book and its Second Edition

EVERY BOOK HAS A HISTORY AND EVERY AUTHOR HAS A STORY TO TELL of how the book came about.

As stated in the original version, *Stones Tell Stories at Osu* has its own history and it must be told in a way that lets readers appreciate and empathize with the soul and spirit, rather than just the letter, of this book. Just as the original had its history, its second edition has added to the original, as extensively described in this preface.

The 1005 copies of the original limited print run were sold out within eleven months of the launch of the book. Thereafter, virtually on a monthly basis, inquirers sent requests in vain and expressed deep disappointment that they were unable to obtain the book.

It was therefore necessary to consider a reprint. However, when a number of typographical errors were discovered in the published book, and new facts came to light pertinent to the improvement of some sections of the book, I eventually decided to consider publishing a second edition to the delight of an old and potentially new readers alike.

But both logistical and technical challenges confronting those preparing the manuscript for the second edition led to undue delays. These delays turned out to be blessings in disguise; for while preparation of the manuscript was dragging, Flora Trebi-Ollennu came on the scene.

Trebi-Ollennu is an accomplished writer and publisher of Ghanaian extraction who calls Canada home. Having read the original *Stones Tell Stories at Osu,* she undertook a critical review of the book and sent her article to a reputable American journal for consideration. The article was accepted and published. Amerley Treb Books, her publishing company, decided to undertake the second edition to make the book easily available to the North American market as well as globally. As the saying goes, the rest is history in this case, it is a history that complements the following history of the original edition.

The history of the original *Stones Tell Stories at Osu,* began with another book which I purchased in December 2004 from the University Bookshop in Kumasi (now Kingdom Bookshop), at the insistence of an academic colleague, Professor Dedei Tagoe-Darko, the then Acting Manager of the bookshop at Kwame Nkrumah University of Science and Technology.

Copies of the book had been delivered for sale at the bookshop, just before the Christmas vacation that year. The manager, who was getting them ready for the shelves when I walked in, thought it would be of interest to me. So she drew my attention to it and persuaded me to purchase a copy as a Christmas present to myself. I did so after browsing through a few pages. As it turned out, the book was about the people, places and past events in Osu, which happened to be my home-town.

The book, entitled *Coast of Slaves,* was written by a Dane, Thorkild Hansen. It told the story of how the transatlantic slave trade proceeded on the Guinea Coast, primarily in the Danish coastal settlement of what was known as "Orsu" in the seventeenth, eighteenth and nineteenth centuries.

Hansen's book, which I read without a break during my Christmas vacation in 2004, awakened an intense desire to know more about Osu so that I could also write a book about my home-town. *Coast of Slaves,* translated from the original Danish into English by Professor Kari Dako, was journalistic in nature but supported with archival data. The images conjured by the writer brought memories of childhood and of historic sites within the community, which had hitherto escaped my curiosity or simply been forgotten.

The inspiration I derived from reading *Coast of Slaves,* was so intense and profound that the title for the one I needed to write came to my mind before I had even finished the book: *Stones Tell Stories at Osu.* It was to be an in-depth account of the architectural history and genealogy of the people and families who occupied places and spaces in the traditional quarters of Osu, now identified as "Danish-Osu," due to the presence over more than two centuries, of old Danish architecture and ancestry.

Thus, in January 2005, I began immediately to research this book, to gather facts, take inventories and refresh my memories of people and my knowledge of places that are still connected to the

Danish past in Osu.

The research quickly transcended the narrow perspective of an Osu citizen and took on the broad dimensions of a heritage scholar. Although I worked with the passion and vested interest of an Osu citizen, I was forced by the material at hand to proceed with a high level of objectivity and with a strong focus on the architectural history of Danish-Osu.

Later, I also went into genealogical profiles associated with the houses and neighborhoods studied, since any task of architectural history at the domestic level is, in essence, about individuals and families, their activities and interactions with the micro-environment (home and community) as well as within the wider socio-cultural milieu (society). By the time I was through, a community history had emerged.

Of course, the great enthusiasm and sense of motivation I brought to the research could not alone constitute the necessary resources required to bring the project to fruition. There was the critical need to mobilize financial and logistical support. Despite the number of project proposals I submitted to various organizations for funding, the support obtained was minimal and inadequate to give the project the boost required.

In addition, there were a number of other limitations, not the least of which include my lack of knowledge of Portuguese, Danish and eighteenth century German. This linguistic handicap made it difficult for me to access extensive and relevant archival materials. A further problem was posed by the poor state of the Ghana National Archives, which frustrated any significant pursuit of nineteenth and 20th century documentation of Osu.

These challenges notwithstanding, I proceeded gingerly, not as a historian but as a heritage scholar with architectural expertise, to gather all the relevant and requisite data for writing *Stones Tell Stories at Osu*. Needless to say, I applied all the principles of historiography, that is, using primary and secondary sources to authenticate unearthed information, respecting chronological sequences, relying on archival sources and investigating oral traditions through interviews.

In the course of examining available writings on the early history of Osu and the Guinea Coast, I was introduced to the late indefatigable and resourceful Dr. (Hon) Selena Winsnes. When she found out about my research and my intentions to write about Danish-Osu, she graciously sent me three autographed copies of the books she herself had translated from the original Danish records of eighteenth and nineteenth century accounts on the same subject. Voracious reading of these books, together with enthusiastic readings of other sources indicated in her bibliography, convinced me to begin writing my own. Thus began the challenge of turning the dream of *Stones Tell Stories at Osu* into a book.

By the end of May 2007, some eighteen months after the major fieldwork had begun, I was able to gather enough information on the history of Danish-Osu to warrant putting together an organized body of research findings from the study that could be shared with others.

Fortuitously, the organizers of the PANAFEST/Emancipation/Joseph Project, who wanted to connect related activities at Osu with the celebration of Ghana's Golden Jubilee of National Independence, got wind of my project and subsequently invited me to mount an exhibition of the research findings. The exhibition took place at Osu to enable the citizenry to participate in the launching of the PANAFEST/Emancipation/Joseph Project.

The Exhibition thus became a precursor to the publication of the book. The overwhelming warm reception the public gave the exhibition generated the impetus I needed to complete my writing. Before the Exhibition closed, visitors, including people whose English language skills appeared weak, were requesting advance copies of this yet to be published book.

Presented at the Exhibition were 137 items, grouped into six thematic sections:

- Danish–Osu Environment as Transit Quarters and Gateway for the Danish transatlantic Slave Trade and as a Home for Local Domestic Slavery;
- Danish Presence, Danish Ancestry and Danish-Osu Family Trees;
- An Unknown Danish-Osu Ancestor;
- Danish-Osu People and Personalities;
- Danish-Osu Architecture and Places;
- Danish-Osu Literature.

Notwithstanding the academic content of the Exhibition, the items visually narrated the story of Danish-Osu to the satisfaction of all visitors. So, as the Exhibition had successfully revealed interest of laymen in these historic exhibits, I decided that this book, *Stones Tell Stories at Osu,* should in no way become an academic treatise, adding yet to the existing plethora of writings on the transatlantic slave trade that catered primarily to the interests of scholars and historians.

Rather, I wanted a book that told stories about the tangible and intangible cultural heritage of Osu; not only as the transit quarters of the enslaved people who passed through on their way to their doom or to the New World, but that of a unique cosmopolitan community marked by the presence of people of divergent origins and family histories. Today, after 400 years, these people are to be found in pockets in communities called Osu Kinkawe, Osu Ashinte Blohum, Osu Alata and Osu Anahor, communities that collectively constitute that famous and attractive place known as Osu, where every year, streams of visitors and tourists trudge down its Cantonments Street, to Oxford Street, to celebrate the world famous August Street Carnival.

I did not only want my book to be popular but I also hoped that it would give a good interpretation of heritage accounts that could be enjoyed by ordinary folk like the majority of the people of Osu, while also satisfying the needs of scholars conducting further research on the community or society that constituted Osu.

Hence, in this second edition, as in the original book, readers will encounter the legendary old man of Osu, known as Ataa Forkoyi, from whose point of view readers can draw authentic and insightful interpretations of a story that spanned 400 years of antiquity and took three years of research to uncover.

Ataa Forkoyi, the protagonist of the original *Stones Tell Stories*, will bring ease of understanding to the raw data of research findings on architectural history and genealogical profiles covering the period of 1607-2007 at Osu.

As Ataa Forkoyi proceeds, he will make the Stones of Osu talk about the past and provide relatively recent information on people, places and events of this historic community called Danish-Osu. And as William Shakespeare wrote in *As You Like It*, there are "Tongues in trees, books in the running brooks; Sermons in stones, and good in everything."

The Stones at Osu, through Ataa Forkoyi, may not have sermons to preach, but they have stories that carry messages and morals, the meanings of which will be readily understandable to all readers of this book. Ataa's narratives will encompass the history of the original Osu, around the 16th century, before it came under Danish-Norwegian administration and cultural influence; the beginnings of Danish Osu in the 17th century through the 200-year presence of the Danes, and thereafter to the time Ghana celebrated its 50th anniversary of independence. To link the historical narratives of

Ataa Forkoyi to the aftermath of the Transatlantic Slave Trade, the story of the Underground Railroad in North America appears in a dream form in the book. These narratives of Ataa Forkoyi constitute the body of *Stones Tell Stories at Osu*.

But who is this legendary old man, Ataa Forkoyi, you may wonder? The "Ataa" prefix to his name is a title usually given to acclaimed wise and knowledgeable old Gã men. The name itself was likely to have been "Ofori Ayi." With time and the colloquial usage of the prefix "Ataa," his proper name was eventually reduced to one word; the "O" dropped from "Ofori" and the "ri" somehow evolved into 'ko,' and eventually, Ataa Ofori Ayi became known as "Ataa Forkoyi," a transformation of colloquial Gã semantics.

In time, the children who saw Ataa Forkoyi walk up and down the neighborhood, sometimes over the wooden bridge to the Klottey Lagoon to perform his usual ablutions behind the mangroves, were fascinated by the poetic sound of his name. *"Ataa Forkoyi, enyiɛ atswa?"* we would say, not only to test the old man's ability to tell the time, but also to enjoy the roll of his name on the tongue, its rhyme and musicality in our ears.

Ataa Forkoyi's origins, his personality and place in the history of Osu will unfold as he fills the book with his narratives. Legend has it that this unique figure is actually the personification of an Osu ancestor called Christian Petersen Witt. Witt was a Danish-Osu mulatto, born in the mid 17th century. He was known to have a profound sense of local history and was admired by both indigenous Osu citizens and the Danes of Christiansborg. He lived to a ripe old age. As will soon be revealed, Ataa Forkoyi's knowledge of Osu lore will seem to be the mythical link to the real chronicle of Witt. Carefully, and presumably through the eyes of Witt, he will imbue the Stones at Osu with the sensibilities required to release their stories.

In order to make the several Gã words and phrases that appear in Ataa Forkoyi's narrations understandable, the reader is encouraged to refer to Appendix III for a translation. Furthermore, the reader will note that Ataa Forkoyi refers to the Danes-Norwegians at times because Norway was then an integral component of Denmark. Ataa Forkoyi uses the phrase "Danes-Norwegians" to remind his listeners of the historical link between the two countries.

H. Nii-Adziri Wellington

Introduction

Introduction

Ataa Forkoyi Unearths the Speaking Stones at Osu

THE SUN WAS ALMOST AT ITS ZENITH AND THE BREEZE WAS NEARLY AT a standstill, blowing neither from land to sea nor from sea to land.

It was warm and humid on the beach at the east side of the Osu Castle, a beach rather bare of coconut trees. So, where else could little ragamuffins such as these ten Osu boys, running around bare-chested in nothing other than their multi-coloured *"piotos,"* go to cool their sweaty bodies, but the brackish waters of the Klottey Lagoon that lay to the east of the same beach.

So, into the Klottey Lagoon we jumped one after the other, like little imps, to submerge ourselves in the cool, muddy, tilapia-teeming waters of the Lagoon.

"Hey, did you see him walking along there?" shouted one of the boys as we resurfaced from under the water.

"There goes Ataa Forkoyi!" A shout from one of the boys, as he pointed his wet fingers towards the east banks of the Lagoon, drawing our attention to the legendary old man of Osu.

Soon, our eyes caught the profile of this lanky, looming figure moving briskly towards his customary midday resting place where the egrets assembled, waiting with eagle eyes to snatch any tilapia that dared break from underneath the surface for a gulp of air.

We began chanting in unison, "Ataa Forkoyi, what is the time? Ataa Forkoyi, what time is it?"

Ataa Forkoyi was known to be a wise old fisherman who had lived in Osu for many years. Exactly how long, nobody really knew. Legend had it that Ataa Forkoyi, who was born in one of the quarters of Osu, knew virtually everything about Osu, past and present. He had seen many Europeans come and go: Portuguese, Swedes,

Danes or Norwegians, Germans, Brits, you name them, he had seen them all. His knowledge of Osu was not limited only to the people and the places. He had a profound knowledge of the complete environment, geography, flora and fauna as well as astronomy.

This was the reason children took delight in asking him the time of the day. If you asked Ataa Forkoyi the time, regardless of the hour, he would simply raise his head, look up at the position of the sun and give you the exact time to the hour, minute and second.

It is Ataa Forkoyi's detailed knowledge of Osu that commands us, as at the touch of a magic wand, to bring his persona to life as he leads us through Osu to hear the Stones tell their stories.

So, imagine Ataa Forkoyi leading an audience to the landing space on the beach; that same space located between the serpentine

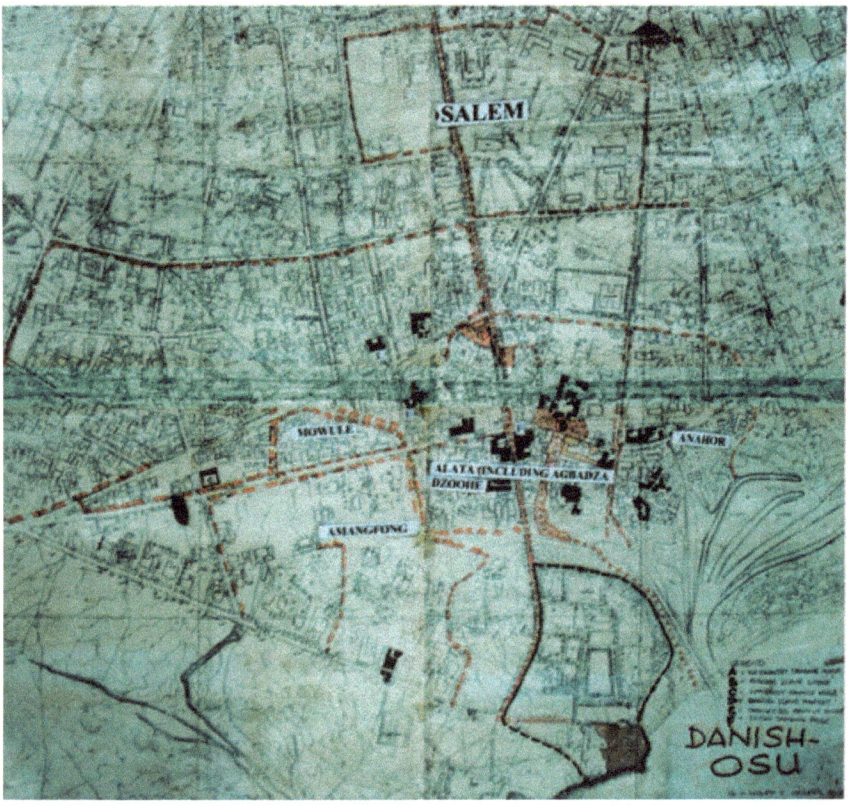

Figure 3: A map composed by the author to show the extent of the geographical space of Danish-Osu as seen today. *Illustration courtesy of author*

Klottey Lagoon on the east, and the high jutting rocky cliffs on the west, where the eastern rampart of Christiansborg castle appears to be precariously but firmly perched.

This is a truly historic and sacred place; a sandy beach on the shoreline of the sea-blue Atlantic Ocean with its boisterous, foamy, white waves. Ataa Forkoyi, with his back now to the sea, points outwards with his right hand, his index finger drawing a geographic outline in the air, and says in his sonorous voice, "There lies before you Osu, Danish-Osu, Ursue, and Wasu."

Then he continues with the confidence and certainty born of long practice and experience, saying:

"*Anyεmimεi*, I mean, brothers and sisters, you have on my right-hand side, beyond the lagoon, the sacred Klottey Lagoon, the Anahor quarters. This traditional residential enclave stretches eastwards and goes along the lagoon in the direction of La, where most of the Anahor people of Osu have relatives with similar names, and are congregated.

"Directly in front of you on the other side of Anahor, you see Osu Alata," continues Ataa Forkoyi as he points due north. "The boundaries of this traditional residential enclave are not distinct, as they flow in and out into sections of Osu Anahor. Within this traditional enclave, one finds sections with curious names such as *Awusai Atso, Tolon, Ogbaame Naa, Songme Naa, Agblanshie, Agbadza Dzoohe,* and *Blogodo.* In these places, you also see standing, a number of old and decrepit stone houses, sometimes referred to as slave-houses, built by Danes, mulattoes with Danish ancestry and Osu families who dealt directly with the Danes."

Somebody from the audience asks Ataa Forkoyi if these curious names have any significance. The person wants to know whether they had anything to do with the Portuguese, or the extensive transatlantic slave trade activities that took place at Osu in the seventeenth and eighteenth centuries. With the teacher's art of systematically presenting information to his pupils, Ataa Forkoyi nods his head and says, "Yes, but I shall explain later." With that, he points his left hand towards the monumental white-washed edifice, located directly on the beach to the west, looking like a sea monster emerging from beneath the waves.

"This is Christiansborg, also known as 'Osu Castle' and in the local parlance, *Karselieh*."

Beyond the Castle, on the west, is the open, undulating ground that appears to be bare. On the contrary, the ground is not bare at all. It is full of Stones that have stories to tell about places such as

Provesten, Touchstone and Amaganaa, and events that lie hidden in history books, and people who lie buried in its grounds. But before the stories come up, Ataa Forkoyi takes us north of these "empty-but-full" grounds to Amangfong, to see more Stones.

We walk by the Wulffs, Bannermans, and other houses standing hale and hearty while others are in ruins, and go through the narrow paths which cut through the old, ruined stone houses of famous Osu families such as the Bergessens, Holmes, Hesses, Lutterodts, Sonnes, Richters, Quists, Riemers, Hansens, Brocks and so on. Going beyond Osu Amangfong, toward the north, is another traditional enclave called Mowule, separated from Amangfong by the road, coming from Accra on the west, towards La on the east.

Meandering north-eastwards, through the narrow lanes between the closely-built houses as found in Fante fishing villages in the Central Region of Ghana, the Awusai Atso Street enters the famous Osu Ashinte Blohum, bordering the northern-most fringes of Osu Alata. This traditional quarter of Osu is comparatively vast, stretching from the north-east to the north-west. Moving westwards, you come across places with names sounding equally strange, like the corrupted Akan name *Ashinte Blohum* (Asante Brono), *Adjumako,* and *Atuwe.* Ataa Forkoyi empathises with the confusion arising in the minds of his audience, with all these non-Gã names appearing in these very indigenous quarters.

"Don't worry," Ataa Forkoyi sets their minds at rest. "The Stones will tell you the stories about all these."

Crossing from Ashinte Blohum, you enter Amantra, the heart of the ancient, early settlement of the Osu-Doku people. Although this is the prime place, its name has been overshadowed by Kinkawe, the royal quarters of Osu kings. Within Kinkawe and Amantra are found the westerly-located enclaves of Adzoate, Anumansa, and Dade We with the domed-shaped structure known as Dadebu, located virtually in the centre of the community, which defines the visual axis between Osu Kinkawe and Christiansborg on the southeast. Ataa Forkoyi takes a deep breath and shouts:

"Here the Stones really shout out their stories. Wait and listen! But first, we do the last walk."

"Where is the last walk?" Somebody asks Ataa Forkoyi.

The last walk takes place on the ancient tamarind tree-lined, long and straight avenue from Christiansborg, all the way to Fredericksgave, the Danish plantations located on the north of Osu, about 25 kilometers as the crow flies. The tamarind tree-lined avenue is the last stretch of the so-called slave route, which the tired feet of manacled slaves from inland had to trudge, to get through the Awusai Atso quarters and to the Christiansborg dungeons or the slave yards and slave-holding stone houses of Osu. Marching northwards of Awusai Atso, Ataa Forkoyi goes up an incline on the road that leads to Salem, another Osu traditional enclave, Salem, without the word "Jeru" as in Jerusalem, the name of the ancient city. "Salem" was the name the Basel missionaries gave to the new traditional quarters they founded.

The sense of community at Salem, as explained by Ataa Forkoyi, was not defined by any traditional affiliations of clanship but by adherence to the Christian faith, the common faith expressed in the Lordship of Jesus Christ by families with a variety of ancestral linkages and connections, stretching to Danish, Krobo, Adangme, Gã, and Fante. Progenitors and forebears of these families were integrated into the Salem community, which had no belief in ancestral spirits but only those based on love and fellow-feeling. Ataa Forkoyi explains that in this community, a neighbour is defined not by kinship, but by 'henɔ,' a Gã word for a fellow human being.

In the Salem quarters, you find family-houses, built in half Danish stone and half Basel mission timber-framed architectural style, belonging to the Lokkos, Clelands, Holmes, Clerks, Hansen-Norteys, Ayetteys, Azus, Reinholdts, Richters, Riemers, etc. These were the families who were encouraged to move out from the four traditional Danish Osu quarters to live, not in accordance with tradition or as custom demanded, but as the newfound faith in Jesus Christ required. Later, other families with European ancestry bearing names such as Coleman, Telfer, Lathbridge, Addington, etc., came from outside Danish-Osu and settled in this area, earning it the sobriquet "Expatriate Quarters."

Among these stone-and-timber houses rises a two-storey architectural edifice, known as Osu-Salem. Ataa Forkoyi, with a sense of pride, points to the building and says with a touch of hysteria: "This is The School!"

"Which school?" Somebody wants to know.

"This is the first ever purpose-built boarding school in this land of ours," says Ataa Forkoyi. "Some of the Stones here have walked away or been carried away. But you can hear those standing tell their stories later, as we encounter them."

With that, he moves further northwards to climb up to Kuku Hill or Fredericksberg. The climb begins to tell on his old bones, which are beginning to creak as he attempts to walk enthusiastically ahead of his listeners. They are at the top of the hill called Kuku, but which the Danes who lived in Christiansborg called "Fredericksberg." On the west side of the tamarind tree-lined avenue, Ataa Forkoyi points to a site. He claims he can see standing four Danish-built stone country houses. But none of his listeners can see anything he is pointing to, in spite of his insistence that the houses are there and the Stones are telling their stories!

"But wait," says Ataa Forkoyi, "When we get back from the beach, you will hear the stories the Stones will tell you about Danish-Norwegian Governors like Carstensen and Wilkens. Do you know that Wilkens was at Osu for a remarkably short time, yet he frequented these houses so often that some people refer to Kuku Hill, where we are, as 'Wliki Goo,' or 'Wilken's Hill?' Why he came here so often, the Stones will tell!"

And with that, he begins to move southwards, in the direction of Danish-Osu.

One | # Long Time Ago At Osu

Osu Kadigbɔi

HERE IS AN INDIGENOUS SETTLEMENT, NESTLING CLOSE TO THE gigantic architectural edifice put up by the Danes and christened Christiansborg, a slave-trading fort named after King Christian V of Denmark. The settlement was there centuries before the Danes-Norwegians arrived on what was then known as the Guinea Coast. It was there before Christiansborg came into existence. But because of Christiansborg, this indigenous settlement called Osu, became Danish-Osu. As Danish-Osu, the settlement acquired many stones that were brought by the various people who came to settle here. The stones that were brought were of diverse sizes, shapes and strengths, which over a period of time, metamorphosed into Stones, and developed memories from which Osu stories of long, long ago can be told.

Now, Ataa Forkoyi, who has been around since time immemorial, is familiar with these stories. So with great enthusiasm, he attempts to interpret what the Osu Stones are saying. As he speaks, somebody listening with rapt attention asks if she is hearing the pronunciation of the word "Osu" correctly, as uttered by the Stones; for she has heard versions such as "Orsu," "Osoe," "Ursu," "Ursue" and so on. Ataa Forkoyi quickly explains that the Stones have not forgotten how the name "Osu" was mispronounced at different times by different Europeans who came to be associated with Osu. He clears his throat and exclaims:

"Osu Kadigbɔi!"

Startled at this exclamation, his audience wonders what he means. Seeing the question marks on their faces, he smiles kindly and assures them that his exclamation will serve to explain how it all began with the word "Osu," which posed so many difficulties for the Europeans who tried to verbalise or write "Orsu," "Osoe," or "Ursu, "as they thought they heard the local people pronounce the name of their community.

Thus begins Ataa Forkoyi's story "The forebears of the Osu people, as a group of families, moved out of their original community due to a quarrel between one Noete Doku family and another family over some precious beads. Noete Doku, who might have been the high priest of the deity Nadu, led the group of families to migrate from Dangme land south-westwards, into the Accra plains.

"It was in the sixteenth century that this group of families was said to have been led to the present location of Osu by a hunter called Kadi, who was in the employment of the chief of Labadey, King Odoi Atsem. Kadi had met this migrating group of families wandering around in the Accra plains in search of a place to settle. In the course of their wanderings, they came into contact with a number of Gã-speaking, scattered communities, which had settled in the Accra plains, having left their home region on the coast at Labadey. The wandering Dangme migrants, who could quickly relate to these Gã-speaking communities because of the similarity of the Gã language to the Dangme language, learned a lot about life along the coast where Labadey was located.

"According to the Stones, Kadi had first met this migrating group around the Adjangote Hills on the north-western fringe of the plains, a vantage point upon a hill, where one could scan the sea. So when Kadi agreed to bring them southwards to find a place to settle in the Plains, they prevailed upon him to do his best to take them to a great location where they could see the sea at any time, having heard so many stories and legends about the awe-inspiring sea.

"Kadi, who through his hunting expeditions, had come to know the plains and coastal area like the back of his hand, decided to take them to a place he knew would be available for them to settle. He knew the Labadey people had earlier pushed out most of the accommodating Kpeshi indigenes from the confines of their original settlement into the spacious and open plains, westwards on the coast. Many were also absorbed into various Gã communities.

With a friendly, now Gã-speaking Kpeshi community occupying the coastal lands, there would be enough room for these strangers looking for a place to settle, Kadi had reasoned.

"Kadi, a savvy hunter, was quite familiar with all the difficult conditions that plagued this coastal savannah, but he wanted to bring the Dangme migrants there anyway. He was aware that it harboured wild animals such as hyenas, elephants, buffaloes, antelopes, bush fowls and pythons as well as dangerous insects such as the swarming driver ants that surfaced now and then to eat up all organic substances and locusts that periodically destroyed crops and leaves.

"He had also frequently seen severe Harmattan weather, which made water so scarce that animals and people alike, had to traverse long distances for it. Confident that these harsh environmental conditions could be survived, Kadi finally led these wayfaring guests who had come all the way from Dangmeland, to the coastal space between the small lagoon on the west and the large lagoon on the east, after seeking the consent of King Odoi Akyem.

"According to the Stones, when the guests of Kadi, termed 'Kadigbɔi,' in the Gã language, realized they had finally arrived at a place of settlement, a place they could call a home, they decided to name the place 'Osu.'"

As Ataa Forkoyi continues to relay what he is hearing from the Stones, somebody interrupts him to find out why the Dangme migrants adopted the name "Osu" for their new location? At this interruption, Ataa Forkoyi frowns to clear the fog in his memory, and says in a deep voice: "One oral tradition has it that these Dangme migrants adopted the name 'Osu' for their new settlement in remembrance of their place of origin known as 'Osudoku,' located on the west bank of the Volta river."

He continues: "Another oral tradition has it that the name evolved out of the Dangme word *'Wasu,'* meaning 'We have arrived.' This might have been because Kadi took them to various different places before eventually obtaining permission from the Labadey state, to settle at this location. The name 'Osu,' an Adangme expression of 'you have arrived,' was adopted probably because this was what Kadi might have said to the migrants when they eventually arrived here."

Ataa Forkoyi then raises his voice to declare: "So whether 'Osudoku,' or 'Wasu,' Osu certainly has Dangme roots. This is affirmed by the existence of Dangme name patterns and the cultural practice of *'otofo-dipo,'* the unique puberty rite of passage for girls in the two indigenous quarters of Kinkawe and Ashinte Blohum quarters."

After this declaration, Ataa Forkoyi relapses into his more informal and relaxed manner and goes on to imitate the various amusing ways in which the Europeans pronounced the name, Osu:

"It is amazing that these Europeans never got the pronunciation right, notwithstanding their interaction with the Osu community which was so intense, that centuries after their departure from the shores of Osu, their handprints, footprints and landmarks are still all over the place. In much of the earlier written correspondence by these foreign-tongued Europeans, Portuguese, Swedes, Dutch, English and Danes, the name Osu appeared, as the Stones rightly recollect, in seven different versions as 'Orsu,' 'Osoe,' 'Ursue,' 'Ursu,' 'Ozzou,' 'Ursow,' and 'Orzu.'"

Why these variations? Is it because the Europeans did not care to learn how to say an African word correctly, an indication of blatant disrespect for the people and their language? Or is it because they were listening to too many divergent accents?

All these thoughts are going through the mind of Ataa Forkoyi, as he tries to explain to his audience the various spellings of "Osu" as found in the records. He knows for sure, however, that the Basel missionaries got it right when they arrived later at Osu around 1828, to initiate their missionary work. No wonder they managed to master the Gã language the Osu community had since adopted as their own, enabling their translation of the Bible from the original Greek and Hebrew into the Gã language. What an achievement, muses Ataa Forkoyi.

By the time Nuumo Forkoyi finishes explaining the different pronunciations of "Osu," and how it came into use, he has brought his listeners to a point where they find themselves standing at the landing space on the beach. Here, all around, they hear the whisperings and whimperings of the Stones. But the guests cannot make any sense of what they are hearing. Ataa Forkoyi then begins to interpret what the Stones are saying by informing his audience in a sonorous voice as follows:

"Before the arrival of the various Europeans on these shores of the Atlantic Ocean, there was the Klottey Lagoon. The Osudoku migrants, who arrived before anyone else, found this body of brackish water at this very location and called it 'Korletey' in Dangme meaning 'first in the land.' It appeared to them to be a remarkable phenomenon and they immediately recognized it as a deity. Possibly, the indigenous residents they met here on arrival warned them not to take this natural phenomenon for granted because it had sustained them up till then. Indeed, it was so precious and regarded as sacrosanct that, as Ataa Forkoyi recalls with amusement, the Osu community once took up cudgels and cutlasses against the Portuguese sojourners when they attempted to win salt from the Lagoon."

As Ataa Forkoyi was telling this story with mirth, one of his listeners asked in all seriousness: "Ataa Forkoyi, if I may ask, when did this take place?"

Ataa Forkoyi smiled and replied with confidence: "This is a historical event that took place sometime in the seventeenth century. If you so wish and you have time after this tour, you can check Ole Justensen's book entitled *Danish Sources for the History of Ghana 1657-1754* (Copenhagen, 2005) Vols. I & II."

So, according to Ataa Forkoyi, this ancient lagoon, a good neighbour of the sea, which they called *'ŋshɔ,'* was reverently provided with its own priest by the early settlers as they began to depend on it for their sustenance. The original name they gave it eventually changed from Korletey to Klottey to become the male counterpart of a similar "feminine" lagoon at Gã-Mashie, known as Korley.

The settlers at Osu depended on Klottey for sustenance. They came to value the fish in it so much they named it *'Didɛi.'* This might have been a corruption of the name Dede, given to their firstborn daughters. At that time, it was the only source of fish, a reliable source of animal protein, easily harvested with baskets made of woven raffia palm fibres. Klottey not only teemed with fish, but it was also the source of their drinking water.

Indeed, Osu people, too, like many of the Gã-Adangme communities that settled along the Atlantic Coast earlier on, confined their fishing activities to the lagoon, although they found themselves so close to the vast and more natural phenomenon of "ŋshɔ," the sea.

It has been said that although some sea fishing was done in the seventeenth century, serious sea fishing among the Gã-Adangme people did not become widespread until the late nineteenth century. This was contrary to what had prevailed for centuries in the Fante communities on the west coast, such as Axim, Shama, Moree, and Elmina established sea-fishing centers much earlier. In these centres, Fantes had developed the art of sea fishing, with the related craft of making nets and canoes.

At this point somebody asks Ataa Forkoyi why the Osu people did not fish in the sea earlier, and only depended on the Klottey Lagoon. He answers with a counter question: "What is the name of the traditional enclave we passed on our introductory walking tour of Danish-Osu?"

"Mowule," they shouted the answer in unison. "Is it not the quarters separated from Amangfong by the road coming from Accra on the west and going towards La on the east?"

"Excellent," says Ataa Forkoyi, with a chuckle. "The name Mowule is the key to your interesting question," he continues.

"Do you know there is a legend about a giant called Kwagya from Moree in Fanteland? He was, according to the legend, one of the ancient founders of the coastal town of Moree and was the first fisherman in the community. He showed many people the art and wisdom of sea fishing and by the power of his knowledge and skill, the practice spread to other coastal communities.

"It was from Moree that Fante fishermen migrated to Osu as remidors (canoe rowers, derived from the Portuguese word remar meaning 'to row') who were employed by the Europeans to use their canoes to bring ashore goods from the ships which anchored a distance from the Osu coast."

To get back to why the Osu people were not engaged earlier in sea fishing, the person who posed the original question interrupts this historical account with another question: "Ataa Forkoyi, what is the relationship between Mowule and Moree? And how does that fit your response to my earlier question?"

Once again, with a chuckle, Ataa Forkoyi raises his right hand and says, "Have patience and listen to the Stones! 'Mowule' is a corrupted pronunciation of the word 'Moree.' The Mowule quarter was the place of settlement for these Fante fishermen and remidors who came to Osu long, long time ago."

In fact, Ataa Forkoyi goes on, this time full of eloquence and confidence, "The existence today of Mowule is convincing evidence that it was the Fantes who came to introduce the art of sea-fishing to the Osu people. To start with, they might have introduced the Akan word *'nsio'* meaning 'water' which later was adopted in a corrupted form, 'ŋshɔ,' by the Osu people as a word for 'the sea.'"

Ataa Forkoyi continues, "Observe the impact of the coming of the Moree Fantes on the word usage related to the business of sea-going at Osu. When the word 'nsio' was adopted and used to describe the sea as 'ŋshɔ,' somehow the Dangme word *'wo'* for the sea, was not totally forgotten.

"Let me explain. The sea, by virtue of its prominence in the territory of the Osu people, cannot be ignored. In fact, the power of the waves and the volume and variety of sounds they make as they tumble up and down, make the sea a revered phenomenon. This reverence has played a significant role in the shaping of the Gã language. For example there are such expressions as: *'ŋshɔnaa'* (the beach or coast); *'ŋshɔnaa shia'* (beach sand); *'ŋshɔ kɔɔ'* (travel by sea); *'ŋshɔ sɛɛ'* (beyond the horizon); *'ŋshɔ ke'* (sea wave); *'ŋshɔŋ loo'* (fish from the sea). However, when it comes to doing business with the sea, the word *'ŋshɔ'* never shows up! Why? I tell you, it has to do with how the sea-going business was shaped by the Fantes."

At this point, Ataa Forkoyi closes his eyes and shouts: "Listen to the Stones, especially you Gã speakers. The Stones are saying that when the Fantes came, they came with the word *'mpo,'* which is the Fante word for the sea. *'Mpo'* features extensively in vocabulary associated with the sea as a resource and a natural phenomenon. Hence there are the common Fante words *'mpoanu'* (beach or coast); *'mponam'* (fish from the sea); *'mpofi fii'* (centre of the sea), and so on.

"Thus, the Fantes, when they came to Osu and introduced the practice of sea fishing, would say in Fante as they set out to sea, *'Yɛ kɔ mpo'*—'We are going fishing.' But the Osu people had not forgotten the word 'wo,' (Gã word for sea), which sounded close to the Fante word 'mpo.' So as they began to learn the trade, they would also use the expression in a Gã style, by saying *'Wɔŋya wo'* as the Fantes would say *'Yɛ kɔ mpo.'* With time everybody in the trade began to use the expression *'Wɔŋya wuo.'* Consequently, in the course of time, the Gã word usage associated with sea fishing evolved into various forms of expressions such as 'wuo yaa (sea fishing), *'wuoyabi'* or *'wolɛi'* (fisher-folk); and *'wolɛi atsɛ'* (chief fisherman)."

Having concluded with this statement, Ataa Forkoyi opens his eyes and says with a deep sigh, "I am done." His audience breaks into applause for such an interesting interpretation to the history of Mowule of Danish-Osu. Energised by their attentiveness, he continues to interpret what the Stones are saying about the landing space on the beach. He defines this space on the beach between the confluence of the lagoon, the sea lying on the east, and the rocky high ground below the feet of the Christiansborg castle as sacred ground.

"What makes this sandy beach with its sparse distribution of coconut trees sacred?" asks a member of Ataa Forkoyi's audience.

"Long, long ago, there were a lot of comings and goings on this beach." The old man clears his throat and softly responds to the question with an obvious look of agitation.

"The Danes-Norwegians arrived in canoes paddled by Fante and, later, Gã remidors; canoes from their own ships that had anchored in the roads, at a distance of about half a mile or so. They arrived with loads of goods, consisting of cheap European and Asian products, guns, gunpowder and numerous kegs of brandy. As the canoes landed on the beach, the Danes were carried out to dry land and the goods were carried ashore on the heads of muscular Fante and Gã carriers.

"The scene was usually characterized by a lot of excitement, shouting and movement as a large crowd of Osu people including mulattoes and natives gather along the beach ready for trade and bartering. A few old coaster Danes-Norwegians, armed with guns on their shoulders, watch the crowds, ready to shoot down anyone who attempted to steal any of the goods."

"How does all this make this beach sacred?" interrupts one of the listeners.

Ataa Forkoyi responds quickly, "Remember I said there used to be a lot of comings and goings? The sacredness of this beach is rooted in the 'goings.' The goods that were conveyed to the ships by the remidors in their canoes consisted mainly of human cargo: men, women and children bound to each other with chains at their hands and feet. As enslaved people, they had been sold and bought earlier at Osu. Moving this cargo of human beings into the canoes and on to the ships anchored in the roads did not happen without drama and tragedy."

He continues in a subdued tone, "There would be desperate, chained men who would fight like wild cats to free themselves before being dragged through the waters of the sea into the canoes. There would be women wailing for not knowing where they were being dragged to. Children would be shouting and screaming at the mere sight of the unfamiliar waves and the booming of the sea. Time and again, there would be shooting incidents with blood spilling from the bodies of hapless and helpless slaves who had been unchained and left to die on the beach, shot for attempting to escape before the canoe trip to the ships. Along this beach, trudged along in a single file, naked bodies with chains on their necks and legs, slaves who had come from the dungeons inside Christiansborg, through the gate of no return that was located on the downside of Christiansborg and facing the east, as if to open to the rising sun that would announce the dawn of a new day.

"From this beach, thousands, tens of thousands, amounting

to 97,850 altogether of men, women and children, and in some cases babies, were bound, bundled and canoed out to European ships as human cargo for sale in the Danish islands of St. Thomas and St. Croix in the Caribbean. On this beach, a motley collection of Africans from the far north, from the far north-east and from the far east of Osu, and also from within the very bosom of Osu, experienced their living-death as they lost their identity, dignity and humanity, dragged from the sands and thrust into canoes that brought them to ships that freighted them away to the new world; a new life, not designed for them as human beings, but as enslaved beings."

Ataa Forkoyi goes on in an apparent trance, until he completes the answer to the question why the Osu beach is sacred, asking almost inaudibly:

"Do you now see why this beach is sacred ground?"

Ataa Forkoyi turns the attention of his listeners to Christiansborg, standing majestically and yet ignominiously on the west side of the sacred beach. He then, as if coming out of his trance, begins to speak poetically. He informs his audience that the human cargo, the chained men, women, and children in whose memory the Osu beach has been imbued with historic sacredness, would always be brought out from the slave dungeons and yard the bowels of this ignominious edifice, to be packed into small canoes to be rowed away from the beach to the waiting slave ships that would transport them to the Caribbean. With the audience's attention now focused on Christiansborg, he continues with poetry:

> It got here stealthily though with presence
> On the Osu shore as Mister Europe,
> It came to exchange goods with us.
> It became more courageous with time,
> And assumed the title: "Master Europe" to dominate us.
> Eventually, Master Europe became ostentatious
> And atrocious and turned Monster Europe;
> To suck us away into its bowels,
> To be regurgitated on other strange shores.
> Master Europe came with a Portuguese face
> Changed into a Swedish outlook and
> Ended with a Danish-Norwegian profile,
> With an English embellishment.

Now Ataa Forkoyi becomes less poetic and continues, "My friends, I hope you understand my emotions. What I hear the

Stones say takes me to a different plane that makes me lose my usual sense for words. But this, in the parlance of the Osu people, is the 'Karslieh,' christened by the Danes as 'Christiansborg.' Many books have been written about this edifice and they are available for your reading, if you wish. Let me therefore summarise what I hear the Stones saying about this building."

He pauses and scratches the right-hand side of his head and cocks his ear, with his head slightly bent, as if trying to listen to something. He then continues, "Christiansborg was built on the site first developed by the Portuguese for their trading post around 1640. The Portuguese who had stayed at Osu for a while, long before all the other Europeans got here, put up their trading post with the forced labour they brought along with them from Allada."

At this point, somebody interjects with the question: "Ataa Forkoyi, where is Allada?"

"I shall tell you more about Allada later on; please, don't forget to raise this question again, when we get to the stories the Stones tell about Osu Alata."

Taking up where he left off, Ataa Forkoyi informs his audience that after the Portuguese had been at Osu for a while, there came other European traders who were better organized militarily, and ousted them. These were the Swedes, who, later, in 1652, put up a trading lodge of a better quality than the Portuguese trading post.

"Soon thereafter came the almighty Danes-Norwegians to sack the Swedes and take over their lodge. The Danes eventually managed to develop the little fort they later built into a prominent structure, a castle by all standards, and named it 'Christiansborg,' after the reigning king, Christian V of Denmark.

"This gigantic and complex edifice was developed by the Danes to serve as their operations headquarters for the east Guinea coast." Ataa Forkoyi continues with a mocking smile on his face:

"Christiansborg, which was built with stones quarried from Labadeye, and some brought all the way from Denmark as ballast in their ships, was erected through the sweat and toil of Osu stone-cutters and enslaved labourers who provided forced servitude to their Danish owners as the construction work proceeded. Christiansborg was built with three faces. To the sea on the south is the faceless face with all the armaments of protection, the canons, ready for enemy ships, which may come to disturb the peace and power of the Dane. To the north side, you can see the hostile front facing Osu Dane. To the north side, you can see the hostile front facing Osu with its huts and houses, armed to the teeth with long range shoot-

Figure 4: Archival photograph of the Danish Slave-Ship "Fredensborg" loading slaves in the road of Christiansborg, 1768.

ing canons on its bastions, ready to show the Osu people their military strength, should it cross their African minds to attack them." Ataa Forkoyi, still with a mischievous, mocking smile, adds, "On the east, the face of Christiansborg showed stony harshness with a hideous single door which opened only in one direction: to the sacred beach.

"Inside Christiansborg, behind the massive, high stone bastions and walls, there were living quarters, crafted with Danish architectural concepts of space to provide for the community of Danes-Norwegians of different social and administrative standing in the Danish management of affairs on the coast. These included governors, merchants, assistants, chaplains, soldiers and other staff. In addition to these living quarters," Ataa Forkoyi continues, "pains had been taken to create within Christiansborg, storage facilities for goods and holding dungeons for enslaved people purchased from local slave traders, waiting to be sold to prospective European buyers or for shipment abroad. And can you believe it? A chapel, where the Danish chaplains on duty tried to remind their Danish compatriots on the coast, of their Christian morality and civilization. There was also a room dedicated to teaching children, which could be referred to as a school."

On hearing of the school mentioned by Ataa Forkoyi, somebody interrupts the narration and poses the question: "What was a school doing in Christiansborg? I thought the castle was for adult Danes and enslaved people on hold till the slave-ships arrive."

Ataa Forkoyi smiles and answers: "Yes, Christiansborg was strictly for the Danes and the enslaved people who were in transit. But you know, the Danes were good planners. They thought about everything that would ensure their safety, comfort and convenience, and guarantee the fulfillment of the objective of establishing their operational headquarters at Osu. They knew their sojourn at Osu would produce offspring that had to be raised according to Danish culture and norms. They therefore made provision for a school, the castle school, about which the Stones have a lot of stories to tell later. But do you know that besides all these facilities they developed within Christiansborg, they also made provision for water reservoirs and burial grounds?

"The Stones have a story about one Danish man, a surgeon called Carl Gustav Engmann, who, due to his medical mind and acute sense of hygiene, when he temporarily acted as a governor in 1753, built an underground water storage with an outer cover of a baroque style polygonal structure to hold about 10,000 gallons of

Figure 5: Showing the old cistern cover built by C. G. Engmann
Photograph courtesy of Leif Svalesen, editor

harvested rainwater."

On hearing the name Engmann, a question comes up: "Does this name have any connection to the Engmanns of Osu Kinkawe?"

Immediately, Ataa Forkoyi responds in the affirmative. "I shall tell you more about this Gustav Engmann later, because his descendants are well known at Osu today. Let me add before I come to that, that the Danes used the courtyard of Christiansborg for a while as a burial ground. Of course, only a few of the Danes that died while in the service of the Danish administration had the honour and blessing to be buried within the confines of the courtyard."

"What happened to the others?" a curious listener asks.

"Oh yes, they were buried alright but had to be taken outside Christiansborg to the west-side, where a cemetery had been developed that came to be nicknamed *'Abentia'* by the Osu people.

Hitherto, the Osu people had never seen a dead relative being buried outside the confines of the family's residence and found the Danes' practice rather strange. The word 'Abentia' therefore became the indigenous word for a cemetery."

Ataa Forkoyi continues to interpret more information from the Stones about the Danish development around Christiansborg and refers to a redoubt built beyond the Danish cemetery.

"This redoubt, named by the Danes in their language as 'Provesten,' meaning 'Touchstone,' to express their superstitious belief in the good luck that a touchstone can bring, was a multi-storey, circular, stone-built watchtower, built as a protective installation for Christiansborg. This was in anticipation that, should their rivals, the Dutch, then living in Gã-Mashie at Dutch Accra, called Kinka, make any attempt to attack the Danes by land, their attack could easily be repelled by the force of the long range cannons installed upon the tower of Provesten."

Ataa Forkoyi elaborately explains this security measure put in place by the Danes as a prelude to some interesting information the Stones have disclosed to him about the traditional quarters of Osu Kinkawe. "Alluding to Kinka, my friends, brings me to the stories of the earliest indigenous community of Osu, where the Osudoku migrants began to set up their new home," says Ataa Forkoyi with a broad smile on his wrinkled, handsome face.

He continues, "Do you know? It is absolutely incredible that the word 'Kinka' should crop up at Osu at all! Listen, in the Gã language, the name for the Dutch Europeans was *'Kinka Blɔfo.'* These Europeans were, at that time in the early seventeenth century, located west of Osu, the settlement developed around Fort Crevecour which came to be known as Dutch Accra, but was called 'Kinka' by the Gã-Mashie. In spite of the frequent contact Osu people had with these Dutch through trade, they never settled at Osu. In fact, in the same Gã-Mashie, next door to the Dutch, were the English, who were residing in the Fort they had built, called James Fort. For the English, the Gã name given to them was *'Ngleshi Blɔfo.'*"

"Then somebody quickly comes up with the question: "What about the Danes?"

To this, Ataa Forkoyi exclaims, "Oh! The Danes? The Danes were known as *'Den Blɔfo.'* But please, allow me to continue the curious story of how Kinka came to be associated with Osu, although the Dutch never stayed at Osu but were at Kinka at Gã-Mashie." With a sudden look of excitement on his face, he clasps his hands and shouts: "Kinkawe! How?"

"Now listen," Ataa Forkoyi says as if to keep his listeners in suspense: "According to the Stones, when the Osudoku migrants arrived years before any of the European traders set foot on these shores, the Kpeshi people were already around, but many had been pushed westward earlier by the Labadeye people when they also migrated to the same coastal area. Kadi, you remember, the Labadeye King's hunter, was the one who brought the Osudoku migrants here. He was an affable person who was by nature, a bridge-builder. So, he did not merely bring the migrants here, but ensured that he quickly created a good relationship between Noete Doku, his family, and the local Kpeshi people."

Ataa Forkoyi continues: "The two groups of people got on so well with each other that in no time the two linguistic forms, Dangme and Kpeshi became a lingua franca for the people of Osu. This spoken Gã at Osu was so perfected that when the attempt was made to translate the Bible from Hebrew and Greek into the vernacular, it was the Gã usage at Osu that was adopted.

"No doubt, without disagreement, both groups had adopted the name 'Osu' to identify their newly-emerged community. This is why the first European visitors, the Portuguese, recorded the name of the place they had landed in as 'Ursu' when they inquired after its name."

Osu-Doku Becomes Kinkawe and Ashinte

"So the Osu community began to grow," continues Ataa Forkoyi, "And quarters began to emerge, spreading eastwards and westwards along the coast. The first two major quarters were composed mainly of the original Adangme migrants. You can see that these quarters retained some of their Adangme cultural practices and naming forms. However, the names 'Ashinte Blohum' and 'Kinkawe' were adopted to describe the quarters they carved for themselves. Now, as Osu stabilized and began to grow, it began also to attract other people from other places. The Stones tell us about some of the interesting things that accompanied this new migration into Osu."

"Please, tell us about these, I am interested," chimes in one of the listeners.

"Well, if you want to know, here we go. According to the Stones, with the attraction the Osu community presented, with their rapid and successful adaptation to the coastal environment, people from Labadeye on the east, and people from Gã-Mashie on the west, began to flock into Osu. Especially, around 1736 and 1738, some people from Kinka, Dutch Accra, with Akwamu lineage, came en masse to settle at Osu. It was said that this large group of people came in as a result of some conflict that had arisen in Dutch Accra. One of the prominent leaders at Dutch Accra, Okaidja by name, had had some misunderstanding with the Dutch and had decided to move his whole household with his strong body of warriors, numbering about 200, out of Dutch Accra and settle at Osu.

"Okaidja was from the Otublohum quarters of Dutch Accra and therefore had in his entourage a great number of people with Akwamu lineage. Hence, as they moved in to settle at Osu, the sections of the quarters they settled were given Akwamu names such as Adjumako and Amantra. Since Okaidja was a prominent person in Dutch Accra, the Dutch administration was not at all pleased with his moving away with such a large fighting force. They became alarmed and jittery, knowing the consequences should a conflict arise between the Dutch Accra people and the Osu people. Hence, they caused Chief Dako, the overlord of the Otublohum people, to pursue Okaidja to Osu, plunder his settlement there and possibly force his return, together with his people, to Dutch Accra."

As Ataa Forkoyi goes on with the story of the coming of Okaidja and his people to Osu, an over-excited listener shouts out to anticipate that Chief Dako would not succeed: "Were they able to get Okaidja back to Dutch Accra?"

Without any hesitation, Ataa Forkoyi responds to the loud voice, almost barking at the questioner: "The answer is definitely no! No, Chief Dako and his warriors had to go back in shame and disgrace." Before Ataa Forkoyi can continue with his narration, another listener again interjects, asking: "If, as you have said, the Dutch who were called Kinka Blɔfo never stayed at Osu, how come we have Kinkawe at Osu?"

Ataa Forkoyi now grins from ear to ear, and with great amusement, responds:

"This is where I have been trying all along to reach in my tale. For me it is very exciting to hear what the Stones say on this matter. Now listen," he says, pointing his right index finger to his right ear, "The Dutch, one day in 1777, with the strong desire to besiege Christiansborg, seize it and sack the Danes, rallied round their Kinka Gã soldiers, armed them with field cannons and flintlock rifles, and marched eastwards through the marsh and the plains towards Christiansborg. To avoid the small lagoon lying west of Christiansborg, they headed north-west of Christiansborg at first and then turned to face eastwards, with the hope of gaining a good firing range on the Danish Fortress. From that vantage point they positioned themselves, pitched a camp at a spot close for the shooting of their two cannons, and began to bombard Christiansborg's apparently weak wall, the north-west side. This vantage point, according to the Stones, was called *'Ofonsrang.'*

"But, between Christiansborg and the north-west where they had pitched their encampment stood the 'lucky' Provesten, tall and indefatigable. Notwithstanding the strong cannon fire from Christiansborg, the Dutch returned fire for fire. This military campaign by the Dutch and their Kinka Gã-soldiers lasted for eighteen good months."

With a sigh of relief Ataa Forkoyi goes on: "But they never succeeded. Frustrated, they dismantled their camp and, like a dog with its tail between its legs, slowly marched back westwards with a deep sense of defeat, for once again they had failed to conquer their competitors and enemies. Meanwhile, sojourning in their makeshift encampment, it was said that the Kinka soldiers dug out a well from which they could get their water supply, knowing that the small lagoon south of where they had pitched camp was brackish. The Stones hint to us that the well they dug was given the name *'Tunma Ayi'* with the belief that the water obtained from this well would provide the soldiers with some supernatural powers to fight the Danes and their Osu allies, when it came to face-to-face combat."

Ataa Forkoyi, having completed this part of his narration, goes on to explain how the Osu Kinkawe quarters got its peculiar and anachronistic name. "In Gã, the word *'we'* stands for a geographical space (a house) or a socio-cultural entity. So 'Kinkawe,' as a matter of fact, means the house of the Kinka people or the clan space of the Kinka people. My friends, the encampment site of the Dutch and their Kinka soldiers, for psychological reasons, was dubbed 'Ofongsrang,' to wit, 'We shall not give up being in camp,' although it was eventually deserted with the defeated army's return to Dutch Accra.

"With this abandonment of the encampment, Ofongsrang became bare, as it should be, after an eighteen-month occupation by warring soldiers. Thus, to take advantage of this deserted campsite, the royal family of the indigenous Osu quarters moved in to occupy it. As leaders of the community, they had to take up a strategic position for future defence against potential assaults from the west. In remembrance, therefore, of the eighteen months of futile occupation by the Kinka soldiers and their Dutch allies, the leadership chose to give an identity to these new quarters that precisely related to defeat of the Kinka at that time. Hence the name of the quarters became Kinkawe."

Ataa Forkoyi goes on to set this historical narration in the context of the collective memory of this significant event and begins to sing and dance to an old *'Kple'* song:

> Kinka moo naa kpataa! Kinka moo naa kpataa!
> Namɔ ya bɛɛ dzɛi, kɛ feelɛ kpataa?

"This Kple song, which is sung as a teasing melody, simply insinuates that the grounds of the Dutch Fort have become bare and desolate. Who went to sweep them up so clean and immaculate?" At this point, seeing the mood in which Ataa Forkoyi finds himself and the expression of pride on his face, his listeners spontaneously join him in the Kple dance and after the fun, they applaud him resoundingly for his immense knowledge and wise interpretation of history.

"Now Ataa Forkoyi, you have brilliantly interpreted what the Stones tell about the establishment of Osu Kinkawe as an indigenous quarter of Osu. You have told us earlier that the two indigenous quarters of Osu consisted of Osu-Kinkawe and Osu-Ashinte. Did Osu-Ashinte come into existence similarly to Kinkawe?" asks one of the listeners who has been keenly listening to the old man.

"All this happened at the time when Osu began to evolve into Danish Osu. But as I have said earlier, the indigenous Osu was one entity, without quarters, occupied mainly by the descendants of the Osudoku migrants. For centuries, it existed as a community of amalgamated Dangme migrants and Kpeshi indigenes, under the cultural influence of the Labadey people living on the east, beyond the Klottey Lagoon.

"Being a pioneering community, the families worked hard to adapt to the environment they came to find; assiduousness and determination spurred them to begin turning the coastal savannah plains, with their peculiar flora and fauna, into a fruitful 'garden of Eden.' They initiated the cultivation of guinea-corn or sorghum, which they called *'ŋmaa,'* and attempted to domesticate the guinea fowl, which they called *'aŋsaa.'* 'Yes, wasu'—'We have arrived'; so said the Osu people in their old Dangme language. 'This is our home and we shall make the best of it, notwithstanding the hyenas, elephants, guinea pigs, the guinea fowls and the guinea worms!'

"So, Osu began to grow and flourish," Ataa Forkoyi continues with his narration. "The size of the community expanded by leaps and bounds, as both adults and children gradually survived the life-threatening environmental diseases and bacteria. As Osu spread eastwards and westwards, the configuration of groups into quarters began to crystallize with their own leadership structures; notwithstanding the fact that they retained their Adangme cultural paradigms.

"So Osu-Kinkawe and Osu-Ashinte-Blohum are virtually one people, only that the royal household was the group that moved eastwards. As they settled at this Kinka deserted campsite, they discovered the well, 'Tunma Ayi,' which the Dutch and their soldiers had dug whilst they were in encampment. To consolidate their occupation of this deserted site, the Osu king and his royal household decided to make the abandoned well their spiritual stronghold and therefore changed the name from 'Tunma Ayi' to 'Dade Bu,' meaning 'The iron hole.' This was to serve as a defensive shrine to ward off any future wicked intentions from the Dutch Accra soldiers.

"Hence Osu Kinkawe became the royal quarters where the Osu King resided. Within Kinkawe emerged an important rallying point for the Osu community which came to be known as 'Adzoateh.' Adzoateh, as a matter of fact, is a colloquial usage that came out of the expression *'aadza tuntɛ'* in the Gã language, meaning 'distribution of gun powder or bullets.' Adzoateh therefore was the central rallying point for all the warriors of Osu who were summoned to gather, whenever it became necessary to get ready to fight and ward off any attack from enemies or to undertake an emergency action by the *Hiiabii*, which is the company name of warriors of the community.

"Now I shall explain how the other quarters on the east, Ashinte Blohum, got its name," continues Ataa Forkoyi. "As I have indicated earlier, this development began when the Danes arrived and Osu began to respond to the influence of the Danish presence in the community, with the erection of Christiansborg. During those early years, a misunderstanding had arisen between a section of the indigenous community and their King, Teinor. As a result of the quarrel which ensued, the aggrieved section moved eastwards, away from the core of the original community. It was this splinter group which constituted the Ashinte-Blohum quarters.

"According to the Stones, Osu Ashinte Blohum gained its name because the indigenous Osu people opened their doors to trading visitors who came mainly from the forest kingdom of the Asantes. The Asantes had heard of the congenial trading environment at Osu, after they had routed the nefarious Akwamus from the coast. Osu therefore became an attractive centre, which the Asantes frequented any time they came down to the coast either to trade or fight. They found the Osu people affable and hospitable. Hence, Osu became their transit quarters when they were down south."

Having shared with his listeners what the Stones have said, Ataa Forkoyi then goes on finally to tell his audience why Ashinte is in Osu.

"You see, because of the hospitality that the Asante visiting traders were accorded, they began to develop one or two guest huts in the courtyard-form of houses they had back in the forest. These were located and concentrated on the east side of Osu, where the community had been expanding. The Asantes began to feel at home and when they went back home, they reported to their King that they now had *'brono,'* a neighborhood of their own at Osu. It therefore became customary that any Asante trader, coming down south to trade, was advised to find lodgings at the Asante Brono at Osu, a home away from home. Asantes were so comfortable with the hospitality of the Osu people that, according to the Stones, one time when they had to bring down people to be used as pawns to purchase gunpowder and guns from the Danes, they arranged to have these pawns domiciled at 'Asante Brono.' With time, this reference to the Asante quarters crept into the Osu word usage and this Osu quarter on the east became known as Ashinte Blohum."

At the end of this long explanation of what the Stones had said, Ataa Forkoyi, with a mischievous smile on his face, concludes and says: "The Asantes not only sojourned at Osu, but they took Osu wives who bore children who were given both Adangme and Asante names."

Somebody then asks: "Is that the reason why at Ashinte Blohum, you meet people today with the hybrid names of Tetteh Owusu and Nortey Yebuah, Nortei Adu, and Norkai Mansah?"

Ataa Forkoyi responds: "Precisely so! The strong social intercourse the Osu people had with the Asantes at Ashinte Blohum, led to some of the Asante cultural concepts rubbing off on the community. Among others, Ataa Forkoyi referred to the use of the Asante expression *'Omankrado'* to describe the office of the community leader as *'Mankralo'* in Osu Ashinte Blohum so as to balance the word usage for the Chief of Osu, as *Mantsɛ,* who resided at Osu Kinkawe.

'Allada' Becomes 'Alata' at Osu

"Long before the Danish presence set in motion the emergence of Danish-Osu, other equally interesting changes were taking place in the Osu indigenous community," declares Ataa Forkoyi.

"According to the Stones, a community began to form on the northwest of the Klottey Lagoon. This community came into existence with the coming of the Portuguese to the Osu shores and grew next to the location of the Portuguese lodge, from where the Portuguese language was to spread into the community and influence the medium of communication at Osu for centuries.

"Meanwhile, to build their lodge in the early seventeenth century, they had brought along with them, groups of able-bodied, enslaved men and women from the regions between the east of the river they named *'Volta,'* meaning: 'We shall return,' and beyond the kingdom of Dahomey. The Portuguese had referred to this geographical space as *'Allada.'*"

At this point, someone among Ataa Forkoyi's listeners asks if he meant *Alata* as referring to Nigerians. With a smile, Ataa Forkoyi responds and says emphatically:

"I meant Allada and not Alata! The word Alata, which came to be used in association with people from Nigeria is actually, a corruption of the word 'Allada.' Now, listen to how this strange word came to be known in the Guinea Coast. The word *'Allada'* is a Bengali word, meaning 'strange.' The Portuguese, who had then already had contact with the Indian sub-continent, were familiar with the word and somehow employed it to describe the coastal regions from where they had brought their enslaved manpower to Osu. It was possible they found this east side of the coast with its peoples rather strange compared to the west of the coast, and employed the Bengali word 'Allada,' which had then crept into Portuguese word-usage, as a nickname for the space they found beyond the Volta River."

Ataa Forkoyi goes on to explain that according to the Stones, the Osu indigenes referred to their new neighbours as "Allada" in keeping with what they heard from the Portuguese. With time, as happened to some other words, the word "Allada" corrupted into the word "Alata." Finishing this long explanation to how Osu Alata came to have its name, somebody asks the question:

"Ataa Forkoyi, how did you know all this?"

Once again, he smiles and with a nod, says simply: "It is all from the Stones, can't you hear? The Osu Alata community in earlier years consisted of the workers who provided the labour for the Portuguese to establish their base at Osu as the first Europeans who came to this side of the Guinea coast. By virtue of the close association they had with the Portuguese, they developed their settlement quite close to the Portuguese lodge."

Having said this, he clears his throat and continues with the narration: "Let me tell you more about the history of this community of people which in the past, some erroneously thought came from Nigeria. Unlike the Osu Kinkawe and Osu Ashinte communities, Osu Alata is very heterogeneous in its composition. You see, culturally, the people of Kinkawe and Ashinte are of the same stock. You remember, according to the Stones, their forbears migrated from Osudoku and because of this migratory history there are a number of Dangme features commonly seen in Kinkawe and Ashinte. This is not so in the case of the Osu Alata community.

"The heterogeneous composition of the Osu Alata community came about as a result of the groups of people which came to join the Allada enslaved worker-settlers during the formative stages of the community. There were the Labadey migrants, who were attracted to the community because of the Portuguese trading lodge that offered trading and employment opportunities. There were the few Akwamus who stayed behind after their military escapades in the Gã coastal areas had been terminated by the Asantes.

"In addition, according to the Stones, in the latter part of the eighteenth century, much later, after the Danes had come to Osu, a few other different groups came in to become part of the Osu Alata community. There was the Fante group, Ataa Forkoyi explains, that was brought in by a Danish merchant by name, J. E. Richter. Richter brought in this group from Fanteland to work in his commercial and slave-trading business as carriers and boatmen. Since they came as a well-organized group, they brought along with them all their cultural goods, including their spiritual protector, in the form of a deity called Ogbaame. Ataa Forkoyi, with a look of seriousness and mock anger, continues:

"Richter used his influence to push this group into the traditional leadership circle at Osu Alata to counterbalance the existing Osu traditional authority centred around the Kinkawe and Ashinte

Blohum quarters. To buttress his intentions, he even went to the extent of allocating a piece of land belonging to him that abutted his palatial house. This palatial residence was later developed into a fort by his descendants."

Continuing with the interpretation of what the Stones are saying, he draws his listeners' attention to the fact that, besides the incoming Fantes from the west, there were also Anlos who came from the east in the place where the Danish outpost was located at Quitta. As he mentions the name Quitta, an Ewe-speaking listener in the group, raises up his right hand to ask a question.

"Ataa Forkoyi, you said the Ewes came from the Danish eastern outpost at Quitta. Did you mean Keta?"

Ataa Forkoyi quickly responds:

"Yes, I mean Keta. According to the Stones, the Danish outpost was called Quitta by the Danes. Since the Danes could not eat the typical Ewe dish of okra stew and banku, called *'fetredekyi,'* their tongues and mouths could not say the letter 'K' in the name 'Keta.' Keta therefore became Quitta in their records." Ataa Forkoyi makes this latter statement with a boyish smile on his old face and the listeners all break into a hearty laugh. As Ataa Forkoyi finishes this historical account on Osu Alata, the question is posed to him once again:

"How did you get to know all this?"

He responds:

"Listen to the Stones. They tell the story and I simply interpret." And he continues, "But let me assure you that as you go through Osu Alata, the evidence is all there to confirm this history. Take for example, the royal household of Osu Alata. It is a configuration of three families that rotate the ascendancy to the Osu Alata stool. It is interesting to note that the names of these three families reflect Akwamu, Labadeye and Fante origins. The name *'Akoto We'* is Akwamu; *'Odoi Tsaakpo We'* is Labadeye and *'Awuley Nfeni We'* is Fante."

He goes on to add: "The customary chief fisherman of Osu Alata comes from the house of *'Djamlodja We.'* Oral traditions at Osu Alata point to the fact that the name Djamlodja was derived from the Portuguese name: 'Azambuja.' In the collective memory of the people, the first European to visit the coast, with the name Don Diego d'Azambuja, has never been erased. Therein stands the historical connection of the name Djamlodja to the original Allada people brought down by the Portuguese in the seventeenth century.

"Furthermore," he continues with the narration, "the Ewe presence is evidenced in place names within the Osu Alata community, such as 'Agbadza Dzoohe' and 'Brogodo.' Agbadza Dzoohe simply means the place where the Ewe-traditional dance of *Agbadza* takes place. Knowing that the Ewes take along their drumming and dancing wherever they go, the Osu Alata community is convinced by the place name Agbadza Dzoohe that the migrant Ewes from Quitta settled at Osu Alata. According to the Stones, a special place was allotted to them for use as a place for ablutions. This place was referred to by the Ewes as *'Nougodo'* that is, a place for attending to nature's call. As it always happened at that time, the word usage corrupted into 'Blogodo.' 'Nougodo' became a livable section of the Osu Alata community, after it had outgrown its function as a place of ablutions."

Ataa Forkoyi's listeners stand there appreciating and admiring his sharp sense of history and the intellectual prowess with which he interprets it. As he observes the delighted impressions on their faces, he goes on with enthusiasm to inform them:

"Because of this heterogeneity in the Osu Alata community, tracing back to what the Stones are saying, it is only in the Osu Alata traditional quarters that the customary naming of individuals does not conform to any recognisable paradigm, as found in the culturally homogeneous traditional quarters of Osu Kinkawe, Osu Ashinte and Osu Anahor."

Osu Anahor

"Wow, Ataa Forkoyi what you have been saying is simply overwhelming. But where does Osu Anahor fit into this fantastic narration?"

"Be patient," he retorts, "I was coming to that. I mentioned Osu Anahor in passing because this is the name of the fourth quarter of the Osu traditional community. This community also has its own story that the Stones are telling and now that you have brought the matter up, let me interpret what the Stones are saying about Osu Anahor."

So he begins with another historical account of the formation of the Osu traditional community.

"In the early part of the eighteenth century, the troublesome and terrible Akwamu warriors began to grow weary as they faced the superior fighting power of the Akyem in the various war encounters. Eventually they had to succumb to the Akyem who defeated them and pushed them over across to the east banks of the Volta River. With the routing of the Akwamu from their original home region, a relative era of peace and stability prevailed in the Gã coastal area.

"When this happened, a group of Gã-speaking people, who had earlier deserted their communities and migrated far away to Little Popo, re-migrated westwards, crossed the Volta and proceeded further west on the coast and eventually settled at Osu.

"These Gã people had earlier migrated away from the paramount Gã town of Ayawaso, around 1680, due to its sacking by the Akwamus. In their search for a safe haven, they had to seek refuge in the Far East in Allada, at Anecho. Anecho, also known as Little Popo, was founded by the Portuguese after they had settled at Elmina to carry out their trade in the region of Allada.

"In this foreign place had settled the Gã-Mashie migrants, who managed to set up their own community under the leadership of the vanquished King Ashangmor. In fact, Ashangmor was the ruler of the Gã-Mashie people, before the primeval capital of the Gã state, Ayawaso, was invaded and destroyed by the Akwamus."

As Ataa Forkoyi continues his narration about the Gã-Mashie returnees, a listener, having in mind what was said about the Ewes, who also came from the east to settle at Osu, interrupts with a question:

"Ataa Forkoyi, may I know if the Gã-Mashie returnees from Anecho were Ewes?"

"No, they were not Ewes. They were pure Gã people; for while on sojourn in an Ewe-speaking cultural environment, they retained their Gã-ness: the original Gã naming traditions, the customary out-dooring (naming ceremony) of babies on the eighth day of birth, and the unique Gã practice of circumcision of male babies also on the eighth day of birth. They never forgot that they were Gã and used the Gã language alongside the Ewe language. In fact, their coming back to join the Osu community strengthened the usage of the Gã language in Osu, since they came back with the original Gã spoken at Ayawaso, the then capital seat of Gã-Mashie."

He continues: "According to the Stones, when the time came for the returnees to head back home, Ashangmor had long since passed on to join his ancestors. The leadership was therefore assumed by a man called Obodai Nyonmo. With the assistance of seven captains, he led the returnees back home, not forgetting to take along with them their spiritual protector in the form of a deity named Egumegya. Having arrived in the Gã cultural environment, Obodai, probably under the direction of Egumegya, selected Osu to be their end-station. So, into the emerging Osu community they settled and because they were coming from the east, passed through Labadey and made their home on the east side of the Osu Alata quarters, near Christiansborg. In remembrance of the place from where they had migrated, they named their quarters 'Anahor.'"

"Why didn't they call it Anecho but Anahor?" Someone interjects.

"It was a case of transformation or corruption of the original over a period of time. This is similar to Allada, becoming Alata, found also in German as Teutsch becoming Deutsch," Replied Ataa Forkoyi, his voice dropping to a whisper; a sign that he needed a bottle of water to refresh his throat and renew his voice. As he hoses the water down, somebody seizes the opportunity to ask a question:

"Ataa Forkoyi, I hear there is another traditional community at Labadey, called Anahor. How did that come about?"

Ataa Forkoyi takes his time to gulp down a few mouthfuls of water from the bottle passed to him. He then closes his eyes, as if searching his mind for a response to the question. After a brief moment of reflection, he responds: "There is Anahor at Labadey, yes. I shall now tell you how that came about."

With a smile on his face, Ataa Forkoyi begins to tell the story behind Anahor at Labadey, distinct from Anahor at Osu.

"According to the Stones, as the returnees neared Osu, they made a short stop on their migratory journey to pay homage to the King of Labadey, who was known to be backed by a powerful deity, La Kpa. The interaction Obodai Nyonmo had with the King of Labadey, made a profound impression on the King. He was full of admiration for the leadership qualities of Obodai and appreciated his tenacity and capacity to lead his people all the way back from Anecho. The king saw in Obodai a great potential that could be used to buttress his own leadership at Labadey. So the King invited Obodai to consider ending their journey at Labadey and becoming part of the Labadey community.

"But Obodai's face was set towards Osu and to Osu he felt he must take his people because that was what Edumegya had declared. Obodai thanked the King but declined the invitation. The King was disappointed, but he respected Obodai's decision and thus accepted his refusal graciously.

"According to the Stones," continues Ataa Forkoyi, "the King then thought of a plan that could link Obodai and his people forever with Labadey. He offered Obodai a beautiful woman from the royal household as a wife. Obodai took the hand of the woman and took her to Osu. It was some of the offspring of this union that went back to Labadey to settle. In time, they grew to become a prominent community due to their ancestral connection to the royal household, and distinguished by their excellent heritage through Obodai the great leader, secured a position as Mankralo of Labadey. This is how Anahor at Labadey came into existence. Although the returnees from Anecho were the last group of migrants to enter the Osu community, Osu Anahor grew into a formidable community. It has all the unique cultural traits associated with people who 'went and came back.'"

Ataa Forkoyi continues to laud the so-called 'returnees.' "The Osu Anahor people took pride in their connections with far away Anecho, and that made them develop an Ewe-influenced naming paradigm for themselves, to distinguish them from the other peoples in the Osu community. That is why one hears names such as Sodza, Torgbor, Sai, Adza, Torto, Torshie and so on, only at Osu Anahor and La Anahor.

"My friends, this spirit of 'going and coming,' the spirit that engenders self-confidence, ideas and initiatives, became entrenched in Osu Anahor. For it happened that the very first Osu citizen to have been sent to far away Denmark and back happened to hail from Osu Anahor."

As he made this statement, one of the listeners who tried to read a little about Osu history before coming to listen, asked: "Ataa Forkoyi, are you referring to Christian Jakobus Protten?"

"Yes. But his full name was Christian Jakobus Africanus Protten. But hold on, I shall tell you later about Protten whose mother was called Aafio Dedei of Osu Anahor, and whose father was a Danish soldier, also called Christian Protten Teiko Saki, *'blofonyo bi,'* (Gã for 'White man's son'), as Christian Protten called himself, was one of the early mulattoes that characterized the intercourse between the Osu community and the Danes, which led to the formation of Danish-Osu."

With this final statement, Ataa Forkoyi claps his hands and shouts: "My friends, it is enough for today; the story is to be continued at another time. Thank you for listening to me. Be there for the next narration."

He raises his head to look at the position of the sun, and says to himself: "It is time to take a break and go for some rest." His listeners applaud him, as he takes a bow, turns around and walks away to his place of rest.

Two | The Making of Danish-Osu

Portuguese Lingua Franca at Osu

ATAA FORKOYI IS BACK UNDER THE TREES WHERE HE HAS BEEN meeting his listeners to take them on another tour around Osu. Today, the sun is shining brightly with the sky almost clear of clouds, so the weather is warm. As a result, the old man shows up with a straw hat on top of his bald head. There are indications that he is in high spirits as he enthusiastically shakes the hands of his listeners with friendly slaps on their backs and hugs one after the other, asking questions about their wellbeing.

Without any notice, he begins his narration:

"Osu as a traditional community was a kaleidoscope of diverse cultural groups located in four different quarters, as I told you the other time. These quarters are located to the west, north, east and south of where we are standing right now."

Before he can continue a listener interrupts, half soliloquizing: "From what we heard you say last time, these divergent cultural groups came with different languages, different deities, and different cultural practices. Is it not amazing that they transcended these boundaries to coalesce into a composite Gã-speaking community called Osu? Ataa Forkoyi, I am really amazed at this phenomenon of social engineering, when I think about how a number of communities in Ghana today, even with similar cultural backgrounds are making war on each other."

After this unexpected but welcome interruption, he continues at full speed: "Yes, it is really fantastic. Of course they had their differences and conflicts that broke out now and then; but notwithstanding that, they were able to create an environment that became a source of envy and jealousy for their neighbours, especially those from the interior in Akwamu." He continues: "Within this relatively peaceful environment, a sort of precursor to the United Nations in philosophy, the Portuguese arrived around the mid-sixteenth century after gaining a firm foothold in their Castle at Elmina. Their arrival further developed Osu as a commercial centre, with the brisk and lucrative trading activities they introduced.

"I hear the Stones saying so much about the Portuguese time at Osu because they settled and interacted well with the community. But today, I want to focus my narration on Danish-Osu So, for now, I will be brief you on what the Stones are saying about the Portuguese time at Osu, but do not forget that their presence was pervasive and powerful." Then Ataa Forkoyi begins to enumerate some of the landmarks of the Portuguese time at Osu. "They were the first Europeans to initiate the so called 'silent trade' or 'silent barter,' by which they exchanged goods without any verbal communication."

With a chuckle he continues, "This is how they did it. For more than a century before any other European appeared at Osu, the Portuguese used to bring out their goods from their boats; goods such as tobacco, rum, mirrors, beads, and fabric (cloths). They lay them on the beach in orderly piles, and then withdraw, hiding close enough to observe the response of the local people. After a while, the Osu people who had been observing, gathered the courage to go and take a closer look; they carefully inspected the goods and found them impressive and desirable. Cautiously they collected them and, certainly, it occurred to them that they should also leave something to replace what they had collected. So they sent the items to the community and brought in exchange food items like guinea corn, guinea fowls and some precious possessions such as ivory carvings and gold nuggets.

"Later, when mutual confidence had been created on both sides, more formal interactions developed and with time, the Portuguese came back with the group of enslaved workers of Allada to build a small lodge around 1640, on the promontory at the beach near the west side of the Klottey Lagoon. They named this lodge St. Francis Xavier and having thus established themselves, the interaction became more intense. With time, the Osu community was able to develop a medium of communication that sounded both Portuguese and Gã, and earned the name 'Negro-Portuguese.' The Akwamus, who later joined in the trade, referred to this trade language as *'portor kasa.'*

"According to the Stones, it was this medium of communication that over time became so refined that it developed into a lingua franca that stayed at Osu well after the Portuguese had left. All Europeans, even the domiciled Danes-Norwegians who attempted to interact with the people, had to master this 'portor kasa.' Some of the Portuguese words that remained in use by the Danes in their written reports in Danish, were *'Kase,'* (meaning: 'house'), *'Caboceer,'* (meaning: 'head leader'), and *'Cassare'* (meaning: 'marriage')."

At this point in the narration, a question arises: "Ataa Forkoyi, why is this language not being spoken at Osu now?"

"My friend, your question makes sense but let me explain that this localized form of Portuguese was a trading language, spoken essentially amongst those who traded with the Europeans. Yes, it became a lingua franca, a kind of a Lyso-African language, but it was used within limited circles. However, it still had some lingering effect on the local Gã language. Some of the original Portuguese words and phrases eventually became entrenched in the Gã language."

"Really?" somebody asks.

Ataa Forkoyi nods and goes on to mention some familiar Gã words, which actually evolved from Portuguese.

The Gã-speakers in the group soon begin to shout: "But hey! Since time immemorial, we have known *'sabolai,' 'aspatre,' 'samala,' 'kaminsan,' 'keesu,' 'tawa,'* as Gã words."

"No, these are Portuguese derivatives. Sabolai (Gã for 'onion') is *cebola* in Portuguese. Aspatre (shoes) is *sapatos* in Portuguese. Samala (soap) is derived from the Portuguese *'ensaboar,'* meaning 'to soap oneself.' 'Kaminsan' (shirt) is *'camisa'* in Portuguese. 'Keesu' (cheese) is *'queijo'* in Portuguese. 'Tawa' (tobacco) is *'tabaco'* in Portuguese. So, you see the Portuguese presence in Gã? Furthermore, do you know that some common family names in Osu, such as *'Djamlodja'* (the corrupted form of 'Azambudja') and *'Nunoo'* are Portuguese in origin?" enquires the savvy old man.

In response, one of the listeners comes up with a reflective comment: "Ataa Forkoyi, from what you have just told us, I get the impression that the Gã language, as has been said by one scholar, is very versatile indeed. Like the sea receiving the muddy waters of the Korle Lagoon without losing its purity, Gã has retained its semantic integrity, notwithstanding all the various foreign words that have been absorbed, adopted and adapted. Yes, the Gã language is as strong and muscular as the Gã people who speak it!"

With this unexpected comment, the old man shakes his head approvingly, with amused satisfaction. He then continues: "Yes, Osu kept on growing with the presence of the Portuguese and attracted a lot of people into its fold, both friends and foes. The foes were those who wanted to take over the brisk trade from the local intermediaries and assume full control of the intercourse with the European traders."

Ataa Forkoyi pauses dramatically and poses an unexpected question to his listeners: "Can you guess who these foes were?"

He does not wait for an answer but supplies it himself: "The foes were the aggressive and war-mongering, uncircumcised Akwamus from the interior. According to the Stones, the Akwamus persistently waged war on the Gã-Mashie, the Labadeye and all the coastal communities located to the east of Osu, up to the River Volta and beyond. Their aggression paid off, because eventually, from the mid-sixteenth to late seventeenth century, all these coastal communities submitted to their imperial authority, after they had virtually destroyed the primeval capital of the Gã state at Ayawaso in 1677."

At this point in the narration, somebody makes a funny sound at the back and everybody begins to laugh. Bemused, Ataa Forkoyi asks: "What is the joke? My friends, what the Akwamus did to the Gã people on the coast was no laughing matter. Do not make me feel bad this morning."

Then somebody standing directly in front of Ataa Forkoyi waves his hand with mock annoyance and tells the old man not to mind them. The one who has made them laugh jokingly refers to the Akwamus as the "Akromanus," likening them to African Romans in their imperialistic exploits on the Gã coast.

When Ataa Forkoyi gets the joke, he makes his listeners laugh even more heartily, by saying: "Yes, the Akwamus were Akromas because they were hawks always preying on our people. They did not even spare the Portuguese they wanted to trade with.

"According to the Stones, when they eventually took control of the lucrative trade, they began to sideline the local Osu traders. Soon after that, they realized that the Portuguese were not easy to deal with in trade."

"And so . . . " One of the listeners impatiently interjects.

"So they devised numerous strategies to outsmart the Portuguese. Their tricks did not work and frustration set in. In their aggression, they began to lose patience with the Portuguese and a confrontation erupted."

Coming of Christiansborg to Osu

With a sad face, Ataa Forkoyi continues with the narration and says in a shaking voice: "To make matters worse for the Portuguese, the Osu community attacked the Portuguese lodge to register their anger over the Portuguese attempts to turn the Klottey lagoon into a salt pond. In the context of this tenuous relationship and tense situation, another set of European traders showed up, the Swedes, on the Osu coast. Having heard what had been going on among the Portuguese, the Akwamus and the Osu community, the Swedes availed themselves of the opportunity and managed to persuade the Portugueses' unhappy trade partners that they would be better and more brotherly partners.

"So they teamed up and routed the Portuguese. They undertook this after they had tried in vain around 1640 to seize the Dutch trading lodge at Anomabu on the west coast. These Swedes totally razed the Portuguese lodge and by 1652, they had replaced it with their own, more solidly built lodge with the Swedish flag proudly hoisted over it, perched on the same promontory where the Portuguese lodge had stood. So ended the era of the first Europeans incursions into the Osu area. But interestingly enough, the Gã-Portuguese lingua franca never ended."

With a cynical smile, Ataa Forkoyi bursts out laughing and says in broken Twi:

"The Swedes forgot that *'Hwin hwim ade kɔ sro sro.'"*

An impatient listener stops him with:

"Old man, please what do you mean by that?"

He stands akimbo and addresses the questioner in a serious tone:

"My friend, why are you so impatient? Do you not know that the Stones never forgot the treachery of the Swedes? I hear the Stones fuming with anger as they recollect the actions of the Swedes at Osu. That is why I have to precede my narration about the Swedish era at Osu with this Twi proverb, 'If you cheat to gain quickly, you will be cheated by others to lose in no time what you have gained.'

"The Swedes thought they had gained a firm foothold at Osu on the east coast after sacking the Portuguese and taking full control of the lucrative trade which had come to include the buying and selling of enslaved people brought down by the Akwamus as war victims and captives from the interior. They, however, never reckoned with the Akwamu capacity for deception and intrigue. In no time, serious conflicts arose between the local traders and the Swedes that led to unfriendly relationships, ending in hostilities.

"Meanwhile, the Danes-Norwegians who had also lost miserably in the attempt to confiscate the Dutch lodge at Anomabu had decided to search for new trading points on the east coast, where they had heard that the British and the Dutch had found good local trade partners amongst the Gã-Mashie people who had began to expand their coastal settlements close to the English and Dutch Forts.

"So, they proceeded eastwards in 1659 by order of Governor Henning Albrecht, who was then residing in Friedrichsburg in Fanteland, with instructions to follow their arch-rivals the Swedes, to capture the little lodge they had built at Osu to replace the Portuguese one. As they arrived on the roads of the eastern coast, they saw in the distance, through the captain's telescope, two forts hoisting the English and Dutch flags respectively. When they observed these landmarks, they knew they were close to Osu where the Swedes had erected the lodge that had replaced the Portuguese one. They therefore got ready to disembark. From their ship, they organized a group of soldiers who took along land cannons and rowed in boats to arrive at Osu in the dark hours of the night. By stealth, they landed on the beach and headed for the Swedish lodge to attack it by surprise. In no time, they succeeded in overcoming the Swedes and forced them out of their lodge."

At this point in the narration, Ataa Forkoyi smiles and asks a rhetorical question: "With the Swedes gone, did the Danes think they had taken control of Osu?"

"No. The Danes could not have Osu so easily and cheaply. The Dutch next door at Kinka in Gã-Mashie learned that the Danes had landed and taken over the Swedish lodge. But the Dutch would not allow them the peace to settle down at Osu. So, getting a taste of what they had done to the Swedes, the Danes were pursued by the Dutch and harassed till they abandoned the little lodge. The Danes however, never gave up. They went back to Osu to reclaim their lodge. After the Dutch were kicked out, they made another attempt to snatch back the lodge from the Danes in 1660 but were unsuccessful this time." At this point, Ataa Forkoyi chuckles and says in an ironic tone:

"My friends I can assure you, with the high profits of the slave trade on the Guinea Coast, this cat-and-mouse game continued for a good while among the Europeans. Then, one day, according to the Stones, the Danes, who were hovering up and down along the east coast watching out for any new incursions from the Dutch, were unexpectedly invited to the English fort at British Accra for an apparently friendly and collegial reception. At this reception, where English ale and Scotch whisky flowed like the waters of the Volta River, the English confided in the Danes-Norwegians that they by all means would wish to assist the Danes to ensure that the harassments of the Dutch became a thing of the past. The Danes got excited, thinking that at last their dream to consolidate their foothold in Osu would be fulfilled.

"Ah! Little did the Danes know that the English had a diabolical plan in store for them, even while they took pains to explain how their assistance would be offered. It would be in an indirect manner so that the Dutch would not know the source of the assistance.

"According to the Stones," Ataa Forkoyi continues, "The Dutch were old rivals of the English and their offer to assist the Danes was not for any love they had for them but rather a conspiracy to get rid of the Danes. This would be achieved by tricking them into a suicidal journey inland to the primeval capital of Gã-Mashie at Ayawaso. They would be advised to go to King Okai Koi to seek his permission for bona fide rights over that promontory at Osu, on which they could develop a formidable fortress to protect their interests at Osu.

"But now my friends, before I proceed, let me give this background information for you to grasp the context of these events. At that time, the two sets of Europeans who had built their trading posts next to the Gã-Mashie settlements, the English and the Dutch, were not aware that the coastal area where both the Portuguese and the Swedes had unsuccessfully attempted to get a foothold was under the traditional jurisdiction of the King of Labadey, Odoi Atsem."

With this explanation, somebody asks a question: "Ataa Forkoyi, could this ignorance be the reason why the English mischievously advised the Danes to go to Ayawaso to see King Okai Koi to obtain his permission?"

"Precisely so," answers the Old Man but then, with a cunning look, he pauses in his narration for a good while.

At this uncomfortable silence, one of the listeners whom he has earlier reprimanded for impatience, blurts out:

"Ataa Forkoyi, what next?"

"Patience! Patience! If you are patient, you will be able to cut up the ant to see its heart!" responds Ataa Forkoyi with a smile. With this proverb, he picks up his thoughts and continues: "As soon as the Danes were given this advice, they did not even wait for the formal ending of the reception which had been given in their honour. In a half-drunken state, they thanked the English profusely for their hospitality and begged for their leave.

"They went back to Osu and hired an interpreter who accompanied them on their first-ever inland march to call on King Okai Koi at his royal abode at Ayawaso. This Gã-Mashie man was a master interpreter in the lingua franca which the Portuguese had left behind. You see, it was a trap since the British knew that the Danes would incur the displeasure of the King if they showed their white faces in his court. But the Danes, in their naivety, went to Ayawaso with the audacity to negotiate with King Okai Koi for the right to occupy the famous promontory at Osu.

"According to the Stones," continues Ataa Forkoyi, "the Danes, upon arrival at the court of King Okai Koi, brought out a lot of fanciful presents from Europe, including a good number of barrels of Danish rum, and presented these to the king, his numerous council of elders, and court attendants. The barrels were immediately opened and extensive carousing began. When everybody had had their fill, the Danes opened negotiations over the promontory at Osu. They desperately cajoled the King to give them that unique site at Osu, insisting they would not leave his court until he did so. The King was not sure what they were talking about for he was not familiar with that part of the east coast. But he was the King of Gã-Mashie and all land in Gã-Mashie, both east and west, belonged to him and his ancestors."

At this point, Ataa Forkoyi gets into a pensive mood. One can see he is agitated and reluctant to continue. However, he pulls himself together and says in hushed tones:

"My friends, I tell you that I feel just as the Stones are feeling as they recollect how the promontory at Osu was given out to the Danes-Norwegians. Osu lands, including the shore, the promontory, and the lagoon, originally stood under the custodianship of Odoi Atsem, the King of Labadey. He had agreed to allow the Osudoku migrants to settle there among the aboriginal Kpeshi people.

So why should the Danes-Norwegians come to negotiate with Okai Koi on the matter?"

Ataa Forkoyi goes on to answer his own question: "In the court of King Okai Koi stood, among the court elders, the *Wulɔmɔ*, the traditional, overall Gã-Mashie high priest, de facto customary leader, who held spiritual and moral authority over both the people and the land on which they lived. As a spiritual authority, he represented *Ataa Naa Nyɔŋmɔ*, the Supreme Creator of the universe in which the entire territory of Gã-Mashie was located. As a representative of moral authority, he had no vested interest in the ownership of the land. As high priest he owned no property; he was above material possessions and was landless. He knew that land, to the Gã-Mashie people, was a sacred entity that belonged to the ancestors, the living and the unborn. Although King Okai Koi had no clue where the Osu promontory was located, it was the presence of this high priest that gave him the authority to negotiate its right of access and usage, and to grant it to the Danes-Norwegians."

Having listened to this impressive presentation on the Gã conception of land as a metaphysical-geographical phenomenon, somebody humorously asked if at the time of negotiation, the King and his elders were sober or still under the influence of the Danish rum. With a smile on his wrinkled face, Ataa Forkoyi responds to the question by dropping a hint of what the Stones had to say on this.

"You see, at such negotiations the wise men, whose chief was always the high priest, the Wulɔmɔ, would remain sober, because they never, by custom, touched alcohol. The king was intoxicated but his wits were around him through the wise men."

A curious listener then asks: "So how much did the Danes pay the King for the Osu promontory?"

Promptly, Ataa Forkoyi responds: "The Danes did not pay anything for the promontory. In Gã custom and tradition, nobody can buy land nor may anybody be paid for land. Land is too sacred to have monetary value. The Danes only gave a token to compensate the King for passing on an inalienable right to them."

"How much was this token?" shoots back the questioner.

Ataa Forkoyi scratches the left hand side of his head with his right hand and begins in an undertone:

"According to the Stones, on the 18th August 1661, one Mr. Jost Cramer, a Danish governor of the then fort Friedrichsborg, offered an amount of 50 benda of gold as a compensation for receiving the right of access and usage of the promontory at Osu.

"On this memorable day," continues Ataa Forkoyi, dramatizing the sense of victory of the leader of the Danish negotiators, "the Danish gentleman was so moved that, through the Gã-Mashie interpreter, (who had been struggling in the local 'portor kasa' to translate between the King and the Danes), he spontaneously declared:

'I shall build for my king and his noble chartered Danish African Company, a fortress and a stone house at Ozzou at the first possible opportunity. The resulting architectural edifice shall have no superior building on the Guinea coast in the years to come.'"

Having made this statement just as it was made by the Danish gentleman on that fateful day in King Okai Koi's court, the Old Man heaves a sigh, closes his eyes and bows his head as if in prayer. His listeners wait patiently for him to continue with the narration. Nobody makes any attempt to rouse him with a question, knowing by now that whenever he gets into this state, he is indicating that he needs time to compose himself.

Then suddenly, Ataa Forkoyi bursts out in a loud voice: "My friends, that day in the court of King Okai Koi marked the beginning of Danish-Osu."

One of the listeners asks:

"Ataa Forkoyi, what do you mean by that?"

"What do I mean? You see, the very moment the king received the 50 benda of gold, Jost Cramer, in his emotional state, began to imagine a mighty Danish Fortress with the name 'Christiansborg' written boldly on its north west façade, facing the Osu settlement. He also saw in his mind's eye Danish soldiers, merchants, surgeons, chaplains, administrators and governors landing from Danish ships and settling at Osu to do brisk business shipping tons of human cargo across the Atlantic to the Danish-owned islands in the Caribbean."

Tarnishing of Osu with Danish Markings

Ataa Forkoyi goes on in a high-pitched voice:

"Jost not only visualized the brisk trade but also the lightening of the Osu coloured landscape as these hordes of Danish-Norwegian men populated the community through African women's wombs. He got very excited and instructed his companions to bring out more rum to celebrate.

"The celebration of the establishment of Danish-Osu went on till the wee hours of the morning, by which time neither the Danish guests nor their Gã-Mashie hosts could stand on their feet or speak intelligibly. When the cool morning breeze blew in at Ayawaso, the Danes began to sober up and eventually Jost Cramer brought out a prepared document and showed this to the King, explaining through the interpreter that this was a treaty to which the King had to append his signature. This was the document to attest that the King had given the Danes the right of access and usage of the promontory at Osu."

At this point, the Old Man makes a dramatic pause, then drops his voice and says plaintively: "King Okai Koi was still half awake but when the interpreter explained what Jost wanted him to do, he agreed and made three crosses on the document where he was asked to append his signature. With this, the deal was done and the promontory at Osu was given to the Danes and Danish-Osu was born at Ayawaso."

Ataa Forkoyi continues: "As soon as the signed document was received by Mr. Cramer, the negotiation ceremony came to an end. The Danes thanked the King and his Council of Elders and hurriedly prepared to depart from Ayawaso. But before then, the King asked his high priest, the Wulɔmɔ, to pray for the blessings of *Ataa Naa Nyɔŋmɔ*, the Omnipotent, upon the agreement and upon the Danes' successful occupation of the promontory at Osu. With these powerful blessings upon the deal, the Danes quickly took their leave and headed south back to Osu, to sail their ship westwards."

At the mention of the westward direction of the Danes, one of the listeners raises his hand. "Yes, my friend. What do you want to say?"

"I do not have anything to say but I have a question," he responds slowly, with some confusion.

In a friendly tone, Ataa Forkoyi encourages him to pose his question.

"Why did the Danes not remain at Osu to start developing the promontory they had been given rather than proceeding westwards?"

To this question Ataa Forkoyi smiles and says:

"According to the Stones, because of the harassment from the Dutch, the Danes had their lodge at Osu in a makeshift state, not the best condition to be used as an operational base. So they sailed westwards back to Fort Fredriksborg to arrange with the Governor to dispatch a ship to Denmark as soon as practicable, to report the good news to the King of Denmark and the managers of the Company in Copenhagen.

"However, I must mention that Jost Cramer left behind Christen Cornelissen, a Danish builder and soldier, with a small gang of staff to start surveying sites from where stones could be quarried to provide materials to embark on the construction of the mighty fortress and stone house he had conceived to honour his King and his Company. In due time, a ship arrived back from Denmark with building materials including bricks, cobble-stones, timber, metals and so on, together with builders to support Christen Cornelissen in the construction of the Fort on the promontory."

Ataa Forkoyi completes this statement with a deep breath, looking tired. Somebody gives him a stool. He gratefully acknowledges this gesture of thoughtfulness and lowers his body slowly, asking for a bottle of water. He takes his time to drink.

Ataa Forkoyi regains his breath, picks up the pitch and continues: "According to the Stones, the construction of the fortress proceeded gradually with labour from the Osu community and the enslaved men and women who were kept by the Danes."

Ataa Forkoyi is suddenly interrupted with a question: *"Nuumoe,* for clarification, may I know where the construction was taking place? Was it on the site of the old Danish lodge?"

With mild irritation, Ataa Forkoyi responds:

"The construction was taking place on the promontory. My friends, the building developed into a massive citadel, a military-commercial architectural edifice, designed, built and equipped to resist any attacks from the sea and land. Now, let me give you some details from the Stones about the history of this Danish fortress. The construction work initiated by Builder Cornelissen in 1661 went on for years with extensions and repairs continuing a century after work had begun.

"In 1751 when the surgeon, Carl Gustav Engmann, was acting as the Governor, major repairs were undertaken and he, as a surgeon, being acutely conscious of water safety and security in the Fort, embarked on an ambitious project to develop an underground water cistern. This cistern measured seven metres deep, six and a half metres wide and seven and a half metres long. The skilled and unskilled labour provided for the excavation and stone-masonry work to line the interior of the cistern was provided by Osu men and women who had to be paid."

One of the listeners with an interest in architecture interrupts with a question:

"Were the stones brought from Denmark to execute this work by Engmann?"

"No, sir," responds Ataa Forkoyi promptly. "As I mentioned earlier, the Danes had carried out a survey to identify sites from where they could quarry stones to complement what they wanted to bring down from Denmark. They found sites on the west of Osu and on the eastern side between Osu and Labadey. This place came to be known as 'Tanshi' from the original 'Teiashi,' meaning under the stones. Most of the stones Engmann used to build his cistern came from there. The total number of stones used amounted to an equivalent of 16,000 Danish bricks."

The listener with the architectural interest enquires about the material used to bind the stones that lined the cistern. Ataa Forkoyi explains that seashells were fired to obtain lime as a bonding material.

"According to the Stones," Ataa Forkoyi continues, "some of the seashells were collected from Ningo, another trading post of the Danes on the far east of Osu, in the direction of Quitta. The Danish slaves collected them and they were brought to Osu in small boats rowed by 'remidors,' the local, professional rowers. Besides seashells, the other building materials collected from the environment were clay and wood. Other ambitious projects undertaken by Engmann included the building of larger slave dungeons, warehouses, more residential accommodation and a chapel."

Somebody at the back of the group shouts out cynically:

"And a chapel? In a slave fortress?"

Ataa Forkoyi replies calmly:

"Yes, a chapel. You know, the Danes-Norwegians retained their religious habits, although the religion they practiced at Osu did not affect their social and business activities. Engmann had to obtain permission from Denmark to undertake these projects in conformity with the established Danish culture of order and decency as determined by their national Christian faith. Accordingly, Engmann was granted permission because the water to be stored in the cistern was to serve the basic needs of the fort dwellers, including the slaves seeking fresh water in the holding dungeons and other foreign ships that would berth in the roads, while the chapel would satisfy the need for contact with their Creator.

"So the fortress was ultimately built to provide storage space for goods in transit as well as dungeons for hordes of human cargo en route to the Danish islands of St. Thomas and St. Croix in the Caribbean. But it was not only a slave emporium; it was a piece of

Figure 6: Christiansborg Castle, Osu; illustrated by W. F. Hedges, F.RI.B.A.
© 1925 W. T. Balmer

Copenhagen, the home of the King and the Noble Chartered Danish Africa Company. It was therefore intended as a small palatial home for the Danes who had to live and work inside it. Hence, it had well-designed spaces including elegant and spacious rooms for the Governor."

Ataa Forkoyi pronounces 'Governor' as 'Gonner,' so somebody immediately asks who the "Gonner" was. Ataa Forkoyi realizes he has been misunderstood, makes a dramatic pause and comes back with a rhetorical statement: "Who is the Governor? You may ask. The Governor was the most senior administrator among the Danish local staff, representing the Company in charge of administration and management of the Danish trading activities and transactions on the Guinea Coast, including the social and religious life of the Danish staff."

Having cleverly rectified himself Ataa Forkoyi continues from the point before the interruption: "As I was about to say, the citadel on the promontory took shape, becoming reminiscent of some of the baroque fortresses in Denmark. With this impressive architectural character, the Danes could not help but christen it 'Christiansborg,' in honour of their reigning King, Christian V. From then on, this massive stone edifice, which became the most significant European trading post on the east coast, served as a Danish emporium and clearing-house, not only to promote the transatlantic slave trade but to perpetuate Danish culture through the governors, administrators, surgeons, merchants, and even the soldiers. Thus arose the pervasive shadow of the massive Christiansborg that befell the indigenous Osu community."

A lady listener now raises her voice: "Ataa Forkoyi, you are being too poetic. Just tell us what the Stones are saying!"

At this unexpected interjection, Ataa Forkoyi clears his throat and says with his eyes closed:

"The shadow, my friends, is the direct and indirect impact of the Danish way of life that was carried into Osu society through the caboceers, the chiefs, the women and their children, and the local Osu workers in Christiansborg. This impact intensified as trading activities expanded and became more lucrative within the courtyard and around Christiansborg. Then came more Danes and other Europeans to Osu.

"As the Danish population increased, there emerged a new breed of Osu people with light skins and black mothers. Their presence was noted in all the traditional quarters and soon they began to function as agents of change. The mothers of these light-skinned children could use them as tickets to obtain easy access to Christiansborg, thus participating actively in both the economic and social activities that took place inside the Danish fort.

"These women were so prolific in their economic and social interaction with the Danes that their activities were documented in the Danish records. Together with their light skinned children, often carried on their backs as they went about their business in Christiansborg, they became the bridge that transferred Christiansborg culture beyond its walls, to embrace the Osu social-cultural landscape. This eventually evolved into a kind of rainbow community that manifested Danish features among the people at Osu Kinkawe, Osu-Ashinte Blohum, Osu-Alata and Osu-Anahor.

"Besides the 'bridge' that brought Christiansborg to the Osu community, there were also the ordinary Danish workers who literally had to depend on the Osu community for their survival. These frequented the traditional community market for their provisions and meals. According to the Stones, some of these Danes became so impoverished that the local people called them *'Poor Orsue Whites.'* Some were even found to be in debt for meals received from Osu women, at the time of their death."

"Ataa Forkoyi, I find the transformation of the Osu socio-cultural landscape into Danish-Osu quite intriguing. Did you say there were black women of Osu who had light-skinned children that mingled with their relatives in the various quarters to effect this transformation of the indigenous Osu community into Danish-Osu?" asks one female listener, in a foreign accent.

"Yes, according to the Stones," answers Ataa Forkoyi emphatically.

The woman continues: "If that is the case, how did it happen?"

At this question, the listeners explode into hearty laughter and chant:

"Ataa Forkoyi, tell us more; Ataa Forkoyi tell us more!"

So Ataa Forkoyi with a straight face and in a mock-serious tone, begins as if at a pulpit:

"I should tell you more? Wait, I shall tell you more. The Stones have a rich memory of how Osu became Danish-Osu; they even have documentary evidence of the Danish agents who turned Osu into Danish-Osu through their social escapades and cultural imperialism. But now, let me have a break."

With this, Ataa Forkoyi walks to the nearby neem tree and sits down. He reclines with his back to the trunk and dozes off, snoring. After a while, the Old Man wakes up, looking fresh after his short nap, and with vim and vigour, picks up his narration with a question for his listeners.

"You want to hear more about how the Danes changed Osu into Danish-Osu, do you? Well, get ready. According to the Stones, the process was slow and silent but salient and varied; nobody really took notice until it all began to show, not only in the appearance of light skinned children among the kids of Osu, but also in the appearance of stone houses among the indigenous adobe houses in the traditional quarters, and the wearing of Danish clothes by Osu women.

"Having firmly established their headquarters within the massive walls of Christiansborg," continues Ataa Forkoyi, "the Danes began to descend in their numbers on Osu, to continue with enthusiasm, the lucrative trade in slaves brought from all over the Guinea Coast. Many of these Danes-Norwegians were soldiers and young men seeking adventure. Christiansborg was, to them, a place for carousing and debauchery to the highest degree, free from the social restraints of the home environment back in Denmark.

"These young men," he continues in a monotonous voice, "to counteract the effects of boredom and the observed anguish of the enslaved prisoners, escaped the confines of Christiansborg's massive walls to venture into town any time they were off-duty, and there were plenty of opportunities. There were numerous occasions to sow their wild oats among the shapely and sparsely-clad, voluptuous young Osu women, resulting in offspring that were neither black nor white. These mixed-race children came to be known as 'mulatto' in the local Portuguese lingua franca."

Ataa Forkoyi clears his throat with some mirth and continues: "The life of freedom and fun was not limited to the younger ones. Senior Danish administrators and merchants also took time off from their strenuous slave-trading activities and visited the various quarters to familiarize themselves with the social life of Osu. Some of the visits were nightly rendezvous which had been arranged with the local women and men who came to the fort to conduct business during the day. These visits were always good opportunities for the Danish workers and merchants to relax outside the depressive walls of Christiansborg, and to taste not only the local dishes but also to share some intimacy with the hospitable women who were always very charitable hostesses.

"My friends," continues Ataa Forkoyi, "these regular European incursions into Osu were great events in the community, although not without pain and anguish for some of these charitable hostesses. Some of the consequences were women getting pregnant and abandoned; women being tricked into marriage only to be sold later into slavery."

Figure 7: A nineteenth century painting of a reception given by the Danes to a visiting French Prince at the Governor's parlour in Christiansborg with dark-skinned nude Osu women serving white-clad European men at table.
Illustration courtesy of Pernille Ipsen's dissertation

Ataa Forkoyi adds, laughing scornfully, "A kind of old-fashioned wife-abuse, if you will." Then he continues: "According to the Stones, the amorous visits that led to the change in coloured landscape in Osu were not always from Christiansborg to the traditional quarters of Osu, but sometimes in the opposite direction."

Somebody immediately asks: "Ataa Forkoyi, what do you mean by this?"

"My friends, let me assure you that the Stones were witness to the numerous visits that came from the Osu community into the fort, almost on daily basis. You see, there was a constant trooping in and out of Christiansborg by different groups of people. There were workers who were employed at Christiansborg that had to come in and out to undertake the various duties they had been assigned. There were also traders, who came from Osu and other communities near or far from Osu every day, except the days when the gates had to be shut for some reason, or to conduct business with the Danes. Among this group of traders were enterprising women whose presence could not escape the keen interest of some of the Danish administrators and merchants. These women also gained the right to frequent the premises of the Fort, even after the gates had been shut at night. They had this singular right because they had become favorites even of the Governors, who were supposed to have left families behind in Denmark.

"Unlike the adventurous young men, some of these Danes took these relationships seriously and went ahead and formalized them by enacting what came to be described as *'Cassare'* in Portuguese word usage. In such situations, the Danes were obliged to pay the exorbitant bride price in accordance with the prevailing Osu tradition of taking a woman's hand in marriage. The Stones also remember other situations where some Danes, in order to get around the expense, chose to marry enslaved women they had bought, who had no family to whom the bride price could be paid.

"As a result of the payment of bride price, the offspring from these relationships were accepted and integrated into the families of these Osu women. In some cases, the children of the Danish men were adopted by the male members of the women's families, in accordance with the Gã customary practice that gave familial responsibility to the male siblings of a woman who bore a child without an identifiable husband. In such cases, the children were given the known Danish father's name but were brought up by the mothers within the extended family setting. In other cases, the women involved were recognized by the Danish administration, giving them the opportunity to engage in direct trade with the Danes. In some cases, these women acted as great supporters to the Danes while they sojourned on the coast. It was this support in the form of food and nursing care that enabled the Danes to survive the life-threatening tropical environment."

While Ataa Forkoyi goes on with his narration about how Osu became Danish-Osu, somebody reminds him that he has promised to show documentary evidence of statistics on relationships between Danes and Osu women. Thus reminded, he breaks his narration, turns his back on his listeners and walks back to the neem tree, where he has left his well-worn leather bag. He opens it and pulls out some sheets of very old documents. He uses his left hand to lift up one towards the sun, to check if the script is still legible. It is, although rather difficult to read; he nods his head with delight and mutters with a smile:

"Huh, these Danes could document things ooh! Their record keeping was exquisite."

He brings these archival documents, all written in beautiful cursive Danish, to his listeners, and pointing with his long, bony index finger, says: "Look at them, here they are; the statistics on the Danes who came to the Guinea coast, starting from the seventeenth century up to the time they left Osu in 1850. You can find out a lot about Danes who once lived at Osu, including those whose offspring are still found around Osu today."

He holds up the first sheet and points to its heading: Basic Statistics on Men, consisting of First Name, Middle Name, Surname; Year of Arrival, Date of Death, Year of Birth, Date of Birth, Place of Birth, Year of Death, Place of Death, Date of Arrival, and Year of Return.

He holds up the second sheet and points to its heading: Family Statistics on Men, consisting of Serial Number, General Number, Male Number according to Basic Statistics, Father's Name, Father's Occupation, Father's Place of Birth, Mother's name, Mother's year of Birth, Mother's Occupation, Mother's Place of Birth, Number of Siblings, and Year of Baptism.

Up goes the third sheet and he points to its heading: Occupation and Education, consisting of Serial Number, Male Number, Type of Occupation, Level of Education, and Type of Employment.

Up goes the fourth sheet, and this time, Ataa Forkoyi, with a chuckle, points to its heading: Marital Relationship of Men, consisting of Serial Identification Number, Male's Identification Number, Wife's Identification Number, Wife's Status (Racial Married/

Concubine), Relationship's Number.

At this point, one of the listeners standing right in front of Ataa Forkoyi raises his hand to stop Ataa Forkoyi. Ataa Forkoyi reacts surprisingly, shouting: "What is the matter, my friend?"

When the person realizes he has disturbed the Old Man he hesitatingly asks: "What is a concubine, a young female chicken or a fully-grown one?"

With this question everybody breaks into hearty laughter that infects the Old Man, because a smile erases the frown on his face.

"Well, I do not know exactly what the Danes had in mind when they documented all this. However, a concubine is not a chicken. A concubine is an adult woman found in a conjugal relationship with a man, without a formal marriage having taken place."

Somebody jokingly asks:
"Is she a woman-friend or a girl-friend?"

Ataa Forkoyi shakes his head with a smile, "These young rascals! How can a concubine be a woman-friend or a girl-friend? Look, a concubine is a wife without a marriage license!"

At this, a roar of laughter bursts from the listeners.

Ataa Forkoyi continues with his presentation, pointing to the heading on the fourth sheet: Basic Statistics on Women, consisting of Serial Number, Woman's Identification Number, First Name, Surname, Status (Racial), Woman's Father's Name, Year of Birth, Date of Birth, Place of Birth, Year of Death, Date of Death, and Place of Death.

Finally, he brings out the fifth sheet and wearily points to its heading: Information on Children, consisting of Serial Number, Relationship's Number, Child's First Name, Child's Surname, Child's Father's Name, Father's Identification Number, Child's Year of Birth, Child's Date of Birth, Child's Year of Death, Child's Date of Death, Child's Place of Birth, Status (White or Mulatto).

When Ataa Forkoyi completes the presentation, he gives a big yawn and sleepily announces: "You the Osu people must pay attention to these statistics. You will see a number of familiar names as you go through the list, names which are still commonly used by local Osu families. The names in these documents I have shown you are names of the progenitors of these Danish-Osu families."

Although he sounded a bit tired, he continues anyway:

"Some of the spellings of these Osu family names have remained as they were originally. Some have been corrupted. For example, family names such as Bergessen, Holm, Lutterodt, Quist, Engmann, Sonne, Hesse, Fleischer, Schandorf, Reimer, Brock, Hansen, Malm, Palm, Wulff, Pedersen, Richter, Reindorf, Rheinholdt, Larsen, Magnussen, and Meyer, have remained authentic in their spelling. However, the spelling of Badger came from Bagge; Briandt came from Brandt; Swaneker came from Svanekjaer; Lokko came from Locko, evolving from Lykke."

Mentioning the name Lokko or Lykke suddenly makes Ataa Forkoyi excited. He says with a strange energy: "You know what, according to the Stones, the Osu Lokko family may have the longest history, in that their progenitor, called Governor Lykke, might have been one of the very first Danish administrators to have had a marital relationship with a local Osu woman.

"Records have it that Hans Lykke (also spelled 'Luecke' in the records), who was born in Jutland, Denmark, came to Osu from the Danish Fort Fredriksborg, to take over the Governorship of Christiansborg in April, 1685. Before coming to Osu, he was alleged to have mortgaged Christiansborg to the English for about seven marks of gold, whilst still in charge at Fort Fredriksborg.

"He had a non-conformist personality with a strong drive for action, making him the first Danish official on record to father a mulatto son with an Osu woman prior to his death at Osu on the 19th of September, 1687. After his death it was also alleged that he had fathered a child with an Osu woman called Djagble (Jamenie). The mulatto son was an Osu King from 1698 until February 1709 under the name Noete Doku."

In the Shadow of Christiansborg

After highlighting some of the outstanding features of the worn, old Danish document, Ataa Forkoyi begins once again to speak to his listeners in a rather depressed mood:

"According to the Stones, the moral life of the Danes-Norwegians was negatively affected by the conditions under which they lived and worked in Christiansborg; and due to the intense interaction they had with the Danish-Osu community, this lifestyle seeped out under the gates of Christiansborg into the community to infect the mulattoes, their mothers, and their kith and kin.

"The long periods of inactivity between the arrival of Danish ships on the coast and their departure, loaded with human cargo destined for the Caribbean; these long periods punctuated by the brutality of keeping imprisoned African men and women in the dungeons posed a psychological challenge that the Danish men would have to overcome to be able to survive on the coast."

Ataa Forkoyi continues in the same dreary tone:

"The poisonous atmosphere inside Christiansborg manifested itself at Danish-Osu in various ways as the growing number of young mulattoes, together with their local clansmen and women, imitated the loose life of sin and debauchery that went on behind the high walls of Christiansborg. Such corrupted and corroding ways of life in Danish-Osu were at times taken to extremes when slave-ships arrived in the roads on the coast.

"According to the Stones, in addition to their cargo of goods for exchange, these ships sometimes brought along short-term visitors, sailors, merchants and adventurers dispirited and emotionally dissipated through long and dangerous sea voyages, who were looking for avenues on land to release their tensions and trials. These visitors found their way into town through the gates of Christiansborg and added their influence to the Danish-Osu social world, roaming about in the community, drinking, pursuing hedonist pleasures and gratifying their lusts. They became models for some of the mulatto youth who in turn began to damage the Gã moral fabric by imitating the things they saw the visitors doing. With pain, one of the Stones recollects the social atmosphere at Danish-Osu characterized by immorality: the wickedness, drunkenness, godlessness, and involvement in some evil religious practices."

With a grim face, Ataa Forkoyi continues his narration:

"The change taking place at Danish-Osu as a result of the emerging numbers of mulatto children that were fatherless but had rich uncles in the traditional community, and their problematic behavior, were causing headaches for the administrators at the fort and began to generate serious thoughts in the minds of the Danish chaplains and their assistants who had to take care of both the moral and spiritual matters at Christiansborg. They eventually came to the conclusion that, although Osu-Christiansborg was far away from Kopenhagen Christiansborg, and although as they used to say, 'Heaven is high and Europe far away,' the values and culture of the King of Denmark and that of the Company must not be dragged through the muddy waters of the Klottey Lagoon on the Guinea Coast.

"Something had to be done about the emerging Sodom and Gomorrah within Christiansborg and the Danish-Osu community. The original chapel in the fort, which had gone into a state of disrepair, had to be renovated and reinstalled to address the religious and moral upkeep of the fort dwellers. In addition, it was thought that there was the need for a school to be put in place in the fort to take care of 'civilizing' and *'Danish-izing'* the fatherless mulattoes who had been running around with bare bottoms, similar to their dark-skinned half-siblings and cousins in the Danish-Osu community. It was hoped that a school could make these non-black and non-white fellows into future Danish soldiers and workers that might serve the Company. Of course, the future of these mulattoes was not seen in relations to the Danish-Osu community but only in relations to the Company and to how it affected its economic operations on the Guinea Coast and in the Danish Islands of St. Thomas and St. Croix in the Caribbean."

At this point in the narration, the Old Man, thirsty and exhausted, beckons a hawker with a head-load of coconuts. He gets to Ataa Forkoyi and lowers the head-load. He selects one large coconut from the bunch, and with his well-sharpened cutlass, chips off the top of the fruit; he removes a calabash from the container attached to his head-load, empties the sweet coconut milk into it and gives it to Ataa Forkoyi. He gratefully receives it with his right hand and puts it to his mouth.

The Old Man gulps down the drink without a break, until there is no drop left inside the calabash. He requests more. As he drinks, his thirst infects his listeners and they surround the young man and begin to buy coconuts as if they are at a jumble sale. They drink the coconut milk with relish. The coconut break comes to an end and Ataa Forkoyi, refreshed, continues:

"So, in February 1722, a motley collection of mulatto children, boys and girls, was gathered by Chaplain Svane from the traditional Danish-Osu community and brought to Christiansborg under the auspices of Governor David Herrn, to start the premiere Danish Castle-School."

At this reference to the start of the premiere Danish Castle School, one of the listeners, who is a retired District Education Officer of the Presbyterian Church Education Unit, impatiently interrupts with a question about how the mulatto boys and girls and their Osu relatives were being educated before the School came into existence in February 1722.

Ataa Forkoyi smiles respectfully and with a pedantic touch, responds to the former education officer's question:

"Madam, there was nothing. The children, as spun in the loom of the memory of the Stones, were doing nothing except playing around with their kith and kin, either on the beach or at the fore court of Christiansborg, and aping the carefree European visitors who frequented Osu to trade in human cargo.

"Of course, at that time, childhood did not last long. By the time these children had reached adolescence, they had already entered the adult world. In that context, the boys were apprenticed in various local crafts and artisanal practices and learned hunting, warring and how to use herbal medicine. The girls were trained in household duties: childcare, cooking and working as traditional birth attendants. The old birth attendants from whom these girls had to learn were well versed in the art of assisting laboring women to a safe delivery. All deliveries in the community, whether of dark-skinned or light-skinned babies, were capably handled by them.

"But note, in some cases, the male mulatto children were taken into the service of the Company and were apprenticed in some European occupations such as becoming soldiers at a very early age. The greatest problem was with the female mulatto children who could not be assisted in any way by the Danish administration at that time. These girls were therefore prone to becoming young mistresses and voluntary chattels to offer cheap services to the visiting Europeans and the fort workers who came down to the community at night to prowl the byways and lanes of Danish-Osu."

"So, in a way, the establishment of the Castle School was an important social welfare intervention to save the mulatto girls from a life of harlotry and prostitution," declares the Madam of the Education Unit, to which Ataa Forkoyi positively responds with a smile but with a slight look of embarrassment at the words "harlotry and prostitution."

To tone things down, Ataa Forkoyi decides to supply another historical piece that the Stones unwillingly speak about, to the credit of the Danish administration.

"Besides introducing the school, the Danes put in place another special welfare scheme to support the management and operation of the school without costing the children anything. The wages of all those suspected to have had children with the Osu women were taxed, and the proceeds from this taxation were put into a common fund, dubbed 'Poor Mulatto Children's Chest' (PMCC). Since most of these children were orphaned or abandoned, they needed all the extra support to survive the challenges posed by the unfriendly environment. The PMCC therefore became a monetary relief fund from which provisions for food, clothing, head-wear, footwear, and sometimes health care were provided for the mulatto children who attended Pastor Svane's Castle School. The PMCC remained an important feature of the school and was maintained for as long as the school was in existence." When Ataa Forkoyi has finished with this account on the PMCC, he picks up again the story of the premier Danish Castle School:

"The Stones recollect that the Osu mothers sent their children to school at Christiansborg every day and the children came home to the community at the end of the day. However, despite these daily visits to the Castle, the children only got far enough to repeat the letters when the Danish teacher pointed to them, since they could not understand a word of what the teacher was saying."

Somebody then jokingly remarks:

"What was going on in the school was just what goes on in the Makaranta in the Zongo Arabic schools of today, isn't it?"

"Yes! Rote learning, "Ataa Forkoyi responds and as if he has gone into a trance, continues in a sudden chant: "You see these mulattoes had been raised until then on their mother tongue, Gã, and knew nothing else. They never really knew their Danish fathers who had either died earlier or had abandoned them even before they were born. So they had zero knowledge of the Danish language before coming to the castle school.

"However, a few of the boys had learnt to read a little by the age of fourteen or fifteen, but they still did not know the meaning of the words. When the teacher attempted to speak to them in Danish, they just shook their heads and could neither understand nor respond since they did not know the meanings of the words they heard.

"But, do you know? The children learnt a lot without the medium of the Danish language. The courtyard of Christiansborg was a big classroom in which the children were exposed to the way of life of the Danes. They saw the debauchery; they saw the brutalities meted out to the recalcitrant enslaved prisoners who were brought out of the slave dungeons now and then to be disciplined; they heard the noises the dangling chains made on the stone pavement of the fort's courtyard and even saw the shackled men and women being dragged through the gate of no return to the beach for boats to ferry them to the waiting slave-ships in the roads.

"What they saw while attending school inside Christiansborg, were practical and poignant lessons in cultural anthropology and psychology to make them feel, as light skinned persons, better than their dark skinned half-siblings and cousins left behind at the forecourt of the fort."

With this last statement the mood of Ataa Forkoyi suddenly

changes; he appears now to be his usual friendly self. He continues with the story in a more relaxed manner:

"The first Danish teacher, Pastor Elias Svane, a typically dedicated and committed educator, trudged on nonetheless. The school schedule was from 7:00 to 10.30 in the morning and again from 2:00 to 5:00 in the afternoon. The time in between was for eating and recreation, since it was too hot to teach in the middle of the day. The curriculum at the school was consistent with the preparation that Danish children received before their confirmation in Denmark. The children were taught to read and recite the Bible and were examined in the catechism and the Lord's Prayer.

"Even though the language appeared to have been the greatest hurdle in their religious instruction, after 1764, when Christian Protten's introduction to Gã and translations of interpretation of passages from the Bible were printed in Denmark, they had an alternative."

When the name Christian Protten comes up, one of the listeners quickly reminds Ataa Forkoyi that he has earlier promised to talk about Protten and then asks:

"Who is this Christian Protten that you keep referring to?"

"Patience, patience," responds Ataa Forkoyi. "I have a lot to tell you about this unknown Osu ancestor. But wait until I come to the point of asking the Stones to pour what they have out of their collective memory. As we wait for that time to come, let me continue to tell you about the castle school."

Before he continues with his narration, somebody impulsively blurts out: "Ataa Forkoyi, were the dark-skinned half-siblings and cousins of the mulatto children coming to school together with the mulatto children?"

"What do you think? The castle school inside Christiansborg was supposed to be Denmark not Danish-Osu. The dark-skinned half-siblings and cousins of the mulatto children could only be in Danish-Osu, not Denmark."

The impulsive questioner then goes on to ask:

"That means the dark-skinned kith and kin of the mulattoes came as far as the gates of Christiansborg and stopped to wait for their mulatto relatives at the end of the day. Is that right?"

Ataa Forkoyi promptly answers:

"Yes. That is right. However, you can be certain that any time the sound of cannon-fire announced the arrival of a slave ship, the mulatto children rushed out of the classroom and joined their siblings and cousins outside Christiansborg, to run down to the beach and await the arrival of the new European visitors and Danish slave traders." He then continues:

"The Castle School was a one-room facility, located in the courtyard of Christiansborg, directly in front of where the doors to the slave dungeons opened. It had little natural light or ventilation and any time the wind direction changed from south-east to south-west, a foul smell wafted from the slave dungeons to the classroom. When this happened, the children would hold their little fingers and thumbs tightly to their noses and hold their breath; and of course they would not listen to anything the teacher was saying."

Getting emotional, Ataa Forkoyi says almost inaudibly:

"My friend, inside this classroom, Mr. Svane was able to pack twelve boys and eight girls. How he was able to train these restless mulatto children day by day for two good years baffled the Stones. He faithfully and conscientiously kept good records of the progress of these children, among whom were Frederich Pedersen, born in 1710, the offspring of the Danish soldier Jacob Protten, Wilhelm Protten, born in 1709, Anna Protten, born on the 2nd of February, 1713, and Uldrich Protten, born on the 1st of September, 1715."

At the mention of the names of the Protten offspring, somebody asks:

"Were these Protten children related to the Christian Protten you have been referring to?"

"Yes. In fact, according to the Stones, Uldrich Protten and Christian Protten were the same person. I will tell you more about this change in name later. Meanwhile, Pastor Svane, a man of conscience and conviction, kept thinking of ways to improve the quality of the teaching environment for his 20-strong mulatto school. He knew, as a religious educator, that teaching these mulatto-Africans in the presence of the daily movement of enslaved African prisoners, shackled and chained in the courtyard of Christiansborg, was not good for their psychological make up and development or their spiritual growth. His deep reflections on this thorny issue eventually led him to a vision. He saw in his mind's eye, a new school erected outside the walls of Christiansborg. When this image became focused, he decided to write down his thoughts on the concept. The Stones, fortunately, have woven deeply into the loom of their memory, some sections of what he wrote. Listen as they speak them out:

> There are supplies enough here of stone and clay, yet it would lead to some expense, in particular since the covering of the case,

especially for fear of fire, should be made of bricks and lime, which must be supported by coconut trunks, if these cannot be sent from our home country, beams are less expensive and longer lasting.

Ataa Forkoyi continues with the narration after sipping some water, since his throat is running dry now. He says:

"Svane became passionate and committed to his dream of building a school outside the walls of the fort. He then began to pester the Danish Governor, H. V. Suhm, to undertake this project by all means. Suhm was thinking about the implications. He knew that if a school building was erected outside Christiansborg, the school would no longer be in Denmark but would be in Danish-Osu and that would mean the dark-skinned half-siblings and cousins of the mulatto children could not be kept out."

At this point Ataa Forkoyi begins to muse and addresses a question to no one in particular:

"How could Denmark afford to train the minds of dark-skinned people, who had to continue to serve as human cargo to be shipped to the Caribbean? "Well," he tries to answer his own question, "Suhm was impressed by the persistence of Svane. He saw the point in improving upon the learning conditions of the mulatto children but the benefits of not doing anything also stared him in the face. He decided on a compromise: to obtain permission to send two of the boys of Svane's school to Denmark for training to become blacksmiths; he badly needed the services of blacksmiths in maintaining his cannon machinery, the ironmongery in Christiansborg and the Provesten Watchtower.

"So, in September 1726, when Svane was due for home leave, he was asked to take along two of his boys to Denmark. According to the Stones, Suhm was so satisfied with himself on this compromise solution that in his dispatch note to Denmark on the historic decision, he proudly, and with great delight, intimated the following:

> ... two boys most likely to learn something are being sent home ... I have made three of the older ones soldiers and sent two smaller ones to sail with the Galliot. Thus we have probably at last found a solution for the boys. But we do not know what to do with the girls.

Provoked by this last statement, the former education officer rattles out like a machine gun:

"What were the names of the boys taken along by Pastor Svane to Denmark? Were they taken as slaves or as free persons? What happened to them eventually? Do the Stones remember if they came back at all?"

At this barrage of questions, Ataa Forkoyi shakes his head slowly thinking about what one great philosopher, Thoreau, said:

"Our life is frittered away by detail. An honest man has hardly need to count more than his ten fingers, or in extreme cases he may add his ten toes, and lump the rest. Simplicity, simplicity, simplicity!" Then he counters: "Madam, are you a machine gun?"

At this joke from the Old Man, the listeners burst into spontaneous laughter and shout:

"Ataa Forkoyi, please answer the questions!"

"Why, did I say I would not answer the Madam's questions? You wait; I shall answer each of them. But Madam, please, don't machine gun me with your questions. I know you are passionate about school children; however, so many questions at a go confuse me. Now to the answers:

"The two boys were called Frederich Pedersen and Jacobus Protten. They were 15 and 10 years old respectively at the time of departure from Osu. In fact, Protten was not originally scheduled to travel with the teacher but the original boy intended got sick and his mother was not prepared to release him for the overseas trip. Protten was roped in at the last minute, about which he was delighted, though his mother was very unhappy and unwilling."

On hearing this, a children's rights advocate among the listeners interrupts Ataa Forkoyi and asks aggressively: "Jacob Protten was only 10 years old at that time. There was his senior brother in Svane's school who must have been about the same age as Pedersen. Why was he not selected instead of Jacob, who was not even a teenager yet?"

Ataa Forkoyi is surprised that while trying to answer the barrage of questions from the Madam, he is interrupted so rudely by another lady listener. He holds his peace at any rate, and with a forced smile, responds:

"Thanks for the interruption. Your question has reminded me of some interesting things the Stones have said about Wilhelm Frederich Protten. You can imagine him sitting big and bulky among the skinny mulatto school children before Svane. Wilhelm Frederich was a trouble-maker and a bully in class. Due to his incorrigible disposition, the Governor had marked him down to be sent out, not to Denmark, but to the Danish islands of St. Croix and St. Thomas in the Caribbean, as was the practice for boys with difficult personalities; Wilhelm was to be sent out there as a soldier or a sailor. He was eventually sent out, but neither St. Croix nor St. Thomas could change his disposition, so he was returned to Osu, somewhat sobered up, to serve as a local soldier."

Having handled this distraction rather diplomatically, Ataa Forkoyi, pleased with himself, continues with his original narration in a cheerful mood.

"The two boys, being offspring of Danes, left the shores of Osu, not as slaves, but as free youngsters, though regarded as heathens, since they had not been baptized yet. When they arrived in Denmark, under the custodianship of their old mentor, Teacher Elias Svane, they were sent to a boarding school in Copenhagen, by courtesy of the royal patronage of the King of Denmark. They were baptized and given the formal names of Frederich Pedersen Svane and Christian Jacob Protten. Later, they chose to follow the profession of their mentor and therefore refused to learn the blacksmithing for which they were brought to Denmark, and rather entered the University of Copenhagen to study theology."

Ataa Forkoyi continues excitedly, with a certain amount of pride:

"Both of them, after a good sojourn in Europe, returned home. Pedersen had to go back to Denmark later with his Danish wife, due to insurmountable challenges they faced from the Danish administration at Christiansborg. Protten, however, came and went back to Europe a few times but eventually returned to settle at Christiansborg with his mulatto wife, called Rebecca, to work in his Alma Mater as a salaried teacher in the employment of the local Danish administration.

"According to the Stones, Protten and his wife did a marvelous job as teachers in the Castle School. Embedded in the temporal memory of the Stones is the account that in 1765, when the Danish Chaplain Hagerup was commenting on the couple's work at the school, he described how the girls at the school were being educated in a manner befitting their gender, in sewing, washing, cleaning and cooking. Chaplain Hagerup was additionally proud of the Prottens for the fact that two of the oldest female pupils in the school at that time, named Dorothea Christiansdatter and Charlotte Moellers, were maids for Governor Resch's wife, both while they were still in school and after their confirmation."

With a boyish smile, Ataa Forkoyi teases the former Education Officer and asks her:

"Madam, are you OK now?"

She courteously but joyfully responds:

"Oh! Yes. I am satisfied. Thank you for taking the trouble to respond to my impetuous inquisition."

Ataa Forkoyi then, in his characteristic style, raises his head up to observe the position of the sun in the Harmattan afternoon sky. He mutters to himself, "closing time," and with that, bids farewell to his listeners and wishes them a good evening. He collects his bag and walks away.

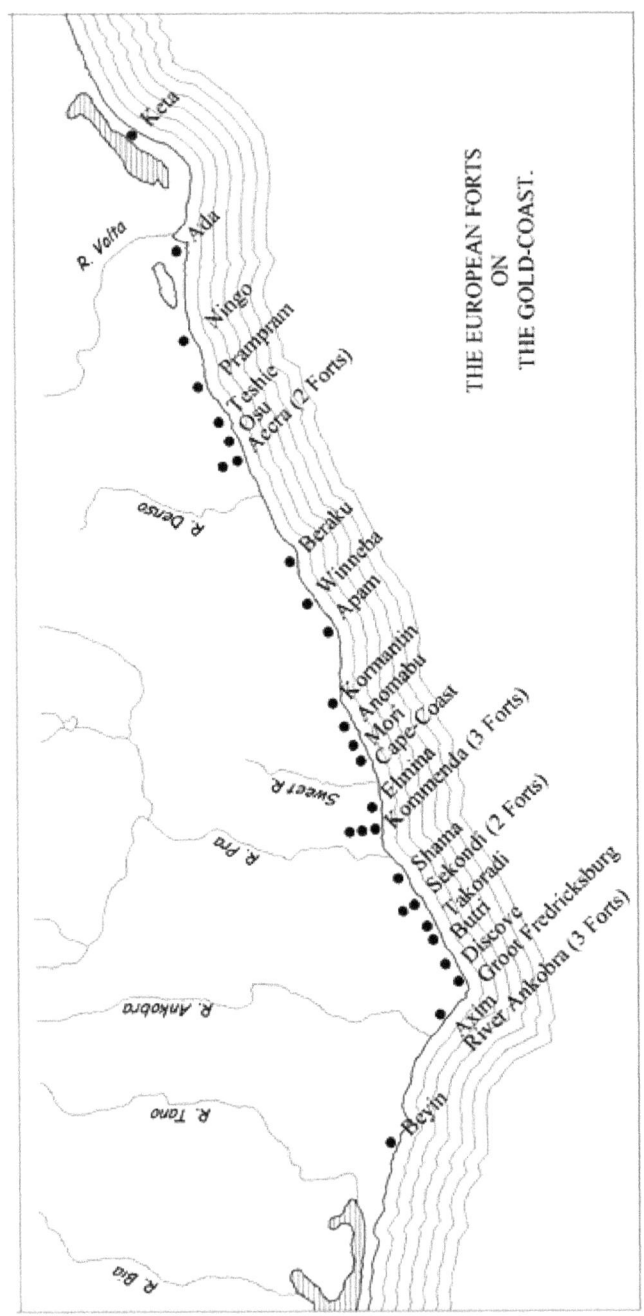

Figure 8: European Forts on the Gold Coast. © 1956 W. E. Ward
Reproduced by Henry Boafo

Three | # Danish-Osu in Paths of Pain and Poise

High Tide at Danish-Osu

BY THE POWER OF LUNAR FORCES, THE IMMENSE WATERS OF THE sea regularly experience the phenomenon of low and high tides. The low tide causes the waters of the sea to recede from the shoreline, while the high tide causes large inflows of sea water to move toward the beach, and sometimes threatens to spill far beyond the sandy beaches. This is an occurrence familiar to all seaside dwellers, including the people of Osu. The symbolism associated with this coastal cultural landscape suggests anxiety and danger to the community when there is high tide and good omen when there is low tide. High tide brings an abundance of life-threatening conditions to coastal dwellers. Low tide brings with it serenity, safety and exposure of a lot of beach sand to make swimming in the sea much more pleasant and safe.

Is it high tide at Osu today?

Ataa Forkoyi is standing with his back to the sea, as he faces his listeners. He is wearing a black cloth with Adinkra icons that depict the 'Manacles,' *Aban ka ba*. Somebody asks him if he has a funeral at home.

He laughs, showing his almost toothless gums, and responds:

"I am wearing a mourning cloth, my friend, not because I have a funeral at home, but because the Stones are ambivalent today."

After a dramatic pause, he continues:

"As the Stones recollect the past of Danish-Osu, they are not sure whether they should rejoice or grieve ..." While formulating his next sentence, he finds himself musing ...

"With the advancing shadow of Christiansborg, Danish-Osu began to grow and develop. Development and change were in the physical environment as well as in the demographics of the community. As the number of Osu people in the community increased, not only Danes and mulattoes were seen around in the traditional quarters of Osu Kinkawe, Osu Ashinte, Osu Alata and Osu Anahor as strange people, as you are about to learn.

"The community began to be populated by hordes of strange looking, dark-skinned people: tall ones, short ones, jet black-skinned people, coffee brown-skinned people, people with smooth round faces and pointed noses, people with high foreheads and broad noses. They were peculiar, because they came into the community in manacles, with shackles and chains around their necks, their hands and their legs. Some of them, men, had iron clamps fastened to their right arm and attached to heavy wooden logs which they carried on their heads or shoulders as they walked along, virtually dragging their bodies; the women and children had their right hands tied to their waist. You could not miss their presence in the community although they came incognito.

"They came, moving together in large companies, but in single files of fifty slaves chained together, accompanied by gun-toting guards and whip-thrashing guides. They cut a pitiful picture, sitting down, completely exhausted from the long walk from the interior and waiting under the trees of the local slave-market that the Osu people referred to as the *Awusāi Atso,* that is, the 'Motherless Orphans' Tree ..."

As these thoughts go through his mind, an expression comes over Ataa Forkoyi's face that indicates he is about to talk about things he would rather not give words to. Finally, he curves his lips and in a melancholic voice half-whispers:

"Christiansborg not only brought Danes-Norwegians and mulattoes to the indigenous Osu community. The trade in human cargo associated with Christiansborg caused Osu to attract varieties of people and volumes of activity in proportions hitherto unknown."

Somebody standing at the back pleads with Ataa Forkoyi to raise his voice so that those at the back can hear him better. In a pensive mood, he picks up his voice and declares:

"I cannot shout at the top of my voice about what the Stones are saying, Slavery? Panyerring? Pawning in the Danish-Osu community? No, no. The memory is too painful, enough to puncture my peaceful mind. But you need to know; so I will speak, but not much; I will speak, but not with joy.

"The selling and buying of human-beings had gone on in the Guinea Coast since time immemorial. But in the Osu community, it was not a very common practice until the Portuguese introduced it through their apparently innocuous attempt to bring forced labour from Allada in the sixteenth century, to help build their trading lodge. When the inland dwellers of Akwamu got wind of how human cargo could be converted this way into guns and gold and barrels of rum, they went all out to get involved in this inhumane business. Thus began the cataclysmic undertaking of the mass collection of enslaved people and their forced march down to the coast for sale at the European slave emporiums by the Akwamus and the other Akans, such as the Denkyeras, Asantes, Fantes and the Akyems."

Ataa Forkoyi continues: "The Akwamus, being the lead warriors that fomented wars and conflicts in the coastal communities to create opportunities to obtain war captives for sale, were the chief slave suppliers to the Danes, having begun with the Dutch and the English on the west coast through the tenuous relationship they had with them, and later with the Swedes, whom they conspired against with the Osu people, to oust people from the east coast.

"By the time Christiansborg was completed and nestled confidently on the promontory on the Osu coast, the Company, under the royal patronage of the King of Denmark-Norway, and with the support of a fleet of different-sized ships equipped with navigational accoutrements and manned by Atlantic Ocean-savvy sea captains, had developed and organized its trading activities into the complex transatlantic slave trade. Operating this triangular, international trade from Copenhagen to Christiansborg to island states of Saint Croix and Saint Thomas necessitated incredibly complex financial, administrative and human resources to harness and harmonize contributions from local merchants, inland slave-raiders, all sorts of intermediaries, and other European slave-trading agents that had also built their own slave emporia along the length and breadth of the Guinea Coast.

"Later, around 1792, the King of Denmark-Norway granted the right to private Danish traders to be involved in the slave trade, leading former employees of the Danish administration to build and settle in the Danish-Osu community. These became the so-called 'free-traders' who lived outside Christiansborg in their own stone houses built in European style, and became the progenitors of latter day Danish-Osu families, such as the Lutterodts, Fleischers, Hesses, Hansens, Larsens, Meyers, Schandorfs, and Richters."

In tune with the mood in which Ataa Forkoyi has been giving his narration, his listeners have been quietly listening, saddened by what they have been hearing, but also enthralled by his profound sense of empathy and depth of understanding of the events. Sensing that no questions are coming to interrupt him, he continues in a subdued tone: "My friends, this business of selling, buying and shipping human cargo went on for centuries, until at the end of the eighteenth century, when the Company had virtually imploded due to its inability to sustain the trade and its concomitant operations, a royal decision was made in far-away Denmark to bring this inhuman economic activity to a stop. By then, somewhere between 85,000 and two million enslaved people, men, women, children and infants had been shipped from Christiansborg across the Atlantic to the Danish plantations in St. Croix and St. Thomas in the Caribbean.

"No doubt by 1803, when the Danes officially disbanded the trade, the Danish-Osu community had configured into a society, consisting of sojourning former slave traders, former local slave merchants, slave-owning families, enslaved and freed slaves."

In an exhausted state, Ataa Forkoyi now closes his eyes, and upon completion of his last sentence, asks rhetorically:

"What sort of culture do you think emerged from Danish-Osu at this low tide? Was it not a slavy and a slavish one?"

Ataa Forkoyi's rhetoric attracts the attention of one of the listeners who is an English Language school teacher; she pedantically confronts him:

"Ataa Forkoyi, you are using strange and unusual words that need to be explained. What do you mean by 'slavy and slavish culture?'"

He smiles wryly and addresses his listeners:

"Who is a slave and what is slavery? The Gã language paints for us a profound picture of the meaning of the word 'slave': an individual who has been deprived of his or her right to be free and is owned and utilized as a chattel. And 'slavery' too: a practice of holding an individual in a permanent state of loss of freedom and personal identity by another human being and utilized as such. 'Nyɔŋ' and 'nyɔŋyeli' respectively mean 'slave' and 'slavery' in English. The word 'nyɔŋ' is the same used to mean 'darkness,' however this latter is distinguished by a lower intonation in pronunciation. The two words must therefore have a generic root. Usually,

Gã culture deems anything associated with *'nyɔŋ,'* that is 'cloak of darkness,' to be evil. A bribe, for example, which is considered an unsavory cultural practice, is *'nyɔŋnii,'* in Gã, literally meaning something belonging to the cloak of darkness. The cultural unacceptability of slavery among the Gã people is also evident in the connotation of the word *'nyɔŋ(ni)yeli,'* literally 'eating under the cloak of darkness.' Only wrong-doers have meals under cloak of darkness."

He continues to address his listeners with passion and pain written all over his wrinkled face:

"This little excursion into Gã semantics, my friends, is to show you that to all intents and purposes, the Osu community, as Gã-speaking people, knew that the keeping of slaves and the practice of slavery were immoral and unethical. But sadly, the whole society was caught up in the greed and gains of the trade in human cargo as introduced by the Danes and their fellow Europeans who came to the coast to obtain strong African people with the sole purpose of conveying them to the Americas to sell as slaves to plantation and business owners.

"The trade generated all forms of enslavement and disposal of humans, beginning with the war captives brought down from inland by the Akwamus, the Akyems and the Asantes after their numerous wars and conflicts, to the coast for the Danes and the other Europeans slave traders. Besides these, there were instances in the Osu community when individuals, female and male, adults and children were kidnapped or forcibly seized and sold to the Danes. The local Portuguese lingua franca referred to this inimical practice as 'panyerring.' It is interesting to note that the word 'panyerring' originated from two Portuguese words *'penhor'* meaning 'pawn' and *'empenhar'* meaning 'to pawn.'

"The Stones remember the dramatic panyerring of a young woman from Dutch Accra who was brought to Osu for sale. When the culprit was discovered, he was forced to replace the missing woman with two relatives. Later the young woman was found being held in a bush behind Christiansborg. This woman was rescued but remained at Osu, in the neighbourhood known as Agbadza Dzoohe, where she was said to have raised a family with an Asante trader who had a trading post at Osu Ashinte. The first stone house, Nartey family house, built by a native local merchant in the Danish-Osu community was owned by the offspring of this woman."

Ataa Forkoyi goes on to add:

"There were also cases of men stealthily arranging to sell their wives to slave merchants. The Stones have in the loom of their memory a dramatic instance in which a Danish-Osu man, by the name of Okwei of Osu Ashinte, sold his Krobo wife to the Danes for a cask of rum. This scandalous episode came to the attention of the Danish administration, which caused a judicial enquiry that took place in Denmark. Quist, Engmann and Reindorf, who had lived at Osu at the time of the incident, appeared to testify."

Ataa Forkoyi holds his breath for a moment, makes the sound "Hmmn," gives a sigh of relief and continues:

"Later, when the trade had totally corrupted the Osu traditional values of sanctity of human life and spiritual value of individual family members, it became a common practice for family members to be pawned, at times, to the Danish slave merchants for cheap European goods, and when the individuals who could be grandparents, parents, cousins, uncles, aunts, children or grandchildren were not redeemed after a period, they ended up as human cargo aboard slave ships to the Danish islands of Saint Croix or Saint Thomas.

"For the local merchants, middlemen and slave agents, the value of this human cargo was in the European goods exchanged by the Danes for the slaves. A male slave cost 96 rixdaler or six ounces of gold. The 96 rixdaler was worth two Danish muskets, 40 pounds of gun-powder, one anker of Danish brandy, and some beads and cowries and other cheap European products. The profit made by the Danish merchant over and above the cost price, was in selling a male slave at 128 rixdaler to the European slave ships waiting in the roads.

"In time, according to the Stones, the trade in human cargo became an institution that led to the emergence of different categories of enslaved people found within the Danish-Osu community. The slaves held in the dungeons of Christiansborg, awaiting the ships, were those whose humanity had been reduced to zero, to the extent that they no longer had any human rights but to be abused. Those among them who tried to assert the little humanity left in them through revolt, were treated like domestic animals gone crazy. In their agony, they cried with the voices of wild animals. Under the dungeon conditions in which they were held, they had to behave as animals without minds and memories."

Now with a mischievous smile on his lips, Ataa Forkoyi slowly and distinctly says to his listeners: "But to appease their conscience and to ensure that they did not lose much on their investment during the transit in the dungeons in Christiansborg, the Danes tried to make these slaves happy. You know what they did? According to the Stones, four days in a week Mondays, Wednesdays, Thursdays and Saturdays each slave was given a tot of brandy."

He continues, now with rage on his wrinkled face:

"The Stones remember that in 1707, when the slave dungeons could no longer hold the large number of slaves delivered to Christiansborg, the Danes created slave-houses built outside the Fort, which had no roofs. These were, in effect, human pens created to hold about 200 or 300 souls in transit to the Danish islands in the Caribbean. Then there were those who had become unpaid workers, known as fort-slaves, inside the walls of Christiansborg. These slaves were kept without shackles and manacles and they lived and worked like Egyptian bulls inside Christiansborg. Around the 1750s and 1760s, they numbered constantly about 100. However, with the increase in the volume of trade, the population became too large, numbering about 442 in the 1790s. Hence, an abode was found at Osu Alata for them from where they had to troop daily to Christiansborg to report for work."

The human rights activist suddenly interrupts Ataa Forkoyi's passionate presentation by asking if the slaves without shackles and manacles living at Osu-Alata were still slaves. Ataa Forkoyi responds to the question indirectly:

"These men and women were slaves because they were Awusai, those who had not only lost their fathers, but their mothers as well, making them nobodies in Osu. Although they lived within the community, they had neither local kinship groups nor families they could turn to." He continues:

"Then there were those who could not match the standards for shipment required by the slave merchants. These were retained in the community and became domestic slaves who were made servants in the homes of merchants and community leaders. Because they had been bought as slaves, working within the family setting, they always had their human rights abused through misuse for all kinds of unimaginable and menial work, without any corresponding compensation.

"Finally, there were those, also, whose freedom had been paid for. Yes, I mean what I have said. These bought-to-be-freed slaves were found at Osu in the latter part of the era when slavery in Osu was coming to an end. Such slaves had come under the favour of the Christian missionaries, and according to the Stones, around 1839, freed slaves were settled at some specific areas within the Danish-Osu community.

"There was the interesting story of a slave who was bought by the Basel Mission. On being freed, he converted to the Christian faith and eventually became a missionary himself. He was an Akyem with the name Jantuah, meaning 'seeking refuge.' Notwithstanding the attempts of the Mission to be exemplary in their involvement with the slave trade, there were instances of local Christians falling foul of the moral expectations relating to attitudes to slavery and the slave trade.

"According to the Stones, when the legal sanctions prohibiting slavery fell out of stringent adherence, even Christians went back to the practice of slavery and pawning, to the embarrassment of the missionaries who had maintained a strong position to uphold the laws banning slavery and its trade in the Guinea Coast. It was discovered that there were families that discreetly held slaves and pawns in their possession and used them as cheap labour at home and on their farms in places outside Osu, at ancestral villages such as Papao, Haatso, Agboogba, and Boi."

All this time, Ataa Forkoyi's audience listens spellbound, without making a sound to distract or interrupt him. He makes his usual dramatic pause, closes his eyes and appears to have gone into a prayerful mood. After a while, he opens his eyes and begins to speak again, but this time in a rather somber tone.

"My friends, for a long time, the Danish-Osu community came under the culture of human cargo business. The sound of this culture was the constant, clanging cacophony of shackles and chains everywhere in the community, as parties of enslaved people were marched on the tamarind-lined road from the north into Osu; the culture was also manifested in the feeble, plaintive wailings of the chained women at the old slave-market at Awusai Atso. These wailings would attract the attention of the old men who would be standing by at the slave market smoking their pipes, making them reflect on what Osu-life had become. The fearful booming of the cannons at Christiansborg, announcing the arrival of the Danish slave-ships, would send chills to the hearts of those mothers whose sons and daughters had been pawned to the Danish merchants, who had threatened to sell the children being kept in the slave dungeons of Christiansborg.

"According to the Stones, besides the general sense of insecurity among the people in the community, created by the practice of panyerring, the culture of the human cargo business in the Danish-Osu community generated many kinds of neurosis and fears within the people. For example, although being a slave at Osu was not considered to be a tragedy, being put on a slave-ship and taken out across the horizon, was considered synonymous with being killed.

"It was commonly believed that Europeans bought Africans to use as bait for fishing in the ocean. Some also thought that when slaves were taken away beyond the horizon, they were killed and their blood collected and drunk as wine, and their skins utilized in making shoes for Europeans, since the shoes they wore looked black. Other prevailing perceptions were that the slaves bought by the Danes were taken away either to be eaten or for their bones to be used in making gun-powder which was sold back to the African traders.

"The heavy and heinous spirit emanating from the slave trading business hung over the community for centuries," Ataa Forkoyi continues. "A thoughtful man at Danish-Osu once attempted to capture this spirit poetically, for it to be passed on to the Stones. I once heard a Stone reciting this poem (see English translation, Appendix II):

Ŋshɔ naa, ŋshɔ hiɛ,
Ŋshɔ yɛ fɛo po!
Shi gbomɛi pii kamɔ mli,
Mɛididzi hu fa tsɔ!
Mɛididzi ni sumɔɔ shwɛmɔ
Kɛ nyɛŋnyɛŋtswibɔɔ tsɔ,
Toigbolɔi kɛ daanulɔi,
Mɛi pii ni aŋo hɔɔ.
"Miyaba eei, miyaba"
"Onyɛɛ oba ekoŋ?
Afi o awo lɛlɛn,
Onaŋ ojaku dɔŋ!"
Mɛi pii hu kamɔ dzɛmɛ
Mɛi ni feko efɔn.
Mɛididzi ashikpon lɛ,
Kaahɔɔ obii lɛ dɔŋ!

When Ataa Forkoyi comes to the end of the poem, he gets an enthusiastic round of applause from his listeners. Without any show of emotion, he takes a bow and when he raises his head, he asks his listeners:

"Was there still a high tide at Danish-Osu?"

Without waiting for a response, he answers his own question:

"Yes, there was, and high tide was always a bad time. Danish-Osu was not only suffering from the weariness and worry that came

Figure 9: Osu Slave Market © 1925 W. T. Balmer
Illustration courtesy of W. F. Hedges, F.R.I.B.A.

from the slave trade. In fact, as a result of the trade, the community attracted so many ills upon its head. The greatest ill came from the Akwamus and they became a thorn in the flesh of the Osu community and all the other outlying coastal communities, stretching from Gã-Mashie in the west to Anlo in the east.

"Around 1733," Ataa Forkoyi continues, "the Stones recall that Osu became depopulated; only about 20 to 25 families could be found living in the vicinity of Christiansborg. What had happened? You may justifiably ask. The Akwamus were waging war with the Anlos on the east coast and many of the Gã-Adangme communities, in solidarity with their eastern neighbours, had packed bag and baggage to move there to lend support to the Anlos in resisting the Akwamus' aggression. Participation in this war campaign by the Danish-Osu community, had therefore taken a lot of people away for the duration of the war."

Ataa Forkoyi then makes a brief pause to catch his breath, since his throat appears to be getting dry. Somebody standing directly in front of him notices and offers him some water. He receives the bottle of water gratefully but only sips a bit and returns the bottle to the owner. He continues to speak, refreshed.

"Before this wholesale move eastwards to assist the Anlos, the Danish-Osu community had been seriously impoverished due to payment of war taxes imposed by some Akyem warlords known by the names Frempong, Kwasi Adu and B. Quakye. These warlords had demanded financial support from all the coastal communities, including Danish-Osu, because they had claimed they were waging war against the troublesome Akwamus to rout them from the coastal regions so that everyone could trade with the Europeans in peace. The Akwamus nevertheless continued with their skirmishes to harass the coastal communities.

"Finally, in 1677, they realized that the trade with the Danes at Danish-Osu was thriving, with the local merchants taking advantage of their position as middle-men. So the king of Akwamu brought down his warriors and ferociously attacked Danish-Osu and other nearby communities, including Labadey, Gã-Mashie and Kinka. Having vanquished the communities, the Akwamus seized power over the area and took over direct control of the trade with the three European forts including those at Dutch-Accra and British-Accra."

With a frown now on his face, Ataa Forkoyi takes a stance, standing firm with legs apart and declares: "Having thus positioned themselves to do business, the Akwamus began, in 1679, to control Danish-Osu and the other Gã towns with full force. While in control, with directives from their monarch, King Akonnor and later King Ansa Sasraku, they made sure that the Osu people felt their oppressive presence and the power of their cultural imperialism. They always found good excuses to demand compensation for the perceived misdeeds of the Osu people, anytime they were in town to carry out business with the Danes in the Castle.

"The Stones recollect how an Akwamu trader would have the audacity to demand one or two slaves from his host as a compensation for the inconvenience of being served with over-heated water for bathing, or being served with food in the presence of the host's domestic animals, or a disturbance from a crowing rooster at dawn. There were also instances when King Akonnor sent down two or three of his concubines to sojourn at Danish-Osu. These women were intended as bait to attract and seduce men. Later, when Akonnor came round on his imperial visits, courts were set up to try the men who had fallen for the bait. Such men were made to pay heavy fines in gold or were sold to the European slave ship captains."

As Ataa Forkoyi goes on with this account of the Akwamus' domination and unfair treatment of their subjects, one of the listeners, standing in front begins to shake his head violently from side to side, saying almost inaudibly but to the hearing of Ataa Forkoyi:

"No! No! No!"

"Young man, what is wrong?" Ataa Forkoyi, surprised, asks

him. The young man responds:

"Where were the Danes, when all these atrocities were going on?"

"Oh, the Danes? The Danes were around in Christiansborg minding their own business, buying and selling slaves, gold and ivory and not caring a hoot for what was going on!" Ataa Forkoyi shouts scornfully and adds with a shaking voice:

"The Akwamus uncompromisingly demanded to be recognized by the people of Danish-Osu as their overlords, disregarding the fact that the community was in direct view of Christiansborg with all its cannons and the Danish flag. Furthermore, they demanded from the Danes, the annual tribute due to the Danish-Osu community, and continued in this imperial position till 1729, when they were defeated by the Akyems who had also become interested in direct trade contact with the Europeans. This long imperial presence resulted in a number of Akwamu cultural footprints in the Danish-Osu community."

A sociology student in the group immediately raises up his hand and says:

"Nuumoe, may I ask a question?"

"Yes, you may. What is your question?"

The young man, trying to show off his academic background, slowly formulates his question in a scholarly manner:

"According to what you have told us, the Danish-Osu milieu was essentially Gã or Gã-Adangme. The Akwamus ethnically are Akans. How could Akan cultural practices then be imposed on Gã people?"

"Young man, you have jumped the gun," says Ataa Forkoyi. "I was about to let you know what the Stones had to say about these Akwamu cultural footprints. But now that you have asked the question, let me give you a little background information on Gã culture. For centuries, the fundamental cultural difference between Gã and Akan people lies in the state of the male organ. The Akwamu, just like any other male Akan, is uncircumcised, whereas all male Gã children have to be ceremonially circumcised, usually on the eighth day after birth, to mark them out as true Gã-born. Because Akwamus did not go through this ritual, they were referred to by the Gã as *Foolɔi,* meaning 'the uncircumcised.' Gã society used to be led by the Wulɔmɔ, the priest-king or priest-leader who remained, sometimes, over long periods of time, in the *Gbatsu,* the oracular room, to receive guidance and direction from the Omnipotent, for the society. This priest-king presided over the Council of Elders to keep law and order and subscribe to all moral and religious obligations in the community. The priest-leader determined the time of the annual celebration of the Homowo festival that reminds the Gã of their ancestral past.

"With the dominant presence of the Akwamu among the Gã on the coast, some of these ancient customary practices began to give way to imitations, as it were, of Akan culture. The gradual change started with the in-roads Akan word-usage made into the Gã language. Words such as *'akatanwiah'* (umbrella), *'asafo'* (company, church group), and *'ntolɛ ahuu'* (discovering a fortune by chance), are all corrupted Akan words.

"Traditionally non-Gã cultural practices began to show influence of the imperial presence of the Akwamu; for example, the function of the priest-king as the head of the society gave way to the *Mantsɛ,* the father of the society, who led the people in time of war and also in peace time, similar to the Akan practice and custom. Related innovations were the institution of the offices of *Mankralo* (Akan: *'Oman Krado'),* and *Dzaasetsɛ (Gyaasehene),* which had hitherto been non-existent."

As Ataa Forkoyi completes his explanation of how the Akwamus influenced changes in the cultural landscape at Danish-Osu, the young academic who asked the question, admiring Ataa Forkoyi's wide knowledge, exclaims:

"Wow! The Akwamus' influence at Danish-Osu was pervasive indeed."

"Yes, indeed. You can call that cultural imperialism! The Akwamus were so audacious that their cultural imperialism was not limited to Danish-Osu but extended beyond to impact Christiansborg. They even managed to take over the Danish fort, to the amazement of the Danes.

"The Stones have a recollection of how this seventeenth century coup d'etat took place. It all happened when a habitual drunkard, a Dane named Peter Bolten, decided to dispose of Christiansborg by selling it to the Portuguese who had been waiting in the roads like vultures waiting to pounce on dead carcasses. It was in 1681 and living conditions in the then modestly built Christiansborg had declined to a very low ebb. Seeing no hope for the Company to continue surviving the stiff competition posed by the other Europeans operating on the coast, Peter Bolten sold Christiansborg to the Portuguese.

"But because this sale had no official approval, the Danes employed diplomacy to get the Portuguese to nullify the transaction.

So, within a year, an agreement was executed to release the fort back to the Danes. By the agreement, the Portuguese were supposed to vacate the fort by August 28, 1682. However, the Portuguese chose to leave ahead of time and left by February 20, 1682. Thus, a vacuum was created. The audacious Akwamus saw this as an opportunity to satisfy their unbridled ambition to take over Christiansborg, consequently filling the vacuum created by the early departure of the Portuguese. "

One of the young men in the group spontaneously shouts:

"This is audacity of ambition!"

Everybody breaks out laughing.

Ataa Forkoyi also smiles and mischievously mutters to himself:

"What is 'audacity of ambition'? I know about 'audacity of hope.'" He continues: "The Akwamus, under the leadership of their king, Akonnor, refused to give up Christiansborg until a year later on February 24, 1683, when the Danes had to buy back their Fort with a handsome amount of gold and a great number of casks of rum. Soon thereafter, a Dane named Peder Hofman was appointed as the Merchant of the fort to be in charge until Governor Hans Lykke came to take over in April 1685. With this failed attempt by the Akwamus to occupy Christiansborg, they decided that they would have more direct trade dealings with the Danes and eliminate the local merchants who always took advantage of their close relationship with the Danes, by cheating the Akwamus. When they realized that it was rather difficult to eliminate the Osu merchants from their direct dealings with the Danes, they conceived an idea of using an Akwamu man called Asomani who had once been in the employment of the Danes and lived and worked inside the fort, to make another attempt to capture it.

"Asomani who had good knowledge of the geography of Christiansborg and was quite familiar with the strengths and weaknesses of the living circumstances of the Danes inside the fort, had earlier been chased out for a crime committed and had run away to seek refuge back home at Akwamufie. King Akonnor had managed to seek pardon for him, for which he was granted a letter of freedom by one Danish man called Erich Tilleman. It was this man Asomani, who later, by subterfuge, managed to attack the fort and seized it with the support of a Danish gunner called Thomas Bentzen. Bentzen, who was married to an Osu woman named Djagble (Jamine), a widow of Governor Lykke, was known to be a habitual drunkard, always intoxicated with brandy before seven o'clock in the morning. He had become disgruntled with the Danish administration so he readily became an accomplice to take over Christiansborg for a period of one year, from December 1687 to December 1688.

"As stored in the loom of the memory of the Stones, Asomani was relentless in his inordinate ambition to occupy Christiansborg, so in June 1693, Asomani, with his gang of robbers, took the Castle again; at that time, Harding Pettersen was the Governor. The fort was thereafter redeemed in June 1694."

Ataa Forkoyi now calls for water; he is given some water in a sachet. He shakes his head to indicate that he does not want sachet water. As his listeners stand around wondering what is happening, knowing that Ataa Forkoyi normally drinks sachet water as many others at Osu do, he announces that he is no longer speaking. He walks away saying virtually to himself, "My soul is agitated and I need to be pacified with a calabash of pure cool water."

Turbulence, Turmoil and Travails at High Tide

Ataa Forkoyi comes back and is found sitting on one of the rocky outcrops at Osu Amangfong, the heritage site which marks the bombardment of Danish-Osu by the British in 1854. Here, looking less distressed and with a wry smile on his face, he picks up his narration and continues:

"When the Akyems sacked the Akwamus and finally vanquished them in 1734, the tide at Danish-Osu began to ebb, with the oppressive domination of the Akwamus having been forever set aside. However, the community's troubles were not yet ended. Conflicts between Danish-Osu and its neighboring communities and other coastal communities continued to haunt the peace and tranquility the people desired in their day-to-day family, social and trading activities. These conflicts, caused at times by flimsy misunderstandings, continued to erupt here and there all the way into the twentieth century. In addition to these came natural disasters like long periods of drought, locust plagues, and earthquakes.

"To make matters worse, constant harassment from the Asantes led to the destruction of farmlands on the outskirts of the communities. The Stones remember an extensive demolition by the Asante warriors of the Danish plantations in the Accra plains in

1811, and even the taking of hostages, including former Governor Flindt, to Kumasi. Later, in the nineteenth century, these Asante skirmishes developed into a full-scale war, which the people of Danish-Osu, together with their kinsmen at Gã-Mashie, La, Teshie, Nungua, Tema and Kpone had to join with other allied forces to fight against thousands of Asante warriors who descended on the coastal communities. This military campaign ended with the Asantes' final defeat in the Katamanso war in 1826. Beyond the inter-ethnic wars were disturbances and disasters caused by tensions that arose between the community and the Danish administration, and later the British administration, which bought Christiansborg in 1850."

Somebody, realizing Ataa Forkoyi is showing signs of tiredness, and flagging in his narration, interjects with a loud question:

"Nuumoe, what were these disturbances and disasters that visited the Danish-Osu community?"

With a long, loud yawn, Ataa Forkoyi, now wide awake, responds: "Why this question, my friend? I was about to tell you of these visitations. According to the Stones, Danish-Osu suffered two major bombardments, in 1845 by the Danes, and in 1854 by the British."

As soon as Ataa Forkoyi alludes to bombardments, one of the listeners, an ardent pacifist, barges in with a question:

"I thought you mentioned that the Danes always minded their business inside Christiansborg, managing their trade in slaves, gold and ivory. How come they turned their cannons not on the Akwamus, when these people were harassing the Danish-Osu community, but on the very community where Danish merchants and Danish mulatto offspring lived?"

Ataa Forkoyi gives his characteristic wry smile, clears his throat and responds to the question: "The Danish bombardment of Danish-Osu in 1845 was, indeed, quite out of character for the Danish administration. In fact, the bombardment was ordered by someone who, by nature, was very peaceful. It should be interesting for you to note that at the time of ordering the bombardment, he had a Danish-Osu woman named Severine Brock as a wife, and had a good social connection to the community because of his kind disposition towards the local people. According to the Stones, this man who ordered the bombardment was Governor Edward Carstensen, the last Danish administrator before the ownership of Christiansborg changed hands in 1850. The genesis of this physical violence meted out to the Danish-Osu community was in the evil spirit of the transatlantic slave trade, which had been the business of the Danes in the Guinea coast for over 150 years already at that time."

Ataa Forkoyi makes another dramatic pause, takes in a deep breath, and continues with his narration.

"As you may know, the Danes had issued an edict in Copenhagen in 1803 to abolish slavery and the concomitant slave trade. The British had followed suit in 1807. The trade had therefore officially died at Danish-Osu and in the other Gã-Adangme coastal communities. However, the evil spirit of the trade had refused to subside. Through illegal and clandestine activities, the Danish slave merchants and their local counterparts, including the middlemen, the Asante traders and all the others, had been collaborating and conniving with some daring European slave-trading ships, to circumvent the abolition by the Danish administration. These interlopers had been managing to get slaves from the interior to the east coast and having these bandit ships carry the contraband human cargo to their destinations in the Americas and the Caribbean.

"The young Danish Governor, Edward Carstensen, had been very much troubled by these clandestine and despicable activities under his administration. To make matters worse for him, since assumption of office from his predecessor, who died unexpectedly, he had been confronted with civil unrest in one of the important communities inland named Akropong Akwapim, which his administration was obliged to deal with. In this regard, he had been called upon to arbitrate in the chieftaincy dispute between the incumbent King, Adum Tokori, a suspected illegal slave-trading accomplice, and his rival, Owusu Akyem. To settle the dispute between these two arch rivals, which posed a serious threat to peace in the jurisdiction of the Danish administration, Carstensen, exercising his talents as an arbitrator, had invited them to Christiansborg for palavering." Ataa Forkoyi warms up to his narration with his eyes closed. Nobody dares interrupt him now.

"The two Akwapim rivals had arrived separately at Danish-Osu on a Friday in November, 1844. Note that it was in the same year in which the Fante Chiefs had met with the British Governor at Cape Coast Castle to sign the bond that brought the Gold Coast under the British Protectorate. So the Akwapim rivals, in company of their loyalists who were secretly well armed, began to march from the north on the tamarind tree-lined route leading south to Christiansborg. Owusu Akyem, the contestant, had brought along his seven young sons, perhaps to demonstrate to Carstensen how prolific and powerful he was.

"As fate would have it, on their way to Christiansborg for the arbitration meeting, the two rival parties coincidentally encountered each other in the presence of some of the Danish-Osu community leaders at Songme Naa, the marketplace. Suddenly, there was an eruption of bitter verbal exchanges which enraged the two rivals to the point of emotional explosion. Owusu Akyem, who felt he had been customarily abused by Adum Tokori, became so infuriated that he brought out a gun and attempted to shoot him; he missed but his bullets seriously wounded some bystanders. As a result, a fight broke out between the two companies.

"When Owusu realized what had happened, he took to his heels, running north-eastwards in the direction of the Klottey Lagoon. He was hotly pursued and was finally caught beyond the outskirts of Danish-Osu by the Adum loyalists, who decided to finish him there and then, instead of sending him as a captive back to King Adum who was waiting at Songme Naa. While the chase was going on, the seven young sons were arrested by some of the other Adum loyalists. Immediately, when he saw what had happened, one of the Danish-Osu leaders, by the name of Sabah Atsem of the Kinkawe quarters, saw an opportunity for an unexpected profit."

Somebody standing at the back with a business mind quickly put the question to Ataa Forkoyi:

"What sort of profit did he think he could gain without making an investment?"

Ataa Forkoyi grimaces and makes some guttural sounds as if he is clearing his throat.

"You should have known Sabah Atsem," says Ataa Forkoyi.

He continues: "This man Sabah Atsem was intelligent and knowledgeable but was also a very sly person. He used to be in the employment of the Danish administration as an interpreter and really learned about the Danes and assumed all their practices. He became fluent in Danish and not only that, he was at home with the local Portuguese lingua franca, Twi and Gã-Adangme. As he found the Akwapims capturing Owusu's sons, he convinced them to hand the children over to him so that he could bring them to Christiansborg. Because of his previous good standing with the Danish administration, the Akwapims believed him and they handed over the children to him.

"But Sabah Atsem, who had also been one of the illegal slave trade agents, had a secret agenda. He thought he could get these boys to an unknown place where he could sell them into slavery as soon as he could arrange it with the middlemen. To cover up his nefarious plan, he deceptively got some of the Danish-Osu community leaders to accompany him with the captured boys to Amanganaa, a ritual ground in the Kinkawe quarter, near the west side of Christiansborg, towards the beach.

"He arranged with the traditional drummers of the King's court to bring the two main *Obonui,* the state-talking drums, to the ritual ground to perform some rituals, apparently to protect these children who had just lost their father. The community leaders who followed him to the ritual grounds had not the faintest clue that Sabah Atsem had in mind to execute a ritual murder, since such acts had since vanished from the traditional practices of the people of Danish-Osu.

"When the drums were brought, Sabah Atsem, speaking as if possessed by an evil spirit, authoritatively instructed the leaders to encircle the boys with the drums laid on the ground in the centre. Then from nowhere, he brought out a slasher, gripped the neck of the youngest boy and slashed his throat, and as the blood oozed out, he let it pour out onto the drums, a ritual act to supposedly reinforce the metaphysical power of the drums.

"The leaders stood there flabbergasted with open mouths. As they stood there, dazed, and watched Sabah Atsem, he gripped the second boy and did the same to him. When the leaders came back to their senses and became fully aware of what had transpired before their very eyes, they took to their heels, leaving behind their native sandals and started shouting out the Gã customary alarm as they ran: '*Ataamɛi, awomɛi, nyɛ baakwɛ aeiiii!*'

"Sabah Atsem, by this time fully intoxicated with a murderous spirit, took the remaining five boys, who had been bound together at their necks, to a secret place he had in mind, and some three days after this gruesome event, he sold the boys to some mulatto agents who sent them to a European slave dealer."

At this point Ataa Forkoyi's voice begins to tremble and as he tries to speak, his voice simply fades away into a hush; no one can hear him anymore. His whole body begins to sway to and fro, like a leaf being blown by the wind. Some of the listeners standing near him quickly move closer to embrace him, to keep him from falling off the rocky outcrop. After a while, he regains his composure. He gets up and stands on top of the rocky outcrop. He shakes his head slowly and sadly says: "My friends, do you see the power of that evil spirit the slave trade released into the Danish-Osu community? Its power was absolute and it corrupted absolutely."

The human rights activist in the group, with anger in his voice, lifts up his head to try to look into the face of Ataa Forkoyi as he stands on top of the rocky outcrop and asks:

"Did Carstensen get to know about this dastardly act and what did he do about it?"

"Yes, he did get to know about it some few days after," Ataa Forkoyi responds with a glimmering smile on his wrinkled face.

"According to the Stones, when Carstensen got wind of what had happened, he arranged for the arrest of Sabah Atsem, Adum Tokori and the community leaders involved in this ritual murder. He then confiscated the drums which received the blood of the two sons of Owusu and after having made sure that the sections of the Kinkawe quarter surrounding the ritual place had been evacuated, he got his Danish military assistant, Sergeant Svedstrup, to climb up to the top of the Danish Watch Tower called Provesten. Provesten, which had been used on a number of occasions to prevent the onslaught of European enemies attempting to attack Christiansborg from the landside, this time had to turn its fire-power on the section of Danish-Osu which had incurred the fury of Carstensen.

"With the assistance of a few Danish soldiers, Svedstrup employed the cannons on top of the circular Watchtower, Provesten, to bombard the houses in the Amaganaa section of the community. The houses were immediately reduced to rubble. The bombardment took place on January 13, 1845; some eight weeks after the children had been ritually murdered. Thereafter, Carstensen personally led a team of mulatto soldiers to the stone house of Sabah Atsem and torched it. As it burnt, the fire spread to neighboring houses, which also burnt down.

"Later when Sabah and Adum were arrested and brought to Christiansborg, Carstensen had them put in the slave dungeon and immediately arranged with a ship to have them exiled to the Caribbean and finally to Denmark as prisoners of the King, not before they had been tried and found guilty of murder and involvement in illegal slave-trading. Thereafter, the two criminals were kept in Denmark as prisoners until they were granted amnesty and returned home at the time the Danish administration under Edward Carstensen was relinquished to the British in 1850."

"Ataa Forkoyi, you had earlier informed us that, while the Danes were establishing the administration of the east coast from Christiansborg at Danish-Osu, the British were in the Central Region and also occupying their modest fort at British Accra in Gã-Mashie. How did it come about that Carstensen relinquished the administration to the British in 1850?" asks an elderly-looking listener who appears to be a history teacher in a senior high school.

While he organizes his thoughts to answer the question from the history teacher, Ataa Forkoyi's mind strays and he begins to hear the whining and silent weeping of the Stones as they reminisce on the dark aspects of the Danish past at Danish-Osu. The Stones keep intimating to Ataa Forkoyi, through their groaning and gnashing, that this dark past had been well chronicled in available Danish records and that those who wanted to satisfy their curiosity should go to the books.

Having regained control of his thoughts, his mind refocuses on the teacher's question and he gets ready to respond. Going back to sit on the rocky outcrop, Ataa Forkoyi declares:

"1850 began in 1803."

The history teacher frowns with a confused expression at this curious statement from Ataa Forkoyi. She politely asks him: "Sir, what do you mean by this declaration?"

"Just listen to me," says Ataa Forkoyi.

"I made this statement to make you aware of how the Danes eventually began to wind up their over 150 years' sojourn on the Guinea Coast."

Then he stands up and climbs down from the top of the rocky outcrop and begins to move up and down while speaking, as if he is teaching in a classroom.

"Before the turn of the nineteenth century, the Company and the King of Denmark had realized that their hitherto lucrative involvement in the transatlantic trade was beginning to experience diminishing returns. Furthermore, there had been a national awakening of a sense of guilt for the inhumane activities leading to the shipment of human cargo to the Caribbean islands of St. Thomas and St. Croix. Arising out of these, debate emerged in Denmark around the need to curtail Danish involvement in the transatlantic trade and look for more acceptable economic initiatives in agriculture on the coast, as the British had also begun to do.

"In tune with this gradual change in the trade activities of the Company, the Danish administration at Christiansborg and many of the local Danish slave traders at Danish-Osu began to divert their energies from buying, selling, and shipping human cargo.

"Thus, the Danish governors began, with a keen sense of purpose, to initiate agricultural development on the northern fringes of Danish-Osu and attempted to acquire lands for plantation cultiva-

Figure 10: A photograph of one of the drums on display in the National Museum in Copenhagen, Denmark. *Photograph by Courtesy of author*

Figure 11: A picture of a drawing of the two prisoners as they spent their prison time in Christianshaven in Denmark. *Illustration by courtesy of Henning Henningsen*

tion, even on the Akwapim Hills and in the Accra plains around Dodowah where Governor Flindt had begun a settlement development. In this nascent settlement were structures such as sawmill, three dwelling houses, a granary and large agricultural buildings. But before moving further inland, they had experimented with intensive gardening on Kuku Hill, which the Danes named Fredericksberg. This was started by Governor Wriesberg just before the end of the eighteenth century, and vegetables, citrus and tamarind were tried there, as well as cotton.

"Later, Governor Wilkens, who arrived at Christiansborg in 1842, together with Edward Carstensen, took a strong liking to Fredericksberg and thus devoted much attention to the gardens there, where he built four country stone-houses. According to the Stones, it was while building these structures that he introduced the practice of laying cornerstones to buildings in the Danish-Osu community. Into the first cornerstone that he laid, he buried a silver coin and picture of King Frederick VI."

Now with a rascally smile on his face, Ataa Forkoyi goes on to add to his lecture.

"Wilkens' frequent movements from Christiansborg to the gardens for recreation and high-spirited relaxation activities caused the Danish-Osu community to refer to this hill as the 'Wliki Goo,' as they saw him frequenting there during the weekends with Danish-Osu women in the company of local traders and friends he was able to make during his short period of survival on the coast.

"Following the example of the Danish administration, the local slave merchants also turned their attention to agriculture, though still engaged actively and extensively in the waning slave trade. Hitherto, the then well-known licensed Danish merchants in the Danish-Osu community, such as Messrs Lutterodt, Richter, Schonning, Dictorle, Truelsen, Meyer, Gronberg, and others, who had settled on the coast, had been investing the profits from their slave trading business in property development for themselves and their Danish-Osu wives and mulatto children. According to the Stones, the houses of these Merchants looked very impressive. They had been developed like citadels, all of them having balconies all around, and flat roofs, providing for lovely walks."

Having referred to what the Stones are saying, Ataa Forkoyi shuts his eyes and bows his head and cocks his ears as if he is listening to a voice. He shakes his head approvingly and then as if speaking to himself, he mutters:

"Yes, H. C. Truelsen bought the late Jen Jacobsen's stone slave-trading house at an auction. Yes, Gronberg installed a corn-mill in the community. Yes, Schonning put up a stone-house for his native Danish-Osu concubine, called Naa Tolon, near where Richter had developed his two-storey, palatial-stone residence."

With a broad smile now on his wrinkled face, Ataa Forkoyi continues with his narration:

"Christiansborg and all these slave businessmen of Danish-Osu began to move to the outskirts to look for land for cultivation of crops such as coffee and cotton. They went to outlying villages such as Dokutso, Legon, Sesemi, Dwaben, Bebiase, and Kponkpo, located at the northern end of the Accra plains, at the feet of the Akwapim hills, to start plantations. It was at the beginning of this new direction away from trade in human cargo toward agricultural cargo that Christiansborg used slave labour to plant a row of tamarind trees along the route that linked it to its plantations and country house, named Fredericksgave, located at Sesemi at the foot of the Akwapim Hills. They had brought the seeds of this medicinal plant, Tamarindus Indica, from India and had planted them as avenue trees to provide shade as they moved along the route to the plantations north of Danish-Osu. The trees not only provided the Danes with shade but the pods were transformed into a potent herbal concoction against malaria for the community as well."

Sounding tired and with weariness written all over his face, Ataa Forkoyi continues slowly now with his narration:

"My friends, I can assure you that, notwithstanding the new direction the Danes began to take at Christiansborg, fatigue and weariness could be seen in their administration. There were illnesses, frustrations and deaths all over. By 1844, they had realized that it was no longer necessary to continue to operate on the Guinea Coast. Most of the Danish trading posts were lying in ruins and the number of administrators and soldiers that had survived the stress of the climatic conditions and environmental disasters had been reduced to a negligible figure. Hence the final decision to pack up, fold up the Danish red-cross on the white flag and go back to Denmark."

With a mocking smile on his tired face, Ataa Forkoyi almost inaudibly says:

"It was not an easy decision for the Danes to take, considering all the investments the Company had made, starting from Christiansborg on the promontory at Osu, all along the coast to the estuary at Keta, where stood their Fort Prindzensten. But the decision was taken at any rate, and in September 1850, Governor

Edward Carstensen sold Christiansborg and all the other Danish properties on the Guinea coast for the amount of 10,000 pounds sterling to a British representative, at a ceremony at the forecourt of Christiansborg. With this sale, the Danes had virtually given up everything that they had on the Guinea Coast, except the Watchtower, Provesten.

"It was this circular mini-fortification that Carstensen and the remaining Danish soldiers and staff found their way to after the handing-over ceremony. They were followed into the small Watchtower by a large group of local Danish-Osu people, including some relatives of Carstensen's wife, Severine Brock, the concubines of Svedstrup, and some soldiers who had come to express their sorrow and sympathy for the imminent departure of their Danish friends and relatives, who would be leaving the shores of Danish-Osu forever after over 150 years of settlement."

With a hint of mockery in his voice, Ataa Forkoyi continues with his narration:

"With no cause for celebrating the end of the Danish presence at Danish-Osu on that day, upon arriving back in the Provesten the Danes, in a pensive mood, slowly changed into their non-ceremonial uniforms and settled down to pack their few personal belongings. The remaining ragged pieces of furniture, faded clothing, and rusted pots and pans that they could not pack or did not want to pack, were auctioned to those who had followed them to their small fortification.

"Until March 30, 1850, their small fortification remained their one and only property, with its rusted cannons, which had helped to defend Christiansborg on its landside for decades, that had been used to chastise the Kinkawe community on the day the fury of the gentle Carstensen was released. This unprecedented application of violent Danish power on Danish-Osu was a bad omen of what would befall the community ten years hence, when the British, who bought Christiansborg, showed their power of intimidation and domination when they took charge to include the Danish east coast in their administrative jurisdiction."

As soon as Ataa Forkoyi makes reference to the phrase "bad omen," one listener, who is by nature highly critical of superstitious ideas, quickly interjects with a question:

"What did the British do when they took over Christiansborg? Weren't they already residing at the James Fort in Gã-Mashie and operating from the Cape Coast Castle? How did Carstensen's bombardment to teach a lesson to the Kinkawe community, predetermine what the British would do ten years hence?"

"Yes, bad omen, bad omen!" retorts Ataa Forkoyi with slight anger coming up through his feeble voice.

"It all began on the last day of the Danes and the first day of the British in the forecourt of Christiansborg in the presence of the dignitaries from Gã-Mashie, Akyem and Akwamu and the chiefs and community leaders of Danish-Osu, at the ceremonial handing over of the power of administration of Danish-Osu to the British.

"Madam History teacher, you see, as the formal negotiations went on between the Danes and the British to dispose of the Danish possessions and sell them to the British, there was no single Danish-Osu soul present at the meetings. All the initial and serious meetings took place far away in Europe and nobody from Danish-Osu was invited to be present to be part of the negotiations. The chiefs, the community leaders and the merchants had only been informed to get ready to have and reckon with the new overlords coming from the west: Gã-Mashie and Cape Coast.

"On the eve of the handing-over ceremony, March 5, 1850, as the final discussions on the detailed arrangements for handing over the properties in Danish-Osu, Kuku Hill, Sesemi, Augustensborg at Teshie, Fredensborg at Ningo, Kongensteen at Ada and Prendzensteen at Keta and other places were going on, it was expected that at least the representatives of the affected communities would have been present as witnesses, since the decisions taken would have a direct bearing on their future living circumstances."

In an infuriated tone, Ataa Forkoyi blurts out:

"Madam, on such an important and significant occasion, the Danes did not consider it courteous even to invite the respectable and knowledgeable Danish-Osu gentleman and a royal of the traditional Osu ruling house, Frederick Noi Dowuona, to grace the occasion. Hitherto Noi Dowuona, a man of great stature in the Danish-Osu community, who had had his formal and theological orientation and some technical training in Denmark and had returned home in 1828, had officially assisted in various deliberations a number of times at Christiansborg. But on the eve of arriving at significant agreements that would determine the future of the people of Danish-Osu and the other Danish settlements, Frederick Noi Dowuona was not considered worthy to be included.

"According to the Stones," Ataa Forkoyi continues, "rather than a Danish-Osu representative, there was a Gã-Mashie mulatto gentleman by name of James Bannerman present at the meeting, at the invitation of the British. The chiefs, elders and community leaders, who were fully aware of what was going on in Christiansborg that night, did not take kindly to this disregard for their important role in deciding on what might affect them and the various communities of Danish-Osu. They felt slighted for not being considered as stakeholders in this matter that dealt with the future of their people, their land and their communities. Thus they felt betrayed by the Danes, and since they thought the British had instigated this, they consequently developed ill sentiments towards them. The atmosphere therefore was poisoned before the British took charge of Christiansborg and the administration of Danish-Osu.

"As a result, when the British eventually settled down and made their presence felt, a number of Danish-Osu citizens, especially indigenous merchants and community leaders began to show hostility towards them and the mulattoes who came along with them from Gã-Mashie. Nothing the British did pleased anyone in the communities, and citizens always had cause to complain about the administrative measures the British began to put in place. Even their good intentions to curtail the domestic violence perpetrated on women by unkind husbands were interpreted to be interference in family affairs and undermining tradition and culture at Danish-Osu. This simmering dislike for the new overlords ultimately came to boiling point in 1854, barely four years after the Danes had left the shores of the Guinea Coast, which the British now officially referred to as the Gold Coast."

At this point in the narration, Ataa Forkoyi, with a whimsical face, turns around and uses his left hand to point towards Christiansborg, standing on his south side, whilst he tries to speak with an English accent, standing with arms akimbo:

"Christiansborg and Danish-Osu, you are no longer in the Guinea Coast. You are in the Gold Coast and you are our protectorate. Do you understand?"

Then with the voice of a Gã-Mashie man speaking English, Ataa Forkoyi vociferously responds: "Yes sah, saah."

After this short theatrical performance, he continues in a more serious manner, "The British had it in mind to undertake some development projects to bring Danish-Osu closer to the standard of development which had began to emerge in British Accra. To achieve this, the British realized that they needed to levy a tax on the communities to raise funds. So, they rallied the chiefs and their elders, the community leaders and local merchants, and announced that all adult citizens of Danish-Osu would have to pay a poll tax.

"The immediate reaction from the community was strong rejection of the payment of any tax to the British, who were considered unwelcome sojourners. The British did not have any mulatto offspring at Danish-Osu to claim any right of relationship, nor citizenship nor lordship as the uncircumcised Akwamus once did several centuries ago.

"To show their disdain for this British move to introduce this incomprehensible and unacceptable tax burden on them, some of the boisterous community leaders organized the youth to march to Christiansborg to let the British administration be informed in no uncertain manner, that Danish-Osu was not prepared to part with a farthing for collection by the British."

Before Ataa Forkoyi can proceed, a young man who appears to be a student hastily poses the question:

"You earlier informed us that both Christiansborg and the Watchtower Provesten were well equipped with cannons that the Danes always used to defend themselves from any attack from the landside. As the youth marched towards Christiansborg, were they not afraid that they could be fired upon from these cannons perched on the bastions?"

Ataa Forkoyi, surprised at the question, exclaims loudly:

"What? Afraid? Afraid of what? The youth of Danish-Osu knew that since the Danes left, the new occupants of Christiansborg had not bothered with those cannons, and almost all of them had become rusty and useless. So, they felt safe and confident in marching to the castle to demonstrate their protest against this tax. They simply could not understand why they should be saddled by the British with such a burden. So on they marched boldly, towards the Castle. As they approached, the soldiers from the Castle realized these young men and their leaders meant to get closer. The soldiers then began to shove back, with brute force, the first batch that had got quite close to the gate.

"When the irate demonstrators saw what was happening, they became infuriated and a mob action gave way to the earlier boisterous singing, drumming and dancing that accompanied their march. The angered youth began to throw stones at the soldiers, who, not armed, took to their heels back inside Christiansborg, when they found that their commanding officer, a Briton, had been badly hurt by a missile. According to the Stones, the atmosphere became tense and after a few days of aborted attempts to bring the situation under control, the British decided to show the Danish-Osu communities and the other eastern communities at Labadey and Teshie, whose support had been solicited by the Danish-Osu community leaders, the power of British rule."

Ataa Forkoyi then suddenly stops talking. He closes his eyes and tears slip out. His listeners realize that he is going through emotional recollections, so, although they are eager to hear more, nobody prompts him to continue. After a while, his emotions abate and he gives his characteristic wry smile. He opens his eyes, and with a gentle voice, says:

"My friends, I must apologise for becoming emotional. You know, the Stones continue to grieve and cry, and I see their tears and feel their pain as they reminiscence about the events of 1854. It was a Wednesday morning at Danish-Osu. The day was September 13, a Homowo Wednesday, when the people of Danish-Osu, and their eastern neighboring communities, Labadey and Teshie, were celebrating the annual Festival of Homowo."

Without waiting for Ataa Forkoyi to complete what he is saying, one of the listeners, who appears to be a foreigner, interjects humorously:

"Ataa Forkoyi what is this festival which has so many 'o's in its name?"

He replies in the same spirit in which the question has been asked:

"My friend, the word '*hɔmɔ wɔ*' in the Gã language literally means 'hooting at hunger,' and hooting customarily goes with a high-pitched sound of oh, oh, oh; hence the frequent appearance of the letter 'o' in the anglicized version, Homowo. But Homowo is a very significant festival accompanied by profound socio-religious activities. The Gã-Dangme celebrate this annual festival to mark their new year by preparing the cult food, *Kpoikpoi,* for communal feasting, to commemorate the historic harvest that ended a severe and prolonged hunger caused by an extensive drought in the Accra plains once upon a time. The preparation of the cult food and communal feasting customarily falls on a Tuesday. The Wednesday thereafter celebrates a solemn family and community event in which mutual blessings and well wishes are exchanged amongst relatives and neighbours. The greeting expressed in Gã on this solemn occasion usually is '*Ŋoo Wala,*' literally 'receive life,' meaning 'may peace, and well-being and prosperity be yours.' The occasion is also used to effect reconciliation amongst individuals and groups that might have been at loggerheads during the previous year."

Having thus explained to the foreign listener the cultural significance of Homowo, Ataa Forkoyi returns to his narration with a grim face and continues:

"Yes, it was a Wednesday morning at Danish-Osu, and although the atmosphere was tense, people were in a festive mood. The weather was relatively cool but the joy of the celebrations had brought cheer and warmth to the hearts of the people. It was a misty morning, so those who were already out in the communities, going around to extend to their relatives and neighbours the customary early morning ŋoo Wala greetings, did not see the British warship, HMS Scourge, anchored quietly in the roads in the sea, on the east side of Christiansborg. Suddenly there was an explosion of fire and fury from the bowels of the ship, 'Boom, Boom, Boom.'

"The bombardment of Danish-Osu had begun. Cannon balls, sizzling and searing, began to fly, landing viciously on the stone and mud houses at Amangfong, where a large collection of family houses were located within the communities of Kinkawe, Ashinte, Alata and Anahor. The houses belonged to both indigenous and mulatto families such as the Brocks, Bergessens, Engmanns, Holms, Swanikiers, Larsens, Briandts, Richters, Riemers, Hansens, Malms, Quists, Sonnes, and the other Danish-Osu families with Danish ancestry."

Shaking his head sadly, the human rights activist in the group of listeners raises his right hand to stop Ataa Forkoyi and asks:

"Nuumoe, did you say September 13 was the day the people of Danish-Osu were exchanging the peace and reconciliation customary greetings?"

"Yes," responds Ataa Forkoyi. The human rights activist, in a tense mood, begins to soliloquise almost inaudibly:

"How could the British choose such a day to visit such mayhem upon people who only had stones as weapons? What a cruel irony to use a ship called HMS Scourge to bombard the coast of Danish-Osu on such a solemn occasion."

Ataa Forkoyi stands there quietly, listening to the soliloquy. The rest of the listeners capture the spirit of the moment and join Ataa Forkoyi in his silence. When the atmosphere has lightened a bit, he clears his throat and picks up the narration again.

"Yes, the bombardment went on for sometime and when a considerable number of houses, including even those of the Basel Mission had been reduced to rubble, the 'Scourge' menacingly moved eastwards towards Labadey and Teshie to release the same explosions of fire and fury on the houses there."

With a trembling voice, Ataa Forkoyi continues:

"When the bombardment ceased, the soldiers stationed inside Christiansborg came out to loot the destroyed houses. According to the Stones, Danish-Osu families lost all their property consisting of money, jewels, furniture and several sturdy stone buildings, twenty-two of which were stated to be worth £1000 to £3000 each at that time in the bombardment and the subsequent looting by the soldiers. In addition, precious items like some of the manuscripts Reverend Zimmerman had produced on Gã proverbs and histories, written in Gã, all perished. Sacred items such as the old church pews the Basel Mission received as relics from the chapel of Christiansborg were reduced to ashes in the bombardment."

When the Rastafarian hears this, he shouts out: "Shame you Brits, for touching Jah's furniture!"

After everybody has finished laughing at this outburst, Ataa Forkoyi gravely continues with his narration:

"After the town had thus been razed, many of the people escaped with wailing and weariness, to seek refuge at their traditional villages located in the Accra plains at Haatso, Agboogba, Abladzei, Boi, Abokobi and Kponkpo. The Basel Missionaries, who had also lost their mission house and school building, followed suit to look for a place of refuge in the surrounding villages for themselves, their school children, many of the mulattoes, and converts. They settled down eventually at Abokobi to continue with the Basel Mission School and made the place a temporary headquarters for their missionary operation among the Gã-Adangme."

Low Tide at Danish-Osu

"Much later, after the dust had settled, the people began to trickle back to see the state of their properties. It was total destruction; there were only stones and rubble lying around and all the houses were gone. They had paid the price for being too close to Christiansborg, their former provider and protector. Christiansborg had now become their prosecutor and persecutor. Danish-Osu dared not be in its vicinity any longer.

"They then realized the enormity of the task of reconstruction and remembered that the leadership structure of Danish-Osu was in disarray. They needed a leader with a peaceful disposition, great organizational abilities and competence. They thought the obvious choice would be that royal scholar and Danish-Osu-born missionary, Frederick Noi Dowuona. So the community leaders decided to approach him and plead with him to utilize his experience and wisdom, knowing that he would be equal to the task of rebuilding Danish-Osu. Noi Dowuona, who was qualified to be a traditional ruler of Danish-Osu, had decided against involvement in chieftaincy matters due to his deep commitment to his mission to bring the Gospel of Jesus Christ to his fellow Gã people. He was, before the bombardment, residing outside Danish-Osu, in the village of refuge he had founded at Santse in the Accra plains, doing his missionary work.

"When he was approached to take up the leadership role, he accepted the invitation without hesitation. His first undertaking was to go around encouraging the scattered communities of Kinkawe, Ashinte, Alata and Anahor to regroup and come back to rebuild Danish-Osu. He then went to collaborate with his old colleagues, the Basel Missionaries, who were the first to return to the demolished town, to undertake a massive reconstruction exercise.

"The Basel missionaries thought they could go back to their previous location but the returning communities wanted to be at a comfortable distance from Christiansborg. In no time, by sheer force of determination and deep love of their ancestral home where their ancestors lay buried under their houses, the people managed to re-erect Danish-Osu out of the rubble effected by the HMS Scourge, to the delight of the British administration in the Castle."

Before Ataa Forkoyi can continue with his narration, the history teacher raises her hand politely and begins:

"Ataa Forkoyi, you have been making so many references to Frederick Noi Dowuona in your narration. You mentioned him in passing, as a man of stature who should have been consulted when the negotiation for the future of the Danish properties was going on between the Danes and the British. You are now referring to him as the one who took the leadership role to embark on the reconstruction of Danish-Osu. Who was Frederick Noi Dowuona?"

"Thank you for the interruption and your question. You have offered us all the opportunity to have a break. I am getting tired and I need some rest now. You see, the sun is at its zenith and it is twelve o'clock. It is time for a bite and a nap. When we come back, I shall tell you about King Fetreke, as he came to be known later at Danish-Osu."

Ataa Forkoyi comes back from his midday break with his straw hat gingerly perched on his bald head for protection from the powerful afternoon sunshine. He gets to his seat on the rocky outcrop at Amangfong but does not sit down to continue his narration, as expected. Instead, he bids his listeners to follow him as he begins to walk slowly towards Osu Kinkawe. When he and the group get to a huge tamarind tree in full bloom standing by the road, he makes a stop and leans towards the rough trunk of the tree. There are some children standing under the tree, trying hard to bring down some of the ripened fruits. As they realize that Ataa Forkoyi is leaning on the trunk, they courteously but reluctantly give up and walk away. Ataa Forkoyi now clears his throat and begins once more to speak, this time with a firm and audible voice:

"Who was Frederick Noi Dowuona?" he asks the question, turning in the direction the History Teacher is standing.

"I promised to tell you about Noi Dowuona, King Fetreke of Osu Kinkawe. King Fetreke was one of the best things that happened to Danish-Osu. His life and work highlighted some of the tangible and intangible blessings that came to Danish-Osu through the coming of the Danes to the Guinea Coast. Now, before I tell you about this remarkable son of Danish-Osu soil, let me speak about some of these good things that the low tide brought along to Christiansborg, to the shores of the land of the Osu Kadi Gbɔi."

The Emergence of a Cosmopolitan Community

In a lively mood, similar to that of a school teacher well pleased with his responsive class, Ataa Forkoyi moves from his leaning position and begins to pace up and down in the comfort of the tree's shade. As he walks up and down with his eyes partially closed, he continues with his narration:

"Besides the turbulences and turmoils and travails, there were also good times at Danish-Osu when Christiansborg came to perch on the promontory at the beach. Low tide at Danish-Osu unleashed fame, favour, and frivolity into the communities, and brought boundless blessings to the environment, the society, and the people. Meanwhile, times had changed and transitions had been made from the painful period of the seventeenth century to the promising and optimistic period of the eighteenth century. Trade in goods, gold, ivory and slaves increased and Danish-Osu grew by leaps and bounds. According to the Stones, during this period, 500 to 600 slaves per month were loaded onto European ships bound for the Caribbean and business was going well for Christiansborg and all its partners.

"With trade booming around Christiansborg, Danish-Osu began to attract traders and people servicing traders. They came from diverse places in the interior and overseas, leading to the configuration and integration of people into a community of Africans and Europeans, a hybrid of peoples and traditions with Gã, Akan, Portuguese and Danish cultural colorations.

"Because of the transatlantic slave trade, the Atlantic system was brought into the local world of Danish-Osu and influenced their everyday life. European ships were seen arriving with people and goods and these ships could later be seen leaving again with other people, many of them enslaved being taken to the Caribbean islands of St. Croix and St. Thomas. This traffic linked Danish-Osu to the West Indies. According to the Stones, due to this close link, in 1708, one Danish Governor, Erich Lygaard, considered the possibility of sending away all Danish-Osu mulattoes to the West Indies.

"The traditional settlement, starting as a small village of the Osu Kadi Gbɔi, thus evolved into a cosmopolitan town, with a townscape influenced and shaped by that Danish architectural edifice, Christiansborg. With this influence, some of the merchants began to build little stone houses that looked like small citadels, with balconies all around. Later, some of these houses had flat roofs which made it possible for the owners to take strolls on them in the evenings when the sun had set. In order to ensure adequate supply of water, underground cisterns, similar to what existed in Christiansborg, were built in the compound of these houses to harvest and store rainwater collected from the roofs.

"There were also the neatly kept family-houses, belonging to the local, indigenous Danish-Osu people. These houses, built in adobe, with their extending thatch roofs that overhung both the streets and the interior courtyards, had clay benches beneath the roofs so that people could sit in the shade during the day. They had several rooms, some with ancestors buried below the floors, and were occupied by members of extended families. The rooms were grouped around numerous courtyards, which were organized into male and female quarters in accordance with the Gã customary separation of the residential environment into *Hii Amii* and *Yei Amii* (as explained in Appendix III). This customary segregation was necessary to provide for ritual and functional convenience for men and women in their living quarters. The courtyards were very significant spaces, and were called *'kponɔ,'* in Gã. The kponɔ was more than a physical entity for the families."

Ataa Forkoyi speaks with a grin on his wrinkled face. "It was a place of gathering for all the days' activities that the families pursued from dawn till dusk and even into the night, when grandparents gathered their grandchildren to tell them stories of long ago, about the ancestors and their heroic deeds.

"It was also here that the extended families gathered for the naming ceremony to formerly welcome newborns into the family. The naming ceremony is known as *Kpodziemɔ,* that is, 'out-dooring.' The out-dooring ceremony served as a customary rite of passage and a mark of Gã identity. It is religious as well as social."

At this point in the narration, Ataa Forkoyi closes his eyes and cocks both ears with his hands as if he is listening attentively to somebody. After a while he takes a deep breath and begins to speak again:

"According to the Stones, Danish-Osu was seen by all who visited as always going through cycles of physical change. At times, it was a city with a large population of different skin colours and cultures. At other times it was so small that one could literally count the population on one hand.

"In its heyday, one could see a number of beautiful, well-built houses surrounding the towering walls of Christiansborg. In times like these, the Danes became at ease and complacent, knowing that there was stability and vitality in the communities to guarantee a good atmosphere for trading and social interaction.

"However, peace and tranquility could not always be guaranteed in Danish-Osu, due to destabilizing incursions by enemies from within and without. When Danish-Osu was at peace, the Danes also knew that there would be enough men available to be used as soldiers to protect their interests and undertake military adventures into the eastern coastal areas where they pursued their trading activities.

"When Danish-Osu was at peace, community life became buoyant and activities stretched from the courtyards of the family houses into the streets, to the forecourt of Christiansborg and far out to the beach on the east of Christiansborg, the landing place for the boats that brought the goods and people from the slave ships, anchored in the roads far out to sea.

"The most important community gathering place in Osu was a square that came to be called *Songme Naa* where people could meet or play games. This square was also a place for the weekly market where everything 'from land and sea' was on sale. It was located on the main route leading to Christiansborg on its north side, from where local mulatto women such as Lene Kuehberg, would arrange for European goods to be brought for sale."

At this point in Ataa Forkoyi's narration, a lady who appears to be of Danish ancestry interrupts with a question:

"Who was Lene Kuehberg?"

With a smile Ataa Forkoyi responds:

"Hold it, Madam. I shall tell you more later about this very interesting character who lived in Danish-Osu, and all her activities that disturbed the Danish administration for a long time."

After this interruption, he continues to talk about Songme Naa and says:

"Lena, together with some of the mulatto women, such as Miss Linekensdorf, Miss Wikstrand, Miss Sodring, Miss Nissen and others, were the chief brokers of the frequent auction sales that took place at Christiansborg. It was customary that as soon as a Dane died in Christiansborg castle or in the community, the deceased's property was auctioned three days after burial. Some of the mulatto women, through the good connections they had with the Danish administration, obtained the auctioned property, be it precious items like silk, or old clothing, mirrors, or cooking utensils, and brought these auctioned goods to Songme Naa for sale at the market."

While Ataa Forkoyi is speaking, one of the young men standing at the back bursts into a loud, whimsical laugh to the surprise of everybody. Ataa Forkoyi, surprised, asks the young man what could have caused this sarcastic laughter. The young man, who appears to be a Rastafarian, responds contemptuously:

"*Obroni waa wu* goods, you have been around since time immemorial. Ei, '*Bend-down Boutique*,' you were there at the beginning. Christiansborg, *ayekoo*." He sings out this response to express his disdain for the popular commercial practice of trading in second-hand clothing in the country.

Having recovered from the unsettling reaction of the Rastafarian, Ataa Forkoyi begins to talk about dress culture among women in the heyday of Danish-Osu.

"The young man was expressing his aversion to the birth of the second-hand clothing trade at Christiansborg. I can tell you that the Stones had an even stronger aversion, not only to the second-hand or used clothing business, but even more so to the new dress culture amongst women in the community, as influenced by the Portuguese. It was said that women married to Portuguese men in the community at that time dressed differently than the other women. To show their perceived status, these women hung many decorative charms and other beads from their bodies, wearing at times, a belt of blue or yellow cloth from which they hung knives, purses with money, and a bunch of keys."

As Ataa Forkoyi makes reference to this peculiar body adornment, his listeners break into loud laughter. He also gives a wry smile and continues to speak after the laughter dies out:

"Later on, life among women at Danish-Osu was influenced by the progress the mulatto women made in learning European household-skills at the Castle school that they had the privilege to attend, unlike their indigenous cousins and siblings. In time, as these women acquired the rudimentary skills of the Danish language and culture that the school offered, they began to develop what became a specific Gã-Danish hybrid culture that influenced Danish-Osu quite considerably, affecting marriage patterns, family life and social behaviour in the communities.

"For centuries, Danish-Osu existed and grew as a community which thrived on the energy of the transatlantic slave trade as directed and administered by Christiansborg. Within this milieu, the people and their cultural practices, together with the social values they built for themselves, evolved gradually as time passed.

"Then, at the beginning of the nineteenth century, came the abolition and outlawing of slavery and the slave trade. The established system began to crack and disintegrate, but not cataclysmically. The end of slavery and the slave trade in Danish-Osu was not so obvious, but it was certainly happening.

"The process began when the edict to end the trade was pronounced in Denmark in 1792, prior to the arrival of anti-slavery-minded people like Paul Erdman Isert, who had arrived in 1783 at Christiansborg in the service of the Danish administration at Danish-Osu. On his arrival he had met a sympathetic governor called J. A. Kioge, who was equally anti-slavery at heart."

Before Ataa Forkoyi can continue with his narration, the history teacher in the group of listeners raises her hand to indicate that she wants to ask a question. Ataa Forkoyi reluctantly stops talking and grants the teacher the chance to come out with her question. The lady begins with delight in her eyes:

"It is a relief to hear you describing how the Danes began to realize the evil in the obnoxious transatlantic slave trade and how they marshaled the moral courage to declare the trade as illegal. I find it interesting that you mention the name Paul Erdman Isert in connection with the historic process that spelled the doom of the Danish trade. I find the name interesting because I have seen a name of a street not far from here in the Ridge area, bearing the name 'Dr. P. E. Isert.' I am curious to know if the man you have mentioned was the man whose name has been given to that street in the Ridge area."

"Yes, 'Dr. P. E. Isert Street' was named after that wonderful Danish man I have mentioned. According to the Stones, Isert, a German by birth, from the town of Angermuende in Brandenburg, came to Christiansborg on his assignment as a chief surgeon of the Danish administration. He stayed in the Danish establishment for three years, during which he gained first-hand experience of the transatlantic slave trade as promoted and controlled by Christiansborg.

"What he saw, as he moved with the other Danish officers, merchants, soldiers and mulatto and African employees up and down the Guinea coast to conduct the business of the Company, deeply upset him. A number of moral questions arose in his mind but any time he tried to discuss his thoughts and feelings about the evil he saw in the activities of the Danish administration, his colleagues laughed him to scorn. They reminded him that doing business was the prime purpose of the Company in this inclement environment and that business was gold, ivory and most importantly, human commodities.

"He felt within himself that there should be an alternative to this inhuman business. Eventually, as his scientific mind propelled him to search for this alternative that his sensitive conscience challenged him to consider, he decided to undertake a private trip inland to investigate the possibility of testing the ideas he had been considering in the uplands of the Akwapim area he had been told about. He also wanted to collect more species of plants that had engaged his attention as a botanist since his arrival on the coast.

"So he left Christiansborg and Danish-Osu with permission to be away for a few days. With the assistance of his servants, he managed to make the trip by using the slave route through the Accra plains and up to the Akwapim hills. Upon arrival in the lush and cool hills, he realized that he had found the appropriate environment for his idea to take seed. Here in the hills of Akwapim, he could establish a colony of farmers that could plant tropical crops similar to those in the Danish islands of St. Thomas and St. Croix, without trading in slaves for export.

"However, the dreams he began to have were rudely curtailed when he was summoned back to Christiansborg. He had become a suspected agent provocateur. Christiansborg needed to observe him closely, lest he start a revolt against the Company in the Guinea coast.

"Isert became very uncomfortable with his new status in Christiansborg and was no longer willing to stay. He terminated his sojourn and left the shores of the Guinea coast to return to Denmark. But, consumed with the resolve to realize his dream of showing that the Company did not need to trade in human cargo from the Guinea coast to the Caribbean, he returned in 1788 with the blueprint to realize his dream of establishing a colony of Danish settlers in the Akwapim hills.

"He christened this colony Frederiksknople, meaning Frederick's City. Just as Isert's dream was taking off, a tragedy occurred. The man with this noble mind and gracious spirit suddenly died on January 21, 1789, ostensibly from the so-called climate fever (malaria), followed soon by his young wife who passed on in childbirth, with the surviving child dying later."

At this point in the narration, Ataa Forkoyi takes a deep breath and in a sorrowful tone, says quietly: "This tragedy sealed the fate of Fredericksknople and that was it."

Speaking now very slowly with eyes tightly shut, trying hard to hold back tears, he continues:

"The news of Isert's sudden death reached Danish-Osu and Christiansborg in no time. In the various communities, a lot of weeping and wailing was heard, as the news spread from home to home. But, according to the Stones, when the news reached Christiansborg, there was a celebration with rum and brandy. After all, the agent provocateur was no more."

Now, with a broad smile on his wrinkled face and a tinge of triumph in his voice, Ataa Forkoyi says loudly:

"Notwithstanding the joyful celebration inside Christiansborg, Isert's death did not stop the low tide that was bringing good fortune to Danish-Osu and the Guinea coast from the Danish administrative headquarters in Denmark. The tide had turned with the pronouncement of the edict in 1792. This had led to the abolition of slavery and the slave trade in the Guinea coast, which began to take effect in January 1803, fourteen years after the untimely end of P. E. Isert at Fredericksknople in the Akwapim hills.

"Although the evil trade continued at Danish-Osu and in the other Danish establishments, the beginning of its end had arrived. So, with the fortunes of the Company having greatly waned, the royal Danish Government assumed full responsibility for Christiansborg to ensure that royal authority was finally enforced on the contraband dealings in the slave trade. The focus of the administration became encouraging local Danish merchants to devote their energies to the development of the emerging oil palm cultivation which the English had been pioneering.

"With that came proactive governors such as Wilkens and Carstensen who employed the dwindling resources of Christiansborg to promote non-slave labour agricultural development and good business among the local merchants. According to the Stones, Wilkens was a charming man, who was able to generate warm friendships. He endeared himself so well to the Danish-Osu community that people associated him with Kuku Hill, since he might have started the construction of the four houses there.

"Incidentally, his gravestone became one of the five now mounted on the remaining wall of the old Danish Cemetery on the west side of the Osu Castle. You have already been introduced to Edward Carstensen who, with firm determination made sure that the evil, clandestine trade was uprooted in the Danish-Osu communities and the other Danish establishments on the Guinea coast."

Ataa Forkoyi is at this point interrupted with a question from the listener who appears to be of Danish ancestry. She begins hesitatingly:

"Nuumoe, you referred to the good fortune that the low tide brought to the shores of Danish-Osu with the declaration of the abolition of slavery and the transatlantic slave trade. Besides Wilkens and Carstensen who came as governors to Christiansborg in the nineteenth century, what other good things came from Denmark to Danish-Osu?"

Hearing this question, he adjusts the straw hat on his head, and appearing to be pondering something, begins to pace up and down whilst speaking to himself:

"What other good things came from Denmark? Hmm, let me listen to the Stones. What are they saying?"

He suddenly stops in his tracks and with a gleam in his dark eyes, says to his listeners:

"From Denmark, before the arrival of Wilkens and Carstensen, had come governors who were the agents of the new Danish conscience with the express intention to let the transatlantic slave business die out completely on the Guinea Coast. There were governors such as Wrisberg, Schionning, Richter, Reiersen, Svanekjaer, Steffens, Thionning, von Richelieu, and Broch. With these came, starting in 1800, the agricultural activities on Kuku Hill, which the Danes named Fredericksberg on the north of Christiansborg. They planted this hill with cash crops such as coffee, cotton and fruit trees. They linked the plantation that developed here to Christiansborg, with a straight avenue lined with tamarind trees that provided shade for the Danish officers as they moved up and down the hill either to supervise the works or to have fun in the country houses they built there, with good views of the sea.

"The governors were followed by Flindt and others numbering nine excluding the last two who arrived before the Danes sold Christiansborg and the other establishments in 1850. My friends, mentioning Flindt's name now brings to mind a memory of a very significant piece of good fortune at Danish-Osu in 1828. With the genuine interest now in discouraging the clandestine trade in buying and selling of enslaved people being perpetuated by the local mulatto merchants and their African relatives and business partners from the interior, Governor Flindt and his predecessors, von Richelieu and Brock, petitioned the royal Danish administration in Denmark to get the Basel Mission to send down missionaries to the Guinea coast to let the light of the gospel of Jesus Christ enlighten the hearts and consciences of the people, to give up their interest in slave trading."

As soon as the Rastafarian in the group hears Ataa Forkoyi referring to the Basel Missionaries as light bearers to the Guinea coast, he gets infuriated and shouts at Ataa Forkoyi rather discourteously, saying:

"Old Man, were the Baselers or Bastards not Europeans like the Danes? Were they not the very people who sent their slave ships in the name of Jesus to the shores of the Guinea coast to collect, pack and ship our ancestors like animals to the Caribbean to be used as beasts of burden? How can these very people become light bearers that would enlighten the hearts and consciences of the survivors of the evil transatlantic slave trade? Ataa Forkoyi, I demand, as a true son of Africa, and an offspring of the millions of ancestors who were dragged as human cargo from these shores here, an apology from you, for putting these objectionable statements in your narration on the good things that came from Denmark to Danish-Osu."

Ataa Forkoyi, visibly shaken by this unexpected verbal attack from the Rastafarian, bows his head and becomes still for a while. To help reduce the tension generated by the Rastafarian's outburst, the history teacher gently turns to the Rastafarian and points out to him that he has behaved disrespectfully toward Ataa Forkoyi by the manner in which he expressed what appear to be his genuine emotions. She goes on to explain to the young man that he should not have spoken in a loud and harsh voice to an elderly person. As a youth, he dares not, by the traditions of the land, demand an apology from such a respectable and revered person in Osu society as Ataa Forkoyi. The Rastafarian listens repentantly as the teacher educates him on cultural expectations and norms that guide how people should speak in public and how the youth must relate to elders in the community.

While the pep talk from the teacher is going on, Ataa Forkoyi keeps his gaze on the ground, shaking his head up and down, indicating that he understands the emotions expressed by the Rastafarian. When the teacher finishes speaking, a heavy mantle of silence falls and everybody becomes quiet.

Ataa Forkoyi then raises his head and begins to speak again without any trace of anger in his voice:

"Ladies and gentlemen, I know these outbursts. I have witnessed even the outbursts from the Stones as they recollect the times of the high tide at Danish-Osu. Young man, I don't hold anything against you by what you have said to me. When I finish the narration, you will understand why I made 'these objectionable statements.' But allow me first to correct your wrong perception that all the Danes and Europeans who were part of the machinery that drove the transatlantic slave trade, were slave masters and inhuman fellows.

"Going back to the high tide at Danish-Osu, the Stones recall the coming of individuals such as Governor Kioge, Dr Isert, Reverend Svane and Reverend H. C. Monrad, and some others, who, although guilty of being employed in the administration of the transatlantic slave trade, were, to all intents and purposes, against the practice of slavery and the business of the slave trade in their hearts. What was in their hearts, showed in the ways in which they responded to the people and situations they encountered while sojourning on the Guinea Coast. The Stones recall one interesting episode in which the Reverend Monrad was involved, and that needs to be told to illustrate the fact that not all the Europeans derided our people. Mr. Rastafarian, please listen."

Ataa Forkoyi then sits after he has taken a gulp of water from his water bottle. He wipes the sweat from his forehead with his left palm and begins to speak as if he is telling a story to a group of children by the fireside.

"Once upon a time, according to the Stones, Monrad was travelling in the company of some of his compatriots and the fort slaves, as they moved from the coast inland somewhere around the region the Danes used to refer to as Kreppe land. This might have been along the Volta River in Ewe-speaking villages. En route, the travel party came to a community that provided the opportunity for a rest stop. The villagers gathered around to receive the party and after a while it was time to move on.

"But before then, the local priest wanted, by pouring libation, to offer his blessings to Monrad and his group. When he got to know that Monrad was also a priest, he urged him also to pour a libation as he handed over the drink offering to him. Without hesitation, Monard accepted the invitation and poured the libation with a prayer just as the local priest had done.

"It was said that although Monard, as a representative of Christiansborg which considered black people as not worthy of the saving grace of God (and hence fit to be traded as cargo and used as beast of burdens) in that moment, displayed his character as a man of great tolerance. But much more, he elucidated his deep respect for and appreciation of the spirituality of the people Christiansborg had labeled subhuman."

Ataa Forkoyi ends this short tale by saying in a rather serious mood:

"There is a lot of information available to exonerate some of these Europeans posthumously, when the perpetuators of the slave trade have to be judged for their crimes against humanity. But we are not in a court of law so let me continue with my narration."

Now, in a relaxed mood, but still looking sprightly, he says:

"So, in 1828, there arrived on the shores of Danish-Osu, a group of four Basel missionaries in the company of an Osu-born young man who was returning home from Denmark after his training there as an officer of the Danish King. This young man was called Frederick Noi Dowuona, a son of the Kinkawe Royal house.

"The four missionaries could not survive the uncongenial weather and passed away so quickly. Noi Dowuona however, could survive, although he had been away for over a decade. He began to teach in the Christiansborg School and with his presence there, indigenous children, with great interest and enthusiasm, began to do what their mulatto relatives had had the liberty and right to do for centuries: enter Christiansborg to attend school.

"The school began to grow and eventually had to relocate from Christiansborg. It could no longer hold the large class of indigenous and mulatto pupils. In light of this, the School was re-established in 1843 in the vicinity of the Watchtower Provesten, outside the massive walls of Christiansborg by the Basel Mission with the able assistance of Frederick Noi Dowuona, who doubled as a teacher and an interpreter in Christiansborg.

"The development of the mission school came with an increase in the activities of the Basel Mission, which included the attempt to teach the Biblical truths and the tenets of the Gospel of Jesus Christ in Gã to the various groups of people in the Danish-Osu communities, including slaves, freed slaves, free citizens, the local indigenous merchants as well as the sojourning Danish merchants. The increase in mission work attracted more Basel missionaries to Danish-Osu, so much so that by 1848, Danish-Osu had become a missionary station from which a systematic evangelical effort extended into the Gã-Adangme speaking environment."

With a twinkle in his eye, Ataa Forkoyi enthusiastically continues with his narration:

"According to the Stones, the horrendous sounds heard around Danish-Osu as the long file of chained slaves were marched into the slave dungeons of Christiansborg, diminished as new sounds began to be heard. This came about with the establishment of the first factory in 1855 by the Basel missionary entrepreneur named, H. C. Rottmann. Other industrial establishments began to spring up, where local young men and women were employed as joiners, wheelwrights, carpenters, locksmiths, blacksmiths, shoemakers, and book binders to produce goods and provide services to support the development of new residential and commercial buildings in Danish-Osu and the surrounding areas.

"The congenial atmosphere created by the emerging, healthy, non-slave labour economy, fuelled by trade in oil palm and other food crops, led to the social and cultural circumstances that made it possible for the Basel missionary, J. C. Zimmerman, to undertake the first-ever attempt of translating the Bible into a local language. At Danish-Osu, with the assistance of young literate persons such as Carl Christian Reindorf and a number of unschooled local men and women whose identities cannot be traced by the Stones, Zimmerman finished the translation of the Bible into Gã in 1865. As a follow-up to this feat, the Stones affirm that within a period of five years, from 1879 to 1883, three Danish-Osu young men, Christian Reindorf, Jeremiah Engmann and Christian Quist, had responded to the call to become ordained ministers in the Basel mission."

As soon as Ataa Forkoyi completes his sentence, one of the listeners, who has Danish ancestry and strong evangelical convictions, puts her hand up to indicate that she has a question. She manages to catch the Old Man's attention and with a nod of approval from him, she clears her throat and speaks:

"All these names you have mentioned obviously have Danish ancestry. As you told us earlier, it was the mulatto children who were attending the Castle school and they were sitting daily at the feet of the various Castle chaplains who were their teachers while they sojourned on the Guinea coast. In a slightly raised voice, she asks the question: "Why did it take such a long time to have some of these mulattoes respond to the call for ordination as ministers of the Gospel, knowing that God had been interested long ago in the planting of a church of Jesus Christ on the Guinea Coast?"

This question from the lady brings a peculiar, loud laugh from Ataa Forkoyi but then with a solemn demeanour, he respectfully says:

"Madam, Christiansborg School was controlled by the governor and the Danish administration in Denmark. The mulatto pupils were not made Christians at school to go and make their dark-skinned half-siblings in town become Christians. Christiansborg did not believe at that time that dark-skinned people as such were qualified to become Christians; if they were qualified, they could not have been human cargo for shipment to the Caribbean. The mulatto pupils who sojourned in Christiansborg School therefore did not have any clue about the need to respond to a call for ordination as ministers of the Gospel. It was only the Basel Missionaries who believed the local people were part of God's salvation plan and it could only be in their school that any call for evangelism amongst the people could be discovered. So the showing up of these Danish-Osu young mulattoes in 1883 was just right."

Having finished speaking, he pauses to observe the reaction of the lady who asked the question. When he realises that the questioner is satisfied with his response, Ataa Forkoyi comes back to pick up on his earlier narration and says:

"With the ordination of the three young men from Danish-Osu, the Christian faith began to take root in the communities and the traditional lifestyles began to alter. Therefore, with the growth and spread of the influence of the emerging small local Christian community, the milieu at Danish-Osu began to move away from the slavery culture. That notwithstanding, the past evil of slavery and the slave trade hung around the communities, although the clandestine slave trading activities ebbed.

"The arrival of the British Union Jack in the community in 1901, after its relocation from Gã-Mashie as the headquarters, caused Christiansborg and Danish-Osu to cease to function, symbolically and finally, as a slave transit point. The slave transit quarters that for centuries provided homes for sojourning Danish slave merchants and enslaved people en route to the Caribbean, became a British administrative centre that fostered progress and advancement, not only at Danish-Osu, but in the whole of the Guinea coast, which metamorphosed into a political configuration by the name 'Gold Coast.'

"Under the British administration, Christiansborg, which became the Castle, served as the seat of government, with Danish-Osu functioning as its operational environment. By this status, it grew extensively and turned into a colonial settlement which assumed the name 'X'Borg,' an English literary corruption of the original Danish. Although the beginning of the British administration at Danish-Osu was marked by a destructive episode in the bombardment of Osu Amangfong, the community later benefited from many significant development initiatives undertaken by the administration. The Stones have in their memory the erection of a 340,000 gallon capacity water reservoir in the community in 1889, located on the north-west corner of the local cemetery, the enforcing of good building maintenance practices in the community, and the effective manner in which the outbreak of the bubonic plague in 1908 was controlled to reduce the number of deaths to only three victims.

"The X'Borg, the ex-slave transit point, with its attraction as the home of the seat of His Majesty's Government, was therefore accorded a new status and dignity within its social milieu. The greyish slave trading centre began to give way to a positive atmosphere that pulled good things into the community. These new virtues gave Danish-Osu, X'Borg, the privilege of hosting a vast array of historic figures and personalities who travelled to and sojourned in its community at one time or another.

"The Stones observed the presence of several good people who were attracted to the community. Some of the known historic figures that passed through included Rev. Hermann L. Rottmenn, who started the Basel Mission Trading Company at Danish-Osu in 1832, Rev. David Asante, the first ordained African Minister of the Basel Mission Church, who was married circa 1845 to a Danish Osu woman by the name of Martha Lydia Otutua; Rev. J. G. Christaller, the Basel Missionary who translated the Bible into Twi, Rev. Theophilus Opoku, one of the pioneer theologians of the Basel Mission Church of the Gold Coast who was sent from Akropong Akwapim to welcome Rev. Christaller, as he arrived by boat at the beach of Danish-Osu on January 25, 1853 to begin his momentous missionary effort, and Rev. Jakob Wilhelm Wert, the last of the Gã-speaking Basel Missionaries who lived at Danish-Osu from 1895 to 1937 and played a significant role in the revision of the Gã Dictionary. Amongst these historic figures who came to Danish-Osu or sojourned in it, one stands on a high pedestal. This person is a national hero and was known as Nii Adza Tetteh Quarshie."

As soon as he mentions the name, the history teacher comes in and asks Ataa Forkoyi:

"Are you referring to Tetteh Quarshie, the man who brought cocoa beans from Fernando Po, now known as Bioko in Equatorial Guinea, and planted them at Mampong Akwapim to start the first cocoa farm in Ghana?"

"You are a history teacher indeed. Yes, I am talking about that man with the eyes to see gold from green pods and hands to turn the soil into a factory of golden pods that made Ghana a land of the brown gold. It all started at Danish-Osu. Tetteh Quarshie, born in 1842, hailed from Teshie where his father, Ataa Mleku Boi was also a native son. His mother, Awo Ashong Fio, was of the La Anahor community (quarters) and through her relatives of Osu Anahor, Tetteh Quarshie gained admission to the Basel Mission Training centre, where he learned blacksmithing.

"In 1870, at the age of 28, when he had become a master craftsman in blacksmithing, he joined some of the Danish-Osu youth and travelled out for an adventure in West Africa that eventually landed him on the Portuguese island of Fernando Po where cocoa was being cultivated. Returning to Danish-Osu in 1876, he brought back a few cocoa beans to try to farm cocoa as he had seen it being done on the island. When he realised that he could not succeed with his experiment, he decided to do what many of the Danish-Osu skilled men did to offer their exquisite skills to the people on the Akwapim Hills: he migrated to Mampong with his remaining cocoa seeds and made a home there. The rest, as they say, is now history."

With a broad grin, Ataa Forkoyi turns towards the history teacher and when he realises that she is satisfied, he closes his eyes and continues cheerfully:

"Besides these historical people that were associated with Danish-Osu, there were also the big political guns, such as Sir Gordon Guggisberg, the great colonial administrator who initiated ground-breaking development projects in the Gold Coast such as the Takoradi Harbour, the initial Railway System linking Takoradi, Kumasi and Accra, and the Achimota College; Sir Charles Noble Arden-Clarke, the British governor who successfully presided over the transition from colonial administration to self-rule; Lord Listowel who was the last governor of British rule in Ghana; Osagyefo Dr. Kwame Nkrumah, the premier President of the nation state of Ghana; General J. A. Ankrah, the first military Head of State; and Flight Lt. J. J. Rawlings, the last military Head of State. Among these were also sons of the Diaspora such as Dr. J. R. Lee, the first African-American returnee to establish a dental practice in Ghana and Dr. W. E. B. Dubois, the first-ever leading African-American scholar and philosopher to spend his sunset years outside the United States. There was also the petite giant, Dr. Esther Ocloo, the first female Ghanaian industrialist, who launched the world famous Nkulenu Food Industries from her backyard at X'Borg."

At this point in his listing of historic figures and personalities hosted by the Danish-Osu community, his throat runs dry and he begins to lose his voice. Seeing this, one of his listeners kindly offers him a bottle of water. He graciously receives it and sips from the bottle. Having regained his voice, he closes his eyes and says, slowly and sonorously:

"My friends, the list is very long. According to the Stones, just as Danish-Osu and Christiansborg shamefully hosted ignoble people at high tide, it welcomed several wonderful people to X'Borg and the Castle at low tide. But I do not need to mention all their names. Many left their footprints behind, bestowing the community its rich endowment of sites and landmarks that mark its historic significance up to today. Meanwhile, the Union Jack, hoisted on top of the Castle, kept waving in the sea breeze until March 6, 1957, when it was lowered to be replaced by the Ghanaian national flag with the stripes of red, gold and green and the shining black star in the centre."

As Ataa Forkoyi reaches this point in his narration, he begins to run out of steam and his voice declines. There are all the indications that he is getting tired. He lifts up his straw hat from his head, looks up to check the position of the sun in the sky and abruptly declares:

"My friends, it is now time to go home for my evening meal. Good night." He then mumbles something, which sounds like, "I shall see you another time," and gingerly walks away in the direction of the setting sun.

Four | Danish-Osu Sprouting Seedlings

Between the High and Low Tides

IT IS NOW ALMOST MIDDAY AND THE SUN IS GETTING TO ITS ZENITH. THE hawkers are going round, trying hard to attract the attention of passers-by to their assorted wares. The ice cream bicycle vendors are also busily cruising around, tooting their bicycle-horns to announce their presence to those who want to taste their creamy iced lollies. There are the housewives hurrying home from the market after the hard bargaining they have done, to go and prepare lunch for their children who will soon be back from school for the midday break. Ataa Forkoyi has been talking the whole morning, while taking his listeners round, showing them places where the Stones have been telling the stories of Danish-Osu.

As they stroll around, stopping here and there, listening intently to Ataa Forkoyi's narrations, they come across streets, lanes and byways with European names that appear Danish in their spelling. One's eyes cannot help catching a number of Danish names such as August Avenue, Richter Road, Sonne Close, Fleischer Lane, Lutterodt Loop, and many more. Now they are about to cross a street with the street sign "Lokko Road."

On the side of the intersection between Lokko Road and Salem Road, there stands a huge neem tree with many branches with lush green leaves, providing cool shade beneath the tree. As Ataa Forkoyi and his listeners slowly approach this place, he branches off and tiredly drags himself towards the tree and eventually stops underneath. He takes off his straw hat and begins to fan himself with it, while he leans his tired body against the tree-trunk.

His listeners realize that the old man needs some rest so they quietly follow him into the shade of the tree. One by one, with the midday heat tearing at their throats, they take out their water bottles from their knapsacks to begin to quench their thirst. Ataa Forkoyi also beckons a sachet-water hawker to buy some water to drink.

While the group rests, the lady with Danish ancestry walks up to Ataa Forkoyi and offers him some of her ginger energy biscuits that she has been munching. He receives the biscuits with gratitude and as he begins to nibble at what he has received, he appears to have suddenly regained his energy and then begins to talk about the history of some of the families whose names appear on the street signs they have been reading as they walk around.

"As you may remember, I mentioned earlier on in one of my accounts that in the seventeenth and eighteenth centuries many of the Danes fathered children with Danish-Osu women while they were at Christiansborg. These children, who were known as 'mulatto' in accordance with the Portuguese coastal lingua franca, always bore the names of the Danish men who fathered them. These were either the surnames of their Danish fathers or derivations of the original surnames, signifying that the child was the offspring of a particular individual; for example, Pedersen being the son of the man called Peder. The Gã Danish-Osu local women who bore these mulatto children knew precisely who their fathers were and they always managed to get the Danish administration to register the names of these men in their records, despite the fact that they knew very little Danish; as you are aware, mothers always know, no matter what."

He gives his customary wry smile after this statement, a little amused with himself; his listeners catch the pun and burst into hearty laughter. He then continues:

"According to the Stones, these Danish names began to show up in the community here and there with the establishment of Christiansborg, when a number of local Gã women began to have intimate relationships with men at the fort. Some of the names used in these early stages to identify the offspring were either corrupted or lost outright due to difficulties in pronunciation. Thus, names that appeared early in Danish-Osu, such as 'Lykke' or 'Brand,' or 'Bagge' changed into 'Lokko' and 'Briandt,' and 'Badger,' while names such as 'Witt' and 'Roemer' virtually vanished.

"Later, with the maturing of a generation of mulatto women in the community, the taste of the men in the Christiansborg castle shifted away from dark-skinned women to these mulatto women. Since these women had closer contact with the Danish administration and the men at Christiansborg, the Danish surnames such as 'Engmann,' 'Sonne,' 'Fleischer,' 'Petersen,' 'Hansen,' including difficult ones such as 'Riemer' and 'Burgessen,' given to their seedlings, were better held in memory and the names thus survived in the Danish-Osu community."

Now, Ataa Forkoyi, looking refreshed and excited, puts on his straw hat and indicates with his right hand that it is time they get moving again. But before they move, the Rastafarian raises his left hand and asks Ataa Forkoyi not to move.

"What is the matter this time, my friend?" Ataa Forkoyi impatiently asks. The Rastafarian, appearing relaxed on this occasion, respectfully says:

"Old Man, you talk about the mulatto offspring as seedlings. I like the metaphor and it is beautiful. To continue with this magnificent metaphor, if I may ask, were these seedlings Danes or Gã? And as seedlings, who was nurturing them? And where were they being nurtured, in the Christiansborg castle or the local women's family houses in the Danish-Osu community?"

At the Rastafarian's barrage of questions, Ataa Forkoyi shuts his eyes and nods his head in approval. Phrasing his words carefully, he begins:

"My friend, I am deeply impressed by these thought-provoking questions. The Stones were equally engaged with these questions. You see, the problem started with the Portuguese lingua franca that was used to categorise these seedlings, which came from the union between Danish men and the local Gã and other African women who found themselves in Christiansborg as fort-slave workers or slave women bound for sale and shipment to the Caribbean.

"The word 'mulatto,' was racially loaded and Euro-centric; it was meant to show that these offspring were neither black Africans nor white Europeans. The word was meant to imply that the offspring of Negro and Caucasian parents were a racial oddity. In fact, although the mulatto in the local community was known as 'blofonyo bi,' to wit, child of 'a white man,' in the oral traditions, the word 'mulatto' was misunderstood to stand for *'mla tolɔi,'* that is, 'law breakers,' that is, children of law breakers.

"But how can an offspring of mixed parenthood not be racially the same as their parents? This is a matter which, when pursued, can only lead to absurdity. After all, what has race got to do with humanity? Are black people superior to white people or the other way round? You see, the Portuguese lingua franca word 'mulatto' was used to categorise these offspring for the convenience of the slave-owning and slave-buying Danes. With the philosophical position that the black person can be made a chattel, an offspring from any union of a Dane and a black woman was tainted. The offspring was racially above the black parent but not as good as the white parent. Do you see the absurdity of pursuing such an issue?"

Ataa Forkoyi continues to expound this wisdom with his eyes still tightly shut as his listeners pay close attention. The Rastafarian is especially enthralled by what he is hearing.

"To the second question," he continues:

"The matter is straightforward; the initial nurturing of an offspring starts with the mother who is biologically endowed to be so. Hence, in the case of the Danish-Osu seedlings, it was the local women who nurtured the offspring. In the instance of a fort-slave or a bound slave delivering a baby, she was sent out of Christiansborg into the community to fulfill her maternal responsibility. The offspring invariably remained in the extended families of their mothers and as you know, in the Gã society as in any other African society, the nurturing of the young ones is the responsibility of all and sundry, with the usual required support from the mothers' male senior siblings or the mothers' father.

"The additional nurturing these Mulatto seedlings received did not come directly from the Danish parents. The fathers responsible for the birth of these offspring might have moved away at any rate by the time the children were old enough to benefit from paternal nurturing. There were also instances when the Danish fathers simply forgot about their offspring and ignored their duty, as the children were being kept by their mothers in the community outside Christiansborg castle.

"The actual Danish nurturing might have come through the Fort school which came into existence by 1723, together with the Mulatto Fund, established to attend to the physical needs of the mulattoes who were brought to Christiansborg by their local mothers. The Fort priests, who were at the same time the teachers, were mandated by the administration to attempt to christianize the children through the pseudo confirmation classes they gave them, with the hope that a religious conversion would prepare the children to be isolated from the local traditional culture and thus embrace the

European culture as practiced in Christiansborg castle. The children nonetheless kept trooping daily to the Fort School from their homes in the community and since they never slept over, the attempted cultural isolation program, never worked; for they always lived with their mothers in the extended family compounds with their black-skinned, Gã relatives and half siblings where the traditional cultural practices were part of the everyday domestic and community activities.

However, in time, as the male mulatto children grew into manhood, they were hired into the service of the Danish administration as soldiers and as such, began to make Christiansborg their home with their fathers' compatriots. Their biological fathers were nowhere to be found because they had since long gone either to their graves or back to Denmark. For this reason, mulattoes in general did not know their fathers and many carried with them the heavy psychological burden of wishing to know their fathers."

With a heavy voice, and getting deeper into his proverbial parlance, he continues:

"The burden of these mulattoes did not arise solely from the absence of their progenitors but also from the waters which nourished these seedlings as they sprouted. There was the water flowing daily from Christiansborg as the children went to see how their dark-skinned relatives were dehumanized, sent into the slave dungeons in chains and manacles or marched through the lower gates to the beach to be forced into canoes that would bundle them to the slave ships waiting in the roads to receive them for shipment to the Caribbean. There was also the water flowing from the community that showed these mulattoes how even their own mothers could be subjected to indecent treatment by Danish sailors and soldiers who prowled around with the arrival of new sojourners."

At this point in the narration Ataa Forkoyi suddenly opens his eyes. He looks at his listeners, searching from one face to another, and with his face shining, announces to them:

"The familiar Danish names known today, some of which are found as street names, belong to the seedlings that sprouted. Against all odds, they survived to become the ancestors of family trees that characterize the Danish-Osu landscape today. The Danish names that were known by the Stones but are not known today are many. I have just been reminded of three such names and I will now tell you about the people who bore them, because they were remarkable Danish-Osu personalities that the Stones are pleased to reminisce about."

The lady with Danish ancestry, hoping that her forebear's name will be mentioned as one of the remarkable personalities, impatiently implores Ataa Forkoyi: "What are the names?"

Smiling only on the left side of his mouth, he slowly responds:

"Madam, why are you so impatient? Let us take time to listen to what the Stones have to tell about these mulatto seedlings that never left trees behind at Danish-Osu. They were personalities who, despite their lack of family trees today, left behind fantastic memories engraved on the minds of the Stones. The names, for your information, are Christian Petersen Witt, Frederik Petersen Svane and Christian Jacobus Protten.

Witt, a Danish-Osu Ancestor with a Withered Presence

"Let us start with Christian Petersen Witt, who might have been among the first generation of mulatto children born at Danish-Osu. His father was Peter Witt who in 1678 became an interim governor in the Danish Fort called Frederiksborg, after he had been on the Guinea coast for 15 years. Petersen Witt was born to an African mother in the Danish-Osu community around 1682. Being one of the early survivors of the mulatto children of Danish-Osu, he stood out conspicuously and was well known to the Danish administration."

On hearing this statement from Ataa Forkoyi, one of his listeners who has relatives at Osu-Alata, makes some funny noises, apparently trying to attract the attention of his co-listeners. Ataa Forkoyi stops talking and angrily asks the young man to justify this unbecoming behavior. With a grimace, the young man poses a surprising question:

"Ataa Forkoyi is it true that Christian Petersen Witt is still around today?"

"Christian Petersen Witt still alive today? Young man, why are you asking this incredible question?" The young man then sheepishly answers: "There is a rumour going around here that Ataa Forkoyi is Christian Petersen Witt. Is this true or false?"

With great amusement, he answers the young man's question with a question: "Do I look like a mulatto?"

The young man, now gaining in confidence, almost shouts: "No, but they say you have come from the time of Pettersen Witt and you speak like him."

"Well, I am not him and I can't be him; but I certainly know him through the Stones. Are you satisfied?"

The young man grunts and waves his hand to indicate that he can proceed with his narration. Ataa Forkoyi heaves a sigh of relief and continues to speak.

"As I was saying, Christian Pettersen Witt was well known at Christiansborg and had the favour of the Danish administration. He was therefore hired as a soldier in 1708. From there, he moved on in 1718 to become a drummer, a respectable, although relatively low position in the Danish administration. In this capacity, he could function as an emissary of the governor and once, in 1725, despite his old age, he was sent to the court of the king of Akwamu by Governor Suhm.

"Due to his astuteness, he occupied several different positions under different governors until his retirement in 1727, having worked hard and faithfully for 30 years, not only as a soldier and a walking encyclopedia on Danish-Osu matters, but also as an arbitrator whenever 'palavers' had to be settled between his local fellows and the Danish sojourners. He had a keen sense of history; having been watered by the outflows of the slave culture of Christiansborg, he easily and unscrupulously provided information to guide the Danish administration in pursuing their slaving business. He knew about the skirmishes that the Danes had with their European neighbours, the Dutch on the west of Danish-Osu, which might have led to the development of the Osu Kinkawe traditional quarter."

Having heard Ataa Forkoyi's account of Christian Pettersen Witt, the young man who asked if Ataa Forkoyi and Witt were the same person interrupts the narration with a jolly shout: "Ataa Forkoyi, you are like Pettersen Witt; you are Pettersen Witt and you are buei!"

This time Ataa Forkoyi pretends not to hear the young man and continues smoothly with his narration.

"From what Pettersen Witt heard about Denmark, he always cherished the dream to see that land of his fathers with his own eyes. This dream became a reality when the governor granted his heartfelt request to visit Denmark in 1730. While there, the Company tried to pick his brain on a number of issues but he was not of much use to them, either because they could not understand his Osu version of Danish or because his memory had began to fail him. At any rate, Pettersen Witt returned home to Danish-Osu having fulfilled his life's dream of visiting the land of his fathers.

"According to the Stones, old man Witt lived long thereafter, actively serving the Danes until he was acknowledged in 1753 as a listed pensioner of Christiansborg. With time, his presence at Danish-Osu simply faded away, as his daughter Anna Sophie and her sister Eva, who attended the school at Christiansborg as classmates of Christian Protten, did not perpetuate the name Witt in the community. However, by a strange coincidence, Anna married a Danish man, whose surname was the middle name of her father. This man's name was Cornelius Petersen.

"Anna, the strong-willed woman with an elevated sense of pride in having a father who was recognized by the Danish administration, married Cornelius Petersen after she had left her two previous Danish husbands. This marriage, which was shrouded in much chicanery, led to the planting of the Danish-Osu family tree with the name 'Petersen.' According to the Stones, unlike the old man Witt, Anna Sophie was highly disliked by the Danish administration, which described her in 1760, as a 'powerful and dangerous person.' Her negative influence inside Christiansborg might have caused her husband to be sent off by Governor Hackenberg to the Caribbean as a punishment."

The lady with Danish ancestry, who has impatiently waited to hear the name of her forebears, now interrupts the narration, asking with an expectant smile:

"Ataa Forkoyi, who was Governor Hackenberg?"

"Have patience, my dear; I shall tell you about Governor Hackenberg when I start talking about the family trees of Danish Osu. Kindly allow me now to finish with the stories of the seedlings that did not become trees."

Svane, Obliterated Danish-Osu Ancestor

Ataa Forkoyi now gives a long yawn, indicating that he is getting tired. He takes a sachet of water to refresh himself. His listeners sympathetically urge him to take a break, but he refuses. The yawn appears to have taken the tiredness out of him and the water has invigorated him so much so that he continues the narration with peculiar exhilaration. He begins to pace up and down, shaking his head from side to side in his excited fashion. "One Danish-Osu mulatto, whose place and position in the community the Danes tried hard to wipe off the memory of the Stones, is the man Friederich Pedersen Svane.

"Pedersen Svane was born Friederich Pedersen in 1710, 23 years after Christian Petersen Witt. He was a mulatto whose mother hailed from Teshie, the easterly neighboring community of Danish-Osu, and his father was a Danish soldier called Hendrik Pedersen, who might have met the Teshie woman at the small Danish fort called Augustaborg on the site the Danes referred to as Tessing. In the pioneer Fort School in Christiansborg, Pedersen came under the tutelage of the chaplain, Rev. Elias Svane, who doubled as the school's teacher from 1722 till 1726. Friederich Pedersen and Christian Protten became the first ever local boys to be sent from the Fort School to Denmark on scholarship. They were sent to be trained as blacksmiths at the request of the Royal Danish Africa Company with the expectation that their training would benefit the Company in the various construction and maintenance work that had to be carried out on the canons, flintlocks and other ironmongery found in the Danish properties on the Guinea coast. This expectation, however, never materialized."

The history teacher, who has been keenly following Ataa Forkoyi's narration, respectfully interrupts and asks:

"I am curious to know why you said the expectation of the Company was never fulfilled. Was it because the young men never got to Denmark?"

With a mischievous smile, he replies: "Not at all. They arrived safe and sound in Denmark and in fact sojourned for over eight years in the land of their fathers. What I meant was that, unfortunately for their benefactors, the plan for them to become blacksmiths to service the fire-power of the Danish slave business did not appeal to these alert young-men. They wanted to follow in the footsteps of their teacher by studying theology, not technology! The influence of Rev. Elias Svane had been strong on fifteen-year old Pederson and twelve-year old Protten. Having accompanied the two young men to Denmark, Rev. Svane witnessed their christening, when Friederich Pedersen adopted the Reverend's name as a token of his gratitude, becoming Friederich Pedersen Svane. Thereafter, both young Svane and his younger compatriot Protten, went to school at a place called Sorterup where they received private tuition to prepare them to enter the University of Copenhagen in 1732, to study theology. According to the Stones, Svane completed his studies and earned himself a Bachelor's degree in 1734.

"While he was in Sorterup, he met a young Danish woman by

name Catharina Maria Badsch and by the good counsel of his old school teacher, Rev. Svane, they got married. Having achieved this respectable status and with a Danish degree in his pocket, he now felt ready to pursue a career, not in Denmark, the land of his father, but in the land of his mother. So Svane resolved to go back home, arriving together with his wife at the Guinea coast in August 1735. In his mind, they had left Denmark behind forever with all the difficulties he had encountered trying to assert himself as a person with his own mind."

With an excitement in his voice and a sparkle in his eyes, Ataa Forkoyi continues enthusiastically, "My friends, the Stones remember that his singular desire was to return home with his Danish wife, an outcome of his conviction as a true Christian, armed with deep faith in God as his provider, to launch his missionary enterprise among his people. He was fully aware that the community to which they were coming had been badly corrupted by the local Danes with their godless life-style and ignoble practice of the slave trade. So they decided not to live near Christiansborg. Rather, they temporarily sought lodgings with an old mulatto schoolmate named Severin, in his two-storey stone house in Danish-Osu, to the displeasure of the then Danish Governor, Schiedlerup."

Before Ataa Forkoyi can utter his next sentence, the Rastafarian comes up with a question, which he poses cautiously: "Why was the governor peeved by the Svanes' decision to lodge privately instead of finding accommodation in Christiansborg?"

Immediately Ataa Forkoyi responds: "How dared this mulatto, bring a Danish woman to the Coast and house her in a community of local people? So thought the governor. You know, Mrs. Svane was one of the very first European women to set foot on the shores of Danish-Osu. The governor thought he had the responsibility to provide a safe haven for a fragile Danish lady who had ventured to the unsafe and uncivilized environment of Danish-Osu. No doubt this audacious decision spelled out a fate of woe for Svane. But before I come to that, let me tell you how he settled back into the community he had left at the age of fifteen.

"Launching his re-integration attempts from his friend's house, he soon began to familiarize himself with the various communities of Danish-Osu, looking up his mother, sisters, brothers and several other extended family members at Teshie on the east of Danish-Osu and beyond Labadey. According to the Stones, his homecoming tour showed him that not much had changed. He had rather changed, having virtually forgotten his mother tongue, Gã. He recognized that he could no longer communicate with his people and this became a great source of frustration for him. How could he make his countrymen understand the Gospel message he had brought from Denmark for their conversion and enlightenment?

"He was also deeply distressed by Christiansborg's lack of concern for the care and training of the mulatto children in the communities. He had gathered that the mulatto educational fund that existed when he was growing up at Danish-Osu had been badly managed and had become dysfunctional, for which reason the mulatto children were suffering abject poverty just as their dark skinned half-siblings. To make matters worse for him, his eventual concession to seek employment and residence at the Christiansborg castle, exposed him and his wife to all the evil machinations that had virtually become the culture of the local Danes. According to the Stones, the wife of Svane became an object of lust for Governor Schielderup. In the face of the governor's attempts to seduce this Danish woman by all possible means, Svane made the hard decision to send his wife, together with their infant son, back to Denmark.

"In 1742, seven years after his arrival at Danish-Osu, Svane made a routine but fateful trip to the Danish Fort Fredensborg in Ningo, in the company of some Christiansborg staff, including Hans Hansen Blass, Klyn, Roemer, August Frederich Hackenburg, Juergensen, and Christian Dorph. Some of these gentlemen would later became Governors of Christiansborg."

At this point in the narration, the history teacher raises her hand with a question. Ataa Forkoyi nods his bald head and smiles for her to go ahead. In her elegant style, she asks: "Sir, I have two small questions. Number one: Why was Svane's trip to Ningo in 1742 'fateful?' Number two: The name August Frederich Hackenburg is usually mentioned at Osu in connection with other names like Reindorf, Engmann and Fleischer. Who was this man who accompanied Svane on his fateful journey to Ningo in 1742?"

Ataa Forkoyi, still cheerful, clears his throat and continues with a smile:

"Teachers are questioners. They are always asking questions, putting questions to their pupils, putting questions to their pupils' parents, and even to the pupils' grandparents."

At this, the group bursts into laughter.

When it ends, Ataa Forkoyi turns to look at the questioner and says gently, "Teacher, I will answer you. Svane's trip to Ningo was fateful because it was this trip that marked the beginning of the series of events that forced him out of his motherland back to his fatherland. But you wait; the Stones will give us the details presently. With respect to Hackenburg, it is true that his name is associated with those you mentioned. He was the Danish man who married Ashiokai, a royal of the Osu Kinkawe Ruling House. You will understand the connections better when the Danish-Osu family trees are presented later.

"In Ningo, a reception took place at the fort for the guests from Christiansborg, including Svane. It was in this festive atmosphere, with rum and wine flowing, that Svane made the fatal mistake of sharing his dreams with the people he mistook as colleagues. He forgot that, although he had been to Denmark and returned to the Guinea coast with a Danish wife, he was still a mulatto; not completely black, but still, with African blood in his veins. His dream was to put up a stone house at Danish-Osu, similar to that of his schoolmate, Severin. He dreamt of how he would bring his wife and child back to this dream house which would become his launching pad for preaching the Gospel message of Jesus Christ among his people. In his dream, he could see how his stone house would become a model to change the landscape of Danish-Osu and the other communities which he planned to evangelize.

"Caught up in these lofty ideas, Svane was misled to believe in the goodwill of his colleagues, some of whom promised to assist him to realize it. Juergensen, who soon thereafter became a governor, even promised to provide him with old gun chests as recycled wood to construct the floors, ceilings, doors, etc. of his house. Later, when he began to organize himself to begin the project, some of them presented him with symbolic gifts such as a man-slave and a dressing gown of calico. Meanwhile, he had suspended his missionary ambition due his difficulties with his mother tongue, Gã. His attempts so far to explain to his people theological concepts such as sin, the Ten Commandments, the wages of sin, the redemptive work of Jesus and the Gospel as the Good news had been futile and frustrating. He simply found it impossible to relate the traditional beliefs of his people to the Biblical truths caricatured by the local Danes in their sham Sunday church services, held in the chapel of Christiansborg.

"With the escape of his wife and son from the crude appetites of the local Danes, he could now work comfortably as a Precentor and Catechist within the slave citadel, Christiansborg, for a small income, about a quarter of what a regular Danish-employed Priest received. Seeing what the other assistants and officers had been doing, he began to supplement this income with monies he earned from selling a few slaves."

The Rastafarian, infuriated to hear that Svane was involved in slave-trading, howls at Ataa Forkoyi: "Do you really mean this Danish-Osu preacher man who came home to enlighten his folks with the Gospel of Jesus, the Saviour, was selling his mothers and fathers, brothers and sisters? God have mercy!" He utters a few obscenities that can only be heard by those standing close to him. One of them pinches him and whispers, "Behave!"

At this new outburst, Ataa Forkoyi bows his head, his bald pate reflecting the sun into the eyes of his listeners. As if joining Ataa Forkoyi's embarrassment in reaction to the question, they all close their eyes. When they open them, Ataa Forkoyi has tears in his. "Yes. Svane also got tangled in the evil network of buying and selling human beings at Danish-Osu. Christiansborg and the Danish-Osu community had been poisoned by the evil spirit of the transatlantic slave trade, and everybody was caught up in it. That was the tragedy of the culture at that time. But Svane needed to realize his dream by all means, and, Gospel or no Gospel, the means had to be found. So he traded in slaves to obtain resources for his project and, additionally, used slave labour extensively for the construction work. Being a well-organized fellow, he made elaborate preparations for the project.

"According to the Stones, he acquired a piece of land next to an old garden that belonged to former Governor Boris, situated in a valley below the north side of Christiansborg, beyond the Company's slave houses within the Osu-Alata community. Next to it was an old, disused stone shelter that belonged to Boris but had been bequeathed to Noye, an Osu Kinkawe member of Christiansborg local staff. Svane bought this shelter and razed it to re-use its special stones with Danish decorations, for construction. With the land then made available, he went on to obtain iron bars to be used as tools to break rocks and dig clay soils and earth. The rocks had to be of different sizes: large stones for the foundation, small ones for the walls, and much smaller ones to fill in the gaps. Most of the stones brought in came from a site north west of La, a place known as Teianshi.

"When the work began, besides the slaves used on site, a number of people from the community were hired to provide both skilled and unskilled labour in the construction, which proceeded under the supervision of a Danish builder called Christian Lochau, hired from Christiansborg by Svane. With admiration, he observed how the stone workers skillfully shaped the pieces of stones to fit into the foundation; with wonder he saw how the masons mixed the wet soil with rum to make the customary mortar to hold the stones together. As he saw his dream being realized with the daily progression of the work, he became so fascinated that he started keeping a journal of the process."

At this point, Ataa Forkoyi makes a dramatic pause and closes his eyes. When he begins to speak again it is as if he is reading:

"According to the Stones, although Svane was not a technical person, the entries in his journal showed how meticulously he followed what was going on; listen to this: 'The foundation of the house has already been laid; the walls almost a whole foot in height, built in a few days; a square plan arrangement with stone wall: 2-3 foot wide in the foundations and later narrower and narrower as the walls grew in height. The building was, according to my preconceived design, to be of three floors with a future garden around it for pleasure and amusement ...'"

The architecture student in the group who all this time has been paying close attention, breaks in to ask: "Would you be kind enough, Sir, to take us later to Svane's building?"

The old man smiles and shakes his head. "My son, what I am telling you now is only a memory lodged in the crevices of the Stones' mind. You know, Svane is the ancestor whose presence was obliterated at Danish-Osu. But wait to hear how that came about through the building of the very dream house I have been speaking about." Ataa Forkoyi then continues to talk about how Svane went about organizing his project.

"According to the Stones, Svane had an old, local hut opposite the building site repaired, where he took his meals, sheltered from the midday sun. He had a flagpole in front of his site, flying a white sheet with a small emblem of the Royal Danish Africa Company at its top right corner. Each day, as he trooped down from Christiansborg to the site and saw the waving flag, he felt exhilarated. Hoisting the flag might have been an expression of his independence in creating his own space outside Christiansborg. At the same time, the flag was also an expression of his need for protection from Christiansborg.

"As work progressed on Svane's building site and the flag fluttered his pride and achievement into the wind, the Danish Administration took notice. Knowing that the owner of this house was a son of the soil, a mulatto, a native with African blood flowing through his veins, the administration did not see an ordinary stone house but a mighty fortress in the making that could challenge the power of Christiansborg. Seeing Svane's building project in this light, the administration decided to stop him, quickly and brutally. He was arrested and confined to the terrible space inside Christiansborg castle known as the 'black hole.'

"Having been brought back to heel through this temporary confinement, he was cautioned and released. Svane took the cue and moved out of his lodgings in Christiansborg, returning to the community at Danish-Osu. He thought once he was out of sight of the administration, and in the secure circle of his kith and kin, he could press ahead with his building. But the eyes and ears of the administration were everywhere."

At this point, Ataa Forkoyi appears to be losing his voice and his listeners have difficulty hearing him. The architecture student raises his hand and asks politely, "Sir, where did you say Svane sought refuge when he vacated his quarters and vanished from Christiansborg?"

Ataa Forkoyi drinks a bottle of water in one gulp and answers the question, re-invigorated: "Svane went to town and hired a room in a local family house near his building site. From here, he would walk daily to the site to be with the workers, staying to observe the construction till nightfall, when he would return home for his evening meal, usually aboboi, a dish made from big, round beans. As he defiantly continued to build, the news came to the Danes in the fort that Svane was building a castle.

"One evening in November 1742, Svane returned from the site exhausted but joyful with the progress of his dream. While enjoying his *aboboi,* a party of about forty local men, headed by a man called Sodza, a local employee of Christiansborg and a resident of the Osu Anahor community, pounced on him and without any explanation, bound him hand and foot like a slave. Humiliated, he demanded an explanation and was told that he had been heard regularly firing gun salutes from his building site, indicating that he was in competition with Christiansborg. He was being taken there to face the Danish administration for his subversive actions. Despite the protests from his neighbours, who vehemently denied ever seeing or hearing Svane firing shots, he was taken to Christiansborg that night. When they arrived at the fort, Svane was handed over to the Danes who first tied him up with pieces of cloth, then clapped him in iron shackles and finally threw him into the Black Hole where he was kept day and night for some time."

Before Ataa Forkoyi can continue with the narration, to which his listeners have been listening with rapt attention, the history teacher interrupts excitedly and asks: "I once read that the Black Hole was a dark room in the basement of Christiansborg, used by the Danes to discipline recalcitrant slaves in transit for shipment. Was Svane going to be shipped out as a slave?"

Ataa Forkoyi shakes his head in frustration and scowls: "Why this interruption? Allow the story of this ancestor to follow the sequence as the Stones remember it. In any case, your question does not apply. The Danes had a policy that mulattoes, though regarded as Africans, should never be treated as slaves, since they had Danish blood in them. No! Svane was not put into the Black Hole as a slave. He was put there to break his spirit and the Danes were successful in doing just that. According to the Stones, as Svane sat in the dark room down there, under Christiansborg, he wondered how he, a free man, a former Parish Clerk in the service of the Danish administration, could find himself here on a Saturday evening, this 24th of November 1742, the day before Sunday when he should have been in spiritual reflection, waiting for God's enlightenment to preach His word to the church. The more he reflected on his plight, the more depressed he became.

"As if the Black Hole treatment was not enough, on Monday the 26th, the Administration arranged to ransack his residence in town and took all his belongings, including considerable amounts of hard cash, put them in a large trunk he had brought from Denmark and dumped them at the entrance of the Black Hole. Right before his eyes, all his belongings including the trunk were auctioned off and the proceeds used to pay off a debt he allegedly owed to the administration. What shocked Svane was the gross injustice of the administration for which he had devotedly worked as a Parish Clerk; for the estimated value of his auctioned personal property was five and half times more than what he was alleged to have owed, which was actually a personal debt to the governor."

Ataa Forkoyi now becomes pensive, and, as if talking to himself, poses a question: "As a theologian, what do you do when you lose all your material possessions?" He answers himself with: "You don't mind, do you? No, Svane did not mind. He merely observed his persecutors auction his goods with a holy scorn that infuriated the Danes. So, on the following day, Tuesday the 27th of November 1742, Governor Juergensen, the man who had promised to assist Svane with building materials when he first announced his intention at Fort Fredensborg in Ningo, sent an order to the Danish-Osu men and women to vandalize the foundation works of Svane's dream house and reduce the walls to rubble, which some of them did with glee. To make sure that Svane's audacious dream never came into being, the Company's slaves were sent to collect all the stones piled on the site for the construction work, to be sent to the out-works of Christiansborg to be kept for future repair work on the walls enclosing the out-works.

"While all this was going on without Svane's knowledge, a fellow mulatto woman by name Helena Kuehberg, an influential personality in the community who also had a recognizable presence in Christiansborg, planned to send word to him about what was happening to his dream house. Realising that Svane had been in the Black Hole without meals for over five days, she decided to send him some bread with pork filling. When the Danish soldiers discovered what she had brought, they seized the loaves and destroyed them. Svane was fed with half the rations normally given to slaves locked in the Black Hole."

At this point in the narration, a heavy sorrow engulfs the listeners and they all become still. In an attempt to liven the atmosphere, the Rastafarian makes the sign of peace and love and when he gets Ataa Forkoyi's attention, he solemnly asks: "Did Svane survive?"

"Yes, he survived but his spirit was broken and the desire to stay in the land of his birth died forever," Ataa Forkoyi responds with a lump in his throat. "After six months in the Black Hole, he was released due to a change in administration, which came about through the sudden death of Governor Juergensen, believed to have been poisoned by the daughter of Witt, Anna Sophia, whose Danish husband Sergeant Cornelius Pedersen had been jailed by Juergensen for a crime of attempted insurrection in Christiansborg. The new governor, Juergen Billsen, released Svane from the Black Hole in an attempt to reduce his various administrative burdens of tension and instability in general living circumstances at Christiansborg and the menace of wars then going on between the Asantes and the Akyems, which affected trading activities on the Coast.

"So Svane got his freedom and left Christiansborg but as a dispirited and despondent person, held together only by his deep faith in the Almighty God. With the hope that he could put his tattered life back in order, he went back to stay in his rented residence in the Danish-Osu community, living on the charity of his benefactor, Helena, and his neighbours. With his dream house gone together with the desire to live in the land of his birth, he hung around between Danish-Osu and Teshie where his maternal relatives lived, trying to find some meaning in his life. When the order came five years later from his Danish sponsors to repatriate him to Denmark, he did not resist, knowing that he was going to be re-united with his Danish wife and mulatto son.

"According to the Stones, Svane left the shores of the Guinea Coast on February 13, 1747, by a slave ship called 'Kronprinsens Oenske,' which took him back to Denmark, to a long and purposeful life working as a local parish priest in a rural community in northern Denmark."

Musing over Svane's life and experiences, the history teacher suddenly interrupts and asks Ataa Forkoyi to explain what he means by "long and purposeful life."

"You see," Ataa Forkoyi responds with sorrow on his wrinkled face, "all was not lost to Svane when he returned, a broken man, to his fatherland, after the raw deal he had received in his motherland. He first found an employment with the famous Danish professor, Ludvig Holberg, in Copenhagen. After the death of the charitable professor, he moved northwards and settled in a small rural community called Havrebjerg, where he worked as a parish priest until his retirement and subsequent death two years later in 1785." Ataa Forkoyi continues, "On February 13, 1747, Svane sailed away from the land of his mother, leaving no legacy behind to show that he ever belonged to Danish-Osu, thus becoming the ancestor whose presence was obliterated."

Upon ending his narration about Friederich Pedersen Svane, Ataa Forkoyi looks exhausted but tries to continue. The human rights activist in the group walks up to him, embraces him and assists him to sit down. She asks for some chilled mango juice to be brought for him. Still with her arm around him and looking into his face she says: "Ataa Forkoyi, you need this; take your time to drink it all." He graciously accepts the bottle, puts it to his mouth and drinks the juice with childlike relish. Refreshed, he gets up and begins to pace up and down, looking at his listeners contentedly.

Protten, an Elusive Danish-Osu Ancestor

"You remember, I was saying at the beginning," he begins to speak again in a cheerful mood, "that Svane, as a teenager, first left for Denmark in 1722 together with another Danish-Osu boy; this boy was the one who sprouted into that remarkable man who came to be known as Christian Jakobus Protten Africanus and gave himself the pen name, Teiko Sacki, Blofonyo Bi."

As soon as the Rastafarian hears the name Africanus, he gets very excited and breaks into a Reggae beat with the refrain, 'Barack, Barack, Barack Obama.' The rest of the listeners begin to sway their bodies from side to side, moved by the rhythm of the song. Meanwhile Ataa Forkoyi stands there patiently, waiting for this unexpected musical interlude to come to an end. The Rastafarian hums a few more lines of the song and everybody applauds enthusiastically. The history teacher turns to him and smilingly asks why he interrupted with his song.

"Mamaa, can't you see my Rasta Man Ancestor Man? He has been there all the time, Mamaa, and nobody has noticed his presence." He then turns towards Ataa Forkoyi and says loudly: "Ataa Forkoyi, give it all to them, please; we wanna know about the man!" Amused, Ataa Forkoyi gets up and without a word, begins to walk in the direction of the beach and as his listeners curiously get up to follow him, he says:

"You see, the sun is already gone down and it is past my meal time but the Stones insist that you must hear what they are saying about Christian Protten tonight. The moon is shining brightly above and the sea breeze is cool. So, if you wish, let us troop down to the beach and find a place there to hear what the Stones are saying."

Immediately the Rastafarian shouts at the top of his voice:

"To the beach, to the beach!"

They all agree to go and so Ataa Forkoyi leads them to a sandy location on the west of the Osu castle and when they arrive, they all sit in a horse-shoe formation, facing Ataa Forkoyi who has his back to the sea as he looks from person to person by the beautiful moonlight. Against the booms of the waves and the glittering of the waters, Ataa Forkoyi picks up his voice and begins:

"Christian Protten, who was originally named Uldrich, was born on September 1, 1715 at Danish-Osu to an Osu-Anahor mother, a royal called Awofio Dedei and a Danish father called Jakob Protten, who served as a soldier on the Guinea Coast from 1707 to 1714. It was said that a senior female relative of Protten's mother was married to the governor at that time and through this relative, Awofio had a good connection to Christiansborg. It was therefore no surprise that Jakob Protten had a long marital relationship with Awofio, with whom he had two other children besides Christian Protten. According to the Stones, although this Danish soldier was around for a long time, he departed Danish-Osu before Christian could have known him as his father.

"When Christian Protten was about seven years old, he was sent to Christiansborg together with his senior siblings to join other mulatto children to constitute the new fort school that had been established by Reverend Elias Svane, the Danish Chaplain. After the School had been running for a while, the then Governor Suhm received instruction from Denmark to select two boys from the school to be sent to Denmark for training as blacksmiths, who would be brought back to assist with the Royal Danish Africa Company's work on the Guinea Coast.

"The fifteen-year old Christian Friederich Pedersen, later Svane, and another boy of about the same age were selected to travel in 1726 in the company of their teacher Rev. Svane, to Denmark, to benefit from this initiative. But on the eve of their departure, this other boy fell ill and the governor, acting on the advice of his Danish-Osu wife, quickly had to arrange a substitute, Christian Protten, a nephew of Governor Suhm's wife, to replace the sick boy. So, although Awofio Dedei was against her twelve-year old son being taken away, Rev. Elias Svane left the shores of Danish-Osu with his two pupils and set forth to Denmark via the Caribbean, on a slave ship."

Before Ataa Forkoyi can continue with his narration to his rapt listeners, the human rights activist in the group comes up with a question: "Why was Awofio unwilling to let her son benefit from this generous offer from the Danish Administration? And what about the young Protten, was he willing or reluctant to go with his teacher?"

With a sparkle in his eyes and his bald head reflecting the beautiful moonlight from above, Ataa Forkoyi responds: "You know, according to the Stones, Awofio was right in showing disapproval of her son being taken away. The administration had earlier sent away her first son, Wilhelm Protten, to the Caribbean as a punishment for his untoward and recalcitrant behavior in the community, thus she was worried about her second son suffering the same fate.

"But with young Christian, the trip with his teacher was a great excitement and he was more than willing to leave his weeping mother behind on the beach as they sat in the boat, rowing towards the slave ship waiting to take them beyond the blue horizon to the land of the father whom he wished to meet one day. After a sea journey of about six weeks with an interim sojourn on the islands of St. Croix and St. Thomas, Rev. Elias Svane arrived in Denmark on the 14th of August 1727 with his Danish-Osu hopefuls, to begin a new chapter that changed the course of their lives forever.

"On arrival in Copenhagen, Christian and his senior compatriot, Pedersen, were soon brought under the patronage of the King. They were thereafter baptized on November 17, 1727, in the Garrison Church in Copenhagen. It was at his baptism that Protten was given the name Christian, which was added to his father's name Jacob Protten. Pedersen, for his part, adopted the name of their mentor, becoming Pedersen Svane."

"When was the name Africanus given to Protten, if that was not one of the names he received at baptism?" the history teacher quickly interjects.

"The name Africanus was added by Protten to his name much later when, with maturity, he became more conscious of his African identity. With time, as he stayed longer in Europe and experienced the negative attitudes of the Europeans he interacted with, he even decided to dramatize his identity by adopting the pen name, 'Teiko Saki, Blofonyo Bi.' He certainly adopted this Gã title in remembrance of a Gã-Mashie man who returned from Little Popo or Anecho to Kinka in Accra, to become a King, when Protten was growing up on the Guinea Coast.

"Together with Svane, Protten was sent to the private school at Sorterup to prepare for entry into the University of Copenhagen after the two had expressed the wish to study theology like their dear teacher, instead of training as blacksmiths. They eventually gained admission to the University and began their studies in 1732. Although Svane was serious with his studies, due to immaturity, Protten had other interests and could not graduate. Although he mastered the theological training he received and as well as the Danish language and some Latin and French, he was too restless to remain in the university and eventually dropped out. Nevertheless, he retained contact with some of his professors and fellow students and maintained the academic discipline of study and reflection as he wondered what to do with his life in Europe. He thought of leaving for Holland to seek employment, or travelling with friends to Sweden where he knew some of the people in the service of the Danish administration on the Guinea Coast had come from.

"Meanwhile, as he lived in Copenhagen, he took advantage of the royal patronage he received from the King on his baptism and hung around the royal court now and then. It was during a festive occasion at the King's court in 1735, a royal wedding that had brought visitors from Germany to Copenhagen, that Protten, then 20 years old, was introduced by one of his university mentors, Professor Reuss, to the German baron Count Ludwig Nicholas von Zinzendorf, the noble religious and intellectual founder of the Moravian Brethren."

Hearing the name Zinzendorf, the history teacher asks Ataa Forkoyi if he is the same one mentioned in an account of a group of Christians who reputedly challenged John Wesley to have faith in Jesus Christ, when they once happened to be traveling to America together and a storm broke out.

Ataa Forkoyi answers in the affirmative and goes on to add that, in fact, according to the Stones, Zinzendorf and Wesley met on a few occasions related to their common belief in the Lord Jesus Christ. "This man Zinzendorf, who had a great passion for world missions, immediately recognized in Protten a potential missionary to Africa. Having taken a strong liking to Protten, the Count invited him to come and visit the home of the Moravians in Herrnhut, located in Schlesien in the north-east of Germany.

"Copenhagen is certainly far away from Schlesien in Germany. Moreover, Protten had never met this German Count before and I am wondering in which language the two communicated. Was Protten ready to accept the invitation to travel that far with a stranger?" asks the listener with Danish ancestry.

"Oh yes, Protten accepted the invitation and was more than willing to travel with the Count," responds Ataa Forkoyi. He continues: "According to the Stones, Protten loved to travel and had a spirit of adventure. Remember, at the age of twelve he was not afraid to leave his mother and defied all the odds to travel by slave ship to Denmark via the Caribbean. But take note that although Protten was a restless fellow, he was also a deep thinker and a reflective person. Hence, he did not jump straight at the invitation to travel with the stranger to Herrnhut. He contemplated his future and sought counsel from his mentor on the matter. Regarding communication between him and the German, there was no problem whatsoever. The Count was a scholar who was competent in Danish and because Protten had studied at the University, he was literate in German to some extent.

"So, the elderly German Count and the young mulatto from Danish-Osu left Copenhagen together and three days later arrived in Herrnhut on July 21, 1735, setting Protten on a new path of life. Two months after arrival and after extensive reflection on his life up till then, he decided to cast in his lot with the community of the 'Unitas Fratrum,' the Moravian Brethren. He documented his reflections and decision to join the community in a formal application written by him in the German language and submitted to the leadership of the community on the 21st of September 1735. This document has been kept and is available in the Moravian Archives in Herrnhut together with 300 other manuscripts of Protten's. According to the Stones, Protten became well integrated into this unique, pietistic, collective Christian community that had been founded by Zinzendorf, whom he began to address as 'Papa.'

"His presence in the community was noticed and his charming features could not escape the attention of the famous Moravian portrait artist who captured his image in a painting in 1735, on his arrival in Herrnhut. By the kind courtesy of the Moravian Archives, I have obtained a copy of this painting and am delighted to show it to you now by this beautiful moonlight."

As Ataa Forkoyi carefully unrolls the painting and shows it to his listeners; a collective "Wow" ensues as they all strain their necks to see it. Then he goes on: "Having thus been integrated, Protten actively participated in the community's work and worship and quickly learnt and assimilated the Brethren's unique practice of faith and deep devotion to the Lord Jesus Christ as the Saviour and the risen Lord. In spite of his strong sense of independence, Protten showed his belonging by subjecting himself to the daily guidance the community members received from the Rhema as given by Zinzendorf from the Scriptures."

As the word "Rhema" is heard pronounced by Ataa Forkoyi, the architecture student frowns and violently shakes his head as if a piece of stone has hit him. Ataa Forkoyi pauses to ask him: "Young man, what is your problem?"

He replies tersely, "Rhema." Surprised, Ataa Forkoyi asks further: "What is the problem with Rhema?"

"Please, Ataa Forkoyi, what is 'Rhema?' Has it something to do with a referee for a football match?"

Smiling, Ataa Forkoyi explains to the young man what the word 'rhema' means to a believer who trusts that he or she can receive the word of God as applying specifically to the situation in which he or she finds him or herself on a given day.

Ataa Forkoyi goes on: "The rhema in the Herrnhut culture consisted of drawing lots in the form of pieces of paper on which scriptural passages had been written down by guidance of the Holy Spirit. This was one of the regular assignments of the Count, begun in May 1728. The drawn lots, known as 'Daily Watchwords' *('Loesungen'* in German), were handed to all and sundry among the community members, who received them for daily direction and guidance.

"The community at Herrnhut consisted of people from various classes of German society as well as many people of divergent races and cultures, due to the world mission orientation of the Moravian Brethren. Consequently, Protten was totally accepted by the brethren, notwithstanding the colour of his skin. However, he had difficulties with the leadership due to his strong sense of independence and self-assertiveness. This made it difficult for him to conform and he found himself sometimes breaking the rules of the community.

"As a result, just a year after his arrival, in 1736, he had the conviction that he should return to the Guinea Coast to bring the message of his Saviour and Lord Jesus Christ to his people. He shared this conviction with some of his fellow community members and eventually managed to persuade one of his prayer partners by the name of Heinrich Huckoff, with whom he lived in the residential quarters of the Count, to come along with him to Holland to look for a ship to take them to the Guinea Coast as pioneer missionaries of the Moravian Brethren. So, without official approval and backing of the leadership as the Count, his 'Papa' was away from Herrnhut at the time the two departed from Schlesien westwards, to Holland."

At this point in the narration, the history teacher, who has been listening carefully, politely interrupts Ataa Forkoyi and asks: "Presumably there would always be ships sailing from Copenhagen to the Guinea Coast at that time because of the thriving transatlantic slave trade. Why did Protten and his friend not travel northwards to Denmark but rather westward in the direction of Holland to get on to a ship from there? I find this rather strange."

"Your curiosity is justified. Since Protten was familiar with life in Copenhagen, it would have been better to have headed there but he did not." Ataa Forkoyi now clears his throat, indicating that he is getting tired with a long yawn. Somebody then asks from the back if Ataa Forkoyi wants a cup of warm Milo drink. He nods and is immediately supplied with a large mug of warm Milo poured out from a flask. After taking a number of mouthfuls, he begins to speak again to complete the answer to the history teacher's question.

"Protten decided against going to Copenhagen with his friend to take a ship from there because, according to the Stones, he was aware that his benefactor, Count Zinzendorf did not have a good relationship with the King of Denmark at that time and he knew there would be difficulties arranging for a ship bound for the Guinea Coast from Denmark. So, to Holland they went and there, at Amsterdam, they entered a Dutch ship sailing to Elmina. While they were waiting to set sail, Protten received a letter from his mentor, the Count, who had heard that Protten had unilaterally decided to go on his first missionary journey to the Guinea Coast with Huckoff as his co-missionary. Count Zinzendorf did not dissuade him from going, knowing that that was the very purpose for which he had invited Protten to Herrnhut; however, being aware of his 'son's' intransigence, he strongly advised him to be focused and remain committed to his faith as a true Christian.

"The two unofficial pioneer Moravian missionaries arrived safely at Elmina on the 11th of May 1737, with a clear vision to bring the Gospel of Jesus Christ to the people of Elmina who were then under the administration of the Dutch, who occupied the Elmina Castle. Protten believed his vision could be fulfilled first and foremost by establishing a school for the mulatto children in the town. He therefore encouraged his colleague Huckoff to join him in learning the local Fante language and within a short period of time he had developed a glossary of Fante words with their German translations, to use in teaching some basic truths of the Bible. His presence in the Elmina community was prominent and the impact he and his fellow Moravian were making on the mulatto children could not escape the notice of the Dutch administration. They could foresee the future consequence of this impact and they grew wary of it. Their decision was to nip the whole thing in the bud. Protten was therefore arrested and deported to an island not far from the Coast of Elmina. He was kept in this prison island for a while and when he fell ill, the Dutch administration had mercy on him and brought him back to the mainland at Elmina.

"He rejoined Huckoff and the two found their way to Danish-Osu. While they were waiting for a ship to sail back to Europe, Huckoff fell ill. Unlike Protten who recovered from his illness during his confinement, Huckoff did not survive. He passed away on June 15, 1740, after a traditional healer known to Protten had done all he could to save his life. With a heavy heart, Protten eventually managed to obtain assistance from the Danish administration at Christiansborg to sail away in 1742, on a slave ship bound for the Danish islands of St. Croix and St. Thomas in the Caribbean. He sojourned on the island of St Thomas for three years by his own volition and from there got a ship in 1745 to sail back to Denmark from where he travelled to Marienborn, the other Moravian community in Germany. While in St. Thomas, although he appeared aloof and as usual non-conforming, he had been carefully studying the Moravian style of mission work and getting to know the Caribbean culture which appeared to Protten to have badly affected many of the Africans he encountered."

Ataa Forkoyi, trying to emphasise how objectionable Protten found the Caribbean culture, continues: "As seen by Protten, the Caribbean culture was dominated by European slave owners and slave traders who ignominiously lorded it over the local Africans they viewed as inferior. With time the Africans high view of themselves diminished, saddled with a slave mentality and an inferiority complex, observed even among church members who professed liberty in Christ.

"By 1745, he was back in Marienborn, now much more mature and better committed to the teachings of the Moravian Brethren. It was in this community that he made one of his profound addresses at a gathering of the brethren to send off the first Moravian missionary to the Inuits in Greenland. His address was written in both the Gã language and in High German. Interestingly enough, while he signed the German version with his name Christian Jakobus Africanus Protten, he signed the Gã version with his pen name, Teiko Sacki, Blofonyo Bi. My friends, the manuscript of this address has been kept in the Moravian Archives in Herrnhut until today It is my delight to let you know that I have a copy of this here with me right now."

Immediately as he says this, the Rastafarian breaks the silence by shouting at the top of his voice, "Ataa Forkoyi, we want to see this precious heritage, now, now, now!"

He opens his worn-out bag and carefully extracts the rolled parchment. He cautiously unfolds it, spreads it out and passes it around for his listeners to see and touch the words of Protten, the elusive ancestor. Ataa Forkoyi now continues with the narration, smiling mischievously:

"When the leadership at Marienborn observed the remarkable change in Protten, he was rewarded with a wife Rebecca Freundlich, the mulatto widow of a former German missionary to the Caribbean. This deeply spiritual woman had lost her missionary husband when they had returned to Marienborn from the mission field in St Thomas. The leadership thought Rebecca's profound spirituality would help stabilize Protten and make him more amenable to the established lifestyle of the Moravians. So, in a group wedding ceremony that included eleven other couples, Protten and

Rebecca got married on January 12, 1746, in the worship hall of the community. A few days after the wedding, Rebecca was given the status of a female spiritual leader in the Moravian community. The couple had a daughter in 1750 but she passed away when she was about three years old, by which time they had moved to Herrnhut. She was privileged to be buried in the world-famous Moravian cemetery known as Gottesacker. Before this child died, a painting was made of her in the company of her parents and because her skin was so much lighter than theirs, the painting, of which I have a copy in my possession, became a great curiosity."

Ataa Forkoyi now pauses; he opens his weathered leather bag and pulls out a rolled parchment. He unfolds it and then raises it up to show it to his listeners by the bright moonlight. As the listeners take in the details, they all spontaneously shout in surprise: "Ah, that is the painting!" and he responds: "Yes. This is the painting of Protten, Rebecca and baby Anna in the middle.

Figure 12: A family portrait of the unknown ancestor with his wife, Rebecca, and their three-year-old daughter Anna, who died in 1754 and was buried in the world-famous Moravian cemetery known as "Gottesacker" in Herrnhut, Germany (Artist: A. L. Brandt) *Illustration courtesy of Moravian Archives, Herrnhut*

Figure 13: Manuscript of a formal speech written by Protten in both the Gã language ('Acraisch') and in German (Tauscht as an old version of the word "Deustch") on the occasion of bidding farewell to the Moravian Missionary Johann Bech going to the Inuits (Eskimos) in Greenland (C. 1746)

Courtesy of Moravian Archives, Herrnhut

"According to the Stones, this painting became popular and even began to be used by the Moravian missionaries as a tool for evangelism. But it was also a time of instability and great tension in the Moravian community. Due to political persecution, the spiritual leader Count Ludwig Nicholas Zinzendorf was living outside Herrnhut because he had been declared persona non grata in Schlesien. The situation was creating distress for Protten as he now and then came back into conflict with the leadership because of his non-conformism.

"Notwithstanding the fact that Protten was married to Rebecca who occupied a high office as a female spiritual leader in the community, the open confrontation between him and the leadership eventually led to an explosion that caused the couple to be ostracized and banished to a small palatial residence belonging to the grandmother of the Count in a village called Gross Hennersdorf, about six kilometers away from Herrnhut. This happened in March 1756 with the approval of the Count."

At this point in the narration the human rights activist, shaking with anger, interrupts Ataa Forkoyi and asks him: "Do you mean they sent their spiritual leader and her husband to Coventry?"

Ataa Forkoyi sympathetically responds: "Protten was a man with a strong mind and without the Count to help them sort out his 'son,' their backs were against the wall and they did not know what to do; Protten had to go. But they were fully aware of the injunction of their Lord that, 'What God has joined together, let no man put asunder.' Protten could not be sent away without his wife. So, due to the great respect they had for Rebecca and her status as a spiritual leader, they sent them to the Count's own grandmother's palatial residence."

Ataa Forkoyi, trying to satisfy the human rights activist, goes on to say appeasingly, "A picture brought to me from Germany of a section of the ruins of this palatial residence in Gross Hennersdorf, shows that Protten and Rebecca were not banished to a hole of misery but to a house of luxury. But you see, the restless soul of Protten could not remain at ease in this place of luxury. He tried to occupy himself with some useful intellectual and spiritual activities by writing. It was during this tense period that he tried to write the Lord's Prayer in the Gã language. The manuscript of this attempted Gã version is still to be seen in the Moravian Archives in Herrnhut. I also have a copy with me.

"Meanwhile, by August of that year, he had decided to return home for another attempt at a missionary voyage to his people on

Figure 14: A portrait of the unknown ancestor, Jacobus Christian "Africanus" Protten, AKA Teiko Sacki, Blofonyo Bi drawn by the famous portrait Artist, J. V. Haidt of the Moravian Brethren ca. 1735.
Courtesy of Moravian Archives, Herrnhut, GS 448

the Guinea coast. As he contemplated returning home, the urge to start a school for mulatto children, this time at Danish-Osu, became more pronounced. He wanted to try something similar to his experiment at Elmina in 1735. He shared his thoughts with his wife and the two prayerfully considered the matter. They both decided that it was not yet time for them to move to the Guinea Coast as a family, but that Protten could go on an exploratory visit and see how he could apply his own approach to evangelize his people independently of the support of the Herrnhut community.

"However, because Rebecca would stay behind, they agreed that the leadership in Herrnhut should be informed of his intention. When the leadership got to know about it, they agreed, and assured Protten of their readiness to take Rebecca back into the community while Protten was gone. To show their goodwill towards Protten's missionary trip, they even provided him with some guidelines for his exploratory mission work. Among these was the strong advice not to live in Christiansborg with the Danes, but to start a new community similar to that of the Moravian communities among his people.

"So on Sunday the 22nd of August 1756, Protten left Gross Hennersdorf, after bringing his wife safely back to the community at Herrnhut. With a few belongings in the knapsack on his back, (according to the journal he kept during the period), he began to hitch-hike through northern Germany to Copenhagen from where he boarded a slave ship that brought him to the Guinea Coast arriving at Danish-Osu on June 27, 1757. I have a map here with me which traces the route of Protten's hitch-hiking from Gross Hennersdorf to Copenhagen."

Eventful Sojourn on the Guinea Coast

Ataa Forkoyi now stops talking and once again pulls up an old map from his bag to show his audience; he gives it to the first person standing in front of him and after the person has finished studying the map, he asks him to pass it around. As it is being passed around, Ataa Forkoyi explains the markings that indicate the route by which Protten managed to move through the various towns of northern Germany, partly on foot and partly by stagecoach, until he entered a ferry that brought him across to Copenhagen.

After he has satisfied himself that everybody has seen the old map, he continues: "Protten's five-year stay at Danish-Osu from

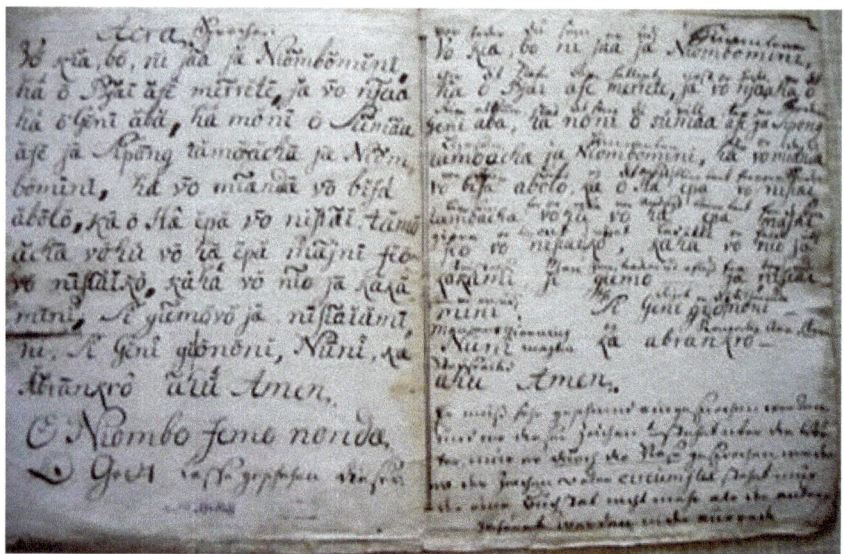

Figure 15: Manuscript of an attempted translation of the Lord's Prayer from German into the Gã language ('Acraisch' as written by Protten) by Protten c. 1754. *Courtesy of Moravian Archives, Herrnhut*

Figure 16: A section of Gottesacker, the world famous cemetery of the Moravian Brethren in which Anna, the infant daughter of the Prottens and historic persons such as the Baron Nicholas Von Zinzendorf, the originator of the Moravian Brethren, were buried. *Courtesy of author*

Figure 17: Part of the ruins of the castle belonging to the grandmother of the baron, Nicholas Von Zinzendorf, located at Grosshennendorf, Germany. Protten and his wife were banished here from Herrnhut, 15 kilometers away, due to a bitter misunderstanding between Protten and his fellow brethren in c.1756.
Courtesy of author

1757 to 1761 has been vividly described in his journal entries which are found today in the Moravian Archives in Herrnhut. He began these entries the day he left Gross Hennersdorf and continued making them till his return to Herrnhut after the five-year sojourn at Danish-Osu. His journal, now known in academic circles, as *'Protten's Diarium,'* throws open a window into the mind and soul of Protten for all who read it. Now my friends, if I were to tell you what are to be found in the spirit and letter of this diary, we would be here till tomorrow morning."

As soon as he says this, the voices of the listeners rise in unison:

"We are ready for a TDB session, go on!"

Ataa Forkoyi, tired and sleepy, asks with a yawn: "What is TDB?"

The architecture student, wide awake and alert, shouts:

"TDB is 'Till day break.'" This is what we do when we are having fun working on engaging design programmes in our studio at the University in Kumasi."

Then somebody shouts: "Do you do it wet or dry?"

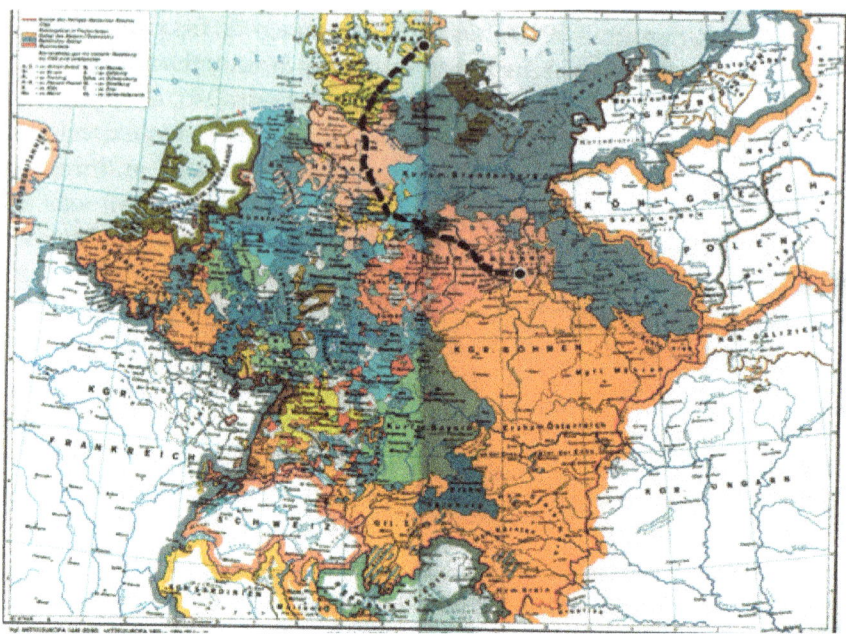

Figure 18: An eighteenth century map of Central Europe with an indication of the route which Protten traversed by hitch-hiking from Gross Hennersdorf, Germany, to Copenhagen, Denmark (C.1756). *Illustration courtesy of author*

Figure 19: The world famous Moravian Archives-Archivum Unitatis Fratrum, Herrnhut, Germany, where Christian Jakobus Protten's portraits, his diary and some of his over three hundred manuscripts written between 1746 and 1761, are kept. *Courtesy of author*

"Wet, of course, with tea, coffee and cocoa flowing like Accra floods in July," shouts back the architecture student.

Sensing the young people's enthusiasm to hear more about Protten, Ataa Forkoyi jokingly asks: "Where are the floods?"

Immediately the lady with the large flask of warm chocolate drink walks up to him and hands him a mug with a steaming and aromatic cocoa drink. He graciously takes it and begins to drink, enjoying every drop. His audience waits patiently, some stretching out their tired limbs and chatting among themselves. After two mugs of the beverage, Ataa Forkoyi gets up in his typical way and begins to pace up and down. Then he sits down contently and begins to fan himself with his hand. After a while, looking tired but alert, he announces:

"We are now going to peep through the window into Protten's time at Danish-Osu between 1756 and 1761, when he finally went back to Herrnhut."

Troubled, Tempting and Trying Times

"Because Protten had been given employment by the Danish Royal Government to work in Christiansborg as a teacher, he did not make his abode in the community at Danish-Osu on his arrival. This was in obvious contradiction to the guidelines he had received from the Moravian Brethren. Instead, he pitched his tent right inside Christiansborg where Governor Christian Jenssen and his fellow Danish officers and soldiers were doing their own thing.

"Life here was shaped not by the ideals of the Moravian beliefs in godly piety and Christian passion for the Lord Jesus. When Protten arrived, what he saw was business as usual at Christiansborg: residents pressuring one another into drinking, for it was prestigious to get as drunk as one could. Anyone who decided not to drink was considered obstinate and evil. It was as if, besides the business of slave trading there was nothing to do but pursue a life of carousing and debauchery. Protten was therefore faced with the challenge to conform to or counteract this situation as he began to work in Christiansborg castle as a teacher for the mulatto school children.

"His passion for teaching the children kept him attached to Christiansborg. However, because his mother and other relatives were living in the Danish-Osu community, his heart was there and he kept up regular visits to express his solidarity and share his Christian faith with his kith and kin. All the same, because of his commitment to the Danish administration, he had to spend a lot of his time inside Christiansborg and found himself in the company of the Danish garrison dwellers most of the time. It was not a milieu conducive to Protten's happiness. Many of these hardened slave traders resented a man of God such as himself and hated his Moravian attitudes. Moreover, as a mulatto occupying space in a Danish community, he was derided for claiming to be a Christian and at the same time manifesting pride in his Gã heritage. The administration kept criticizing him for using the Gã language to teach the children."

"What was Protten teaching the children in his school?" asks the history teacher on hearing this.

Seizing the opportunity of this interjection, Ataa Forkoyi pauses and requests another mug of warm cocoa. He drinks it all, licks his lips and responds to the question: "Protten was teaching some basics from the Christian Book of Faith and the Danish ABCs. Because the Danish words sounded strange to the children, he had to compose a glossary of Gã and other local words from which he explained the words to the children.

"Of course, this attempt by Protten to contextualize his teaching and make his pupils literate Gã mulattoes, and not Danish mulattoes, did not go down well with the administration and the people of the garrison community. They did everything to make him become like them, while he tried to persuade them to submit to the authority of his master, the Lord Jesus Christ. No doubt the pressure they mounted on him proved to be greater than the Christian influence he attempted to wield. Hence, he eventually succumbed to the common practice of heavy drinking, although he maintained his integrity as a Moravian Christian."

"Ataa Forkoyi, from what you are saying, it appears Protten succumbed to pressure because he was confined to Christiansborg," interjects the Rastafarian who seems rather uncomfortable hearing about Protten's plight inside Christiansborg.

"Not at all; Protten was not confined to Christiansborg," Ataa Forkoyi vehemently responds. "According to the Stones, besides his teaching duties and some pastoral responsibilities which included preaching, assisting the chaplain to administer the sacraments and conducting the baptism of infants in the Christiansborg castle, Protten spent time travelling between Danish-Osu and the neighbouring Danish and other European settlements. He undertook trips up-country and to places as far as the banks of the Densu River and forests such as Mblakoo, where he used to go on hunting expeditions.

"He shared his life also with his relatives by visiting the various Danish-Osu communities to observe their way of life and to participate in some of the family activities. According to the Stones, when his relative and friend, Adja Torgbor's funeral took place on December 28, 1757, he was present in the community at Osu-Anahor to give the customary donation of drinks to the family. Through these regular visits, he was able to observe a number of cultural practices such as the celebration of the Homowo festival, observance of widowhood rites and of Tuesday, as the day dedicated to the sea on which no fishing or going to sea took place, etc. He carefully documented all these in his journal and diligently discussed them with the Danes in Christiansborg whenever the Danes, due to lack of understanding, tried to ridicule these practices.

"His deep love of his African-ness made him take great delight in some of the community festivals and activities. With a sense of pride he carefully observed how the newly installed king of La, Nii Maale, was brought in a colourful procession to the Castle, to be introduced to the Danish administration. With joy, he recollected how this new La Mantse, installed after the death of the long-reigning King Okpoti, was accorded recognition by the firing of seven cannon shots as he entered Christiansborg, to be welcomed by the governor. But you must note that in as much as Protten was an African at heart, his spirit was very much Moravian and he had a strong Christian outlook on life. This made him question at times some of the traditional practices he saw in the community. He was often displeased to see the mulatto women who had been baptized and schooled at Christiansborg dressed just as their Danish-Osu local relatives.

"In his day-to-day activities in Christiansborg, he had dealings with individual Danish officials such as Ferdinand Roemer, Augustt Hackenberg, Carl Engmann, Joergen Sonne, and Esau Christensen Quist. He travelled on a number of occasions with these Danish gentlemen to Ningo and Keta to the Danish forts on expeditions to carry out slave business. It is interesting to note that all these gentlemen left their offspring behind at Danish-Osu from which sprang various family trees that are well known in Osu today.

"Besides these officials, Protten also had a close relationship with the then Governor Jessen who was married to his former school mate, Anna Sophia. One day, Jessen had the opportunity to observe Protten as he conducted a baptismal service in the Christiansborg chapel. He was greatly pleased by the excellent manner in which

Protten performed the service, which was for a mulatto baby girl born to a Danish-Osu woman by the name of Korkoi and a Danish man called Schmidt. Jessen saw much spirituality in Protten, in contrast to the Danish chaplain."

When the history teacher hears about the contrast between Protten and the Danish chaplain, he quickly asks Ataa Forkoyi if Protten was a priest. He takes his time to explain that Protten was never ordained but his theological training at the University in Copenhagen, his exposure to the pietistic Moravians, along with the saintly influence of his wife, Rebecca, virtually made him a priest. He further explained that Protten knew how to preach and pray with power and meaning and could administer the sacraments.

Having convinced the teacher that Protten possessed the spiritual credentials to justify the contrast drawn between him and the chaplain, he goes on with the narration, saying, "Because of the positive impression Protten made on him, Jessen, the Danish Governor, took Protten the mulatto of Danish-Osu into his confidence and once asked for his advice. This was when he was contemplating giving his wife's dead child an expensive funeral. Protten advised him to use the intended money instead to purchase clothing for the children in his school, numbering about twenty, most of them haggard-looking orphans. Through this advice, Protten set in motion a significant social institution that persisted for a while in Danish-Osu.

"His keen interest in the welfare of his pupils stemmed from his strong desire to see them educated at all costs. He was therefore much committed to his teaching post, which he fulfilled with zeal and assiduity. When he realised he lacked teaching materials that could help him teach better, he began to develop some in the Gã language which in later years were refined, and published as a teaching manual. As a good teacher, he stimulated his pupils' interest not only in reading and reciting the scriptures as he taught them, but also in learning to sing and express themselves. The Stones recall how he used to organize the children to sing Christian songs from house to house in the community to raise funds when Christmas was approaching. His commitment to his pupils made them very fond of him. They were always in his company and hung around his abode even when classes were over. As a result, one day in 1760, when he was at home relaxing and servicing his hunting flintlock, a terrible accident occurred that led to the death of one of the pupils by the name of Friedrich Magnusen."

As Ataa Forkoyi reaches this sad point in his narration, one can hear a spontaneous moan of "Aooo" from his audience, against the background of the chirping night insects. As if woken from a nightmare, the Rastafarian shouts: "Hei! Wait a minute, Old Maaan; what happened?"

Ataa Forkoyi gets up and stretches his body far backwards as if his old limbs have turned into a piece of Indian rubber. After he has done a few more bodily exercises to chase away the drowsiness he was feeling, he turns towards the Rastafarian crouching on the sandy beach, and with a sad voice begins to speak in a monotone:

"As I have mentioned earlier, Protten loved to hunt in the forest called Mblakoo, located on the north of Danish-Osu. With his flintlock he could bring home antelopes without much difficulty because he was a sharp-shooter. He always had his guns loaded. So that fateful day as he serviced his guns, his finger touched the trigger and 'Pow!' went the gun and because Magnusen was standing very close to Protten, the fiery gunpowder went straight into his chest and Protten suddenly found his dear pupil sprawled before him with blood oozing from his small body. Immediately, Protten became dazed and as if in a trance, he began to see the dead boy's late father lying in his arms as he breathed his last just a year before this terrible accident. Protten asked himself how he could gun the orphan of his departed mulatto friend, to whom he gave the last rites as he lay dying in his arms.

"When the Danish soldiers standing around saw what had happened, they immediately pounced on Protten and arrested him and brought him before the governor. The governor could not believe what he was told so he assembled the Secret Council to interrogate him. With the prevailing prejudice against Protten, he was tried and found guilty of manslaughter. For this offence, he had to be put in the black hole just as they had done to Svane a couple of years earlier. You could imagine his misery. Governor Jessen also felt bad about Protten's plight, especially as he daily came under pressure from his wife, Anna-Sophia, who was Protten's school mate. Anna-Sophia had a lot of sympathy for her former school mate and believed in his innocence so she tried hard to influence her husband to free Protten. He was kept in the black hole for over five weeks but was eventually released to await his banishment from Christiansborg after paying a heavy fine.

"The misery of Protten was deepened when he found out from some of the European traders that his benefactor, Baron Nicholas Ludwig von Zinzendorf had passed away that year in Herrnhut. Protten was almost at the end of his rope; his deep faith in God and intimate fellowship with the Lord Jesus Christ, however, kept him in one piece until he was sent out on a slave ship that took him back to Europe through the Caribbean. According to the Stones, Protten arrived back in Herrnhut on August 15, 1762, penniless and a broken man, having tramped back 300 miles from Denmark by the same route he took when he left Gross Hennersdorf on August 22, 1756."

Ataa Forkoyi's eyes are virtually closing now and his voice is hushed. The architecture student walks up and gives him a slight jerk. "Ataa Forkoyi, you promised to let us have a look into the mind and soul of Protten. You have not yet finished but you are dozing. Do you need more cocoa?" he asks.

Ataa Forkoyi responds, exhausted and yawning: "No, I don't need any more to drink. Sufficient unto the day is the evil thereof. We bring the curtain down tonight. I shall see all of you tomorrow afternoon at this very beach and I promise to tell you then about the mind and soul of Protten. Good night and have a sound sleep." With this parting, Ataa Forkoyi collects his bag and walks away, eastwards towards his house at Osu-Anahor.

Another Sojourn in Europe

It is midday and there is a cool sea breeze wafting around the lush grove of coconut trees on the sandy beach where Ataa Forkoyi and his listeners are taking it easy. A coconut seller is making good business; with his sharp cutlass in his left hand, a coconut in his right, with great dexterity, he cuts the top off so the sweet milk can be drunk by his thirsty customers. He then cuts the empty coconut shell in two halves so the juicy flesh can be scooped out.

While the coconut eating and drinking are going on, Ataa Forkoyi gets up and begins as usual to walk up and down. "My friends," he begins with a broad smile, "as I was saying in the early hours of this morning, after that devastating experience at Christiansborg, Protten retraced his steps back to Herrnhut. There he reunited with his dear wife, Rebecca, as well as with the community that he always believed was part of his life.

"While he had been away in Africa, Rebecca had been active in the Herrnhut community, having rejoined her former sisters, an ordained team of six deaconesses. They were leading the women in the community with their scriptural teachings and diaconal prayers. The spirituality of Rebecca had been noticed by all through her words and deeds, and her presence in the community had made a tremendous impact. Together with her spiritual sisters, she had helped the male spiritual leaders in all matters, including the administration of communion and the schooling of the women in the principles of Christianity.

"So, Protten walked back into a community which to some extent, had been influenced by his own wife. This brought a lot of healing to his broken spirit. But the intellectual atmosphere had not changed much and with the passing away of his benefactor, Count Zinzendorf, who had always been Protten's lighthouse in his turbulent intellectual life, the old tensions between him and the leadership in Herrnhut, began to surface again. After his experience with the Danes in Christiansborg, he was not prepared to submit himself to any European who might think of himself more capable than he."

The architecture student impudently interrupts Ataa Forkoyi, reminding him of his promise to tell his audience about his insights into the "mind and spirit" of Protten. With a scowl he says, "I know, I know. Now, young man, allow me to finish what the Stones have to say before I come to what I have to say.

"Protten began to keep himself busy by actively participating in all the religious gatherings of the community. Inspired by his wife's exemplary life of faith, he took seriously to the worship and prayer sessions held in the Great Assembly Hall located in the centre of Herrnhut. The customary religious procession at the Moravian cemetery, Gottesacker, during Easter, took on a new meaning for him; for in the Gottesacker, he was confronted by the inexorability of death and the hope of the glorious resurrection in Jesus Christ, as he saw the tombstones of his infant child Anna Maria and of his benefactor, Count von Zinzendorf.

"Protten made sure to attend all the meetings of the Brethren, but you can be certain that at each meeting, when a theological issue came up to which he had contrary opinion, he never hesitated to speak his mind. This situation aggravated the tension between Protten and the Moravian leadership and caused a lot of agitation in his spirit. Being a reflective person, he was driven to use the moments of agitation to employ his mind positively by doing a lot of writing. In addition to spending his time translating Luther's Catechism into Gã and Fante, by 1764, he had undertaken a seminal attempt to develop grammatical principles of the Gã Language. He sent the manuscript to Denmark and it was printed and distributed in Copenhagen under the title *A Useful Grammatical Introduction to Two Completely Unknown Languages, Fante and Gã.*

"As he worked on these translations, the urge to go back home to the Guinea Coast came back to him. He therefore began to correspond with Frederick V, the Danish King, to petition him for a pardon and request a re-appointment at Christiansborg. He wished to pursue his programme of teaching and evangelizing the mulattoes, to serve his God and his countrymen. He wanted, more especially, to bring the Gospel message to the poor and forsaken mulatto children at Danish-Osu.

"Eventually, Protten's petition was granted and he received pardon from the King after it had been established that the shooting incident was merely an unfortunate accident. The King then issued the directive to the Danish Trade Board to re-instate Protten and also appoint his wife to Christiansborg on the Guinea Coast. Protten was to teach the boys in the Castle School reading and writing, while Rebecca was to teach the girls housecraft. His annual salary was set at 250 gold Rixdaler, plus an additional allowance of 150 gold Rixdaler to meet the needs of identifiable needy pupils.

"When he received the formal appointment from the King, he and his wife brought the matter before the leadership of the community. Lengthy discussions of their intentions were undertaken, and because of the great work Rebecca had been carrying on in the community, there was reluctance to release them. However, with the hope that her presence with Protten in the Guinea Coast would lead to the fulfillment of the Moravian's hope of planting a church in Danish-Osu, the decision was taken to grant them the mandate to go in the name of the Herrnhut community.

"According to the Stones, after the leadership had thus given its approval for the Prottens to go out as missionaries of the Moravians, they began to take Protten through a series of counseling sessions to help him deal with the drinking habit he had picked up during his earlier sojourn at Christiansborg. But because of the intellectual difficulties Protten had with the leadership, these counseling sessions did not go well. That notwithstanding, Protten and Rebecca were taken extensively through the Moravians' guidelines for missionary work, including how they should develop a community with social and physical environments similar to Herrnhut. They were advised to try and build a house for themselves as soon as they arrived at Danish-Osu. The house, the hub of an 'African village for the Lord,' should be close enough to Christiansborg to offer refuge in times of unrest in the community, but far enough away from the evil influence of the Christiansborg community.

"In March 1763, the great day came to bid farewell to the Prottens, as the first Moravian missionaries to Africa. There was an emotional gathering of the community in the assembly hall in the centre of the community. The atmosphere that day, was very similar to the gathering in Marienborn on February 28, 1746, when Protten, aged 31 years, had made a speech in Gã to encourage the Moravian missionary Johann Bech, who was being sent to the Inuits in Greenland. After a moving service and powerful presentation of the Word of God, the Prottens were prayed for, and having been given enough provisions to make the journey back to Danish-Osu, they were sent off with the blessings of the community. Besides their luggage they had the tombstone for the departed brother Heinrich Huckoff who had died at Danish-Osu while accompanying Protten on his unofficial missionary expedition to the Guinea Coast in 1737."

When the history teacher heard that the tombstone of Huckoff was part of the Prottens' baggage, she stopped Ataa Forkoyi and asked him how they had managed to carry such a heavy piece of stone along. He solemnly explained to the lady that the Moravians had a standard tombstone that was flat and customarily placed in the earth, parallel to the surface of the ground; it did not measure more than fifteen by twenty centimetres. So the Prottens could, with ease, take Huckoff's one along to mark his burial place at Danish-Osu.

"According to the Stones," Ataa Forkoyi continues with the narration, "the Prottens were advised to travel to Zeist, near Amsterdam in Holland, to arrange to board a ship travelling to the Guinea Coast. In Zeist was a Moravian community that had been instructed to assist the Prottens as they looked for a Dutch slave ship bound for the Guinea Coast. The wait was not easy and frustration set in for Protten who had prepared his mind to go back home to settle with his wife Rebecca. Days turned into weeks and soon it was a whole year. Protten's restless soul could not stand the tension and he succumbed to the old temptation of Bacchus, which had haunted him all along; he began to drink again, and this time heavily."

The Rastafarian is agitated and shouts: "But what is wrong with drinking, Maan?"

With head bowed and voice trembling, Ataa Forkoyi responds:
"My friend, anybody at all can drink but not a pietistic Moravian. The strict self-discipline and spirituality of the Moravians forbade insobriety. In this regard, the Stones found it

out of character for Protten to be found drinking and getting drunk. Rebecca, who found the situation rather embarrassing, was all the same very sympathetic because she knew that the litany of deep-rooted psychological problems confronting Protten were the cause of his alcoholism."

Ataa Forkoyi adds pensively, as if speaking to himself, "Through the various letters Protten had written to her in the past, and through their quiet hours of family devotion, Rebecca had discovered the extent to which Protten carried the burden of events and issues that had plagued him since childhood."

Ataa Forkoyi pauses, takes a deep breath and utters a long "Hmmm," after which he continues: "She knew that her husband kept hanging on to the illusion that he would one day meet his Danish father; that he kept on wondering if he led his fellow Moravian, Huckoff, to his early death in Africa; that he kept on questioning the accidental death of his pupil; that he always wished he had been able to fulfill the expectations of his benefactor, Count Zinzendorf, who saw great potential in him when he first encountered him in Copenhagen; she knew that he kept on wondering who he was, an African or an European? Rebecca knew that her husband was caught up in the confusing nexus between his Danish theological mind, his compelling Moravian spirituality and his deep-seated African emotions; she knew …" Ataa Forkoyi's voice trails out and he cannot be heard any longer.

Still pensive, he turns to the Rastafarian and says:

"You see, Protten was a very intelligent man but when he lost control with alcohol, he virtually lost control of his senses. In his state of insobriety, nothing Rebecca said to him made sense and eventually the Zeist community had to report the matter to the leadership in Herrnhut. In response, Jonas Weiss was asked to write a letter to Protten on March 1, 1764, strongly advising him to reform while the community made intercessory prayers on his behalf."

Turning to the rest of his listeners, Ataa Forkoyi goes on, "Just at the time Weiss's letter came to Protten, a ship became available for him and his wife to board. When they got on board, they realized that the ship was still not ready to set sail. Protten confronted the captain about the delay. In the confrontation, a serious argument ensued, which led to a fight. The captain decided to throw out the Prottens, with bag and baggage. The Zeist community thought Protten had crossed the Rubicon this time with his aggression; he was no longer qualified to be a Moravian missionary so they arranged to have his license revoked and decided to send him and his wife back to Herrnhut.

"Protten refused to comply with the directive to go back to Herrnhut. Where else could he go? Of course he could go to Denmark to see his employers about the problem of going back home. So instead of heading eastwards to Herrnhut, he dragged Rebecca northwards to Copenhagen. From Copenhagen, he wrote a strongly-worded letter to the leadership in Herrnhut expressing his hurt at the way in which he felt the brethren had handled his plight. He also informed them defiantly that he was not coming back to Herrnhut. He had decided to take his wife with him back to the Guinea Coast to serve his Lord and God and nothing would stop him, not even the denied assistance of the Moravians.

"Soon thereafter, one morning as Rebecca led him in a family devotion, the Moravian Watchword for the day spoke impressively to Protten to repent and restore his relationship with his Saviour. While Rebecca prayed after this Watchword, according to the Stones something unusual came over Protten and he began to weep bitterly. When it was over, he got up from his knees, embraced Rebecca and solemnly said to her: 'The new has come.' Suddenly, alcoholism was gone and from that day onwards, he distanced himself from anything alcoholic."

As if dramatizing Protten's emotions, Ataa Forkoyi's mood now lightens and he continues cheerfully. "Now fully sober and back in his reflective mood, Protten took Rebecca along to the Trade Board to bid farewell to his employers. While there, a slave-ship bound for Guinea Coast was found in the schedule of slave-ships about to travel out of Copenhagen, and my friends, can you believe it? The name of the ship was Christiansborg. You can imagine Rebecca's joy as she saw her husband's beaming response to this act of providence. This was for her a sign that indeed, the "new had come," as stated by the Watchword that day. Immediately, the Board arranged a place on board for the couple together with all their baggage and provisions. In addition, Protten was presented with a package of the newly printed and published copies of his seminal book, for use in his teaching work at Christiansborg.

"With a deep sense of gratitude to God, they entered the Christiansborg and set sail for the Guinea Coast. The journey was long but it provided the couple quality time together. As they watched the vastness of the ocean they reminisced on the paths down which their Lord and Master Jesus had led them over the past years, and on the times they had spent together in Europe and separated from each other. As the slave ship moved from one shore to another along the Guinea Coast, Protten would point out some of the familiar places he had visited during his six years' absence from Herrnhut.

"When they passed the shores of Rio Junk now called Sierra Leone, Protten shared with Rebecca the remarkable experiences he had, stranded there on his way to Christiansborg in 1756. He repeated, to the amazement of Rebecca, some of the words he had learnt from the language of the people on that coast. Talking about these things led them to think about and plan for the teaching work they were going to embark on when they arrived at Christiansborg.

"The six weeks the ship spent on the high seas also gave Rebecca enough time to help Protten deal with his past through the deep counseling and prayer sessions she had with him. These counseling sessions helped Protten let go of all the hurts he felt he had received from the Moravians and through Rebecca's encouragement, he came to the decision that he would restore his relationship with the community in Herrnhut. By this time, the urge for alcohol was completely gone and there was a renewed desire to make the Lord Jesus Christ known to his people as he had resolved to do in September 1735, on the day he submitted his written testimony to the Moravian Brethren in Herrnhut in the presence of his benefactor, Count Zinzendorf."

Ataa Forkoyi now stops talking and requests some coconut milk. It is brought, and having satisfied his thirst with two coconuts, he continues cheerfully. "By the time the ship docked in the roads at Danish-Osu on May 10, 1765, Protten had become a transformed man. With his wife Rebecca at his side, he felt confident to go ashore to meet his relatives, the mulatto children and the whole Danish-Osu community for whom he and Rebecca had spent long hours praying at sea.

"As they stood on the deck of the slave ship and awaited the surf boats to take them ashore, he could see a bright future ahead of them; he could see his teaching work growing to embrace not only the mulattoes but all the children in the local communities; he could picture himself baptizing his Gã relatives to make it possible for him to administer the Holy Communion to them as followers of Jesus like himself.

"Unfortunately, despite these positive reflections in Protten's mind, the boat carrying their luggage to shore capsized due to the roughness of the breakers, and all their belongings, including the package of Protten's books and Huckoff's tombstone, were lost to the sea."

The lady with the Danish-Osu ancestry, hearing of this tragedy, spontaneously cries out: "What a warm welcome to Rebecca and homecoming reception for Protten!" There is an outburst of laughter from the rest of the listeners, but when they think about what happened, they stop laughing and become quiet and moody.

Ataa Forkoyi is quiet for a while.

Settling Down at Christiansborg

When he finally finds his voice, he begins to speak with some heartiness: "This tragedy did not dampen the spirits of Protten and Rebecca. According to the Stones, they took the loss of their luggage as a sign that God was assuring them of his readiness to take care of them as they embarked on this missionary enterprise. Governor Tysche received them and quickly arranged to provide them with lodgings in Christiansborg. Later on, relatives and old schoolmates at Danish-Osu who heard that Protten had returned with a mulatto wife, trooped to Christiansborg in droves to welcome him.

"The elders of the community at Osu-Anahor, the quarters to which his mother belonged, came with alcoholic drinks to pour libation to thank the ancestors for bringing him and his wife back home. Protten was deeply touched by this gesture but found himself torn between accepting or rejecting this show of traditional gratitude to the ancestors for his safe arrival back home. However, with tact and respect, he managed to convince his relatives that thanking the ancestors with a drink offering was not necessary. Instead, in fluent Gã, he said a moving prayer of thanksgiving to God and ended it with the Lord's Prayer. His relatives were amazed to see how his face glowed with joy as he prayed with them in Gã. When it was all over, they embraced him and Rebecca and returned to the community with great joy, singing and dancing on the way.

"Without wasting any time, the Prottens settled down at Christiansborg and began to re-organize the fort school. In no time, the number of pupils had grown to about forty. Some of the children known to have been on his list of pupils were Erich, Carl and Friederich Engmann, and Jacob and Johann Quist. The Danish fathers of these children were old acquaintances of Protten who had by then returned to Denmark. Protten, using the contents of his own book, taught his pupils in the Gã language. While he taught them everyday except Saturdays, Rebecca would gather the girls around her on Saturdays and develop their housecraft skills. Everybody was impressed by the Prottens' management of the school except the Danish chaplain, who complained about Protten teaching the children in Gã, and that the girls particularly were very weak in Danish.

"As the school work progressed, Rebecca had to remind her husband that he did not come back to Christiansborg only to teach but also to lead his people to know God and to love Jesus intimately as he had experienced. With this nudge from his loving and spirit-filled wife, Protten began to go around the community to explain to them how they could turn from their traditional beliefs and serve Jehovah God and love Jesus Christ.

"Of course, while they listened to him as he spoke his Gã with a German accent mixed with some of the local Portuguese words, they laughed and scorned. They always had to remind him that the white man's God he was telling them about was far away from them. They needed to pour libation to the local deities they could see and feel everyday around them in their communities. Moreover, they reminded him of the behaviour of the Danes, whose God he was persuading them to serve; had they not been fighting among themselves, carousing and cursing? Were they not the buyers of the slaves brought down from the interior in chains? Had they not even been consulting the local Danish-Osu deities?

"In his frustration, he was encouraged by Rebecca to write to Herrnhut for assistance. So in 1766, he wrote a passionate letter to the leadership of Herrnhut. In this letter, which was very conciliatory, he appealed to the Moravians to send missionaries down to Danish-Osu to join them in making Christ known among his people."

"With all the history between Protten and the leadership in Herrnhut, did they take any notice of him?" asks the history teacher.

"Yes. According to the Stones, the brethren were delighted to receive Protten's letter and his appeal found a good hearing. They were, however, not in a rush to send down missionaries as Protten had requested. They took into consideration what the Count used to assert, that the opportune time for the people of the Guinea Coast had not arrived. There was therefore the need to pray earnestly about Protten's appeal and take time to prepare the right people to respond to the call. As the Prottens waited for support from Herrnhut, they went on with their tasks of teaching and trying to reach the communities with the Gospel. Every morning when they had their devotion, they prayed fervently to the Lord to move the hearts and minds of the people to accept the message of the Gospel and turn from their idols to serve the living Christ.

"But Protten had to realize that as the Scriptures assert, a prophet is not accepted in his own country. He felt they were not making any progress in the Danish-Osu community with their missionary attempts and obtained permission from Governor Christian Tychsen, with whom he was on friendly terms, to move with his wife to the community of Dutch-Accra, where he had some good friends.

"So for a while, the Prottens made their abode in the house of Mantse Oto Brafo at Kinka. There, Protten discovered how much better it was to live outside the walls of Christiansborg. Hence, when they returned to Christiansborg upon the death of his friend Governor Tychsen, he discussed with the new governor, a Lower Saxony German called Ruhberg, his intention to move out into the Danish-Osu community. With the hope that this German-speaking governor would be sympathetic, he passionately shared his intention to develop a home and a school for both the mulatto children and their African siblings. This development would hopefully constitute the nucleus of a Christian village in accordance with the Herrnhut model.

"Protten's intentions were frowned upon. Hence, when he requested permission to build outside Christiansborg, he was refused. However, the governor appreciated the good work he and his wife were doing in Christiansborg and in the Danish-Osu communities. In light of this, he followed up on Protten's request to get missionaries from Herrnhut by writing to the Company to arrange with the Moravians to send missionaries to the Guinea Coast. On March 22, 1767, a formal request was sent from Copenhagen to Herrnhut in Schlesien, for missionaries to be sent to Danish-Osu."

When the Rastafarian, who has been listening attentively, hears that a request was sent by the Company to Herrnhut, he sarcastically shouts out: "Did they add to the letter any life insurance coverage for the missionaries that would go? And did the letter ask for any guarantee that the missionaries would not compete with the Danes in the lucrative transatlantic slave trade?"

A spontaneous shout comes from the rest of the listeners: "Mr. Rastaman, what a question!"

In a reflective mood, Ataa Forkoyi pauses awhile before responding to the Rastafarian's outburst. "My friend, your questions are insightful. When Huckoff followed Protten in 1735, he was buried a few months after arrival. So life insurance coverage would not be out of place. But the Royal Danish Africa Company knew that the Moravians were people of faith who did not require life insurance; the providence of God was their sufficiency."

The Rastafarian, embarrassed by Ataa Forkoyi's succinct answer, shoots back quickly: "What about the guarantee not to trade in slaves?"

With a smile at the corner of his lips, Ataa Forkoyi says:

"You need to know the history of the Moravians. According to the Stones, their founding leader, Count Ludwig Nicholas von Zinzendorf, notwithstanding his noble birth and wealthy upbringing, was deeply influenced by his pious and pietistic grandmother, with a spirituality that was totally free from racism. He was able to stamp this freedom from racism on the movement he initiated and directed in his lifetime, attracting people of different races to Herrnhut as their spiritual home. This explains, for example, the unique presence of tombstones of people of almost all races in their world-famous cemetery, Gottesacker."

He continues: "Furthermore, it is worthy of note that the Moravian missionaries who were sent to the Danish islands of St. Croix and St. Thomas actively worked against the slave culture that was entrenched there at that time. In fact, Rebecca's first husband, a German, was jailed for marrying her because she was a slave. It took the intervention of Zinzendorf, who was on a supervisory tour, to get them released from prison and from the islands. This German missionary by the name of Martin Freundlich, stood by Rebecca, with whom he had an infant daughter, until he expired on their return to Germany.

"My friend, the Company knew this history very well and they were certain that the missionaries from Herrnhut would not be involved in any way with the slave trade at Christiansborg, although they would come in the name of the Company." When Ataa Forkoyi ends his brief lecture, there is spontaneous applause from his listeners for his brilliant response to the Rastafarian's impertinent questions. The Rastafarian himself nods with satisfaction.

"In response to the request from Denmark, five missionaries, Jacob Meder, Daniel Lemke, Gottfried Schultze, Sigmund Kleffel and Sanyek Gakk were sent from Herrnhut in June 1767 and arrived safely at Danish-Osu on July 5, 1768. According to the Stones, they were heartily received by the Governor and the Prottens. Like the Prottens, they were housed in three small rooms in the storage quarters of Christiansborg. They came with great expectations and were heartened by the enthusiastic songs of the remidors as they rowed them ashore in their canoes: 'Fear not, you are landing on a good land, a blessed land. Fear not; you will have a good home here.'

"Despite the songs, however, the harsh environment and climatic conditions that had caused the early death of Huckoff, still prevailed. So, by September, three of the missionaries, who had been taken seriously ill, passed into eternity. According to the Stones, Protten and his wife did all they could to nurse their Moravian Brethren, to the admiration of the two surviving missionaries. In the face of all this uncertainty, the surviving missionaries observed the laudable attempts of the Prottens to bring Christ to Danish-Osu. So, despite the fate of their colleagues, they went ahead and requested for reinforcements from Herrnhut to support this work. However, before the new group arrived on February 9, 1770, the elusive and indefatigable Protten had, himself, died."

"Aoooh!" exclaim the listeners at the death of Protten.

"When did Protten die and where was he buried?" asks the young architecture student with some agitation, adding sorrowfully, "Oh my! Why did he have to die when there were now helpers to assist him in fulfilling his heart's desire of making Christ known to his people?"

Ataa Forkoyi emotionally clears his throat and pulls himself together. He dolefully responds to the student's questions:

"Protten passed away unexpectedly on August 23, 1769, in the arms of his wife, after a brief illness. Some of the Stones thought he died of a broken heart as he saw his three young Moravian brothers buried one after the other. Rebecca was shocked by his death but remained strong. She informed the governor, who quickly relayed the sad news to Protten's relatives in the Danish-Osu community. As the news spread pandemonium erupted, especially in the Osu-Anahor community, and immediately the drums began to beat sorrowfully, to announce that a great baobab tree had fallen.

"The head of the community along with his elders, followed by wailing women, hurried to Christiansborg with ritual drinks to inform the Governor that they had come to collect their royal for burial in the family house. When Rebecca got wind of the wish of Protten's kinsfolk to give him a traditional burial, she managed to convince the governor and the Secret Council to refuse the request. Her argument was that Protten died as a practicing Christian and should be accorded a Christian burial, despite being a royal in the local community. The governor was sympathetic to Rebecca's pleadings and refused the kinsfolk's request.

"In order not to hurt their sensibilities, he assured them that, in recognition of the great work Protten had done to advance the Fort School, he would be buried in the yard of Christiansborg as the Danish administration's last respect to him. They found this arrangement agreeable and thought it was equally honorable for a royal such as Protten who should otherwise have been buried in the family house. But in order to ensure that proper burial rites were performed, they requested to inspect Protten's possessions so that they could select appropriate things with which he could be buried.

"The governor conceded to this request and ordered Rebecca to allow access to Protten's belongings. When they entered the small quarters in Christiansborg, which Rebecca and her husband had used as their home since they returned from the palace of Mantse Oto Brafo of Kinka in Dutch-Accra, they were shocked to realize how frugally their relative had lived. Apart from thirty-four feet of embroidered taffeta, six Dutch books, ten Latin books and twenty-five French books which he purchased from the estate of the late Governor Tychsen, there was nothing they considered worthy for the royal funerary rites they wanted to perform for Protten.

"When the governor had issued the permit to select a place in Christiansborg's courtyard for the burial, the relatives came and dug the grave and the body was made ready for burial. That day, throngs of people from all the Danish-Osu communities including some in Kinka turned out, together with relatives and pupils of the fort school, to pay their last respects to the teacher and theologian, Christian Jacob Africanus Protten, alias Teiko Sacki, Blofonyo Bi.

"At the burial, amidst sobbing and dirges, Governor Ruhberg gave the eulogy, Rebecca said a moving prayer and the Danish chaplain finally committed him to his grave, while female relatives rolled on the ground, wailing in Gã: *"Nkɛlɛ baaya ei, nkɛlɛ baaya ei!"*

At this point in the narration, Ataa Forkoyi becomes silent, closes his eyes and bows down his head, as if listening to some voices coming from behind him. Then slowly he begins to speak again: "As I hear the Stones repeat the Governor's eulogy, I recollect the glimpses I made into the mind and soul of Protten while going through his 1756-1761 Diary." He makes a dramatic pause to attract the attention of his listeners, who have become sorrowful and are beginning to lose concentration. Then, he says reflectively:

"Protten had a great mind and he valued education. He went round the Danish-Osu community to encourage the mothers of the mulatto children to send their children to school. The education of the mulatto-child was his greatest concern just as girl-child education is our concern today. He was not an intellectual only concerned with matters of the mind, but showed profound interest in the welfare of his pupils and initiated social activism in the community, collecting clothing, food and money for the upkeep of the mulatto orphans. Knowing the value of the trained mind, he made sure that the mulatto adults at Christiansborg, mostly soldiers who had missed school growing up, received some adult literacy."

The Rastafarian comes in quickly with: "Protten was doing mass education way back then, eh?"

All the others, including Ataa Forkoyi, applaud heartily although one is not certain for whom the applause is meant, Protten or the Rastafarian.

Ataa Forkoyi clears up the uncertainty by thanking the Rastafarian for his crisp remark and continues with his reflections on the mind and soul of Protten:

"The Europeanized mind of Protten created a lot of tension in his soul as he sought to come to terms with the cultural inconsistencies he observed at Danish-Osu. It concerned him how some of the mulatto women after being introduced to European culture through Christiansborg, reverted to the local lifestyle and dress culture. In spite of his deep theological convictions about God as the Supreme One and Jesus Christ as the Saviour of the world, he prayerfully engaged himself with the traditional religion of his people and constantly debated with himself, the merits and demerits of the local practices he observed around him in the communities."

Ataa Forkoyi stops with some irritation for a question from the lady with Danish ancestry. A bit embarrassed, the lady inquires: "Is it really true that the Moravian Christians who arrived at Danish-Osu in 1845 from Jamaica came because of the missionary work Protten started about a hundred years earlier?"

"No. Not directly," says Ataa Forkoyi, "But there is a divine connection between Protten's failed attempts to plant a Church at Danish-Osu and the coming of the Jamaicans. As you might have heard, the one who actually invited these freed slaves from Jamaica to help him plant the Basel Mission on the Guinea Coast was Andreas Riis. He was a Danish man who belonged to the Moravian Brethren in Denmark. Riis might have learnt about Protten and

Rebecca as Moravians. I am certain that he might have been told when he was a student about Rebecca particularly and the great spiritual influence she once had among the Moravians in the Caribbean. From the records, Riis might have known that Rebecca and Protten, together with a number of other missionaries from Herrnhut, were buried in Danish-Osu so as to become the seed of the Guinea Church. This historical fact would have stuck in Riis' mind and might have energized him as a Moravian, to seek support from the Moravian Church in the Caribbean.

"Hence, after a series of fruitless attempts to convince the people of Akwapim to accept God as the Supreme Creator, *Onyankopong*, the only true deity worthy of worship, he might have been divinely guided to go to the Caribbean to seek support from the freed African Moravians. It was these freed slaves who returned home and successfully supported Riis to win the hearts and minds of the local people, for Jesus. I believe this was in response to Protten's and Rebecca's incessant prayers to God a century earlier, for the salvation of the people of the Guinea Coast. Herein lies the connection between Protten and the coming of the Jamaicans in 1845." Ataa Forkoyi is about to continue with his recollections when he hears the Rastafarian shouting: "Yeah maan. Jah is good!"

The listeners begin to laugh while Ataa Forkoyi speaks: "The evils of the local slave trade and what Protten saw going on in Christiansborg afflicted his mind as he reflected on why such an inhumane trade should be perpetuated by people who claimed they had a superior knowledge of God. But he was also a keen observer who was not blinded to other things by his horror of the slave trade. Acutely aware of his environment, he noted a number of details in his journal with interesting comments. The two water cisterns built in an earlier century attracted his attention and he noted that in spite of their age, they were still functioning. The fact that fish were in abundance in the Kpeshi, Klottey and Korle Lagoons in the months of June and July did not escape his attention either.

"Despite his emotional instability, he was a good, faithful and caring husband. In all his long periods of separation from Rebecca, through his journeys away from her, he kept contact by writing to her and having her constantly in his thoughts. Notwithstanding the pressures he was confronted with, he maintained his moral integrity and never once was unfaithful, even when a strange woman was forced on him when he found himself stranded in Rio Jonk on his way to the Guinea Coast in 1756. As a true Moravian, Protten practiced fasting and regular devotional prayers, using typical

Moravian expressions such as 'Desiring to go into the side wounds of the Saviour' (a common Moravian expression of strong devotion to the Lord Jesus Christ). He sought God's guidance by using the casting of lots as customarily practiced by the Moravians. During his five-year stay at Christiansborg, he kept with him a portrait of his benefactor, Count Zinzendorf."

Ataa Forkoyi abruptly ceases his recollections, and looks up at the position of the sun. As he realizes that it is midday, he picks up his bag, puts on his hat and begins to walk away. When the history teacher realizes that Ataa Forkoyi has come to the end of his narration and wants to go home, she quickly walks up to him and gives him a bear hug, saying contentedly:

"Ataa Forkoyi, on my own behalf and on behalf of my friends here, I wish to express my profound gratitude and deep appreciation for what you have shared with us about this wonderful ancestor of Danish-Osu. As a historian, my mind has been greatly enlightened and I am highly inspired to teach my students about our people who lived in the period of the Danes on our shores. But my dear sir, I cannot let you go without pleading that you let me know what happened to Rebecca after the death of Protten."

He smiles and takes off his hat to fan himself since it is midday and he is feeling the heat. "My dear teacher, honestly, if I consent to your pleading, you will have to stay again with me throughout the afternoon and the night till tomorrow morning. The story of Rebecca is longer than that of her husband. Fortunately, it has all been captured in a book called *Rebecca's Revival,* written by somebody called Jon Sensbach or something and therefore I need not start any narration of her story today. But, before you allow me to go home for my midday rest, it might interest you to know that Rebecca survived Protten and all the other Moravian missionaries who came after his death.

"According to the Stones, she continued to live at Christiansborg and later moved to Kinka to live in Mantse Oto Brafo's palace, where she was looked after in her old age. When she became weary and fell ill, she expressed the wish to go back to St. Thomas to spend her last days on earth with her Moravian Brethren. The Secret Council at Christiansborg approved her wish to migrate to the Caribbean but she was not able to undertake the trip. She was too weak to travel and finally passed on in 1780 at the gracious age of 62 years. Unlike her husband Protten who did it several times, if she had managed to make the journey, she would have completed the ignominious triangle between the Guinea Coast, the Caribbean and Europe, brought into being by the transatlantic slave trade."

Concluding with this terse statement, Ataa Forkoyi bids farewell to his listeners and walks slowly away, towards his house at Osu-Anahor.

Five | # Blossoming of Danish-Osu Family Trees

Beginnings

Accordingly to the season, it is time for the harmattan to show its presence. The harmattan that blows in with the dry, dust-laden winds from the Sahel, changes the micro-climate at Osu. The salty, humid atmosphere caused by the ocean winds from the south-west, gives way to the chilly, foggy dawns that make sleeping pleasant here at Osu. The children do not have to wake up early to sweep the compounds because the sun does not show its bright face so early in the morning; it shines only hazily as its face has been covered with a thin veil of harmattan mist. Harmattan brings the dry, dusty days that make housewives fret about the continuous dusting of living room furniture. If they neglect it, they risk the embarrassment of guests sitting on dusty chairs when they come round for afternoon chit-chat.

But these days, the power of the Harmattan is no longer felt at Osu, thanks to the phenomenon of climate change; people's skin no longer gets so dried up, requiring the regular be-smearing of shea butter cream on their bodies. In earlier years at Osu, if one went around in the harmattan season with severely dry skin, one was said to have assumed the image of the harmattan deity *"Aharabata Wɔŋ"* and ridiculed, since a dry-skinned, drab-looking person was always frowned upon. Children, who, because of the chilly morning weather did not like to have their baths and thus would not be smeared with shea butter, became the popular "Aharabata Wɔŋ." To avoid this indignity, they would try to brave the cold baths in order to have their skins smeared with shea butter cream.

So because of the mild harmattan, one hardly sees 'harmattan deities' around these days. Even the old trees that have seen several harmattans, have become evergreens; they refuse to shed their leaves at this time of the year, indicating that although the harmattan is present, there is still a lot of moisture in the atmosphere. It is therefore not too stressful today as Ataa Forkoyi goes around showing his listeners the various family-houses at Osu. He explains to his listeners that whenever they come across a family-house, they are seeing the physical manifestation of a family tree. When the architecture student hears this, his architectural mind quickly reacts and he asks:

"Ataa Forkoyi, my education up to now has made me understand that a house is different from a tree. A house is a non-living entity and a tree is a living entity. How can a house stand for a tree? I do not get the metaphor you are employing here."

At this amusing interjection, Ataa Forkoyi gives the ghost of a smile and stops in his leisurely walk along the street; he turns towards the young architecture student and addresses him: "Students will be students. You are always splitting hairs over small matters. Now let me explain what I mean. The expression 'family tree' is only an analogical description of a socio-cultural phenomenon."

As the listeners hear this, they all shout "Wow!" spontaneously.

Unperturbed by this show of appreciation of his scholarship, Ataa Forkoyi goes on: "This phenomenon embodies the genealogy of a living and dead group of people who are linked together by blood and marital relationships. When the names, periods of birth and status of the individuals of the group are graphically presented on paper, a tree-like chart appears. This tree-like form becomes what is commonly referred to as the 'family tree.' I must emphasize here that a family tree is not observable except when graphically manifested on paper. The compilation of the information that may constitute a family tree, is usually done by a knowledgeable person in the family but it has to be authenticated by the counsel of elders in the family under the chairmanship of the Family Head. Compilation of information for a family tree is a complex matter."

Ataa Forkoyi adds this to his explanation with a chuckle and continues pedantically, "The presence of a person on a family tree chart, who does not qualify to be a member can generate a lot of trouble, sometimes leading to legal battles."

"Why is it so?" somebody asks Ataa Forkoyi.

"For the sake of inheritance," he explains, "only qualified bona fide members' names should appear on a family tree chart. Qualification is either by being an offspring, or having been married or adopted into a family. It has nothing to do with length of time of association. In some cases, the adoption came about because a former slave, who was very much liked by a family, was accorded a customary right to become a family member. This is how, for example, a person may have Danish family name without having a Danish ancestry." He continues awkwardly: "There have been cases when persons whose forebears happened to have been associated with a family over generations did not appear on a family tree chart. This came about because their forebears came into that particular family as slaves and were never adopted into the family."

The human rights activist immediately shouts out: "Does slavery ancestry still play a role in one's status in Osu today?"

Ataa Forkoyi scratches his head, feeling a bit embarrassed at the question. With a grimace, he attempts to answer this difficult question: "Yes and no, but in Osu, nobody should talk about that. As it is said in Gã, *'Atsii mɔta.'* So, please, let's not talk about it." With that he goes into a poetic mood to continue on the subject of family trees. "Metaphorically, the 'family tree' is used to illustrate how the 'roots,' that is, the unseen ancestors and their progenitors, are actively joined to the living. The living members constitute the 'branches.'

"The 'branches' are the various individual families, and together form the 'trunk' or the 'main stem,' which defines the extended family or clan. The people that constitute the 'trunk' may bear common characteristic features and traits as well as a common family name or a surname, employed to give an identity to the family tree. The metaphor is further extended to let the 'leaves' stand for the notable accomplishments associated with the extended family. Any important family heirlooms such as the philosophy of names, physical properties, etc. constitute the 'flowers' that characterize the family tree."

The architecture student nods his head as he listens attentively to Ataa Forkoyi, but realizing that the essence of his question has not been addressed, he politely interrupts with: "I understand all this and appreciate the good explanation you have given. But I still do not see the link between the inanimate house and the animate tree."

Ataa Forkoyi, now with eyes closed, shakes his head gently from side to side. "Young man, patience, patience. I am yet to come to that link. First things first! You must understand the notion of the family tree and then you can see the link between the 'house' and the 'tree.' You see, in the Gã language, we use the phrases *Shiatso* and *Wekutso* to talk about the family unit and the extended family respectively. Shiatso literally translates as 'house tree,' and Wekutso as 'house group tree.' In this light, the house in which the ancestors dwell and which the living use as a place of abode and gathering place for all important family activities and events, such as child naming ceremonies, customary weddings, Homowo festival, as well as funeral celebrations, is more than an architectural entity or a housing unit. It is the Family House and it is a psycho-social entity that represents the genealogy. Hence at Osu, when you come across a Family House you see a Family Tree with all that the Tree stands for.

"Now let me add that the 'family house' as such, also has its metaphors similar to those of the 'family tree.' The 'foundation' which is buried in the ground and invisible, constitutes the ancestors and progenitors. The 'superstructure' is the extended family with the living members usually with a common family name by which the family is recognized and known. The 'infrastructure,' not visible but tangible, is the sense of attachment or belonging that comes about through the common inheritance of blood or marital relationship. The house's 'decoration' and 'heirloom' become the notable achievements and accomplishments associated with the extended family."

When Ataa Forkoyi comes to the end of his pedantic exposition, the architecture student admiringly applauds and exclaims: "Ataa Forkoyi, this is fantastic. Where did you get all this stuff?"

Ataa Forkoyi smiles contentedly and points with his right index finger to the ground, saying simply, "From the Stones!"

It so happens that today's excursion of Ataa Forkoyi and his listeners is taking place on a Friday. Fridays at Osu are the days when one sees the gathering of people at their family houses for funerals. Funerals act as a strong force that pulls members of extended families together to demonstrate their sense of solidarity and belonging, a social catalyst that facilitates reunions that strengthen the bonds imperceptibly linking the various branches of the Family Tree.

All around the open spaces, the streets, the nooks in between houses, stand the black and red coloured pavilions under which gorgeously dressed funeral guests and relatives sit to celebrate the passing away of loved ones. The loud music, a mixture of gospel and traditional, coming from giant loud-speakers helps create the right ambience for the mourners to dance away their sorrow and heartily enjoy the *"Gbonyo Party,"* with its plentiful snacks and free drinks.

As Ataa Forkoyi and his group walk along the Osu Awusai Atso street westwards towards Osu Kinkawe, they see a number of old houses with brightly coloured posters pasted on some of their walls. On these posters, which usually announce the passing away of individual family members, are printed beautiful pictures of deceased persons at the top left-hand corners of the posters. At the top, one typically finds in bold capital letters, all sorts of inscriptions such as: OBITUARY, or CALL TO GLORY, or CELEBRATION OF LIFE or TRANSITION.

Below this bold heading will usually be a long list of names of people with their corresponding titles or positions in the extended family. If one looks carefully, one will see that at the end of this long list of names follows a short statement: "announce with gratitude to God the home call of their beloved …" giving the full name of the deceased relative. In addition, the poster has a long list of names of people in various relational categories such as brothers, sisters, cousins, nephews, nieces, uncles, aunts, etc. Concluding the information on the poster, placed at the bottom of the sheet is another long list of names, the so-called "Chief Mourners."

On the way along the Awusai Atso Street, Ataa Forkoyi comes to a standstill as his attention is caught by one such prominent poster, fixed on the wall of a family-house. As his listeners realize that he wants to talk about this poster, they curiously gather around him and with rapt attention, get ready to listen.

"You see this poster?" He begins to speak, tracing the writing with his skinny index finger. "If you want to see the family tree to which the deceased belonged, you must carefully follow the names appearing under the various categories on this poster. By this you can easily compose the branches and the stem and roots of the deceased's family tree."

His listeners stand amazed at what he is saying because they can only see a glossy poster and not a family tree. "So, obituary posters are important cultural artifacts at Osu," says the history teacher.

"Yes, absolutely," says Ataa Forkoyi, "and that is why I collect them all the time. I collect them and file them to help me update what the Stones tell me about the Danish-Osu families."

Early Graftings

"As I once told you, the mulattoes who were fathered by the sojourning Danish men and mothered by the local Gã women, were given Danish names in accordance with the demands and dictates of the Danish administration. But they were nonetheless totally part of the kith and kin of their mothers and were regarded as integral members of the extended family. As a result, extended families in the four communities began to be 'Danish-ed' and a number of family trees at Danish-Osu were grafted with Danish offspring, names and histories."

Before Ataa Forkoyi can continue, the Rastafarian, who missed the earlier exposition on family trees and family houses at Danish-Osu, interrupts with a question: "What is this 'Danish-ing' of communities and grafting of family trees with Danish names and histories? I am sorry, but I don't understand what you are saying. Will you be kind enough to illustrate what you are trying to tell us?"

In an attempt to respond to the Rastafarian's query, Ataa Forkoyi realizes that his throat has become dry. He beckons a little girl hawking sachets of iced water in a plastic bowl on her head. Since the weather is fairly dry and there are a lot of people milling along the Awusai Atso Street because of the various funerals taking place, the little girl has been making brisk business and is in no hurry to respond. Ataa Forkoyi loses his patience and shouts at her to come immediately. She turns around quickly to obey but stumbles and the bowl falls off her head and all the sachets land on the dry ground. This waste of water he needs infuriates Ataa Forkoyi even more. The lady with the Danish ancestry now walks up and gives him some fruit juice from her cooler. With gratitude and delight he accepts the offer. After he has taken a number of gulps, he is refreshed and ready to respond to the Rastafarian's query.

"I will now give you some illustrations of this 'Danish-ing' and grafting business as I received it from the Stones," he begins. "But first, let me explain to you how grafting actually takes place in trees for you to appreciate the illustrations I am about to present. We talk about 'grafting' or 'budding' in agriculture and horticulture as a technique or if you prefer, as biological engineering. The technique is applied to reproduce a particular tree, usually a fruit tree, by inserting a cut section of its stem with leaf buds, known as a scion, into the stock of another tree to allow it to grow and develop. Grafting is undertaken to achieve a variety of purposes, including top-working an established tree to one or more different cultivars. For example, by top-working, an undesirable cultivar can be changed by grafting a preferred cultivar to the branches. By this means, novelties in fruit trees can be developed."

Now, Ataa Forkoyi, looking a bit tired, takes a few steps towards one of the pavilions with empty chairs, possibly waiting for late-coming funeral guests. He takes a seat and beckons his hearers also to sit down. As soon as they take their seats, a team of nicely dressed young ladies, wearing colourful sashes across their chests with the bold inscription 'USHER' come and serve them with some neatly packaged snacks and bottles of assorted drinks. The group is surprised at this show of hospitality and conviviality since they know that they are not funeral guests. Ataa Forkoyi encourages them to accept the service since this is how things are done at funerals in Osu. He then takes a bite of snack and continues with his exposition on the grafting of family trees at Danish-Osu.

"Metaphorically speaking," he says, licking his lips, "this was what began to happen centuries ago to some of the family trees found in the communities at Danish-Osu. Initially, the grafting was taking place in pure Gã families. However, as the population of mulattoes in the communities increased and more generations of mulattoes emerged, the grafting shifted to families with second, third and so on, 'Danish-ed' ancestries.

"The Stones tell how the family tree of the Sonnes of Danish-Osu sprouted and began to bloom, starting way back in the early eighteenth century. Joergen Sonne, a Danish man in the service of the Danish administration at Christiansborg had a very good relationship with the Osu-Anahor community and fraternized regularly with Sodza, a prominent citizen of that community. It happened that Sodza was also the chief messenger and courier of Christiansborg. He had procured this important position because his relative, Nii Sodza Duamoro, the Chief of Osu-Anahor, had given his sister, Nyuenywerewa, in marriage to the Danish governor.

"Because of his official duties, Sodza frequented Christiansborg, going there at times accompanied by his beautiful daughter. The beauty of this Sodza damsel always attracted the attention of the soldiers and officers who saw her enter and leave their abode while in the company of her father. Many of them therefore sought to win her love but they never succeeded. However, Joergen Sonne who had the privilege of fraternizing with Sodza, became a worthy suitor and eventually, in 1751, he married the young lady in accordance with the Gã customary rites and with the approval of the governor and the Secret Council at Christiansborg. Children were born out of this union and the Sodza family tree was thereby grafted with a Sonne. It was out of this grafted tree that blossomed and matured generations that have come down to the present day.

"The well-known Sonne family of Danish-Osu therefore has its roots in the Sodza family of Osu-Anahor. The Stones recollect that other well-established Danish-Osu families such as the Lokkos, Engmanns, Malms, Palms, Briandts, Riemers, Holms, Quists, Meyers and others, have genealogies with similar characteristic features. I have some of these family trees with me for illustration. The first one I wish to show you is that of the Engmanns of Osu-Kinkawe.

"Look carefully at it. No doubt it is complex and unwieldy but if you follow the chart carefully, you will see how the coming together of Carl Gustav Engmann with the former wife of Governor Hackenberg, Ashiokai from the house of Chief Adjovi at Osu-Kinkawe in the eighteenth century, has led to an extended family that goes over six generations, occupying a geographical space that transcends even the borders of Ghana to date."

With rapt attention the group listens as Ataa Forkoyi deftly goes into the genealogy of the Engmanns. "The roots of this family are traced to a pure indigenous Osu female progenitor and a Scandinavian male progenitor with Swedish and Danish heritage. The Stones have clear memories of these two ancestors and they talk about them as people with outstanding personalities. Before Awo Ashiokai, the female progenitor of the Engmanns came to be married to Carl Gustav, she had previously been married to a Danish governor at Christiansborg of German extraction, by the name of Hackenberg, with whom she had had a son.

"This female forebear was from a royal home. Her own mother, called Koikoi Bonte, was herself a princess of Gã-Mashie. Ashiokai's royal background provided her with the advantage of access to the Danes at Christiansborg. In her business and social interaction with them, she displayed much astuteness; this of course impressed the Europeans who found her to be an excellent partner. By virtue of her strength of character and personal attributes while living outside Christiansborg at Danish-Osu without the support of Carl Gustav, she was able to raise the two strong mulatto sons she bore him, besides the sons she had with Hackenberg and the other European called Reindorf. Erich Engmann was born in 1753 and Frederick Engmann in 1754 and they were christened on November

28, 1779, ten years after the death of Christian Africanus Protten. According to the Stones, the survival of these two sons ensured the successful sprouting of the Engmann seedlings into a full-grown and thriving family tree today.

"After the birth of Erich and Frederick, the restless soul of Carl Gustav Engmann led him away to pursue his trading activities in the Caribbean and Denmark. Thus, he left his sprouting seedlings behind in Danish-Osu. But as an illustrious ancestor, he stamped his legacy on the destiny of the Engmann family tree."

At this point in the narration, the history teacher comes with another interruption, asking Ataa Forkoyi why he asserts that Carl Gustav stamped his legacy when he left the Guinea coast. In answering her, Ataa Forkoyi closes his eyes, seeming to see a video documentary of the growth of the Engmann family tree. For a moment he holds his silence but then begins again to speak, with eyes still firmly shut.

"Madam you see, Carl Gustav came to the Guinea coast initially as a surgeon. When he saw how the Danish slave trade flourished, he put medicine aside and converted his passion for healthcare into passion for business. He became a merchant and, powered with the skills of precision and efficiency learnt in medical practice, he quickly distinguished himself as an astute trader and administrator. While acting as an interim governor, he was visionary in embarking upon development projects at Christiansborg, including the construction of a water cistern that has remained in existence until to today. Look at the leaves of the Engmann family tree and you will see Carl Gustav's traces all over.

"Although the Engmanns are of Swedish-Danish extraction," continues Ataa Forkoyi with a mischievous smile on his face, "they have grown and become firmly established as a typical Ghanaian extended family. At Osu today, they constitute one of the large patrilineal clans rooted in the Osu Kinkawe traditional community and have become prominent and well known in Osu society."

At this point in the narration, the lady with Danish ancestral background who bears no Danish family name indicates to Ataa Forkoyi that she has a question. Hesitatingly, she formulates her thoughts and says: "Ataa Forkoyi, I am wondering how the Engmanns, after all these centuries at Osu, have not lost their identity and can be recognized as such."

Before Ataa Forkoyi responds to the lady's reflective question, he asks for some water. He is provided with a bottle of cool water; he graciously takes it, slowly opens the top and drinks it all. Someone in the audience observes him and offers him another bottle but he declines it. Now looking satisfied and refreshed, he gives a lively response:

"You see, the Engmanns retained their identity because their ancestral roots at Osu Kinkawe had a physical expression in the legendary family house referred to as *'Shia Wulu'* at Osu Amantra. This legendary family house might have been one of the stone houses used for both family members and slaves during the period of the trans-Atlantic slave trade. The house no longer exists today except for its site which has become a landmark and a memorial ground where the Engmanns and other relatives converge to hold funerals. The existence of this site gives substance to the legend that is intertwined with the name 'Engmann' and that has been passed on from generation to generation to make the identity of the Engmanns distinct and enduring.

"The Engmann family, characterized by frequent births of twin children, kept on proliferating to become an Osu clan. The clan now embraces over 200 individuals who consider themselves part of the lineage, Nii-Lomo We, and who cherish the use of indigenous Gã names with the prefix 'Lomo,' which might have evolved from the Gã word *'lumɔ'* meaning 'the great one.' So, many Engmanns today carry middle names such as Lomote, Lomoete, Lomomensah for males, and Lomole, Lomorkor, Lomokai, Lomortsoo for females.

"Over a period of time, the large clan group has organized itself into three patrilineal houses under the names of earlier forebears: Charles Engmann, Jeremias Engmann and Sonne-Engmann. Each of these patrilineal houses has its own family head to preside over all matters that pertain to the interests and survival of these houses. Notwithstanding the existence of these known houses, a number of Engmanns have tenuous links to their patrilineal connections due to migration and translocation of residence outside Osu, the ancestral home. There are now families bearing the name Engmann in faraway places such as the United States of America, Canada, Holland and the United Kingdom. But no matter where Engmanns are found today, excellence in character and achievement are closely associated with them. Strong religious orientation and love for education and scholarship are the hallmarks of most family members."

The history teacher now courteously asks Ataa Forkoyi to illustrate the earlier point he made about Carl Gustav leaving his stamp on the Engmann genealogy. Beaming with delight, he responds almost in a shout, "Carl Gustav was a trained surgeon and when he became an administrator at Christiansborg, he initiated a number of important civil works which stood the test of time, to underscore his engineering ingenuity. Is it not interesting that on one of the lines of the family tree, there have been several generations of medical officers, including a professor of anatomy? There have also been generations of civil engineers.

"In addition to this, a number of individual Engmanns have distinguished themselves as high-fliers. The history of Ghana abounds with Engmann achievements; for example, there was a Reverend Jeremias Carl Engmann, a local Basel Mission pastor who, in the early part of the twentieth century, caused rain to fall after a long period of drought at Osu, through his intercessory prayer; there was Reverend E. Augustus Wilkens Engmann who, as a headmaster, successfully pioneered the establishment of the famous Presbyterian Secondary School, besides the number of books he published in the Gã language in his lifetime and posthumously; there was Yorgen Ernest Engmann, who became an accomplished civil engineer to direct the Ghanaian Public Works Department for several years; there was Professor Frederick Nii-Lomote Engmann, the accomplished baritone singer who became the first Ghanaian trained anatomist, later to head the premier Ghana Medical School as the youngest ever Dean of the School.

"I can go on and on with the list of Engmann achievers but I also need to show you the family tree chart of the Malms. So, I have to stop here for now. Before I do so, however, let me add this fact from the Stones. Although the Engmanns have a low profile in society, their clan constitutes a nucleus of the elite class at Osu today. In spite of their royal maternal ancestral connections, they have never been involved in chieftaincy and traditional community leadership. Their known community leadership roles have been church-based and mainly in the Presbyterian Church of Ghana."

With this last statement on Engmann genealogy, Ataa Forkoyi requests two earthenware pots from the ushers serving the funeral guests. His audience is startled, wondering if he is going to throw up into the pots. Probably the long period of talking has made him weary and nauseous. Or does he want to perform some rituals to pacify the ancestors whom he has been talking about? At any rate, the pots are delivered by the young ushers, who are also curious to know what Ataa Forkoyi is going to do with them. He places them side by side on the table next to where he is sitting. He now gets up and, in a philosophical manner, begins to speak.

"You see these two pots? They remind the Stones of the two sisters of Osu-Kinkawe, who side by side, became the commissioned

Figure 20: Engmann Family Tree

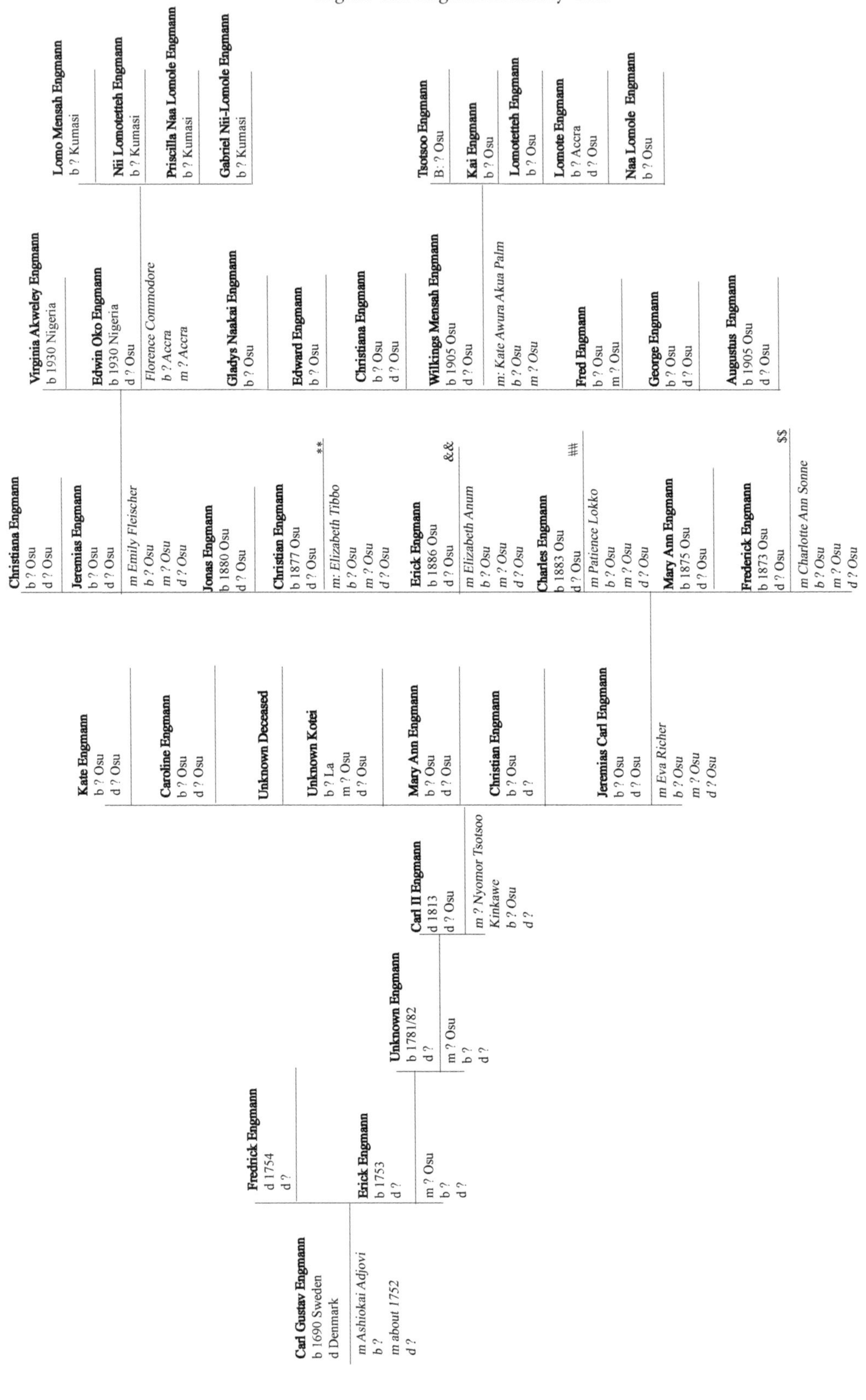

Engmann Family Tree

Carl Gustav Engmann
b 1690 Sweden
d Denmark
m Ashiokai Adjovi
b ?
m about 1752
d ?

Fredrick Engmann
d 1754
d ?

Erick Engmann
b 1753
d ?
m ? Osu
b ?
d ?

Unknown Engmann
b 1781/82
d ?
m ? Osu
b ?
d ?

Carl II Engmann
d 1813
d ? Osu
m ? Nyomor Tsotsoo Kinkawe
b ? Osu
d ?

Children of Carl II Engmann:

Kate Engmann
b ? Osu
d ? Osu

- **Caroline Engmann**
  b ? Osu
  d ? Osu

- **Unknown Deceased**

Unknown Kotei
b ? La
m ? Osu
d ? Osu

- **Mary Ann Engmann**
  b ? Osu
  d ? Osu

- **Christian Engmann**
  b ? Osu
  d ?

Jeremias Carl Engmann
b ? Osu
d ? Osu
m Eva Richer
b ? Osu
m ? Osu
d ? Osu

Children of Jeremias Carl Engmann & Christiana Engmann (b ? Osu, d ? Osu):

Jeremias Engmann
b ? Osu
d ? Osu
m Emily Fleischer

Jonas Engmann
b 1880 Osu
d ? Osu

Christian Engmann
b 1877 Osu
d ? Osu **
m: Elizabeth Tibbo
b ? Osu
m ? Osu
d ? Osu

Erick Engmann
b 1886 Osu
d ? Osu &&
m Elizabeth Anum
b ? Osu
m ? Osu
d ? Osu

Charles Engmann
b 1883 Osu
d ? Osu #
m Patience Lokko
b ? Osu
m ? Osu
d ? Osu

Mary Ann Engmann
b 1875 Osu
d ? Osu

Frederick Engmann
b 1873 Osu
d ? Osu $$
m Charlotte Ann Sonne
b ? Osu
m ? Osu
d ? Osu

Virginia Akweley Engmann
b 1930 Nigeria

Edwin Oko Engmann
b 1930 Nigeria
d ? Osu
- Florence Commodore
  b ? Accra
  m ? Accra

Gladys Naakai Engmann
b ? Osu

Edward Engmann
b ? Osu

Christiana Engmann
b ? Osu
d ? Osu

Wilkings Mensah Engmann
b 1905 Osu
d ? Osu
m: Kate Awura Akua Palm

Fred Engmann
b ? Osu
m ? Osu

George Engmann
b ? Osu
d ? Osu

Augustus Engmann
b 1905 Osu
d ? Osu

Further descendants:

Lomo Mensah Engmann
b ? Kumasi

Nii Lomotettsh Engmann
b ? Kumasi

Priscilla Naa Lomole Engmann
b ? Kumasi

Gabriel Nii-Lomole Engmann
b ? Kumasi

Tsotsoo Engmann
B: ? Osu

Kai Engmann
b ? Osu

Lomotettsh Engmann
b ? Osu

Lomote Engmann
b ? Accra
d ? Osu

Naa Lomole Engmann
b ? Osu

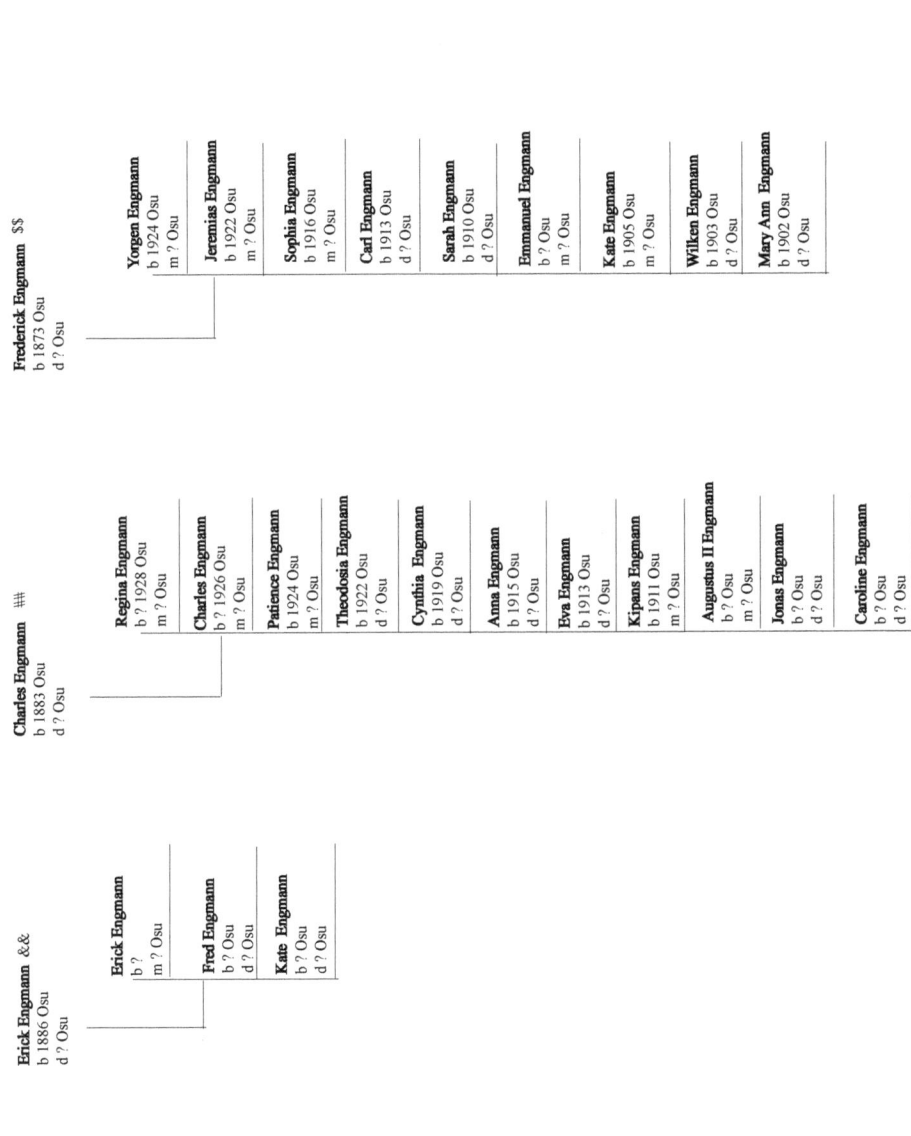

carriers of offspring of Danish men in the eighteenth century." With a naughty smile he continues, "I am talking about the two sisters, Ashiorkor and Ashiokai. They were not twins, but as their names suggest, they were born directly one after another, with 'Kai' coming on the heels of 'Kor.' Together with their senior sister Shormeh, they went through the rigorous traditional puberty rites for young girls, *Otofo*, customarily practiced only at Osu-Kinkawe and Osu-Ashinte. To add to this rite of passage and for the purpose of being given to the Danish sojourners in marriage, they were specially groomed in the court of their prominent father, Ataa Ado Ayi known to the Danish administration as 'Adjovi or Adoui the cabuceer.'

"With his shrewd business acumen, he had extensive and profitable interactions with the Danes and other European traders who came to Danish-Osu. He learned from experience that he would be able to advance his business goals if he could have these sojourners as his in-laws. His first attempt to pursue this strategy proved successful after his first daughter, Shormeh, was given in marriage to a Danish slave merchant called Peter Meyer. This encouraged him to follow suit with his two other daughters. This is how it came about that Ashiorkor, the second daughter, married the Danish administrator and trader, Malm, and Ashiokai, the third born, married the German, Hackenberg, and later, the Swedish/Dane, Gustav Engmann."

When Ataa Forkoyi ends the story of the two earthenware pots, he pulls out from his old bag, a sheet of paper with what appears to be a computer-generated chart on it. He lifts up the chart and points it out to his audience, saying: "This is the family tree of the Malms of Osu. Look carefully, and as you recollect the Engmann's family tree chart, you will see how the two sisters, the two earthenware pots, similarly provided the containers for these Danish-Osu trees to sprout." He runs his thin and ragged-looking forefinger over the chart, stopping here and there to talk about the people whose names appear on it as if they were his intimate friends.

The young architecture student impudently asks:

"Old man, did you live in the eighteenth and nineteenth centuries? I can see from the structure of this chart that the Malm's genealogy goes back to those centuries. Some of the names you are mentioning now, according to the chart, might have lived at Danish-Osu from 1750 to 1850. How can you talk about these people so intimately? Or are you after all the legendary Pedersen Witt come back as has always been rumored at Osu?"

The listeners burst into spontaneous laughter at these questions, laughing all the more as the Rastafarian adds his voice to the barrage of impudent questions: "Hei man! You'd have to be a Jahman or a Shaman or a Conman to know all these people down the centuries as friends!"

Responding to these rather impudent interruptions in his narration, Ataa Forkoyi simply says:

"My friends, I am not Pedersen Witt; I am not a Jahman; I am not a Shaman and I am not a Conman. I rely on the memory of the Stones and they knew the people I am talking about."

Irritated by the interruptions of the student and the Rastafarian, the history teacher shouts in support: "Well said!"

Nonchalantly, Ataa Forkoyi proceeds with the narration. "According to the Stones, a Danish administrator who doubled as a trader, by the name of Johannes Benedict Malm, became interested in Ashiorkor as he used to see her follow Ataa Ado Ayi now and then to Christiansborg to do business. With the approval and support of the Danish governor, A. F. Hackenberg, who had already become Ataa Ado Ayi's son-in-law through his marriage to Ashiokai, a marriage was arranged and Johannes Benedict took Ashiorkor as his lawfully wedded wife.

"Out of this wedlock came the only offspring, a male, given the name 'Abraham,' with the hope that, following the footsteps of his biblical namesake, he would become a father of many nations. So began the sprouting of the Malm family tree at Danish-Osu. Abraham Malm grew up quickly into a young mulatto man, to become part of the soldier community at Christiansborg. Since he had a close relationship with his relatives at Osu-Kinkawe, he always frequented there with his eyes fully open and his ears to the ground. It is thus not surprising, that he one day became attracted to a Danish-Osu mulatto by the name of Anna Bishop whom he married as his first wife. Anna bore Abraham three children, two daughters and a son.

"One of the two daughters, Sarah Malm, got married as a young woman to a Jewish Danish administrator called Wulff Joseph Wulff. Sarah bore Joseph three children adding new shoots to the Wulff family tree, which is well-known and has now attained international fame through its unique early nineteenth century stone family house known as Frederiksminde. The young Wulff, who felt discriminated against by his compatriots because of his religion, built Frederiksminde at Osu Amangfong to provide a home for himself and his family outside the unfriendly Christiansborg."

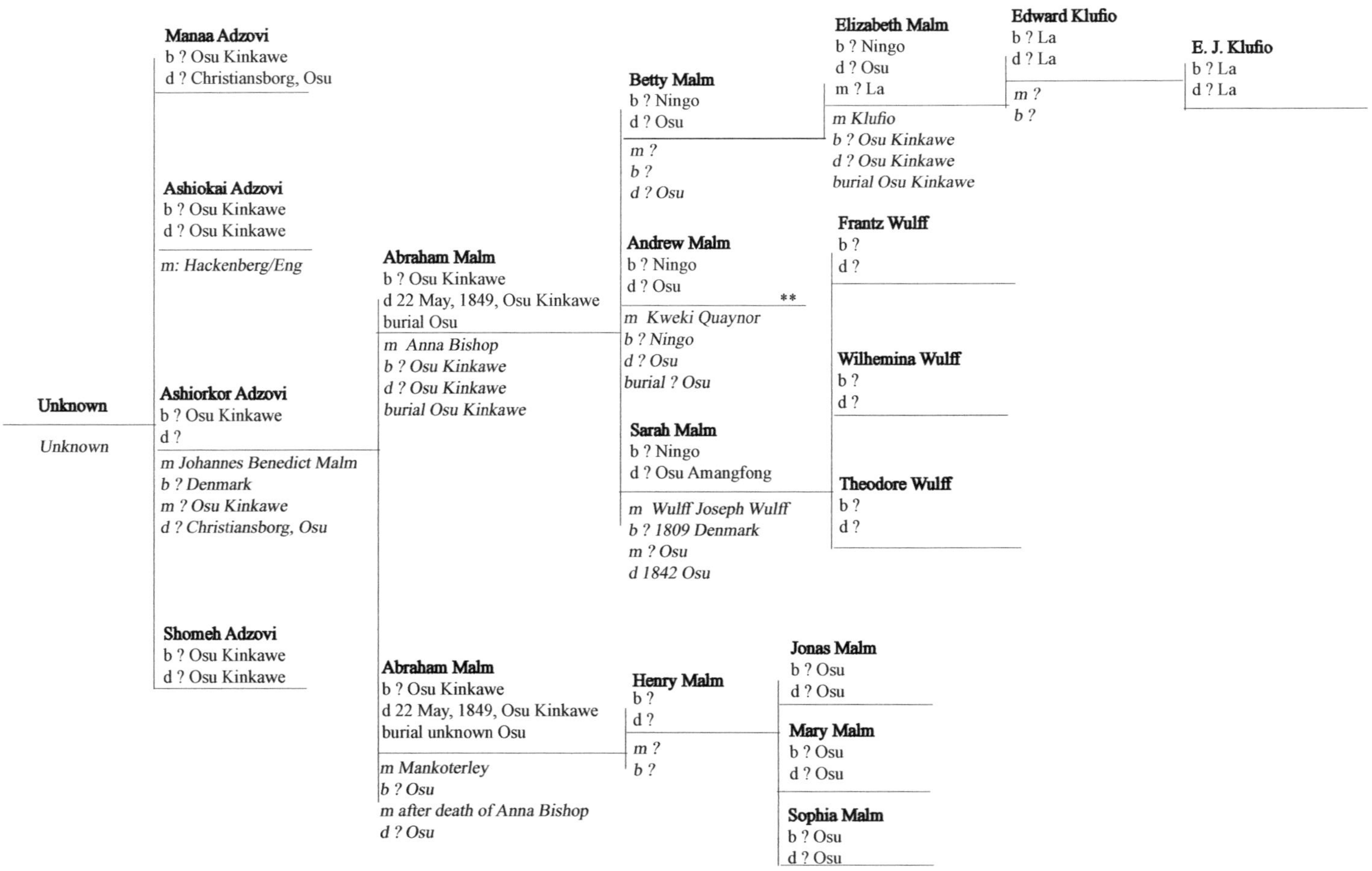

Figure 21: Malm Family Tree

Manaa Adzovi
b ? Osu Kinkawe
d ? Christiansborg, Osu

Ashiokai Adzovi
b ? Osu Kinkawe
d ? Osu Kinkawe
m: Hackenberg/Eng

Unknown

Ashiorkor Adzovi
b ? Osu Kinkawe
d ?

m Johannes Benedict Malm
b ? Denmark
m ? Osu Kinkawe
d ? Christiansborg, Osu

Unknown

Shomeh Adzovi
b ? Osu Kinkawe
d ? Osu Kinkawe

Abraham Malm
b ? Osu Kinkawe
d 22 May, 1849, Osu Kinkawe
burial Osu

m Anna Bishop
b ? Osu Kinkawe
d ? Osu Kinkawe
burial Osu Kinkawe

Abraham Malm
b ? Osu Kinkawe
d 22 May, 1849, Osu Kinkawe
burial unknown Osu

m Mankoterley
b ? Osu
m after death of Anna Bishop
d ? Osu

Betty Malm
b ? Ningo
d ? Osu
m ?
b ?
d ? Osu

Andrew Malm
b ? Ningo
d ? Osu
m Kweki Quaynor **
b ? Ningo
d ? Osu
burial ? Osu

Sarah Malm
b ? Ningo
d ? Osu Amangfong
m Wulff Joseph Wulff
b ? 1809 Denmark
m ? Osu
d 1842 Osu

Henry Malm
b ?
d ?
m ?
b ?

Elizabeth Malm
b ? Ningo
d ? Osu
m ? La
m Klufio
b ? Osu Kinkawe
d ? Osu Kinkawe
burial Osu Kinkawe

Frantz Wulff
b ?
d ?

Wilhemina Wulff
b ?
d ?

Theodore Wulff
b ?
d ?

Jonas Malm
b ? Osu
d ? Osu

Mary Malm
b ? Osu
d ? Osu

Sophia Malm
b ? Osu
d ? Osu

Edward Klufio
b ? La
d ? La
m ?
b ?

E. J. Klufio
b ? La
d ? La

Malm Family Tree

Eva Barbara Malm
b ? Osu
d ? Osu

Cornelius Malm
b ? Ningo
d ? Osu
m Sophia Meyer
b ?
m ? Osu
burial Osu

Andrew Malm
b ? Ningo
d ? Osu **
m Kweki Quaynor
b ? Ningo
d ? Osu
burial ? Osu

Joana Zonia Malm
b ? Osu
d ? Osu

Elizabeth Virginia Malm
b ? Osu
d ? Osu

Diana Malm
b ? Osu
d ? Osu

Sarah Malm
b ? Osu
d ? Osu

Henry Herbert Malm
m Lily Kuorkor Dzani
b ?
d ?

m Beatrice Adubea Okantey-Ayettey
b ? Osu
d ? Osu

m Eva Vida Narki Quaynor
b ? Osu
d ? Osu

m Felicia Kutorkor Kotey
b ? Osu
d ? Osu

m Esther Nkulenu
b ? Peki Blengo
m ? Osu Kinkawe
d ? Osu

m Catherine Nmai Lomotey
b ? Osu
d ? Osu

Riemer Malm
b ?
m ? Osu
b ? Osu

Richard Otto Malm
b ? Osu
d ? Osu

Jonas Malm
b ? Osu
d ? Osu

Andrews Malm
b ? Osu
d ? Osu

Sarah Malm
b ? Osu
d ? Osu
mother Lily

Cornelius Andrews Malm
b ? Osu
d ?
mother Beatrice

William Malm
b ? Osu
d ? Osu
mother Eva

Sophia Malm
b 1944 Osu
d ?
mother Felicia

Vincent Malm
b 1946 Osu
d ?
mother Esther

Meyer Malm
b ? Osu
d ?
mother Catherine

Henry Herbert Papa Nii Malm
b ? Osu

Esther Kweiki Malm
b ? Osu

Kweikor Malm
b ? Osu

The human rights activist, excited by what he hears about Wulff Joseph Wulff suddenly exclaims:

"Wow! This means the Malm's family tree has roots in positive defiance against discrimination."

The Rastafarian raises his clenched right fist and shouts, "Right on, brother, I hear you."

After these interesting and amusing interruptions, Ataa Forkoyi continues with the narration. "Out of the blue, soon after the birth of his third-born, Abraham became a young widower with the sudden death of Anna. However, being reminded that he would be a 'father of many nations,' he decided to marry again.

"Probably with the counsel of his old mother and the assistance of his maternal relatives, he found an indigenous Osu-Kinkawe woman called Mankoteley who was prepared to mother his poor boys and entered into a customary marital relationship with her. This union produced a male offspring to be the first to receive the name Henry, which repeated itself as a first or middle name in ensuing generations of Malms at Osu.

"While Johannes Benedict's descendants were beginning to be established at Danish-Osu, a brother of his, Andreas Malm, who came together with him, had been posted to the Danish Fort Prinsensten at Keta as a sergeant of the Danish fort guard, and while there, had married an Anglo princess, settled, and never came back to Danish-Osu. The Malms of Keta and Togo sprouted from this branch of the Malm family tree that was drawn to Fort Prinsensten.

"Another Malm that went beyond the family space of Danish-Osu to extend the growth of the Malm family tree was the son of Abraham Malm and Anna Bishop. This son, Andrew Malm, brother to Sarah and Betty Malm, was sent to the Danish Fort Fredensborg at Ningo as a mulatto soldier of the Danish administration. While there he became attracted to an Adangme royal by the name of Kweiki Quaynor. From this union came a male offspring who was given the name Cornelius, similar to the name of the pious Roman general from the Book of Acts in the Bible. Cornelius, who married a distant cousin of his, by the name of Sophia Meyer, was prolific in procreation. Through his four sons and five daughters he contributed immensely to enlarge the stem of the Malm family tree. Most of the known branches of the Malm extended family today trace their roots to this prolific forebear."

As Ataa Forkoyi continues to speak, many of the funeral guests, hearing him, have become interested and have taken seats all around him and his audience to join in listening. One of these guests, who has drunk a lot of beer, suddenly exclaims: "Ataa Nii, you must have some drink. You cannot tell this story about the ancestors with a dry throat. Sommmebody, give the old man beeeer!"

Unperturbed, Ataa Forkoyi smiles and says: "My son, thank you. I drink only water and fruit juice." Somebody then offers him a sachet of water. He takes a sip to lubricate his throat and continues with his narration.

"The Malms are well known at Osu as well as Abokobi, where they have an old family house." As he mentions "Abokobi," one of the listeners who is not familiar with the history of Osu raises his hand and politely asks Ataa Forkoyi where Abokobi is located. He goes on to request an explanation as to how the Malms came to be connected to the place. Most of the old listeners are now familiar with the name of this historic town so they begin to murmur at the questioner since they find his question an unnecessary interruption in the narration.

Ataa Forkoyi clears his throat and compliantly begins his explanation. "My friend, your questions are valid and in fact useful in telling the story of the family tree of the Malms. So this is a welcome interruption. You see, historically, Abokobi is closely linked together with Osu. There are many Osu families, especially at Osu-Kinkawe and Osu-Ashinte, who have strong family ties at Abokobi. It all goes back to 1854, when Danish-Osu was mercilessly bombarded because of the people's refusal to cooperate with the newly-arrived British colonial administration. As the town reeled under the power of the cannons, the people deserted their ancestral homes and some ran northwards to seek refuge in the farming communities in the Accra plains. Eventually many, together with the Basel missionaries who were also affected by the bombardment, settled at Abokobi, which for some time functioned as the headquarters of the Basel missionaries. As a result, many Danish-Osu families who connected with the mission made Abokobi their home.

"The Malms, who had been involved in the work of the mission, also joined the exodus to Abokobi. That is how the Malm family house there came into existence. This relocation of some of the Malms from Danish-Osu to Abokobi was spearheaded by the prolific Cornelius Malm. He had become a well-groomed agent of the mission after being trained as a teacher and a catechist. After a trip to Nigeria for exploratory mission work, he returned home to teach at the famous Osu Salem Boys' Boarding School. Later he was promoted to head the pioneering work at the Abokobi Salem Boys' Boarding School.

"Among his nine pupils were Richard Otto and Henry Herbert, who both later joined the British colonial administration. Richard Otto, inspired by his father's excellent results in organizing farming activities for pupils of the Abokobi Salem Boarding School, took to agriculture and spearheaded a number of successful agricultural projects in rural communities in the Eastern region of the Gold Coast. This famous agricultural officer fathered the female progenitor of the Quist family of Osu 'Yellow Store.'"

Ataa Forkoyi now makes a dramatic pause. As his listeners wait for him to continue, they realize that he has shut his eyes and bowed his head. Seeing him in this state, the tipsy funeral guest again shouts, "Beeer! The old man neeeds beeer!"

Hearing this, Ataa Forkoyi suddenly raises his head and, opening his eyes, turns to the drunken guest and reprimands him, saying: "Naughty boy. Who tells you I need beer? The Stones are speaking and I must listen to them attentively and that is the reason why I close my eyes and bow my head. Don't disturb me again, otherwise you will have to go back to the funeral grounds to drink more of your beer."

The lady with the Danish ancestry then addresses Ataa Forkoyi: "Please, don't mind that man. Sorry for the interruption. By the way, what happened to Henry Herbert Malm? Did he also become an agricultural officer in the colonial civil service like his brother Richard Otto?"

"No. He did not." Ataa Forkoyi responds, "Henry Herbert became a civil servant and as a result of the excellent administrative skills and disciplined way of life which he acquired from his teacher-catechist father, he was able to progress quickly in the civil service to be promoted to the ultimate stature of the first African Assistant Colonial Secretary of the Gold Coast. In his capacity as the first African Clerk of the Gold Coast, he made a tremendous contribution, laying a solid foundation for the civil service of the Gold Coast that became the envy of the other African countries in the British Empire.

"Similarly to some of his forebears, he had his own impressive office space in Christiansborg and because of his status as Assistant Colonial Secretary, he functioned as a Deputy Governor from 1930 to 1946. In recognition of his meritorious work in the British administration, he was accorded the title 'Member of the British Empire' (MBE), which he received in 1935 from King George VI of England. On ceremonial occasions, when the people of the Gold Coast were celebrating important events such as Empire Day, one could see Henry Herbert dressed up in his official regalia as the Colonial Secretary. It was a sight to behold as he walked elegantly in his all-white uniform with his sword of honour strapped to his waist and hanging from his left hip, with his white, ostrich-feathered helmet to match, in the company of the other British colonial officers."

Figure 22 : Portrait of H. H. Malm (MBE/OBE)
Courtesy of author

Now, Ataa Forkoyi pulls out of his bag an old picture, which he shows to his audience and says: "This is a portrait of Henry Herbert in his colonial uniform. The picture was taken when he had returned home from an official function. Because of the heat of the day, he took off his feathered helmet, which is why it is not in the picture; the hilt of his sword of honour can, however, be seen under his left arm. If you have time to visit the National Museum, you may see colonial feathered helmets on display."

"I must say that although H. H. Malm (MBE/OBE), as he came to be popularly known, rose to a high office in the colonial administration, he was never cut off from his roots as an indigenous Osu citizen. He became a role model in the Osu society and opened his English manor-like house to the community, inviting both young and old to tea parties and to play tennis and croquet in his home."

The young architecture student, who has been reading about typical English lawn games back at the university, interjects: "Aha! H. H. was really *'colo!'*"

Angered by this curious expression, Ataa Forkoyi turns towards the student and asks: "My friend, and what is this commotion supposed to mean?"

In typical student style, he jokingly apologises for the interruption but goes on to say: "But Ataa Forkoyi, if my friends back at the university hear about these recreational hobbies of Mr. H. H. Malm, they will say the man was really aping his colonial masters as Kobina Sekyi criticized in his play *The Blinkards*. This is what I mean by saying that he was *'colo paa.'* He really adopted the British lifestyle."

Now, with a relaxed face, Ataa Forkoyi apparently speaking to himself says: "These young people are sharp. In fact, according to the Stones, H. H. Malm became a perfect British gentleman. He even moved away from his father's Basel Mission background to become an Anglican in order to attend Sunday church services with his British colonial fellow administrators at the Osu St. Barnabas Church of England, and now and then, appeared in their company at the prestigious Holy Trinity Cathedral. Hmmm ..."

He awakens from his soliloquy and continues the story: "However, the Stones recollect that he was very much an African at heart. Henry Herbert certainly stood tall among the Malms but he was not the only one who added fame to his family tree. The achievements of the Malms also came through descendants of female progenitors whose family names were eclipsed by the names of the men they married, such as H. H. Malm's paternal grandaunt,

Sarah Wulff.

"For example, a branch of the family from the progenitor Betty Malm later became the 'Klufio' family of La. This family produced the outstanding scholar and educationist/novelist Rev. Enoch Joseph Klufio, who became the headmaster of the Presbyterian Secondary School at Krobo Odumase from 1948 to 1966. In addition to an important historic drama entitled *Odoi Din, Legon Mantse,* he wrote a Gã classic, called *Adote Shelenkome,* which is still of great interest to Gã literary scholars today.

"There was also the elitist Wuta-Offei family of Osu, which descended maternally from Eva Barbara, another offspring of Cornelius Malm. The Wuta-Offei family produced a prominent Ghanaian journalist by the name of Robert Benjamin Wuta-Offei. He was a successful journalist who functioned as one of the vanguards of the pre-independence political struggle against British colonialism in the Gold Coast. He was the editor of the Spectator Daily, and the famous Africanist percussionist Kofi Ghanaba (Warren Gamaliel Kpakpo Akwei, a.k.a Guy Warren), then a young and budding musician, worked under his editorship in 1943 as a reporter.

"R. B. Wuta-Offei was one of the West African intellectuals and political stalwarts, similar to Kobina Sekyi, Awoonor Renner, I. T. A. Wallace-Johnson, George J. Perigino-Peters, A. J. Ocansey and others, who created a conducive milieu for the freedom movement. As a mark of his successful journalism practice, he built the imposing palatial residence along the Osu-Cantonments Road, which has come to be known as 'Koala House,' the popular supermarket. The Malm name still appears often in society, especially that of young Henry Herbert Malm. He is one of the sixth generation members of the family tree and being an ace newsreader, his face appears almost daily on one of the national television stations in Accra."

As Ataa Forkoyi makes this last statement, he plunges his right hand into his bag and pulls out yet another chart with a family tree. When the lady with Danish ancestry realizes that he wants to move on to another genealogy, she courteously asks him to hold on and inquires: "Excuse me, Ataa Nii; is it true that the famous lady industrialist who set up the Nkulenu Food Industry at Osu was a Malm by birth?"

He shakes his head vigorously and says impatiently, "No, no. This is why I asked you earlier to have a close look at the Malms' Family Tree chart. Dr. Esther Ocloo's name certainly shows up; not as a consanguine but through matrimony. The late Esther Ocloo of Peki Dzake, born as Nkulenu, sojourned at Osu. As a young lady having completed her formal education at the prestigious Achimota School, she met Henry Herbert in the forties and had a son with him. Vincent Malm, he is called, and he is a prominent industrialist today, with partners in the financial metropolises of the world. Esther achieved fame through her own efforts but her business foundation was supported by Henry Herbert's influential connections to the colonial administration, which provided the milieu to nurture her successful drink enterprise. Let me add for your inquisitive interest, that Esther by the way, was one among a large group of other charming ladies who bore the offspring of Henry Herbert.

"With this, Madam, I think I have clarified the picture of the Malms' Family Tree, and can show you the next family tree chart and it is that of the Briandt family of Osu-Ashinte Blohum. This Danish-Osu family tree traces its roots as far back as the early eighteenth century, but it almost got metamorphosed in structure due to incorrect spelling of the name of the Danish progenitor and inadequate information on the original union of the two progenitors available to the Stones.

"Ambiorn Christensen Brandt, the Danish progenitor, arrived at Christiansborg with his Danish wife around 1715, about the time Frantz Boye was the governor at Christiansborg and Christian Africanus Protten was born at Danish-Osu. According to the Stones, Brandt, who had come from a worthy Danish merchant family, came to the Guinea coast with the single ambition to extend the traditional family trading activities to exotic goods such as ivory and gold.

"Since he did not want to be involved in the Danish slave-trading business, he chose to live with his wife outside Christiansborg and found a home in Kinka, Dutch Accra. As fate would have it, Ambiorn Christensen lost his Danish wife to what was then known as 'climate fever.' Undeterred by this great loss, he decided that he would continue with his trading business in ivory and gold. But he realized that the only way he could make headway with his resolve to trade on the coast was to do what his Danish compatriots had been doing at Christiansborg. He had to marry a native woman.

"Although he frequented Christiansborg to fraternize with his compatriots, he never really had any strong social contacts in Danish-Osu, so when he had to take a wife, he looked for a Kinka woman. It was a mulatto woman from Asere in Gã-Mashie with the name Tsua Tsuru. Before Christensen Brandt passed away around

1723, he had fathered two mulatto sons with Naa Tsua. The names given to these boys were Christian and Frederick. After the death of Brandt, Naa Tsua decided to move to Danish-Osu to be closer to the Christiansborg Danish community, to take advantage of the Mulatto Fund which was in the process of being established by the Danish administration to take care of needy mulattoes and orphans."

As Ataa Forkoyi talks about the Mulatto Fund, the human rights activist is stimulated to wonder how the Briandt name changed from Brandt, if they had a known Danish progenitor. He finally stops Ataa Forkoyi for an explanation. He asks, "Ambiorn Christensen Brandt originated from a well-known Danish family with the surname spelled as *Brandt*. If that was the case, I am puzzled to notice that the family tree chart you just showed us, has the name written with an 'i' inserted between 'r' and 'a.' Why is it so?"

Ataa Forkoyi is amused and turns to the human rights activist, smiling: "So, as a human rights activist, you are not only concerned about human rights abuse, but also about name rights abuse. Is that right?" The audience appreciates his pun and breaks into a loud laugh. When the laughter is over, he assumes a serious posture and goes into his pedagogic mode. "You see how time and tongue collaborated to abuse the integrity of some of the Danish names that appeared in the local community at Danish-Osu, eh? 'Lykke' became 'Lokko' and 'Bagge' became 'Badger' and 'Svanekjaer' became 'Swaniker.' In the case of the Briandts, this is what might have happened or could have happened to make 'Brandt' become 'Briandt.'

"By custom, the Gã people have a deep veneration for the memory of their forebears. It manifests itself in their practice of calling upon the ancestors by name as they pour libation in prayer to God. As a result, no Gã will ever speak the name of an ancestor without adding the respectful prefix *'Nii'* for male forebears and *'Naa'* for female forebears. In the course of time, to conform to this customary practice, the name of the Danish progenitor had to be accompanied with the traditional prefix any time his memory was invoked. But, somehow, the Gã tongue could not bring the name 'Brandt' together with the prefix 'Nii,' without it coming out as 'Nii Briandt' instead of 'Nii Brandt.' So, the repetition of 'Nii Briandt' in libation pouring led eventually to the transcription of Briandt as the family's surname. The Stones have no documentation of when this transition occurred but they are aware of family documents going back to the mid-nineteenth century that bear the name 'Briandt.'

Before Ataa Forkoyi makes his next statement, he hears a voice from one of the Stones nearby telling him that the corruption of the Briandt name came from a sloppy Castle School teacher's miswriting of the original name 'Brandt' into the school's register of names of pupils. That English-speaking teacher inserted the letter 'i' in between the letters 'r' and 'a' as he wrote down the surname of his notable bright pupil. He ponders this information from the Stone but does not pass it on to his audience. Instead, he goes on with his narration and says: "Having given you an account of the name change of the Briandts, let me now go on to explain how the stem of the family tree was formed. As I began to tell you, the Danish progenitor, Ambiorn Christensen Brandt, married Naa Tsua Tsuru of Asere. The union was blessed with two sons, Christian and Frederick. Naa Tsua made Danish-Osu her home where she raised her two sons. Although they never forgot their Gã-Mashie connections, the two mulatto boys settled at Danish-Osu while they found work at Christiansborg as soldiers of the Danish administration.

"Frederick married a local Osu woman who bore him a single mulatto daughter, named Merya Briandt. Merya married an Osu native with whom she had three sons and a daughter. One of her sons by name Kojo Wolenyo, distinguished himself as a successful fisherman. Her daughter, called Fofoi, bore a daughter and a son called Armah who became an accomplished local goldsmith. In terms of enlarging the stem of the Briandt's family tree, it was the other son of the Danish progenitor, the forebear Christian, who did that yeoman's job. Christian married a woman from the La Abese community, by the name of Odoley Odjono, a royal. Together, they brought twelve children into the world, including two sets of male and female twins. The most senior of the children, Juliana Emma Dede Briandt, later married a Gã-Mashie up-and-coming gentleman by the name Brown, creating the branch that sprouted the Brown family at Osu.

"The male twin, William Douglass Akwetey Briandt, enlisted as a soldier in the Danish administration at the time of Governor Frederick Siegfried Mock at Christiansborg. He took part in many of the campaigns the Danes undertook during their time on the Guinea coast between 1835 and 1850. By virtue of his experience and bravery, the Osu-Ashinte-Blohum community took him as their warlord, thus giving the Briandts the honour to assume the traditional title of Sei Asafoatse, Flagbearer of Ashinte Blohum.

Privileged with frequent twin births, the Briandt family expanded rapidly into a prominent patrilineal clan that occupied large sections of Danish-Osu before it was bombarded by the British.

"In the rebuilding of Danish-Osu after the bombardment, the Briandts saw the need to symbolize the continuous presence of their clan in the community. Therefore, the eldest male of the twelve children of Christian and Naa Odoley, also known as Nii Yull, led his siblings to acquire a piece of land from the Richters, which was located at Osu Blogodo, to put up a new family house. To this was later added the first-ever two-storey stone house in the style of the new Basel Mission domestic architecture in 1859."

When the architecture student hears about the Briandt family house at Blogodo, he makes a mental note to go and visit the building to study its architectural character and detail. To make it easy for him to locate the building, he respectfully asks Ataa Forkoyi for directions to the house.

"I am sure you are curious to find out if this nineteenth century stone house is still standing," he says as he hears that the student wants to see the Briandt house. "But let me tell you this before you go on your architectural expedition," he continues with a tone of admonition. "The Briandt family-house annex, which was crafted into a two-storey structure next to the original adjacent single storey compound house, made provision for the traditional male and female quarters, whereby the males occupied the two storey unit and the females occupied the single storey compound unit. The two-storey structure had two distinct parts.

"The ground floor, intended for commercial purposes, was built in the Old Danish building style; massive stone-masonry walls bonded in lime and sand mixture. Above the ground floor is located the residential unit constructed in a lightweight wood-framed structure, with split travelers-palm stems to hold the floor slab on which are placed hardwood planks. Over and above the rooms is a flat roof of treated mud on wooden boards. But you know, sadly, due to family feuds and rivalry over ownership, this magnificent building has fallen into a bad state of disrepair. You should certainly go and see it and find out how it can be preserved.

"It is a great shame that it has been neglected for so long. This house, for several years, as intended by Nii Yull, served as the symbolic patrilineal home of the Briandts, male and female. A number of important family events took place here. The Stones remember that in this home, Mercy Briandt, granddaughter of Rev. Adolf Briandt, tragically lost her life in childbirth, leaving her only

Figure 23: Briandt Family Tree

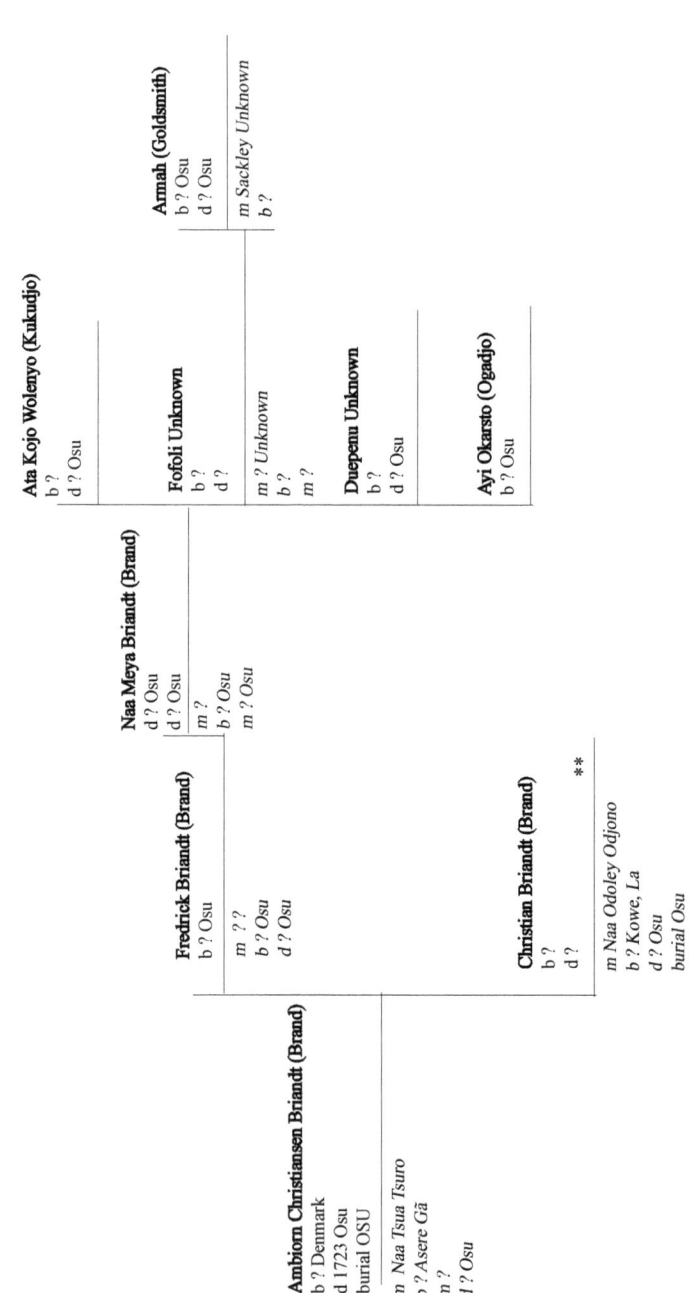

Christian Briandt (Brand)
b ?
d ?

m Naa Odoley Odjono
b ? Kowe, La
d ? Osu
burial Osu

**

Children:

- **A. Hannah Briandt (Brand)**
  b ? Osu
  d ? Osu

- **Patience Briandt (Brand)**
  b ? Osu
  d ? Osu

- **Akweley Aklu Briandt (Brand)**
  b ? Osu
  d ? Osu

- **Evelina Briandt (Brand)**
  b ? Osu
  d ? Osu

- **Dede Bow Briandt (Brand)**
  b ? Osu
  d ? Accra

- **Edgar Christian (Owula Bedu) Briandt (Brand)**
  b ? Osu

- **Francis Briandt (Brand)**
  b ? Osu
  d ? Osu

- **Williams Douglas (Akweley Blofonyo) Sergeant Briandt (Brand)**
  b 1835 Osu
  d 1858, Teshie House
  burial Osu

  m ?
  b ? Osu
  m ? Osu

  - **Victor Ago's father Briandt (Brand)**
    b ? Osu
    d ?
    m ?
    b ?
    m ? Osu
    - **Victor Ago Briandt (Brand)**
      b ? Osu

- **Adolf Briandt (Brand) - Reverend**
  b ? Osu
  d ? Osu
  burial Osu

  m ?
  b ? Osu
  m ? Osu

  - **Unknown Briandt (Brand) Reverend (Grandfather)**
    b ? Osu
    d ? Osu
    m ?
    b ?
    m ? Osu
    - **Emmanuel Christian Briandt (Brand) (Black Stars Captain)**
      b ? Osu

- **Julius Ceasar (Nii Yull) Briandt (Brand)**
  b ? Osu
  d ? Osu

  m ?
  m ? Osu

child Vivian as an orphan. By divine intervention, this orphan child survived in the care of her grandfather to become the mother of Cynthia Quaynor (Mrs. Martey), the current queen-mother of the Osu-Alata traditional quarter."

"Now, going back to the family tree, let me draw your attention to the fact that besides Nii Yull the builder and William Douglass the soldier, another of the twelve children whose name comes up prominently in the Briandt genealogy and Danish-Osu history, is the aforementioned Reverend Adolf Briandt. As a young man, Adolf became strongly attracted to the Christian faith upon the arrival of the Basel Mission at Danish-Osu. Through the teachings of the missionaries, he experienced a personal conversion as he accepted Jesus Christ as his personal Lord and Savior. Consequently, he got himself baptized to nullify the earlier christening ceremony he had been through when he attended the Castle School at Christiansborg. His life of piety and reflection eventually got him involved in the work of the mission, which later ordained him a Reverend Minister of the Basel Mission Church. His legacy to the Church includes the Ghana Presbyterian Church Hymn 192, which he composed and wrote the Gã lyrics for in 1856.

"About a century after his significant and creative work for the church, his great grandson, Emmanuel Christian Briandt, also became an outstanding personality. Emmanuel Christian, popularly known as E. C., displayed great intelligence and dexterity in football to be accorded the honour of captaining the first-ever gallant national football team, the Black Stars. In the immediate post-independence era, when many African countries did not even have national football teams, Captain E. C. Briandt was able to lead the Black Stars to popularize the Ghana colours, as the team successfully toured Britain, the historic home of football, while playing with their bare feet.

"The commercial, entrepreneurial spirit that brought the Danish progenitor to the Guinea coast has run through the branches of the Briandt family. Frederich Richard Briandt who descended from one of the twelve forebears, successfully worked with the famous British cocoa brokers and commercial houses, Messrs Cadbury and Fry and John Holt. These companies pioneered the buying and exporting of cocoa beans from the Eastern Region, where the eldest son of Richard Briandt, Victor Ago Briandt, the current head of the Briandt clan, grew up to become an astute business man. Under the wise leadership of Ago Briandt, the Briandts of Osu-Ashinte have played their role as traditional community leaders quietly, acting as a unifying and pacifying force in the unhappy chieftaincy affairs of Osu-Kinkawe and Osu-Ashinte-Blohum."

When Ataa Forkoyi is about to move on with his narration, the intoxicated funeral guest interrupts with a question. "Nuumoe, I love the story of the Briandts and their historic involvement in Ghanaian soccer. Are some Briandts playing today in Ghana or have they migrated to Denmark to play in the big European leagues?"

Latter-Day Graftings

He hears the question but ignores it, and instead, with closed eyes, embarks on an account of latter-day graftings. "According to the Stones, towards the end of the eighteenth century, the shifting of the grafting to families with second and third generations of mulattoes was intensified as the mulattoes began to intermarry and the sojourning Danes became more interested in mulatto women as partners in marriage and business. That is how it happened that a mulatto woman such as Lene Kuehberg became a prominent forbear of the Richter family."

As soon as the history teacher hears this statement she interjects excitedly with the question: "And Ataa Forkoyi, who was Lene Kuehberg?"

With a smile on his wrinkled face, he answers the lady's question in his characteristic pedagogic style: "According to the Stones, this woman was born at Danish-Osu around the early part of the eighteenth century, of African and Danish parentage. She happened to have been a contemporary of Christian Jacob Africanus Protten and she sat in the same classroom with him in the Fort School at Christiansborg. In the course of time, this woman developed her remarkable skills and competence in the local trade and became a force to reckon with as a trader. The clout she obtained from trading gave her much influence on both the social and political affairs of the Christiansborg community.

"In addition, her regular involvement with the Danes made her more often than not a mistress of one or two different Danish sojourners. Later, as an influential widow with business suaveness, she attracted the attention of a Danish officer by the name of Frantz Kuehberg, who decided to marry her in 1757 to promote his business interests. Kuehberg, who arrived on the Guinea Coast as a surgeon, later rose to the position of interim Governor of Christiansborg. He fathered Anna-Barbara.

"Lene Kuehberg became a notable ancestor of the Richter genealogy because the daughter she had with Frantz Kuehberg grew up to marry the Danish trader and administrator, Johan Emmanuel Richter, around 1780. The Richter family tree by and large, bears resemblance to that of the Lutterodts, Brocks, Svanikiers, Heins, Hesses, Fleischers, Hansens, Quists, Schandorfs, Wulffs, and other similar ones whose Danish progenitors were the latter-day sojourners at Danish-Osu.

"Now, before lowering the curtain on today's narrations, I will show you what one of the family trees of the latter-day grafting looks like." With that, Ataa Forkoyi plunges his right hand into his bag and carefully pulls out a computer print-out showing an elaborate chart with the heading, "Lene Kuehberg's descendants." He asks one of his listeners to help him spread it out for viewing and as they do so he explains that it is the family tree of the Richters.

Looking weary from talking almost the whole day, Ataa Forkoyi begins with the Richters' genealogy first by following the upper part of the chart with his right index finger, as he gingerly traces the outline of the family tree. As he does this, he turns to his audience and asks with a twinkle in his tired eyes: "Do you see the mango tree's taproot and the palm tree's adventitious roots?"

The impertinent architecture student quickly responds, "Ataa Forkoyi, we can't see what you are seeing."

In his characteristic style, Ataa Forkoyi pedantically begins to explain what he meant by his question. "Trees as we know them have different parts as I have already mentioned while speaking metaphorically about the family tree. A tree basically has roots, a trunk, branches, leaves and flowers. Is that right?" He asks the rhetorical question and continues: "Roots of trees appear in different forms and they are rather complex in nature. Basically, there are two different root systems: there is the taproot system and there is the fibrous-root system, usually referred to scientifically as the 'adventitious root system.'

"The taproot system has at its core, besides other minor root offshoots, a single root that is an enlarged, straight tapering section of the stem or trunk that grows verticularly far down from the base of the tree to anchor it. However, the adventitious root system is characterized by several, moderately-sized branching root offshoots, growing down not far from the base of the stem in similar sizes. The mango tree with its delicious yellowish fruit has a taproot system and the palm tree, which produces the sweet sap that can be made into intoxicating palm wine, has a fibrous-root system."

After this laborious description of the two root systems, Ataa Forkoyi goes back to the chart and, with his index finger, circles the Richters' progenitors, Johan Emmanuel Richter and Anna Barbara Richter, saying, "This is the taproot of the Richter family tree." He then encircles the cluster of forebears located on the upper right hand side of the chart, with names such as Akua Basua, Asante Slave woman, Kasky, Henrich Richter, Wilhelmine Nicholine Hein, Christian Richter, Robert Richter, Johan Emmanuel Richter II, Mulatto woman, Henrich Richter II, Robert Wilhelm Richter, and declares: "These are the adventitious roots of the Richter Family tree." Then he turns to the architecture student and poses the question to him: "My friend, do you now see what I see in the Richter family tree?"

Without waiting for the student to respond, the Rastafarian shouts out: "Man, for Jah's sake, your metaphors are fantastic, flummoxed and flabbergasted!"

Once again, the audience bursts out laughing. While the laughter goes on, he seizes the opportunity to drink some water and then continues with the narration when it has died down.

"Do you know why the Richter family tree is characterized by the two different root systems?" Not expecting any answer, he proceeds to explain this phenomenon. "By the time Johan Emmanuel Richter arrived at Christiansborg around 1782, the famous Lene Kuehberg had passed away thirteen years earlier. However, in the Christiansborg community to which Richter came as an assistant in the Danish administration, the name of Lene and those of her daughters, with the business acumen they inherited from their late mother, were always the subject of conversation and gossip. So when Johan Emmanuel decided to settle and do business in addition to his work as an administrator, he quickly struck up an acquaintance with Anna Barbara Kuehberg. He knew that his marriage to her would further his business ambitions. They were married some three years after his arrival on the Guinea Coast and their son Henrich was born on August 30, 1785. Johan Emmanuel Richter and Barbara Kuehberg thereby became the progenitors of the Richters of Danish-Osu. This was how the taproot of the Richter family tree was formed.

"According to the Stones, Johan, who became deeply involved in the local Danish trade in gold, ivory and especially slaves, moved around a lot between the western coast and the eastern coast to carry out business. From Fanteland, he brought a company of

Figure 24: Richter Family Tree

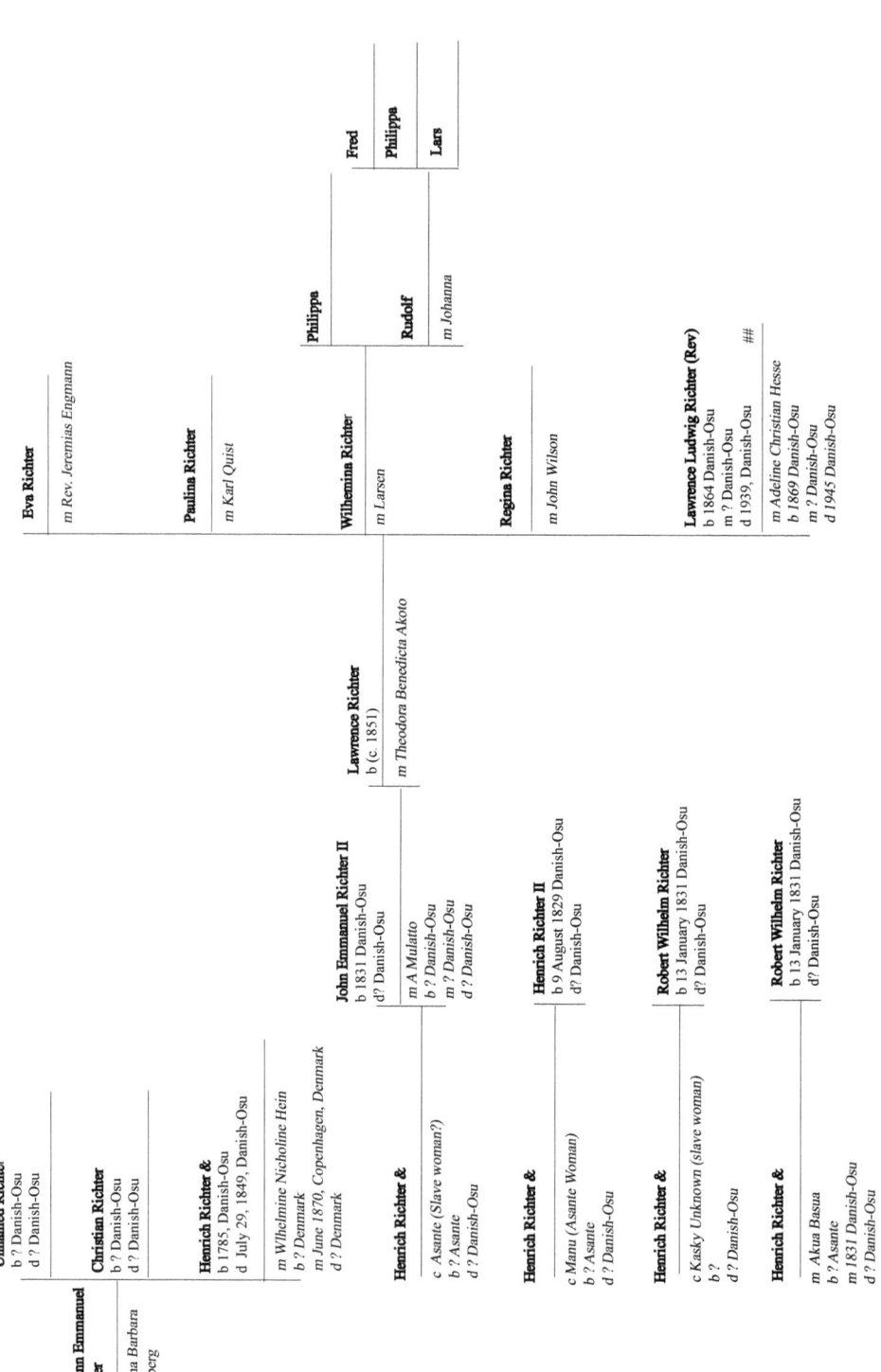

Richter Family Tree

Lawrence Ludwig Richter (Reverend)
b 1864 Danish-Osu
d 1939, Danish-Osu
m Adeline Christian Hesse
b 1869 Danish-Osu
m ? Danish-Osu
d 1945 Danish-Osu

Children of Lawrence Ludwig Richter and Eva Richter (b ? Danish-Osu):

Gilbert Richter
b ? Danish-Osu
d ? Danish-Osu
m Gladys
b ?

Vincent Richter
b ? Danish-Osu
d ? Danish-Osu
m Sophia
b ? France

- **Johann Richter** b ? Danish-Osu, d ? Danish-Osu
  - Benedicta Richter
  - **Julius Richter** b ? Danish-Osu, d ? Danish-Osu
  - **Christian Richter** b ? Danish-Osu, d ? Danish-Osu

Regina Richter
b ? Danish-Osu
- **Henry Richter** b ? Danish-Osu

Rev. Philip Christian Richter
b ? 1903 Danish-Osu
d ? 1977 Danish-Osu
m Jessie Trounischek
b ? Danish-Osu
m ? Danish-Osu
d ? Danish-Osu

Children:
- **Lawrence Richter** b ? Danish-Osu, d ? Danish-Osu
- **Vincent Richter** b ? Danish-Osu, d ? Danish-Osu
- **Wilhemina Richter** b ? Danish-Osu, d ? Danish-Osu
- **Ernest Richter** b ? Danish-Osu, d ? Danish-Osu
  - **Edward Adjei Mensah Johnson** b ? Danish-Osu, d ? Osu
    - Peter
    - **Anyeley Johnson** b ? Danish-Osu, d ?
  - **Catherine (Kate) Johnson** b ? Danish-Osu, d ? Osu
    - **George Lawrence Richter Johnson** b ? Danish-Osu, d ? Osu

William Richter
b ? Danish-Osu
d ? Danish-Osu
m Adeline Swaniker
b ? Danish-Osu
d ? Danish-Osu

Eva Richter
b ? Danish-Osu
d ? Danish-Osu
m John Peter Johnson
b ? Danish-Osu
m ? Danish-Osu
d ? Danish-Osu

Continue ▼

Continue

Ernest Richter
b ? Danish-Osu
d ? Danish-Osu

Henry Richter
b ? Danish-Osu
d ? Danish-Osu
m Clara Steiner
b ? Danish-Osu
m ? Danish-Osu
d ? Danish-Osu

Lawrencia Richter (Reverend)
b ? Danish-Osu
d ? Danish-Osu
m A. Clarke
b ? Danish-Osu
m ? Danish-Osu
d ? Danish-Osu

Ludwig Lawrence Richter II *
b ? Danish-Osu
d ? Danish-Osu
m Mary Coleman
b ? Danish-Osu
m ? Danish-Osu
d ? Danish-Osu

Ludwig Lawrence Richter II *
m Unknown

Descendants (right column):

- **Ernest Richter** b 1951 Danish-Osu
- **Gilbert Richter** b 1949 Danish-Osu
- **Mary Richter** b 1946 Danish-Osu
- **Irene Richter** b 1944 Danish-Osu, d 2013 Danish-Osu
- **Eva Richter** b 1941 Danish-Osu
- **Vincent Richter** b 1939 Danish-Osu
- **Philip Richter** b 1937 Danish-Osu, d 2010 Danish-Osu
- **Lawrencia Paulina Richter** b 1935 Danish-Osu, d 2002 Danish-Osu
- **William Richter** b 1933 Danish-Osu
- **Herbert Richter** b 1931 Danish-Osu, d 2016 Danish-Osu
- **Adeline Richter** b 1930 Danish-Osu, d ? Danish-Osu
- **Ludwig Richter (Red)** b 1928 Danish-Osu, d 2000 Danish-Osu

- Emma
- Paulina
- Dora

'remidors' and their families to settle at Osu-Alata to support his shipping business. He was also in Fredensborg as a factor and eventually became an Acting Governor at Christiansborg in 1817 shortly before his death in October of that year. Around the end of the eighteenth century, he acquired land at Osu-Alata, in the area where Governor Schionning had built a house for his concubine, Naa Tolon, to put up a palatial two-storey residence for himself and his official spouse, Anna Barbara; to reassure her of her position as his wife, he named this residence, 'Barbara House.'

"But due to his frequent dealings with the local Danish-Osu community, including the numerous women engaged in trade, he had several opportunities to father other children besides Henrich, the first born-son of Anna Barbara. The women he had children with were both mixed-race and indigenous. In 1809, to streamline his domestic affairs in the hope of winning the respect of the Danish administration and being promoted to the office of Governor at Christiansborg, he arranged for a statutory recognition of the paternity of his two sons with Anna Barbara, Henrich and Christian."

"Aha, now I see how the formation of the fibrous root-system began," exclaims the human rights activist when he hears how Johan Richter gave selective statutory recognition of the paternity of his offspring. Amused by this outburst, Ataa Forkoyi feigns surprise and asks the activist to explain himself. "From what you have been telling us, I can imagine a number of second generation Richters, besides Henrich and Christian, living at Osu-Alata in the early nineteenth century; all these could have constituted the fibrous roots of the palm tree."

As soon as he finishes speaking, the Rastafarian loudly responds: "Brother Jah, you are damn right on."

Ataa Forkoyi, invigorated by these comments, continues: "Yes, according to the Stones, it was Johan Richter who offered Henrich Richter the model of creating a swarm of forebears to constitute the fibrous roots of the Richter family tree in the nineteenth century. Henrich became closely attached to his father and took after him in business and life style. His father made sure that he was introduced to all the contacts and connections associated with trade in the Guinea Coast as well as in Denmark and other European centres.

"Between 1827 and 1829, he sojourned in the United Kingdom and also visited his ancestral fatherland to take the hand of a Danish woman in marriage. Her name was Amalie Wilhelmine Nicholine Hein but she never really became part of the family tree because she was later divorced without any offspring. In all the places Henrich lived, he contracted marriages and at Danish-Osu he had children with local women including mixed-raced ones, as well as with some of the Asante slave women in his possession.

"Henrich Richter was a prominent ancestor in the Richter family tree. After the death of his father in 1817, he took over his business and the Barbara House. To serve his business in the slave trade, he extended this house into a mini-fort to compete with Christiansborg, enclosing the yard with solid stone outworks fitted with bastions and defense contraptions. He gave the fort a formal entrance with a portal gate on which he had the insignia 'HR/CR' inscribed on a shield to commemorate the year in which his late father statutorily recognized the paternity of himself and his uterine brother, Christian. He moved into this mini-fort in 1829 when he returned from his sojourn overseas, making sure that the fort, which came to be known at Osu as *'Tolon Mɔɔ,'* functioned as a palace, similar to Christiansborg. In this palace, Henrich held important political and social meetings with historic figures such as the British Governor Maclean, Queen Dokua of Akyem and King Addo Dankwa of Akwapim in the 1830s to discuss the peace accord that had to be signed with the Asantes after their defeat in the Katamanso war.

"Barbara-House was not only developed for social reasons but also to foster Henrich Richter's trade pursuits. As I have earlier stated, he enlarged the compound to hold the increasing number of slaves and hostages he had to keep in transit. The Stones remember that at one point, he had as many as 400 slaves in transit. Furthermore, in order to ensure water security for his large household and the slaves in transit, he developed two large underground water cisterns, one on the north-east premises and the other outside on the south-west. Although this stone palace is in disrepair today, it bears a number of interesting marks of the events and people who passed through it.

"For example, the elegant hanging stone staircase leading apparently nowhere tells the story of the glorious banquets and dinners that took place upstairs, to which guests were frequently invited to partake of sumptuous meals and drinks imported by Henrich Richter from all over the world. To the west of the foot of the staircase, in the forecourt of the fort, is an Asante traditional marble game, Oware, which was scooped out of the flagstone pavement of the yard. This confirms the fact that Henrich Richter used to hold large companies of hostages and Asante slaves waiting to be sold through the back door after the Danes had abolished the slave trade in 1803."

While speaking, Ataa Forkoyi pulls out of his wonder-bag what appears to be a re-constructed architectural plan and shows it to his audience, explaining that it is an image of what Richter fort once looked like. He passes it on to the architecture student who wants a closer look.

He continues with his narration: "Determined to follow in the footsteps of his father, Henrich worked hard to establish himself as the wealthiest merchant of his day and accumulated vast resources in human capital, trading goods and arms. He also made certain that he played a decisive role in the politics of the Danish governance of Danish-Osu. This gave him the confidence to request that the Danish administration make him a governor, when he realized he had become more powerful than the declining Christiansborg. He was refused, but in recognition of his clout in the local community, he was accorded the office of Danish Principal Inspector of Recruits.

"In this capacity, he was able to distinguish himself as a capable resource person who supported the Danish campaign in the Dodowah war, which led to the final defeat of the Asantes by the Gã-Adangmes and their European and other allies. For his successful participation and gallantry, he was accorded the Knighthood of the Order of Dannenborg by the Danish Governor, F. S. Morch, in

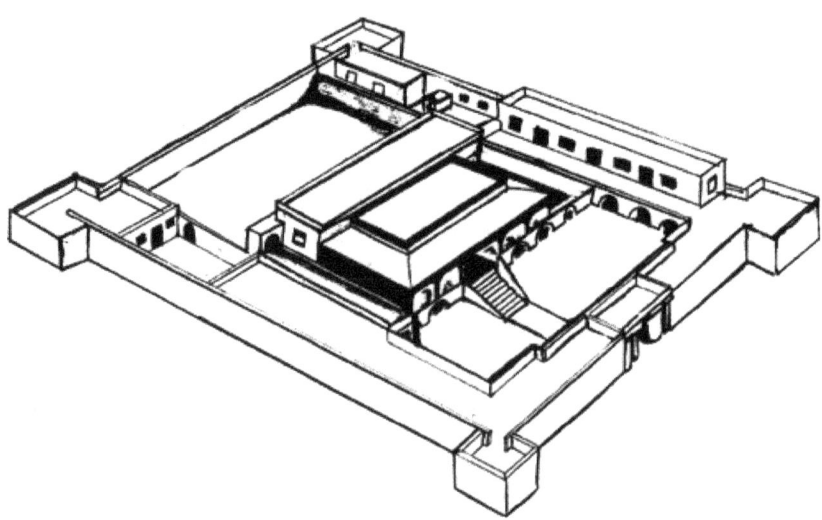

Figure 25: A three-dimensional projection representing a reconstruction of Richter Fort at Osu-Alata. *Illustration courtesy of Neils Bech*

1836.

"Although Henrich Richter fathered numerous children, by the time he joined his ancestors on June 29, 1849, it appears that only John E. Richter Junior had survived him to continue with the management of his remaining property. According to the Stones, this J. E. Richter was the one who signed the land title transfer document in 1857, for the Briandts to acquire and develop the property at Osu Blogodo. It was the same J. E. Richter who, two years earlier in 1855, had petitioned the British administration for compensation for loss of his property through the bombardment of Danish-Osu in 1854. From the stock of J. E. Richter, whose mother was not known, sprouted the present Osu Richter family whose forebear is the renowned Reverend Ludwig Lawrence Richter, born in 1864."

When the lady with the unknown Danish-Osu ancestry hears about this renowned Richter forebear, she experiences a sudden spark; a sense of connection with the Richter family. She says to herself, "I sense within me that my father's mother's ancestry can be traced to the Richter roots in the nineteenth century. I must undertake some DNA research." While this passes through her mind, she is overwhelmed by a strange urge to stop Ataa Forkoyi from going on with the narration. She feels she needs some quiet to capture the thoughts floating through her mind. So she signals to Ataa Forkoyi to hold on.

"Do you have a question?" asks Ataa Forkoyi.

She nods but does not utter a word.

Sensing what is going on in her head, Ataa Forkoyi sympathetically asks: "My dear, what is your question?"

But she still stands there speechless. After a while, she composes herself and decides that Ataa Forkoyi can go on so she hesitantly utters the first question which pops into her head: "What made Reverend L. L. Richter a celebrity in his time?"

Ataa Forkoyi smiles and walks up to the lady, puts his frail hands around her and says to her: "I understand your feelings. Pursue the thoughts going on in your mind. You may one day find out whom your ancestors were. But for now, I will answer you."

Ataa Forkoyi reformulates the question, asking himself: "What made L. L. Richter a well known man in his time?" He then goes on to answer the question: "L. L. Richter bridged the gap between the diffused fibrous root system of the nineteenth century Richter family tree and the slim stem of the family tree of today. This slim family tree is now, with the support of the octogenarian Katherine

Ellenora Ayele Botwe, a granddaughter of Rev. L. L. Richter, born on March 6, 1922 as a Johnson, is headed by a fifth-generation descendant by the name of Ernest Richter, a retired international diplomat.

"Ludwig Lawrence was also the ancestor who caused the lineage to move from the family tradition of commercialism to ecclesiasticalism. Becoming an ordained minister of the Presbyterian Church of Ghana, he distinguished himself as a great man of God and a sound theologian as he worked tirelessly to propagate the gospel of Jesus Christ in the land. He ultimately became the head of the church when he was elected to serve as the Moderator of the Presbyterian Church from 1929 to 1931. His marriage to Adeline Christine Hesse (1869-1945) produced nine children consisting of seven males and two daughters, sprouting the stem from which branches of the Richter Family tree are known today.

"All seven males and two females survived him and his wife, Adeline Christine, after their deaths in 1939 and 1945 respectively. They all settled at Osu and raised offspring to build the Richter lineage. The seventh child, Philip Christian Richter, born in 1903, followed in his father's footsteps to become a clergyman of the Presbyterian Church of Ghana. Starting as a trained teacher-catechist, he taught at the famous Osu Salem Boys' Boarding School from 1923 to 1926, after which he received further training in Basel and London to become a theologian.

"He was ordained as a Reverend Minister of the Presbyterian Church on January 6, 1936 at the age of 33 years. Later, he lectured at the newly established Joint Theological College in Kumasi from 1944 to 1949. As an eminent theologian and scholar he was recommended for appointment as the pioneer chaplain of the newly established Kumasi College of Technology, later Kwame Nkrumah University of Science and Technology, from 1953 to 1962.

"Having served his term of office in academia with honour and excellence, positively influencing the lives of many students who became prominent international professionals and national leaders, he went back into pastoral work at Osu, where he peacefully joined his ancestors on May 28, 1977 at the good age of 74 years. Besides Reverend Philip Christian Richter, his other male siblings Ludwig Lawrence Richter Junior, William Albert Richter, Vincent Richter and Gilbert Richter constituted the five main family groups that define the stem of the Richter Family Tree today. Within the context of these five groups, the Richter family maintains a tenuous relationship with the Engmann Family as a result of the consanguine relationship through Eva Richter, one of the nine children of Reverend Ludwig Lawrence Richter, who through marriage, became one of the forebears of the Engmanns. In addition to the Engmanns, the Richters have family ties to some other Danish-Osu families such as the Hesses, Quists, Augustts, Swanikiers, Larsens, Burgessens, Colemans and Ashies.

"Due to the strong Christian traditions laid down by the Presbyterian teachings which were adopted as the moral and social framework for the family life and culture of the Richters, the Richter family has not cultivated its patrilineal connections. For this reason, it has not grown into a clan. It has thus not pursued, for example, its ancestral rights and entitlement to the Osu-Alata Stool through the gate of Akoto We, to which the Richters have a maternal ancestral link. In the same vein, they have not laid claim to the right to ascend the Mankralo Stool of Osu-Ashinte to which they also have an ancestral link. The typical customary practices related to traditional events at Osu such as the Homowo festival and *Kotsa gbamɔ,*' funeral rites for the dead, are not observed by the Richters.

"The Richters' attitude to traditional life and culture is characterized by the general absence of Gã names among family members. Instead, the common names appearing as middle names are Lawrence, Wilhelm, Vincent, Henry, Ernest, Ludwig, and Philip. However, in remembrance of the Asante connections in the family's genealogy, Asante names, such as Osei and Owusu do show up in few instances. The continuous delimiting of the family tree to the five ancestral groups has caused the Richter family composition and structure to take the shape of a palm tree with its characteristic straight and single stem. It appears also that the size of the family tree stem is dwindling due to the limited birth-rate prevailing among the Richters at the moment."

At this point, the architecture student, thinking about the things Ataa Forkoyi has said about the root system of the Richter family tree, makes an observation that makes everybody laugh. With an impish face, he says with a stuttering voice: "The Stones are right. The adventitious root-system of the Richter family tree grown in the nineteenth century, has nurtured it in the twenty-first century into a palm tree single, straight, and strong."

When the laughing ends, Ataa Forkoyi picks the narration up again: "Yes, indeed. The Richter family tree has become single, straight and strong. The Stones bear testimony to the strength of this family which, because of its relative size, appears to be incognito in the Osu community today."

The lady with the unknown Danish-Osu ancestry, still deeply moved by the thought that she could have shared ancestry with the Richters, excitedly asks Ataa Forkoyi to illustrate the strength which the Richters have demonstrated to date.

Ataa Forkoyi now appearing hungry and drained, begins jadedly to recount the achievements of the Richters over the years with his eyes closed. In his mind's eyes, he sees the dilapidated old bastion on the south west of the fort. "You see," he says with a deep sense of conviction, "the rocky bastions and walls of the Richter fort within which Henrich Richter lies buried today stand as a symbol of the strength of the Richter family. No wonder the family abounds with high achievers. Note that Reverend Philip Christian Richter was not the only one who made his mark in Ghana. There was his brother, Vincent Richter, who became the first General Manager of the Bank of Ghana. There was also his senior brother, Dr. William Albert Richter, the first person ever to qualify as a Veterinary Surgeon in Sub-Saharan Africa."

Having given his audience this remarkable, hitherto unknown historical fact, he picks up his bag and puts on his hat; he is about to walk away but remembers that he has not quite finished with his narration so he stops in his tracks and absentmindedly says:

"Along the line in the Richter family, there have been professional musicians, pianists, architects, accountants, economists, medical officers, who had, like Henry Austin Richter, academic letters such as FRCS (Lond), FRCOG (Lond.), FRCS (Camb.) after their names and civil servants of international standing. But to the Stones, the amazing navigation of the Richters from the inglorious and muddy waters of the culture of trading in human cargo, to the high and saintly waters of theological excellence and exemplary leadership in ecclesiastical vocation, is a testimony to the strength of the family tree."

As he finishes speaking, the history teacher begins to shake her head slowly from side to side, saying to herself: "Wonders of wonders!" and then turns to her fellow listeners and says to them in a barely audible voice: "Friends, do you realize that in all the family genealogies Ataa Forkoyi has introduced us to since he began to speak this morning, there has been the appearance of at least one ordained minister of the church? Are these not the families whose forebears took part in the transatlantic slave trade? Is that not amazing, for descendants of slave-dealing progenitors to become soul winners?"

At this, the Rastafarian enthusiastically responds:

"Jah woman, for me this is a beautiful picture of a Jah-influenced paradigm shift: from "commerce to Christ."

When the lady of unknown Danish-Osu ancestry hears this beautiful expression, she breaks spontaneously into a hymn written by John Newton, an ex-slave trader who was changed when he encountered Jesus Christ in the mid eighteenth century:

> You are coming to a king;
> Large petitions with you bring;
> For his grace and power are such,
> None can ever ask too much.
> With my burden I begin:
> Lord, remove this load of sin;
> Let your blood, for sinners split,
> Set my conscience free from guilt.

While she sings, Ataa Forkoyi walks away solemnly in the company of two of the funeral ushers, who are taking him to one of the family houses at Osu-Amantra for his dinner.

Figure 26: A picture of the dilapidated bastion on the South-West of the Richter Fort. *Courtesy of author*

Figure 27 : A wall in ruins at Briandt's house at Osu.
Courtesy of author

Figure 28: Danish architectural conservator, Nik Hallestad looking at a disused canon in front of Osu Anahor Chief's House. *Courtesy of author*

Six | Sung and Unsung Heroes of Danish-Osu

Assembling for a Durbar

IT IS AN AUGUST MORNING AND THE WEATHER IS COOL AND REFRESHING. The sun is shining but its heat is not felt because of the strong sea breeze blowing into Danish-Osu. The cool weather has brought a lot of fish and the fishermen and their wives have had a field day; a lot of fish have been caught and the price has gone down so everybody can afford to buy fish. That is why the Homowo festival has been celebrated in grand style this time around.

Today is ŋoo Wala, a day after the Homowo festival, an occasion on which people express their goodwill to one another in the community. That is why the spirit of goodwill is felt all around. The chiefs and people of Danish-Osu have decided to commemorate this special day. They will hold a durbar to celebrate their dead and living heroes. There are notices all around pasted on the backs of cars, lotto-kiosks, wooden chop-bar structures, fence walls of houses, and even on house walls where the owners have put up written signs, boldly reading, "POST NO BILLS." There are brightly coloured posters inviting all and sundry to attend this historical durbar to commemorate Danish-Osu heroes of bygone-days and of today.

The cocks have not yet begun to announce the break of dawn with their second phase of crowing. And the cool August pre-dawn weather has caused Ataa Forkoyi to go into a lower level of sleep consciousness before waking from his well-deserved slumber.

Before coming out of this sweet and serene slumber, he finds himself hovering above the Niagara Falls, far away from the Osu shores of the Atlantic Coast and on the other side of the Atlantic Ocean boarded by the United States and Canada—dreaming or flying on a drone?

Far above the Niagara Falls' clouds of turbulent whitish foaming mist, his eyes move around like the eyes of the chameleon, and observe virtually 360 degrees across the states of Kentucky, Ohio, Pennsylvania, New York, New Hampshire, and Maine in the United States, and across the provinces of Ontario and Nova Scotia in Canada. In his chameleon eye-view, he sees hordes of pockets of dark-skinned men and women and children; some of the women carry little children either strapped on their lean broad backs or on their bony sides. What is he seeing? The invisible Underground Railroad?

In the dream, he finds himself listening to the Stones' inaudible murmurs, as they solemnly converse and reminiscence about the Underground Railroad. Ataa Forkoyi scratches one side of his hairless head and asks himself which Underground Railroad the Stones are talking about. Is it the visible or the invisible one? Then he feels a series of vibrations from the underside of the drone on which he is sitting and the vibrations begin to compose words which he slowly and steadily and steadfastly identifies as 'passengers," "conductors," "stockholders," "stationmasters," "depots," "routes," "stations," "North Star," "lines," "Joseph Alexander," "heavenly end station," and …

As these words eventually take on meaning and significance in his dreamy mind, Ataa Forkoyi gets the total picture. The picture that emerges shows the Underground Railroad as a network of people who assisted to facilitate the movement of enslaved Africans. The network also included secret passageways and safe houses used in the nineteenth century by African enslaved persons in the United States who defied all the odds to escape slavery as they departed by foot, wagons, boats and night trains to Canada, the "Freedom Land"—the land of the maple leaf, where the enslaved runaways eventually landed to enjoy freedom from their atrocious slave masters and mistresses. As this vast picture sharpens in focus, Ataa Forkoyi quickly and quietly instructs the drone to take note of names of persons, groups of people, and places that come up as the Stones continue to murmur, because all the associated persons, people and places in the Underground Railroad saga will be among the heroes to be celebrated on Heroes Day at Danish-Osu.

The drone deftly uses his digital stylo and hastily writes down in the open palms of Ataa Forkoyi "Harriet Tubman (Araminta Minty Ross, 'the Moses of her people'), Frederick Douglass, John Brown, John Fairfield, Levi and Catherine Coffin, William Still, Charles Turner Torrey, Josish F. Huttoon, William van Ransalier, Harriet Beecher Stowe, Josiah Henson, John Freman Walls, Jermain Loguen, Joseph Alexander, Mary Ann Shadd, Samuel Ringgold Ward; the Quakers, the Abolitionists, the Vigilance Committees, Native Americans, Blacks, Whites, Free, Enslaved, house in Oxford Ohio, the banks of the Niagara River in Lewiston, Dresden in Ontario, Preston, Hammond plains, Africville, Halifax in Nova Scotia, and ..."

Suddenly the drone on which Ataa Forkoyi is sitting stops writing and turns into a bed. And Ataa Forkoyi wakes up lying outstretched on the bed in his bedroom. He lifts himself up slowly but determinedly from the bed and says to himself: "go get ready for today's Durbar at the Mandela Park at Danish Osu."

Ataa Forkoyi, walking majestically ahead of his group of listeners, has turned up in a resplendent white kente cloth with an immaculately white tunic shirt to match. Today is Community-Heroes Day, and he is the master of ceremonies. He must therefore be appropriately dressed. Under his *Fruit of the Loom* cotton underwear, he is also wearing the special garb of Gã heroes: a beautifully hand-crafted *sliki terkleh*.

As they walk along, the history teacher, whom Ataa Forkoyi had privately intimated to that he is wearing sliki terkleh, walks up closer to him and whispers in his ear: "You told me earlier that you are wearing a 'sliki terkleh' under your shorts. I know from my history lessons that silk cloths were introduced into the Danish-Osu community by the Danes as some of the textiles they brought from India for trading. I have also been informed that the word *terkleh* is, as a matter of fact, *toerkloe* in Danish. It means 'a napkin or a piece of cloth.' Why are you using something which is so foreign on such a culturally significant occasion?"

Hearing this question from the teacher, Ataa Forkoyi suddenly comes to a stop in his majestic stride; he smiles and says to her: "You inquisitive beauty, the answer to your question cannot be for your ears alone. Your friends must also hear it. In that case repeat your question, not to my ears but for the hearing of them all."

Slightly embarrassed but with the delight of a teacher who loves to know what is not known, she confidently repeats her question for the hearing of all.

Ataa Forkoyi now takes a few steps to come into the shade of one of the old tamarind trees standing by the side of the road leading to the durbar grounds, and begins to speak as if he is giving a public lecture.

"We must start with the cultural history of this 'sliki terkleh,' that you have been told I am wearing under my clothing," he slowly formulates his words. "According to the Stones, silk as a textile had been introduced to the Danish-Osu community by the Portuguese but was popularized by the Danes who traded it with the local community in the seventeenth century.

"The Danes brought it from India to use as a precious commodity to trade for slaves. Silk therefore had been known as a fabric for clothing since time immemorial. With time, the Danish-Osu people began to use the silk material for making loincloths for ceremonial wear after they had earlier nicknamed their usual loincloth 'terkleh,' which they adapted from the Danish as a word for a piece of cloth. So, in the course of time, this ceremonial loincloth assumed the name 'sliki terkleh' in the tradition, to accord it a certain dignity and prestige. Fortunately, I have with me in my pocket an old picture of two Danish-Osu warriors in their battle dress. Have a good look at it and you will see, hanging between the thighs of the warriors, 'terkleh' pieces.

"As ceremonial wear, the 'terkleh' was used as military attire as well as civilian men's clothing. Hence, the dignity it assumed in local dress culture, together with its association with war and warriors' celebrations, gave it a symbolic function. By this symbolism, the 'sliki terkleh' became synonymous with chivalry, bravery and honour, usually accorded to victorious warriors. Out of this evolved its use as traditional funerary underwear for elderly males in the community, who by virtue of dying at a ripe old age, achieved the status of heroes."

As Ataa Forkoyi continues to speak, they draw closer to the vicinity of the durbar grounds, and one can see a large crowd of people also making their way towards the durbar grounds. Ahead of him and his company of listeners, are the various Asafo groups in their ceremonial uniforms. The Osu-Kinkawe group is wearing dark red with a number of the youth wearing red headbands.

Some are dragging along the old, rusted Danish field cannons, and now and then they fire them to make an awful boom, making the singing and dancing women shout out with fright, "Ei! Hiiabii, nyɛkaba gbeiawɔ ei!"

Behind the Kinkawe group comes running the Osu-Alata group

Figure 29: A picture of two Danish-Osu warriors in their battle accoutrements with "Terkleh" hanging between their thighs.
Illustration courtesy of Selena Winsnes, translator

with war songs. They are wearing dark red and black striped uniforms, with the *Alata Ntɛn* around their necks. The young men in the group are carrying on their shoulders the decrepit Danish flintlocks which are known in the community as *Kafugben.* As they march about, they fire sporadically, with the guns making their characteristic funny sound "Kafugben!" to the cheering of the Osu-Alata women singers.

The Osu Mantse, the paramount chief, and the other divisional chiefs of the various traditional communities of Danish-Osu, are in the company of their gorgeously dressed queen-mothers, being followed by a large crowd of singing and dancing women as they troop majestically down towards Mandela Park. As they walk down the street, the women standing by cheer and hail them loudly with all sorts of appellations: *"Hei, Nii oh! Hei Nii oh! Bo ni, oo boni"*

Slowly, they inch their way towards the Durbar grounds, the traditional plaza in the community, known as Songme Naa, located behind Christiansborg on the north side where the Community Heroes Day will be celebrated this morning. The dais, decorated in the national colours of red, yellow and green, is at the moment empty because the dignitaries invited to the function have not yet arrived. It is getting to nine o'clock when the durbar is scheduled to start but on such occasions, nobody minds the time.

Meanwhile, a thick crowd has formed with many school children in their brown and cream-coloured uniforms milling around, together with a large body of young boys and girls, a number of them wearing assorted forms of white T-shirts over faded blue American jeans. Some of the white T-shirts these young people are wearing carry a variety of interesting inscriptions, such as: "Terminator," "Tune in and drop out," "Turn around! Jesus is coming soon."

Seated under a special canopy reserved for very important personalities is a motley collection of dignitaries, including reverend ministers wearing black suits with their white clerical collars and local politicians wearing gorgeous flowing gowns in brightly coloured made-in Ghana fabrics. Also seated among these dignitaries are special guests from the American Virgin Islands. These African-American guests of honour are here to represent the ancestors who were once heroes of the Danish-Osu community before the transatlantic slave trade took them away to the Danish-Caribbean islands.

Durbar to Celebrate the Sung Heroes

The stage is now set and Community-Heroes Day begins in earnest. Formal prayers are said; a number of speeches are delivered; a number of musical shows are performed. Then it is time for the highlight of the celebration. Ataa Forkoyi is respectfully invited to the rostrum to begin his well-known narrations about the heroes of the Danish-Osu community. He has been telling these stories since time immemorial and therefore, although he takes his long scroll bearing the story of the heroes along to the rostrum, he begins to speak with his eyes closed and his head turned slightly to one side as if he is keenly listening to voices coming from that direction:

"*Agoo tsɛmɛi, kɛ nyɛmɛi; agoo tsɛmɛi kɛ nyɛmɛi; agoo tsɛmɛi kɛ nyɛmɛi!*"

The crowd booms a response with a loud "*Amɛɛ!*"

When the lady with the unknown Danish ancestry hears these calls and responses, she becomes unsettled because she simply cannot decipher what it is all about. She turns to her neighbor, and smiling a little bashfully, asks for an explanation. The neighbor enthusiastically explains in simple English that Ataa Forkoyi is calling for the attention of the fathers and mothers who have gathered; the positive response from the gathering is expressed as "Amɛɛ."

"*Niimɛi, Naamɛi*, my honorable brothers and sisters from the Diaspora, my dear young ones, ladies and gentlemen," he continues with the usual felicitations. "Today, as we mark our Community-Heroes Day, I wish to let you know that we are here to listen to the exciting, invigorating and inspiring stories of ten heroes of this community. Eight of these are no more alive but two are still with us. Our heroes are the role-models of our youth and the next generation. I am happy that many of the school children and the youth are here. May I ask you in particular, to lend me your small, restless ears."

At full throttle, he proclaims: "According to the Stones, there was a Danish-Osu son called Frederick Noi Dowuona who was born around the time the Danes had officially abolished the transatlantic slave trade. This was the time Danish Governor Johan P. D. Wrisberg was at Christiansborg. To show goodwill to the Danish-Osu community, the Danish King instructed the chief of Kinkawe and the other customary heads of Osu-Ashinte, Osu-Alata and Osu-Anahor to present young, non-mulatto boys for selection with the four brightest amongst them to be sent to Denmark for schooling.

"Noi Dowuona, who was a son of the Kinkawe paramount chief, and three other boys were selected and dispatched to Denmark in the early nineteenth century. According to the Stones, the other three boys could not survive the long trip through the Caribbean to Denmark. Noi, however, arrived safe and sound and began his schooling in Copenhagen. He distinguished himself as a conscientious and intelligent young man and took his studies seriously. He attracted the attention of his teachers as a sensitive and reflective person. He later expressed a keen interest in the Christian faith and established a personal relationship with Jesus Christ. As a result, he was baptized and took the name Frederick. With his new-found faith, he decided to study theology at the university, which he did with distinction.

"At the university in Copenhagen, one of his professors, the philologist, Rasmus Rask, was so impressed by his mastery of and dexterity in the Danish language that he decided to team up with him to write and publish a book in the Gã language. This took place in 1828 and the professor hoped that the publication could be used as a text-book by Frederick Noi on his return home as a qualified teacher. While in Denmark, our hero Frederick Noi Dowuona, heard about the Moravian Brethren in Zeist and, knowing that his ancestral compatriot Christian Africanus Protten had been a Moravian, decided to acquaint himself with them. So he traveled to Zeist, to this famous missionary, pietistic Christian group.

"Sojourning with the brethren, he got to know them as fellow Christians. Later he found out that a group of four young men who had completed their missionary training at the Basel Mission in Switzerland were about to embark on a missionary journey to the Gold Coast. He was encouraged to join the group to support their work in his home country. Noi Frederick, being a reflective person, found the arrangement perfectly in line with his ambition to return home with the salvation message of Jesus Christ for his people. Thus, he joined the missionary party and arrived back in Danish-Osu on eighteenth December 18, 1828."

At this point in the narration, Ataa Forkoyi pauses, opens his eyes and signals for water. One of the young lady ushers dressed in a beautiful kente skirt with a silky white blouse daintily walks up the dais with a bottle of water and a glass covered with a white lace napkin. When she gets to Ataa Forkoyi's side, she makes a slight bow, removes the napkin and respectfully pours him some water.

Ataa Forkoyi, well refreshed, continues: "On arrival home, he was greatly hailed as the first indigenous son of the soil to become a European scholar. He was the pride of his father, who immediately made Noi Frederick his heir apparent. But Noi had other things on his mind. He decided to concentrate on assisting the missionaries by acting as their interpreter. He was then offered employment as a teacher at the Castle School at Christiansborg.

"As he continued with his teaching and interpreting work in Christiansborg, he found himself with so many conflicting challenges. Life inside Christiansborg disturbed his Christian sensibilities; traditional life in his father's court also made him unhappy as he saw what he considered as unchristian religious practices. The conflicts in him were heightened when his father passed away in the 1840s and he was called upon to ascend the stool as the Kinkawe Mantse, the paramount chief. He could not reconcile his faith as a Christian and a theologian with handling traditional customary rites, which at times involved the offering of sacrifices to unknown deities. He decided to turn his back on Christiansborg, also refusing to be enstooled as a paramount chief."

When some of the youth in the audience hear that Noi Dowouna refused to be enstooled, they are surprised and begin to murmur their dissatisfaction at his nonconformist attitude. The rumbling goes on for a while. Ataa Forkoyi hears it but ignores it, because he is used to hearing such mumblings each year when he gets to this part of his narration. He continues:

"Noi Dowuona's refusal to inherit his father's stool caused serious dissatisfaction in the family and in the community; he incurred the displeasure of his people and this led to his decision to move out of the Danish-Osu community. According to the Stones, Noi Frederick sought a new abode in one of the ancestral villages called Papao to pursue a life of contemplation and prayer. From here, he began his own missionary journeys inland to the surrounding Gã villages, moving further inland into the Adangme-speaking areas to make Christ known to the people there. He later settled in the Accra Plains and developed his own community that he named Santse.

"At Santse, where he practiced scientific agriculture and undertook improved building construction, he developed a community to give expression to what he considered his life's calling, namely to protect and provide for the underprivileged in society. According to the Stones, he might have named the settlement he established 'Santse' because he regarded himself as the father of the orphans. Not surprisingly, the community became a 'city of refuge' where runaway enslaved people found solace and protection. The community also attracted a number of people who wanted to realize their life's potential.

"When the famous Basel missionary, Rev. J. G. Zimmerman, the translator of the Bible from the original Hebrew and Greek into the Gã language, visited Noi Dowouna in his village, he was highly impressed with what he saw. According to him, he stayed for a night and found Santse to be a neat and pleasant village and Noi's reflections and thoughts on the Christian faith to be of great interest.

"It was from this 'city of refuge' that Frederick Noi Dowuona emerged in 1854, in response to the plea of the people of Danish-Osu to come back and lead the community to rebuild the bombarded and demolished township.

"The leaders of the four quarters of Danish-Osu, Osu-Kinkawe, Osu-Ashinte, Osu-Alata and Osu-Anahor had unanimously agreed that they needed a capable leader to organize the rebuilding of their shattered town after the British bombardment. Having been informed how Noi Frederick had successfully established a model village, they were convinced that he was well qualified to lead them in the reconstruction of Danish-Osu. They therefore came with the purpose of enstooling him as Danish-Osu Mantsɛ to accord him the authority and mandate to lead the rebuilding of the devastated community. But Noi Dowuona would not accept this honour and responsibility unconditionally. According to the Stones, he gave some conditions on which he would accept being enstooled. These were that he would pour no libation for any deities and that he would have the freedom to wear his European clothing."

Hearing this, a spontaneous exclamation of "Colo! Colo!" bursts from the section of the crowd where the young people are standing, causing Ataa Forkoyi to pause in his narration. The expression they are using means that they find Noi Dowuona to have been a reactionary.

When their shouts die down, he turns in their direction and addresses them: "You think Noi Frederick was reactionary? No, he was not. He became a hero because as an independent thinker and a deeply reflective person, he employed his Christian faith, his world-acquired knowledge, and his practical experience to fight victoriously, the battle to rebuild the bombarded Danish-Osu. His organizational approach and experience in construction guided the people to rebuild their houses within the shortest possible time, to the amazement and admiration of the British administration."

With a twinkle in his eye, he concludes his narration on Frederick Noi Dowuona by virtually singing into the microphone: "As a result, he endeared himself so much to his people that he earned the name 'Mantsɛ Fetreke,' the traditional ruler with a European name corrupted from 'Frederick.' No paramount chief of Osu has since been able to endear himself to his people to that extent."

As soon as the Osu-Kinkawe Asafo Company hears Ataa Forkoyi extol Mantsɛ Fetreke, it fires three shots from the old Danish field cannon which has been set up on the north fringe of the durbar grounds, to salute the memory of this great hero of Danish-Osu.

Ending the narration, Ataa Forkoyi takes a cursory glance at the list of heroes on his long scroll, to check who should be the next hero to be talked about. His eyes catch the name Reverend Carl Christian Reindorf. So he enthusiastically begins his next round of narration:

"From Kinkawe, we now move to Ashinte-Blohum to remember another outstanding Danish-Osu hero. This hero needs no durbar to introduce him. His memory and memorabilia are all over in books written about him and by him. Those of you who worship every Sunday at the Ebenezer Presbyterian Church see him cast in stone, fixed on the north wall of the sanctuary, looking down over the choir. On this occasion, I wish to give you only a few reminders of Carl Christian Reindorf of Sanshi We of Osu-Ashinte-Blohum. This prominent man of history was a mulatto who became the first Ghanaian to undertake a monumental work on the history of this nation. He began his primary education at the Castle School at Christiansborg when he was baptized in 1844, the year of the bond that made the Gold Coast a British colony.

"In keeping with his strong and independent mind, three years after he had been enrolled in the Christiansborg School he decided to quit without the approval of his parents, to enroll at the newly established Basel school because he preferred to learn in the English language instead of Danish, the language of his forebears; this was when he was only thirteen years old. Later he abandoned school altogether, because he was not happy with the Basel missionary Rev. J. G. Zimmerman, who had begun to use the Gã language as a medium of instruction. He then headed towards Prampram in Gbugbla with the aim of joining his uncle who was doing brisk business in the oil palm buying and export trade. But two years later, his intellectual inclinations rebelled and he returned to school in Danish-Osu.

"He was at Danish-Osu as a young man of twenty when the

bombardment took place and so he joined the Basel missionaries with their converts who fled the town, to seek refuge at Abokobi. Now more serious with academic work and committed to the teachings of the mission, he trained as a catechist teacher and eventually became an ordained missionary of the Basel local church. It was in fulfillment of his calling to the Basel Mission that he discovered his multi-faceted talents as a thinker, writer, rural evangelist, community organizer, cultural activist, self-taught herbalist, military strategist and ordained minister. Of all his great pursuits over his long life, his most outstanding achievement was his successful scholarly project, the monumental book, *History of the Gold Coast and Ashanti,* which he wrote in both Gã and English. By the time he passed away on July 1, 1917 at the ripe old age of 83, he had distinguished himself not only as a hero of Danish-Osu, but also as an eminent historian of the Gold Coast."

As soon as Ataa Forkoyi completes the narration about Reverend Carl Christian Reindorf, the drummers of Osu-Ashinte-Blohum community begin to beat their huge drums with praise songs accompanying their women singers. This goes on for a while as the women dance to the beat of the drums.

During this interlude, people move around looking for iced water and ice-cream to quench their thirst and cool down in the midday heat. Some fan themselves with copies of the Durbar programme.

Ataa Forkoyi, who has in the meantime taken a seat next to the Osu Mantse, the paramount Chief, is enjoying a cool bottle of pineapple juice. With the sea breeze blowing around his bald head, he begins to doze off. The Chief hears his faint snoring and gives him a gentle goad, whispering to him, "It's time."

He jerks awake, gets up and walks briskly to the podium, vigorously resuming his narration as if he never dozed off. In a rejuvenated voice, he announces without looking at his scroll: "The next hero on our list hailed from Osu-Kinkawe. His name was Sir Charles Emmanuel Quist."

Without allowing him to continue, the Asafo-Company of Kinkawe begins to chant loudly: *"Kinkawe, Kinkawe, Kinkawe, osee yie, hee yiee; Kinkawe oo, heei Kinkawe oo; osee yiee oo!"*

Ataa Forkoyi raises his right hand to silence the group. When the chanting dies down, Ataa Forkoyi continues: "As you can see from the name, this hero of ours had Danish ancestry but he was a true son of the soil, born here on May 21, 1880. He gained the title 'Sir,' not because he was British, but because he was made a knight of the British Empire in 1952, for being the first African Speaker of Parliament in a British colony south of the Sahara and, of course, for his meritorious contribution to the development of the Parliamentary Institution in Ghana.

"Being the son of a reverend minister, he had a strong Christian upbringing, and having gone through the rigorous Osu Salem Boys' Boarding School, he opted for a theologically advanced education at the Theological Seminary at Akropong, Akwapim. It was there that he sat in class with Dr. C. E. Reindorf, the second son of our hero, Reverend C. C. Reindorf. Graduating from the seminary as a teacher, he made teaching his career and brought knowledge and the love of God to many children growing up at Danish-Osu and other communities of the Gold Coast. Later when he observed the need to influence national development which had begun in earnest, he decided to study law so that he could participate in enacting laws that would guarantee an orderly society in the Gold Coast.

"His decision to leave his teaching career for legal practice appeared to be divinely inspired because this change created the opportunity for him to make his monumental contribution to the establishment of a national democratic system to replace colonial rule in this country of ours. As a representative of the then Eastern Province in the Legislative Council of the Gold Coast, he distinguished himself as an excellent advocate for many improvements in the social and economic conditions of the citizens. This effective advocacy role he played in national development, endeared him to the chiefs and people, especially in the Eastern Province and the Danish-Osu community.

"It was as advocate that he attracted the attention of the colonial administration as a man of sound judgment and insight. He impressed the then governor, Sir Charles Arden-Clarke, as a man with a clear legal mind and a great heart. The governor therefore had no reservations when he appointed him as an extraordinary member of the Legislative Council and subsequently as the Council's first African president in 1949, when the governor relinquished his post as president of the Legislative Council. With this shining track record, it was not surprising when Charles Emmanuel Quist, our hero, was unanimously elected Speaker of the august House when the Gold Coast had an all-African Legislative Assembly in February 1951. He held this high office until November 14, 1957 when he retired, not before he had presided over the first Ghanaian Parliament as the Speaker.

"According to the Stones, Sir Charles Emmanuel Quist performed his duties with dignity and finesse on the ceremonial occasion of the special state opening of Parliament on Independence Day, March 6, 1957, in the presence of dignitaries such as Queen Elizabeth of England, the Duchess of Kent, the second special representative, Vice-President Richard Nixon of USA, and Rev. Dr Martin Luther King Junior, the Black American freedom activist. By the time he became an ancestor on February 28, 1959 at the post-biblical age of 79, he had consistently demonstrated the unique qualities associated with Danish-Osu citizens as persons of deep Christian conviction, high moral standing, excellent behavior and great achievement."

Concluding his narration about Sir Charles Emmanuel Quist, Ataa Forkoyi immediately proceeds to the next hero on his list, not wishing to be interrupted by more chanting from the youth. "Distinguished listeners, my dear young friends of the Danish-Osu community, it is my great delight now to tell you about the next hero. His name is Nii Kwabena Bonne III, Osu-Alata Mantse, *Oyokohene* of Takyiman and also known in Ghana as 'Boycotthene.'" As soon as the youth of Osu-Alata hear the title 'Boycotthene' mentioned they begin to exclaim to the displeasure of Ataa Forkoyi, *"Boni ee boni. Alata Ntɛn lɛ nɛ."*

Realizing he has caused this spontaneous exclamation, Ataa Forkoyi relaxes and smartly incorporates the shouts of the Osu-Alata youth into his narration, continuing thus: "Yes, Theodore Taylor was the one and only acclaimed ruler of the Osu-Alata community. He was the pride of Osu-Alata because he rose to national prominence as the traditional leader who, as a conscionable merchant, was able to organize a mass national boycott of commercial goods brought into the Gold Coast by the exploitative Asian merchants.

"Theodore Taylor, as Nii Kwabena Bonne III was named at birth, was born at Danish-Osu on January 26, 1888. He had his basic education at Saint Thomas, the famous Presbyterian Primary School at Danish-Osu. Later on he was sent to Aburi to further his education. Family circumstances forced him to abandon school and enter into commerce. By dint of hard work and what he considered to be divine providence, he became a successful, self-made businessman and merchant who did business with partners in a number of overseas countries. Later, through his maternal lineage, he ascended the Osu-Alata stool to become Nii Kwabena Bonne the third.

"As a traditional leader, he employed his business acumen

and entrepreneurial experience to elevate the social and cultural responsibilities of the Osu-Alata stool to a high pedestal, through the innovations he introduced. By virtue of his political and social experience, he broadened the perspective of his ruling council to link up with other chiefdoms outside the Gã traditional environment. Through this, he earned the recognition of the Asante state and was accorded the title 'Oyokohene of Takyiman,' to give substance to the mythical connection of the Osu-Alata people and the town of Bono Manso in Brong Ahafo. In appreciation of this honour, Nii Kwabena Bonne invited Otumfuor Nana Asantehene Prempeh II to visit Accra as his guest. According to the Stones, in 1946 he was able to bring the Asante King down to Accra to meet him at Avenor on the outskirts of the town, at a historic place which thereby earned the name *'Kpeehe,'* meaning 'meeting place.'

"As a traditional leader he did not only pursue sentimental activities but also addressed a number of important issues relating to the social advancement of his subjects. He asserted that there was a need for the traditional authorities of Danish-Osu to undertake careful planning of land tenureship and land utilization to secure the interest of the future citizens of the Danish-Osu community.

"A mark of his foresightedness, development sustainability had become his major concern long before the concept ever appeared in the development literature. His heroism transcended the national arena when he embarked on his crusade to mobilize the country to rise against the exploitative dealings of the local Asian merchants, who had congregated themselves into the monopolistic hegemony known as 'AWAM,' an acronym for the Association of West African Merchants. He went round the country and sensitized the chiefs and their subjects to boycott goods sold by the Asian shops in the communities.

"The successful boycott action was to culminate in a mass demonstration in Accra, scheduled to take place on February 28, 1948. This date coincided with the Second World War ex-servicemen's march on the Christiansborg or Osu Castle, to demand fair retirement and pension benefits from the British colonial administration. The resulting incident, in which three of the ex-servicemen were shot at the Osu crossroads, led to disturbances in Accra, with attendant looting of Asian shops. All this tied the ensuing political agitation that constituted the last stage of the struggle for independence, to the mass boycott action organized by Nii Kwabena Bonne III that earned him the national nickname, 'Boycotthene,' a title he cherished until his death in 1968 at the ripe old age of 80 years."

Ataa Forkoyi, whose eyes have been shut the whole time he has been speaking, now opens them and makes a dramatic pause in his narration. The audience awaits his next words with bated breath. Unexpectedly, a shout emanates from the side where the Osu-Alata youth have been standing: *"Boni, boni oo boni. Alata Ntɛn lɛ nɛ."* Ataa Forkoyi, as if he has been waiting for this exclamation, quickly responds: "Yes, Nii Kwabena Bonne was the pride of Osu Alata and of Ghana. As we celebrate our Community-Heroes Day today, we salute his ability to use the Osu-Alata traditional authority as a platform to launch such a remarkable feat in national politics."

With that, he pulls his scroll out of his pocket and takes another look at the list of heroes. At about this time, the Osu-Alata youth begin to shoot their old Danish flintlocks but Ataa Forkoyi stops them by raising both hands and waving them violently, saying, "It is enough. Now we move on to the next on the list."

"We remember today a medical giant who became the first in almost everything in the history of medicine in Ghana. Affectionately known as Charlie Easmon, this medical hero who became Professor Charles Odamtten Easmon was born outside Danish-Osu on September 22, 1913 at a little town called Adawso in the Eastern Region. He had his roots in the Danish-Osu community through his mother, Kate Salomey Odamtten and grand-aunt Betty Lokko, the wife of Sir E. C. Quist. Both of these women belonged to the Osu-Alata quarter. His father, Victor Farrell Easmon, also traced his maternal lineage to the Danish-Osu Richter family.

"Typical for all Danish-Osu boys growing up at that time, Charlie Easmon was sent to Saint Thomas and to Osu Salem Boys' Boarding School for his education. Having won a scholarship, he went to Achimota School as one of the pioneer students. At Achimota School he displayed remarkable artistic talents as well as scholarly achievements. A mural painting he made of Christiansborg was kept in the School's dining hall for several years.

"Having completed his pre-university training at the Achimota College, he proceeded to the Edinburgh University Medical School where he discovered the talents that would push him to the forefront of medical practice back home. Although he was the third qualified Ghanaian medical officer, he became the first Ghanaian Surgical Specialist, the first Ghanaian Surgeon General, the first President of the Ghana Medical Association, the first Dean of the University of Ghana Medical School. In that capacity, he became a co-founder of the Noguchi Memorial Institute for medical research, established at

Legon to immortalize the Japanese medical scientist who died from yellow fever whilst researching in Ghana, a cure to that dreadful illness.

"Professor Charles Odamtten Easmon was also among the first Trustees of the Osu Medical Foundation (OMF), an organization established to enhance the professional knowledge and expertise of Osu Salem trained medical practitioners and to conscientize these to offer medical advice and services to the elderly of Osu who needed medical help but could not afford it. Easmon's prominence in the medical field was attained not only by virtue of his intellectual brilliance but also through hard work, perseverance and divine favour. As a young African doctor he defied the odds to work with dedication in the face of subtle discrimination and discouragement amongst European medical officers.

"The colonial administration at the Korle-Bu Hospital thought that, being an African, he could not become a surgeon. Hence, when he requested leave to go for further training to obtain his membership at the Royal College of Surgeons, he faced stiff opposition. Eventually, the then Governor Sir Alan Burns himself had to authorize his release. In 1948 he obtained the surgeons' highest honour as a Fellow of the Royal College of Surgeons, Edinburgh (FRCS), to the surprise and amazement of his senior European colleagues.

"In 1964 when he was commissioned by the President, Osagyefo Dr. Kwame Nkrumah, to establish the Ghana Medical School, he had only a few dedicated local staff to work with in the face of limited resources and without state-of-the-art equipment to train the first batch of medical students. Instead of complaining, he responded to the challenge with tenacity and innovation and together with his team, turned out an excellent first crop of medical graduates in 1969 to fulfill Kwame Nkrumah's aspiration of having an all-African, indigenous medical school. Among this '69 Year Group are some notable names such as T. C. Ankrah, G. Ankrah-Badu and J. Oliver Commey, who have since become professors in their various areas of specialization.

"The Danish-Osu community regards him as one of its most outstanding heroes because, besides being the 'medical first,' as a pioneer surgeon and medical officer he left indelible footprints of quality and humane service, characteristic of Danish-Osu citizens, in all the health centres where he worked, in the Northern and Upper Regions, in the Western Region, and in the Central Region. At the Korle-Bu Teaching Hospital, he performed miracles with his scalpel and endeared himself to both his patients and his medical colleagues as a man with blessed hands and an affable heart. In the 1960s when he led a team of surgeons to perform the first ever heart operation in Ghana, people realized that his heart and hands had indeed been in the hands of the Almighty God, with whom he had become well acquainted growing up at the Osu Salem Boys Boarding School.

"His love for medical practice made him continue to work as a doctor many years after his retirement. Not surprisingly, he breathed his last on May 19, 1994 at the ripe old age of 81 years, in the hospital to which he had continued to offer his medical services for two decades after retirement."

As Ataa Forkoyi struggles to end his narration, his voice starts to tremble with sudden grief. The audience senses his deep emotion. Silently and spontaneously, they rise up in honour of the memory of the medical hero of the Danish-Osu community. After a while, the Osu-Alata Asafo Company gives one or two shots into the air with their decrepit Danish flintlocks.

The sorrowful atmosphere breaks and Ataa Forkoyi continues with the next narration after taking a few gulps of water. "You members of Osu-Alata Asafo Company, give me a break and hold back on firing those decrepit Danish things. The next hero on the list is an Osu Alata man and a real soldier. He did not handle flintlocks."

The audience breaks into loud laughter at the irony of this scathing remark. "According to the Stones, real soldiers have rarely been seen in Ghana. Among the few was the Osu-Alata man called Major General Neville Alexander Odartey Wellington." Before Ataa Forkoyi can continue, the women and youth of Osu-Alata rise to their feet and begin to chant: *"Osu Alata, Osu Alata, osee yei! Osu Alata ooo, hee eei!"*

This goes on for a while and Ataa Forkoyi patiently waits for them to stop. After shouting themselves hoarse, they take their seats.

"The father of this General was a well-known royal of Osu-Alata, by the name of Archibald Mensah Wellington. It was he who compelled his fourth son, Odartey Idan, born on June 18, 1937 in Idan, Cape Coast, to follow his footsteps into the Ghana Postal Service after his secondary school education at the Accra Academy. This was contrary to the General's dream of studying pharmacy at the Kwame Nkrumah University of Science and Technology, then known as Kumasi College of Technology. As an obedient son who had been strongly disciplined through his home upbringing and training at the Osu Presbyterian Boys' Day School, he conceded to his father's wish and attended the Ghana Post and Communication Training School. He qualified as a postal clerk in 1954, and as fate would have it, was posted to the Burma Camp Post Office.

"It was here that, through the interaction he had with the British army personnel, he was influenced to enter the army to become a commissioned officer. The brilliance and bravery he displayed during his training at the Military Academy at Teshie, together with his acute sense of loyalty, marked him out as a potential military leader, suited to the infantry. Therefore, soon after qualifying as a junior officer of the Ghana Army in 1959, he was sent to the prestigious Royal Military Academy at Sandhurst in the United Kingdom, for further military training.

"At Sandhurst, where he rubbed shoulders with young British nobles and the offspring of foreign monarchs, he was exposed to the best in military scholarship and tradition. He was able to acquire special skills including competence in French and Spanish. He completed his training with distinction on December 22, 1961 and returned home immediately to begin his military career that ultimately took him to the zenith of the command structure of the Ghana Army. His track record as a serving officer in the Ghana Army included positions such as Company Commander, 4th Battalion of Infantry; Deputy Assistant Adjutant and Quartermaster General, 2nd Infantry Brigade Group; Commanding Officer, 4th Battalion of Infantry; Acting Commandant, Military Academy and Training Schools; Commander, Ghana Army.

"When the Armed Forces became involved in national politics, he served in civilian positions such as Managing Director of the Timber Marketing Board, Commissioner for Health and Commissioner for Agriculture. In these civilian positions he distinguished himself as a man of integrity who made sure that the policies he implemented enabled the respective organizations he directed to progress and to make useful contributions to national development without any benefits to himself and his family.

"In the Ghana Army, he earned the sobriquet *'Sumsum'* as a result of his strong sense of military discipline and decorum. So, when he served on the reconstructed Supreme Military Council to rule the nation, he received great respect from all his colleagues including the then Chairman of Council and Head of State, General Kutu Akyeampong. By virtue of this high regard he enjoyed, when it became necessary to remove General Acheampong from office in 1978, General Odartey-Wellington, as the Army Commander, was able to mastermind a palace coup to get Acheampong out without shedding a single drop of blood. By removing General Acheampong, he made it possible for General F. O. Akuffo to take over the governance of the nation without any hindrance.

"The apogee of his heroism was in his response to and consequent action regarding the events of the June 4th 1979 mutiny in the Ghana Armed Forces that removed the Supreme Military Council through the Armed Forces Revolutionary Council." As Ataa Forkoyi comes to this point in the narration, he begins to speak hesitatingly, as if he is being somehow restrained. The Osu Mantse, thinking something is wrong, sends one of the elegant ushers to enquire if he needs water. Ataa Forkoyi indicates to the Chief that he does not need water but rather to know if he should declare all that he is hearing from the Stones. He is reminded that today is Community-Heroes Day and the audience that has gathered, especially the youth and the school children, must know whatever the Stones have to say about their hero.

Encouraged by the Chief's response, he continues with his narration but in a voice full of stress and sorrow. "According to the Stones, General Odartey-Wellington as the Army Commander, was careful to monitor the events that preceded the June 4th Revolution within the Armed Forces. With the mind of a Sandhurst-trained infantry soldier dedicated to the maintenance of military law and order, he insisted, to the dissatisfaction of his colleagues on the Supreme Military Council (SMC), that the arrested culprit of the earlier May 15, 1979 revolt to unseat the SMC, of which he was a member, should not be summarily dealt with but court-martialed to grant him a fair hearing.

"Beyond this insistence, to encourage his men to remain loyal, he organized a durbar at the 5th Brigade to award military honours to the loyal soldiers and officers who quelled the 15th May 1979 mutiny. Notwithstanding his attempts to ensure the loyalty of the Army, on June 4th 1979, anarchy broke out at one of the barracks and beyond, in the Ghana Broadcasting House (GBC), where the leaders of the insurrection announced that they had taken over the government.

"In light of this, some of the loyal officers and their men entered armored cars to drive to General Odartey-Wellington's bungalow at Burma Camp to alert him. When they arrived at the General's residence at about three o'clock in the early hours of the morning to inform him about what was going on, the General was already up, dressed in full battle gear. As a commissioned officer of the Ghana Army in charge of the command structure, he had sworn to defend Ghana with his life and was ready to fight to restore order in the nation.

"In the true spirit of an infantry soldier, he entered one of the armored cars together with his military assistant and drove with the contingent of armored cars to the Broadcasting House, at the helm of affairs. Upon arrival at GBC premises, they were able to outmanoeuvre the stiff opposition they encountered from the troops in support of the revolt and finally entered the newsroom, where the General made his heroic and historic announcement that the coup d'état had been foiled and that he had taken over the governance of the nation.

"Having thus brought the situation under control, he left the GBC for the Police Headquarters, to strategise further on bringing stability to the fragile order he had restored with his victorious announcement. At the Police Headquarters, where he had expected to meet members of the SMC and the unit commanders, he realized that things were in disarray because his colleagues had gone into hiding and were nowhere to be found. To make matters worse for him, there were threats coming from the revolt soldiers to bombard the Police Headquarters building to dislodge the General and his loyal troops.

"To counteract the threats and to assure the people of Ghana that he was still in control of the security of the nation, a recording was made of his earlier announcement which was sent back to the GBC to be broadcast. Intelligence available to him suggested that he should move his operational base to the Nima Police Station where there was a state-of-the-art communication system that could be used to reach all the command posts in the country. So the General left the Police Headquarters in one of the armored cars in the company of his young Aide-de-camp (ADC). Meanwhile, in the midst of this battle situation, he thought about his aged father who might be concerned about him. To assuage any fears of his father, he sent his military assistant with a note for his father at Osu-Nyaneba Estate.

"Not knowing that the revolt had gained ground in spite of his apparently successful quelling of the coup d'état, when he got to the Nima Police Station, he decided to take some rest whilst he waited for his military assistant. It was while resting in one of the offices at the Police Station with his ADC that they were unexpectedly attacked. The General was mortally wounded and so he asked his

ADC to surrender. When the revolt soldiers entered the room where he lay bleeding, they began to unload bullets into his body to make sure that he was really dead; being a strategist infantry soldier, they thought he was trying to outwit them so they riddled his body with several rounds of bullets.

"By the time the General's military assistant returned for the rendezvous with his boss, the General was dead and no more. According to the Stones, by this time, the jubilating soldiers were doing surreal things with the lifeless body of the General which were too despicable to be described in words. Ahead of the group of soldiers carrying the dead body of the General was another frenzied soldier wearing the General's military hat and shouting with an uplifted gun to the large crowd which had gathered at the Nima Police Station: 'This is General Odartey-Wellington, the Army Commander. See? We have finished him!'"

With this statement from Ataa Forkoyi, a great hush descends on the audience. It becomes so quiet that one can hear the booming of the waves from beyond Christiansborg, to the south of the Durbar grounds. Against this sorrowful silence, Ataa Forkoyi proceeds with his narration and with a certain amount of defiance in his voice, utters loudly: "But our hero was not yet finished in his death at the battlefront at Nima." He continues:

"For several weeks after this tragic death, whilst his body was being kept at the 37th Military Hospital Mortuary, the leaders of the Armed Forces Revolution Council rigorously investigated the assets of his widow, his octogenarian father, his grief-stricken siblings and most of his mourning relatives to see if they could find any evidence of corruption associated with his command posts and the public offices he had held. They finally had to come to the embarrassing conclusion that General Odartey-Wellington was not only a brave and loyal soldier but also a man of integrity.

"So, to the delight and sorrowful satisfaction of his father, and against the spirit and sentiment prevailing at the time, our hero was given a state burial with full military honours including the customary gun salute. The coffin bearing his mortal remains wrapped with the national colours, was pall-borne by a group of soldiers including Major Boakye-Gyan, one of the prime movers of the June 4th coup d'état."

When he comes to the end of his narration, Ataa Forkoyi, with suppressed emotion, quickly asks, "Who is the next hero?" He waits for a few moments and after turning his head from one side of the audience to the other for an answer, he begins to speak. "Our next hero was from the Nii Okantey Shikatse We at Agblanshie, Osu-Anahor. His name was Michael Francis Okantey. In his heyday, he was simply known as M. F. Okantey. At the Osu Presbyterian Boys' Day School, his physical education teacher realized he was endowed with an excellent athletic physique. The teacher therefore decided to develop his athletic potential while encouraging him to take his academic work seriously.

"Soon, running in the school's athletic competitions, he was identified as a talented sprinter and by the time he completed his middle school education and joined the Ghana Army, he had won many sporting victories for his school in the Inter-Schools' Athletic Championships. These championships, which offered the school children wholesome avenues to develop their athletic talents, were organized by the ace sporting administrator, Ohene Djan. He worked together with school sports teachers to establish the National Central Organisation of Sport (COS) under the auspices of President Kwame Nkrumah, to make sure that talents were found in all areas of sports, including football, boxing and athletics.

"President Nkrumah gave strong backing and encouragement to Ohene Djan to use the national Central Organisation of Sport (COS) to fish out talent through the athletic championships events, to build national teams for Ghana. Osagyefo believed that the development of sports would forge a national identity and generate international recognition for Ghana, the emerging star nation of Africa. Hence, the political support Ohene Djan received in the 1960s enabled the COS to make giant strides, especially in track and field. Consequently, superb performances by Ghana at the Commonwealth Games and the All-Africa Games brought track stars such as M. F. Okantey, Mike Ahey, Bukari Bashiru and B. K. Mends to the sporting world's attention.

"These great stars constituted the elite sprints quartet that came to be known as the fearsome four. The quartet, with M. F. Okantey as the anchor-leg, won so many laurels for Ghana as they collected gold medals in Games stretching from Perth in Australia to Kingston in Jamaica. Of all these achievements, the most dramatic was the quartet's sharing of the Commonwealth Games record with England in the four by one hundred yards relay at Perth in Australia in 1962. Michael Francis Okantey, a son of the soil of Danish-Osu, became a treasure of the nation in sports. By his sporting prowess he brought pride to the community and to Ghana. This same prowess took him to faraway Canada and while he was sojourning there, he passed away on September 1995 as a sports legend known in all the continents of the world."

It is about midday and the sun is at its zenith. But it is not so hot because of the cool August breeze. With the exception of the school children who are growing weary and fidgety, people are glued to their seats, eagerly waiting to hear more from Ataa Forkoyi.

However, when he realizes that it is noontime, he decides to speed up his narration as the day is advancing and soon Durbar will be over. "Some of you may be surprised that I have the next person on my list as a Danish-Osu hero," Ataa Forkoyi begins, looking up at the position of the sun to determine how much time he has left. Realizing time is no longer on his side, he hurriedly continues:

"Emmanuel Noi Omaboe, who later became Nana Wereko Ampem II, our next hero, was fortunate to have a bi-cultural ethnicity like some other Danish-Osu citizens. His father was Peter Nortey Omaboe, a strong Presbyterian of Adzuateh at Osu-Kinkawe. His mother was Mary Opeibia Awuku, a royal of the Asona family of Amanorkrom, brought up in accordance with the Presbyterian traditions as they prevailed on the Akwapim Hills. The royal Asonas of Amanorkrom are matrilineal whereas the Osu-Kinkawe people as original Gã-Adangmes are patrilineal. So by virtue of his bi-cultural ethnicity, our hero was both a son of the Danish-Osu soil as well as an Akwapim. The place of his birth offered him the space to benefit from the privileges of this bi-cultural ethnicity.

"The man, Peter Omaboe, in pursuit of his vocation as a skillful goldsmith, traveled from Danish-Osu to sojourn at Amanorkrom and while there, due to his admirable character and excellent craftsmanship, was able to make inroads into the Asona royal home and win the heart of the royal, Nana Opeibia Mary with whom he raised Osu-Kinkawe offspring with Emmanuel Noi as the first born.

"The Omaboe children were raised as Gã-speakers who grew up in an Akwapim cultural milieu with Presbyterian traditions. So our hero, born Emmanuel Noi Omaboe on October 29, 1930, remained a Gã and a Danish-Osu citizen, although he became enstooled in August 1975 as the chief of Amanorkrom and the Gyasehene of Akwapim, with the stool name of Nana Wereko Ampem II, by virtue of his maternal lineage. Oyeeman Nana Wereko Ampem II, after completing his basic education at the Presbyterian Junior and Senior Schools at Mamfe and Suhum respectively, came down to Accra to attend Accra Academy for his secondary education. From here he went overseas for his training in Economics and Statistics and qualified with flying colours as an economist.

"When he returned home to begin his career in the government civil service, his phenomenal progression in public life never abated. From the appointed position of Deputy Government Statistician in 1959, he was promoted in 1960 to the post of Government Statistician at the age of twenty-nine years, becoming the youngest ever to head a government department. In this capacity, he supervised the first national population census in Ghana."

At this point, he makes his characteristic dramatic pause and holds the audience in suspense. When he feels the tension is enough, he declares exhilaratedly, "The trajectory of his heroism began to unfold as his local, national and international achievements were manifested in various ways." With his eyes still firmly shut, he begins in an oratorical style to enumerate some of Nana's achievements.

"According to the Stones, Nana Wereko Ampem II, known at that time as E. N. Omaboe, was the one who directed the first ever devaluation of the Ghanaian currency, the cedi, in 1967."

The audience delivers an ovation amidst the drumming and blowing of horns by the Asafo companies.

"According to the Stones, Nana Wereko Ampem II, for his bold, economic policy to devaluate the cedi, received the Grand Medal (civil division) in 1968."

The audience gives another ovation amidst more drumming and horn blowing.

"According to the Stones, Nana Wereko Ampem II was awarded the fellowship of the royal statistical society in 1973."

Again the audience repeats the ovation with the drumming and horn-blowing getting to fever pitch.

"According to the Stones, Nana Wereko Ampem II became chairman of Barclays Bank of Ghana Ltd."

Another ovation with drumming and horn-blowing follows.

"According to the Stones, Nana Wereko Ampem II, as an appointed member of the UN Investment Committee, became chairman on January 1, 1997."

Again the audience claps loudly amidst drumming and horn blowing.

"According to the Stones, Nana Wereko Ampem II, was appointed Chancellor of the University of Ghana in 1998 and in 2005. On the occasion of embarking on his second term of office, he bequeathed the multi-million dollar Asante Brass Works Heritage Collections to the Institute of African Studies of the University."

Another round of applause and drumming and more horn-blowing erupts from the audience.

Now, Ataa Forkoyi, having raised the emotions of the audience, opens his eyes with a bright twinkle and slowly says: "Last but not least, Nana Wereko Ampem II, with his love of soccer and deep attachment to his roots in the Danish-Osu community and the city of Accra, accepted the chairmanship of the Council of Patrons of Accra Hearts of Oak."

As soon as the youth in the audience hear the name of the nation's premier football club, they break into a chant of, "Way Hearts!" with the response, "Never say die, Phobia, Phobia!"

When the chanting abates, Ataa Forkoyi goes on in poetic style: "This great royal hero of Danish-Osu, having gloriously fulfilled his life's calling, was called to join his ancestors on November 28, 2005. His funeral took place not here at Danish-Osu, his paternal ancestral home, but at his chiefdom in Amanorkrom. A large crowd of mourners from different parts of the world gathered that day at Amanorkrom to pay their last respects as he was laid in state at his palace. A number of tributes were read to his memory. The Stones vividly recollect a particular one read by an unknown mourner. It said:

> Nana Wereko Ampem II, alias Emmanuel Noi Omaboe, was a financial mogul, a business magnate and an astute traditional leader.

The big drums now begin to boom as the women singers from all the Danish-Osu quarters begin to sing dirges to honour the memory of Nana.

When the singing and drumming end, Ataa Forkoyi pulls out his scroll and takes a long look at it, moving his head up and down as if counting. Having satisfied himself that there are only two names left on the list of heroes, he smiles, shuts his eyes again and begins to speak. "Niimɛi and Naamɛi, honorable, distinguished visitors, young people and my dear school children; we are almost at the end of our proceedings for today. I have two more heroes to talk about. These are living heroes so I shall make my narration brief because these two heroes have not yet received their 'sliki terkleh.' A hero without a 'sliki terkleh' has no long narration, since the yarn of his life is still being woven and must be allowed to unfold.

"Our first living hero, who is not present at this occasion today, is in the person of that intellectual giant with a small stature by the name of Professor Frederick Torgbor Sai of Osu-Anahor. He was born on June 23, 1924, but lost his father early and was raised by his mother and grandmother at Songme Naa at Osu-Alata. Both were, however, supported by his paternal uncle who made sure that he remained a true citizen of the Osu-Anahor community. Coming from a humble home, he made sure that he worked hard and lived frugally to justify the expenses as he attended the famous Osu Presbyterian Boys' Boarding School, known as Osu Salem. At Osu Salem, he was able to wear his first pair of shoes, not without difficulty, but discovered with ease his talents and intellectual endowments.

"His brilliance showed in all things and by the time he was in his senior class, notwithstanding his diminutive size, his intellectual prowess gained him the position of senior prefect of the school, to the displeasure of some of his mates who were twice his size. By the time he won a scholarship to leave for Achimota College in 1939, he had so impressed his teachers that his name was inscribed on the Salem School's Honour List, which hung in the School's Assembly Hall. At Achimota College it became obvious that he was gifted in science and by the time he completed his secondary education, another scholarship had fallen into his lap, to study medicine. So, our hero left for overseas and on his return home in 1954 qualified as a medical officer with distinction.

"He worked as a dedicated physician in the major health centres of Ghana such as Korle Bu and Okomfo Anokye Hospitals. With his academic inclinations and endowments, Dr. Torgbor Sai ultimately went into academia to become a Professor. His specialization thereafter opened doors for him to enter the international arena and as a typical Danish-Osu achiever, he established himself as a world-class authority in his field of Preventive and Social Medicine. Since then, having risen to the upper echelons of his profession with international recognition, his achievements and pioneering exploits have known no bounds. Professor Frederick Torgbor Sai, working as an international civil servant, once served as Assistant Secretary General of the International Planned Parenthood Federation. From 1978 to 1982, he served also as the International Coordinator for Africa and Europe for the United Nations University. From 1985 to 1990 he was Senior Population Advisor for the World Bank in Washington, USA.

"In addition to the many things he has done to advance the progress of Ghana in the area of public health, in 2001, he was appointed Chairman of the National Population Council and he became the Presidential Advisor on Population, Reproductive Health and HIV/AIDS. In recognition of his meritorious achievements and contribution to the well-being of humanity, he has received several awards and citations, including the UN Population Award in 1993, and the Prince Mahidol Award from Thailand in 1995. In response to the divine blessings showered upon him, he has remained a consistent and generous philanthropist. Characteristically, Professor Sai donated the prize money of his Prince Mahidol Award to the University of Ghana, Legon, as seed money for a fund to assist women interested in studying the basic sciences."

Ataa Forkoyi now opens his eyes and looks towards the sky to tell the time. He realizes that he has gone beyond the time he allocated to talk about the diminutive medical giant. He therefore shuts his eyes and with a mischievous smile ends his narration by saying simply:

"Niimɛi, Naamɛi, distinguished listeners, my dear young people and school children; the time is far gone but allow me to inform you that our hero, Professor Frederick Torgbor Sai, is an octogenarian and is still intellectually and socially active." With a gesture, he now requests something to drink. The lady usher brings him a bottle of chilled coconut juice. He flinches at the sting of iciness on his weak teeth and, on the verge of spitting it out, remembers that he is standing in front of a distinguished audience of the Danish-Osu community. So he swallows what is in his mouth but courteously declines the rest of the drink and takes up his narrative.

"The last Danish-Osu hero on my list is also a medical giant and a professor. He is from Mowule, Osu-Kinkawe and was born in 1935 at Duadetsean outside Danish-Osu, to royal parents named George and Victoria Ashitey. From Duadetsean, a village near Nsawam, he embarked on an eventful and life-changing journey that brought him from the backwaters of a Gã farming community to the historic Osu Salem School when he was twelve years old.

"It was here, in 1947, that Gilford Amarh Ashitey found himself among a group of boys in Standard Four, marching gingerly into their senior school education in the Presbyterian Boys' Boarding School, which had existed since 1865. Hanging on the back wall of their classroom, which doubled as the Assembly Hall for the whole school, was the 'Honours List' placed on a beautifully framed wooden tablet. On this tablet appeared the inscription:

1. C. J. Bannerman 1926
2. Casley O. Mate 1926
3. Emmanuel Evans-Anfom 1934

4. Frederick Torgbor Sai   1939
5. Edmond A. Moffat   1941
6. Philip A. Odjidja   1944

"The headteacher of the school Mr. A. M. O. Ayettey, constantly drew the boys' attention to the Honour List, as those who studied hard and were disciplined enough to win scholarships to continue their education to college level. Inspired by this tablet of honour, our hero subjected himself to the rigorous, proverbial Osu Salem discipline and also studied hard to obtain a scholarship to enter the prestigious Achimota College in 1950. From Duadetsean, through Osu Salem to Achimota, he now took the gigantic step of crossing the ocean to gain admission to Medical School at Queen's University of Belfast in Ireland."

The way in which Ataa Forkoyi keeps pronouncing the name "Duadetsean" causes mirth among many of the youth, who shout, *"Duadetsei lɛ amli,* among the cassava trees." He refuses to be distracted by this youthful clamor and continues with his narration, conscious that time is no longer on his side. Slightly agitated, he yells out: "Whether it was from the 'Duadetsean' or the 'Duadetsei le amli,' the Stones confirm that the village boy Gilford Amarh Ashitey, rose to follow the giant footsteps of Professor Frederick Torgbor Sai when he returned to Ghana in 1970, as a qualified Medical Officer and Medical Scientist.

"At the newly established University of Ghana Medical School, he additionally entered into specialized areas such as Epidemiology in Medicine; Preventive and Social Medicine; and Public Health, when he returned to Ghana in 1970. Soon after his arrival, he was tasked to team up with senior colleagues to control the cholera epidemic, which broke out in 1970/71 in the nation. With his specialization in epidemiology, he was a kingpin in the team, which fought a relentless but vain battle, to prevent cholera from taking root in Ghana.

"Beyond this great national effort, Professor Ashitey persisted as a pioneer to move the frontiers of social and preventive medicine in Ghana through the proactive research projects he undertook that translated into action to impact the major health problems of several communities in both rural and urban areas. His academic work, for over three decades after he had become a Professor in 1988, strengthened medical students to appreciate the value of epidemiology in medicine, as he headed the Department of Community Health at the University of Ghana Medical School. In order to practice what he had been teaching as a Professor of Public Health and Social Medicine, he teamed up with Osu and Osu Salem Old Boys who were doctors, to establish the Osu Medical Foundation in 1985. The laudable objectives of the Foundation, among others, were to deliver help, health and hope to the people of the Danish-Osu community that were in dire need of medical care.

"The pinnacle of his heroism to date is his passionate leadership of the Osu Salem Old Boys' Association which undertakes activities and projects to cherish and sustain the fabric of that historic Alma Mater, Osu Salem." When the white-haired members of the Osu Salem Old Boys' Association in the audience hear this, they rise spontaneously and begin to sing their school anthem:

>   Ani dzee Salem School otee loo?
>   Kɛdzi dzɛmɛ otee lɛ
>   Nolɛ teeshi ni oba, ni obafata wɔhe
>   Kɛye gbi dzuro nɛɛ
>   Ni wɔyeo ŋnɛnɛ nɛɛ
>   Koni wɔkɛ kai
>   Koni wɔkɛ kai
>   Wɔ yoomo, nidzi Salem lɛ
>   Koni mɛi fɛɛ ana ale akɛ
>   Salem nyo dzi oo
>   Koni mɛi fɛɛ ana ale akɛ
>   Salem nyo dzi ooo!

As the young school children see the white-haired Old Boys enthusiastically singing their school anthem, they get excited and begin to cheer Ataa Forkoyi for his beautiful narration on Danish-Osu community heroes. He raises both hands in acknowledgement and waves back at them. At the end, he thanks the audience for their attention and patience in listening to him. He makes a gentle bow and with that, speedily brings the day's proceedings to a close. With a sigh, he slowly descends the steps of the dais and walks away.

The Unsung Heroes

As soon as he gets to the bottom of the dais, the human rights activist, who has been in the audience listening attentively, walks up to him and with much emotion, expresses disappointment that there was not a single female mentioned in the lengthy narration about Danish-Osu heroes.

"My friend your problem has to do with your lack of understanding of the concept of heroism," says Ataa Forkoyi in response to her criticism. "So now, let us try to put in context what you have observed and heard today at this Durbar. What is heroism?" Assuming his pedantic style of speaking, he begins to answer his own question. "One time or other, everybody seeks a hero. There are favourite childhood heroes who become role models. There are teenage heroes adored as pop-stars. According to scholars, the distinguishing essence of any heroism is that intrinsic stature associated with people whose personal achievements provide inspiration for others.

"In the distant past the majority of achievements that provided inspiration for others, especially the youth, were essentially accomplished in the context of warfare or conflict against enemies of the community. It was believed that these achievements stemmed from courage that provided moral, mental and metaphysical strength to venture, persevere, and withstand danger or difficulty. Because of this traditional perception, heroism in the Danish-Osu community has been gender-biased since it has always been appreciated essentially only from the viewpoint of women. It was women who made men heroes as they returned from war. It was women who cheered the heroes as they returned home bearing their war trophies with their 'terkleh' in the right place on their bodies. It was the sisters, aunts, mothers, grandmothers and wives who hailed their brothers, nephews, sons, and husbands as they distinguished themselves in various achievements within the community."

Ataa Forkoyi continues with his voice becoming rather strident: "It was the mothers and sisters and daughters who hailed their returning male relatives as they came back home from the battle fronts. It was the elderly women who had seen several seasons of harmattan that put the 'sliki terkleh' on the loins of their deceased male relatives as they prepared them for burial. It was the queen-mothers who approved the list of names of heroes in the community that was prepared by a committee. Hence, there are no female heroes at Danish-Osu.

"However, it does not mean that tradition neither recognizes nor celebrates the achievements of women; on the contrary, tradition places the heroism of men far below the achievements of women in the community.

"For example, the title given to the mother of twins is *'Haadzi anyɛ.'* The word *'haadzii'* in itself, is very intriguing. Although it means 'twins,' in Gã, it does not connote the notion of 'double' as in some other Ghanaian languages that recognize twins as special. Its singular form, *'haa'* is similar to the word *'ha'* which means 'give.' Twins are believed to give or bring blessings to the family into which they are born. In this light, with the title 'Haadzii anyɛ,' a mere mortal is accorded a status which comes with a metaphysical capacity and recognition placed far above heroism. Another example is in the custom of 'Sleeping on the mat of the tenth,' or *'Nyɔŋma saanɔ wɔɔ,'* in Gã.

At this point in the explanation, the architecture student cuts in to ask Ataa Forkoyi about this custom: "In my study of 'History of Cultures,' I have never come across any information about this practice you are referring to; what is it?"

Ataa Forkoyi grimaces and exclaims: "My goodness! Is this young man still so impatient? Today is Community Heroes-Day, not the day of the 'Greats of the Community.' But because of our young friend's impatience, let me briefly explain this customary practice that honours and celebrates the great achievement of a mother of ten children.

"In the days of High Tide at Danish-Osu, the survival of the community depended on how populous it was. People were needed to resist the frequent attacks of rival groups from neighboring communities. Men were needed to go into battle with the Akwamus, the Akyems and the Asantes, who sought to dominate the coastal communities. People were also needed to replace the able-bodied who were sold away by the Danes. For the chiefs and leaders of the community, the nagging question always was, where would the people come from? Was it not from the wombs of daughters, wives and mothers of the Danish-Osu community?

"In light of this survival issue, prolific wombs had to be recognized and appreciated. So, tradition began to honour mothers who could give birth to, nurture and raise at least ten surviving offspring in their lifetime. It was in recognition of this great achievement that the husband of such a woman, acting on behalf of the community and with the support of both maternal and paternal extended family members, would present the 'Mat of the Tenth' or *'Nyɔŋma saa'* to his wife, to sleep on. This was a symbolic act accompanied by a grand celebration and the presentation of gifts, including the customary 'Goat of the Tenth' *('Nyɔŋma Too')*, to let the mother of ten children know that the survival of the community depended more on her than on the heroes who returned from war. The 'Mat of the Tenth' signified that such a worthy mortal deserved to have rest, a kind of holiday, for herself.

"Such women constituted the Greats of the Community. If you would like to know more about them, come to the next celebration of Day of the Community Greats. But I wish to let you know that there are several women of Danish-Osu whose names could have been deservedly mentioned on this occasion of Community Heroes-Day." Ataa Forkoyi, now appearing highly elated and with eyes wide open as if watching something, begins to read out an unseen list:

"We have, for example, Maa Sanku, alias Mrs. Mina Holm (born Hesse of Danish ancestry), the mother of the talented, blind civil servant and organist Adzei Holm. Maa Sanku also earned the nickname 'Mother Organ,' because she could sing from memory, all the hymns of the old Gã Presbyterian Hymn Book. Then there was Teacher Mota, born Sarah Mota Welbeck, the indefatigable educationist who touched the lives of many Osu school children when they were at the primary schools. Auntie Dedee, alias 'Happy Corner,' born Josephine Dedei Odonkor, a national political figure who helped Kwame Nkrumah to launch and sustain the Convention Peoples' Party in Accra; 'Chez Julie' Kweifio-Okai who achieved fame as a trail-blazing fashion designer and fashionista, whose influence extended beyond the boundaries of Ghana into Francophone West Africa; Dr. (Mrs.) Elizabeth Naa Masoperh (of Danish ancestry), the accomplished first female dental surgeon of the community."

Ataa Forkoyi pauses for effect and adds "And finally, Alice Anum, the woman who achieved both national and international fame in sports because of her unusual speed despite a small and frail structure. I can continue with the list but let me end for today."

As soon as he finishes his last sentence, the human rights activist comes in exclaiming disenchantedly: "These did not and do not qualify as heroes because they could not don 'sliki terkleh.' Is that right?"

Ataa Forkoyi emphatically answers, "Precisely, but they are the unsung heroes. That notwithstanding, it will not be right for me to say they do not qualify as heroes because they do not don on 'sliki terkleh.' I accept that I should have included the Community Greats in the list of the Heroes of the Community. As a Hindu scripture is said to assert, 'when women are revered, there the gods are pleased, when they are not, no rite will yield any fruit.' The mentioning of such Female Greats was a lost opportunity of presenting great role models for our beautiful and bright girls. Apologies to you my dear and all those whose sensibilities have been sorely touched. My mind was somewhat still stuck in the 'sliki terkleh' centuries."

The lady laughs and with a great sigh of relief says: "It is refreshing to hear such outmoded male chauvinistic views are fading from our society."

After his gracious statement, he raises his right hand as if to bless his listeners and says: "It has been a long day. Thanks for participating in Community Heroes Day. I shall see you another time. Ŋoo Wala."

With that, he gently walks away into the twilight which, has already begun to engulf the Durbar grounds and the outline of his small image. Shining in his white kente cloth and white silk tunic shirt, he gradually vanishes from the view of his listeners.

Seven | Sites of Significance at Danish-Osu

Discovering an Out-Of-Sight Architectural Heritage

T HE YOUNG ARCHITECTURE STUDENT WHO WAS IN THE AUDIENCE when Ataa Forkoyi addressed the Durbar for the celebration of Community Heroes Day at Danish-Osu was struck by the remarkable significance of Osu Salem in the lives of most of the heroes mentioned that day.

This led to a keen curiosity to find out more about the building and its history. He made a mental note to arrange for a site visitation. When he discussed his intention with Ataa Forkoyi after the Durbar, he was immediately encouraged to schedule a date for the visit. He thought a fine day in December would be appropriate.

The scheduled date is today. As expected, the weather is dry and dusty at Danish-Osu. The young architecture student, together with his mates from the university in Kumasi, are walking around the sites of significance in the community, in the company of Ataa Forkoyi, who at every spot stops and delivers an academic exposition on the construction of the site where they are standing.

They walk around in good humour, visiting several sites of memory with architectural significance. Inside Christiansborg, they stand and stare at the old courtyard, the slave dungeons and Engmann's eighteenth century water cistern baroque stone cover; outside Christiansborg to the west, they behold the archaeological site of the Provesten Watchtower.

Along the Awusai Atso street, they come across the Fleischers' and Hesses' stone houses in ruins; the almost hidden stone two-storey courtyard of Nii Tetteh We at Agbadza Dzoohe; the ruined Hansen's stone cottage at Anahor; the rickety Osu-Alata Stool House abutting the Richter Fort; the ruined Richter's public water cistern stone cover. From the tamarind tree-lined old Danish slave route, they catch glimpses of the Opinta two-storey stone townhouse and the dull old Quist family-house at Amantra comes into view.

Stories of the Stones in Construction

They are now heading towards Osu Salem but Ataa Forkoyi brings them back to "Frederichs Minde" first, the nineteenth-century family stone house built by a Danish Jew by the name of Wulff Joseph Wulff.

Ataa Forkoyi regains his breath after the long and circuitous walk and begins to lecture again: "My friends," he says in his characteristic pedagogic tone, "I have brought you here to show you just three objects of interest that accord this site a heritage status. I do not need to talk extensively about the architectural configuration of this house. Architects who have studied it have written about it, and if you want to know more about 'Frederichs Minde,' you have to go and consult your journals.

"Wulff Joseph Wulff, the original owner of this house, was a Danish Jew who arrived at Christiansborg on November 3, 1836, to work as an assistant in the Danish administration. Besides living within the walls of Christiansborg, he also tasted life in the Danish-Osu community. In fact, it was as a result of the discrimination he endured from his compatriots as a Jew that he decided to build a house for himself and his Danish-Osu wife and their mulatto children.

"In this very house, which he named 'Frederichs Minde,' are found the three objects of cultural and historic interest I have mentioned. Before he left Denmark, he had a portrait made of him in his uniform as an assistant of the Danish administration in the Guinea Coast. This portrait arrived after his death, and as intended was hung in the living room of the house as you see now. He also ordered a stone name-plate with the inscription, 'Frederichs Minde: built 28 May 1840 by W. J. Wulff.' It is the very one you see on the wall above your heads. When you descend from where we are now into the room located on the north-west of the ground-floor, you will see the third object of interest.

"While Wulff was living in the Danish-Osu community, he observed how the local people buried their dead beneath the rooms of their houses. Wulff found this practice most unacceptable and primitive. However, because he did not wish to be among his compatriots after death, since they had not accepted him in life, in his last testament he expressed the wish that barring any objection, his body should be interned in a room of his house, in case he did not make it back to Denmark alive.

"Now, you see two unnamed graves in the floor of this room in which we are standing. One is marked longitudinally with tiles and the other is marked squarely. The longitudinal one is the grave of Wulff's daughter called Wilhelmine Josephine Wulff who became Cochrane by marriage. The square marked grave bears the mortal remains of Wulff J. Wulff who became an ancestor on December 16, 1842."

Fascinated to see graves inside the room of a house for the first time, the impertinent architecture student turns to Ataa Forkoyi for an explanation of the squarish form of Wulff's grave.

Bemused, Ataa Forkoyi responds, "Indeed your inquisitive mind will let you learn a lot. You see, according to the Stones, in the time of Wulff at Danish-Osu, the dead who were buried in rooms of houses, were buried standing instead of lying down."

Immediately the student exclaims, "My goodness! That makes sense. Standing takes less space than lying down, which could take about thrice the space."

The student's colleagues break into laughter and begin to hail him: "*Woye buei!* You are good! You are a master!"

After this, Ataa Forkoyi invites the students to follow him to another heritage house. They walk eastwards to Osu Agblanshie to the Nii Okantey Shikatse We, a stone house built by a Danish merchant by the name of Jen Jacobsen in the early nineteenth century.

Stone House with a Living Memory

As they walk, Ataa Forkoyi begins to tell them the history of the house. "The house we are going to visit was built by a Danish merchant, with the skilled labour provided by local stone masons and other experienced artisans who had been involved in construction work at Christiansborg. He put up this building to serve as a residence as well as a trading facility, with bedrooms and a living room upstairs and a slave-holding unit with a warehouse and a shop downstairs. Soon after putting up the house, he passed away and within three days the Danish administration had to auction his belongings, including the house.

"The house was bought by another merchant called Hans Christian Truelsen who had been living and trading in the Danish-Osu community and in other places as far as the islands in the Volta River. An Ewe island village named 'Trusckerwunu' meaning roughly 'Truske on the sand,' marks the fact that Truelsen sojourned there. After buying the house, Truelsen moved in with his Danish-Osu mulatto wife and together they raised their four daughters here. The names of these four daughters were Johanne, Caroline, Charlotte and Birthe.

"According to the Stones, Caroline married a Danish merchant and administrator by the name of Neils Brock, and gave birth to a daughter named Severine. It was Severine Brock that was married to Edward Carstensen, the last Danish Governor of Christiansborg, around 1843.

"The four daughters unfortunately lost their father in 1814 and became dispossessed of their house. Apparently, due to several debts Truelsen owed to his many trading partners, his property, which should have gone to his wife and children, was auctioned together with his other belongings. It was even reported that as his estate stood under the gavel, a woman debtor by the name of Apalee, sent a debt-collector all the way from Ada to the auction at Danish-Osu to claim her share of Truelsen's estate."

One of the colleagues of the architecture student, who happens to hail from Ada, quickly asks Ataa Forkoyi if Truelsen's house was obtained by Apalee.

Ataa Forkoyi shakes his head vigorously from side to side and says: "No, no. The auctioned house was bought by that wealthy young merchant, Henrich Richter. Later, when his father bequeathed his Barbara's House to him, he decided to sell the house, but was not able to do so before he passed away on June 29, 1849. His son, Johann E. Richter, inherited the house and in turn sold it to one of the up-and-coming Danish-Osu local merchants, Nii Okantey of Osu-Ashinte-Blohum.

"This merchant found the house ideal for his trading business and slave-holding for the internal slave-market. He expanded the house by adding female living quarters to abut the main house on the south west."

The architecture student interrupts with an observation: "Ataa Forkoyi, I now see why the house, built by a Dane, has no Danish name and is rather called Nii Okantey Shikatse We, which I understand to mean 'The House of Nii Okantey, the rich man.'"

Ataa Forkoyi gives a broad smile, nodding his head in admiration and says to the young student: "You are perfectly right. Since its purchase and occupation by Nii Okantey in the latter part of the nineteenth century, the building has become a family-house for the Nii Okantey line."

Hearing about the Nii-Okantey lineage, a female student on the tour quickly asks: "Who was this Nii-Okantey? Was he a mulatto or an indigene? Ataa Forkoyi, you must excuse me for bothering you with these questions. I cannot help asking because my boyfriend's surname is 'Okantey' and I know he comes from Osu but I do not know if his family is part of this lineage."

Ataa Forkoyi slows his walking pace and begins with amusement to tell the young lady about her boyfriend's forbears. "You see, all Okanteys of Osu sprouted from this prolific ancestor," he declares with certainty and confidence.

"This is how it all began. According to the Stones, this progenitor hailed from Osu-Ashinte-Blohum from the Okaileytse We, located not far from the old slave market, Awusai Atso. His father, Okaileytse Okai, was a renowned blacksmith who was married to a woman of Gã-Mashie with the family name Hammond, suggesting European ancestral origin. Nii Okantey was born in the 1830s, when the Danish administration was in its sunset years. The transatlantic slave trade had been officially abolished by then, but the trade, running both as an internal and external business, was very much alive in the Danish-Osu community. Nii Okantey, standing on the platform of his family's successful blacksmithing business and strengthened by his experience from sojourns in places such as the Congo, Cameroon and Nigeria, ultimately found his feet in the local trade and became a prominent merchant.

"According to the Stones, from his numerous trading activities in gold, arms and ammunition, foreign goods and human cargo, in addition to his blacksmithing workshop, he amassed a lot of wealth, earning him the title of *'Shikatsɛ,'* that is, a 'rich man,' anglicized as *Shikatse*. He also earned the accolade *'Atofotsɛ'* given to philanthropists of Danish-Osu at that time, for his generosity in sponsoring community projects. The Nii Okantey Shikatse We, which was his residence and business operation base, now serves as

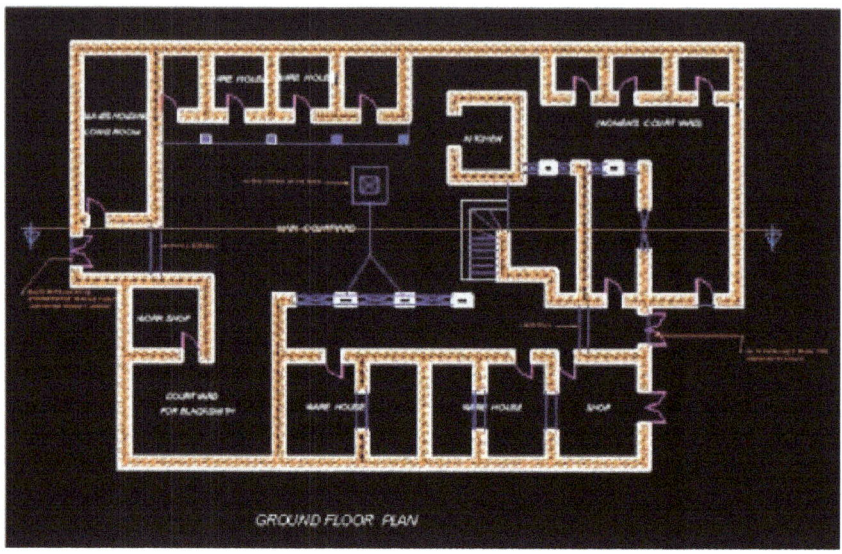

Figure 30: Computerized image of the ground floor plan of Nii-Okantey Shikatse We. *Illustration courtesy of author*

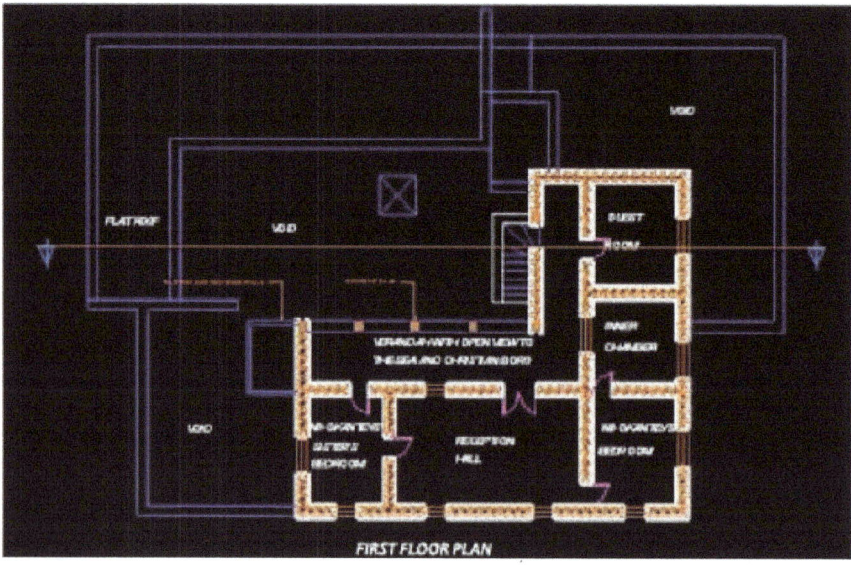

Figure 31: Computerized image of the first floor plan of Nii Okantey Shikatse We *Illustration courtesy of author*

the ancestral home of the extended family, which includes a large body of offspring that he fathered with several women, including some of his women-slaves."

When the male students in the group hear this detail in the narration, they burst out laughing. The female students, however, become incensed and strongly reprimand their male colleagues for shamefully amusing themselves with such an ignominious piece of information.

Ataa Forkoyi cannot help giving a chuckle as he observes the divergent responses of the students to Nii Okantey Shikatse's story. "Ladies and gentlemen, we are now at the historic house," he announces, bringing his touring group to the fore ground on the west side of the main entrance to the house. With the air of an architectural scholar lecturing his students, he continues, "Let me show you around and explain the architecture of this heritage building. This house covers a total area of 160 square metres and is spatially divided into two building masses, making the morphology of the house manifest two L-shaped units. These units help define a large stone-paved courtyard with two other minor outdoor spaces, located on the north-east and on the south-west as you can see (as in Fig 30).

"The main entrance, located on the west, has well-ornamented two-leaf door panels. The doorway leads directly into the house through the covered corridor defined by an archway. This corridor runs the length of the courtyard on the north, and acts as a transition space between the ground floor rooms on the north and the courtyard. Along this corridor are located the four massive stone masonry columns which carry the three arches upon which the first wooden floor slab is anchored. At the south end of the courtyard, about one and half metres away from the south side of the single storey component of the second L-shaped unit, is located the square-shaped baroque style outer stone cover for the water cistern you can see standing over there (see Fig 32).

"The second doorway located on the east leads from outside into the courtyard through an arched entrance space, linking the north-south aligned long room to the main courtyard. The north-south oriented long room found on the east of the courtyard has no verandah to it, in contrast to the east-west oriented room located on the south of the courtyard, which has a colonnaded verandah fronting the courtyard. This verandah appears to be a later addition introduced to the rooms abutting the outwork wall on the south.

"On the west of the courtyard, linking the ground floor rooms on the north and the upper rooms directly above the ground floor, is the stone masonry one-flight staircase." At this point, Ataa Forkoyi begins to climb the staircase and invites the students to follow him. He continues to speak while climbing. "This stone staircase has fifteen steps that link the ground floor and the first floor on a wide covered verandah on the upper level. The verandah, fronting the rooms on the first floor, opens out towards the south with a good view to the sea and the gardens of Christiansborg.

"As seen from the spatial organization of the first floor, there is direct access from the corridor to the room opposite the staircase located on the north-south axis. This room, which served as a guest room, abuts the inner chamber of the bedroom that was occupied by Nii Okantey himself. From the wide verandah, from which good views can be obtained of activities in the main courtyard as well as of the sea and castle garden, a two-leaf entrance door leads into what served as the reception hall and living room of the house. On the east of this hall is located Nii Okantey's sister's bedroom, with a very ornate door. Almost opposite this door is the other well-crafted door that leads to Nii Okantey's bedroom."

After showing the students the various rooms on the first floor, he comes back to the staircase and carefully descends the steps to the ground floor. He continues to show them around as he explains the functions of the rooms here. "The first room on the ground floor located on the west, next to the entrance doorway, was used as a shop in which European goods were sold in exchange for gold and in some cases, for pawned local people and slaves. The shop was serviced by warehousing facilities found in the three adjoining rooms. On the southwest corner of the entrance is a massive stone wall rising to a height of two and a half meters, to enclose a small courtyard space designated as the Yei amli, that is the section of the house where the women and children of the household lived."

The impertinent student, attempting to tease Ataa Forkoyi, jokingly interjects: "Was Nii Okantey keeping a harem here?"

Everybody laughs and Ataa Forkoyi shaking his head disapprovingly, says: "I will not answer such naughty questions. But now let us move into the main courtyard to see some details which tell interesting stories. As you can see, this yard, which has a massive brown stone pavement, served as a popular meeting place where all the members of the household, including pawned indigenes and domestic slaves, met to undertake daily household chores and perform cultural rites such as naming ceremonies and funerals. It is now the place where the lineage gathers at Homowo

Figure 32: Picture of baroque-style stone cover for a water cistern in the courtyard of Nii Okantey Shikatse We. *Courtesy of author*

Figure 33: Picture of courtyard showing residential block on the north and slave holding longroom on the east of Nii Okantey Shikatse We.
Photograph by courtesy of author

to eat the festive meal together.

"According to the Stones, in the lifetime of Nii Okantey Shikatse, it was believed that due to the enormous volume of gold trade he handled, pieces of gold stubs used to be found in this courtyard. So, visitors who came here at times had gum under their feet with the hope that as they walked around, their feet might pick up a few idle stubs from the floor of the yard.

"This courtyard, which acted as the private community centre of the house, is well drained as you can see. In the yard, you can see the well-positioned, square, baroque-style stone outer cover for the underground cistern below the courtyard. The cistern, which could hold about 5,000 gallons of water, is connected to two underground drainage pipes into which rainwater spouts channeled from the roof, are connected. The openings of these underground pipes have been blocked and the access from the outer cover to the underground cistern has also been sealed.

"On the south side of the courtyard is a sheltered space which has four stone masonry columns. The space abuts the southern outwork and appears to have served as a warehouse for commodities such as gold, ivory and oil palm, which Nii Okantey used to export. Linked to this open, sheltered space on the east is an enclosed long room with access through a door located in the east entrance loggia that has an arched doorway. Since you are architecture students, you can see that the spatial configuration of this long room and its high level, small size fenestration suggests that it used to be a holding place for slaves in transit. As you can see (Fig 33), the east doorway could easily have served as the point of entry and exit for the human cargo who had to be brought into the house without, so to speak, disturbing or upsetting the normal household activities in the main courtyard."

One of the students lets out his feelings at this detailed explanation of the architectural configuration of the house, shouting:

"This is the architecture of slavery, an edifice to inhumanity!"

Ataa Forkoyi, nodding in approval at the student's outburst, continues to speak with a certain amount of discomfort as he reflects on what the student has expressed.

"The structural integrity of the building fabric of this historic house is based on the use of massive stone masonry walls, measuring between forty and forty-five centimeters in thickness. The stability of the walls, which might have allowed the house to survive the 1939 earthquake that leveled a number of stonewalled houses at Osu, including the Richter Fort, is attributable to the lateritic rocky

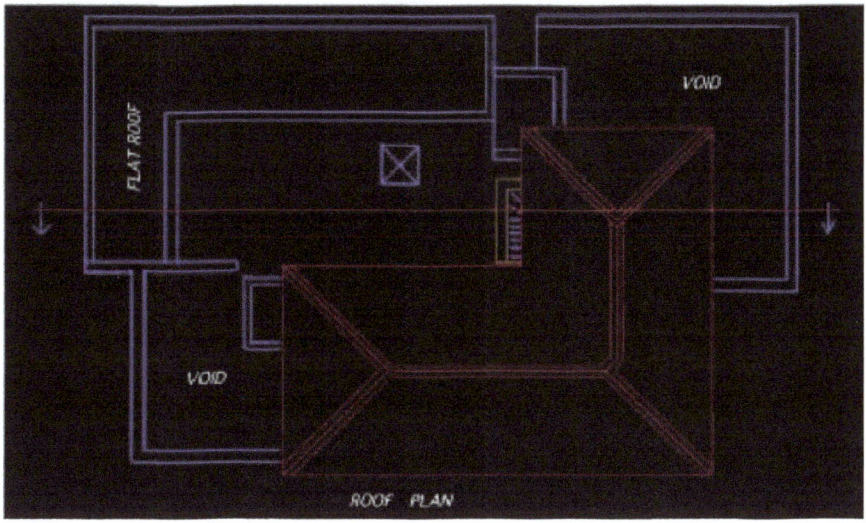

Figure 34: Computerized image of roof plan of Nii Okantey Shikatse We.
Illustration courtesy of author

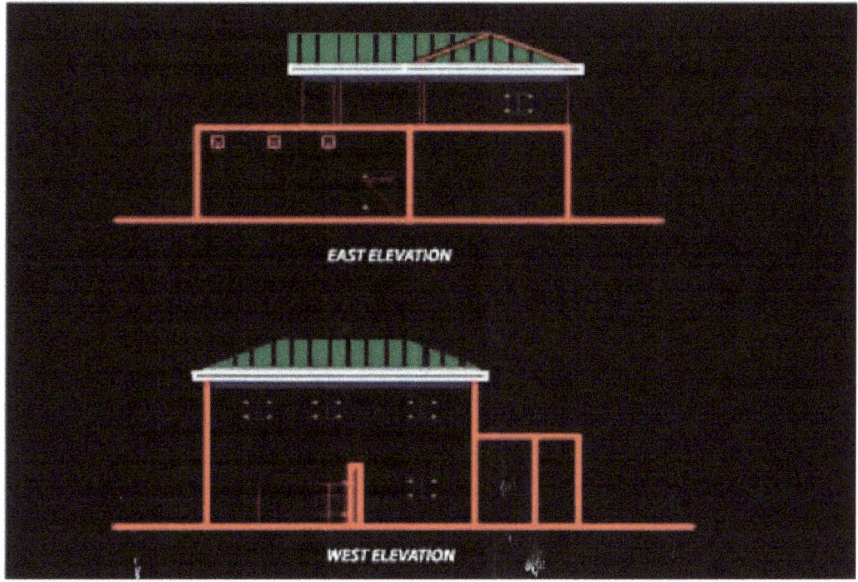

Figure 35: Computerized image of east and west elevations of Nii Okantey Shikatse We. *Illustration courtesy of author*

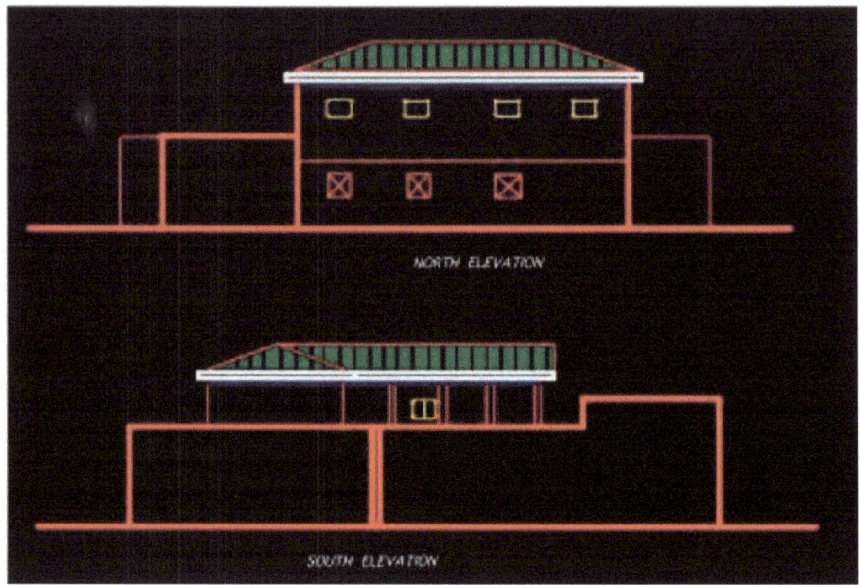

Figure 36: Computerized image of north and south elevations of Nii Okantey Shikatse We. *Illustration courtesy of author*

ground on which the house was built.

"The original structural framework of the floor deck of the first floor, together with the main roofing members and wooden pillars above the massive stone masonry arches on the ground floor, consisted largely of planks cut from the traveler's palm tree. Some of the original timber planks serving as floorboards and ceiling members have been replaced over the years. However, the timber door frames, door and window panels have survived, together with the attached ironmongery which might have been from Denmark.

"The architectural character of this historic house, as you have seen, (Figs 30-37), should, no doubt, suggest to you its original function. The building design was not originally conceived as the ancestral family house that the Nii Okantey Shikatse We has turned out to be. It was built as a fine example of a Danish stone-masonry trading house for ensuring the residential comfort as well as the safety and security of the household and the goods including the human cargo, which had to be held in transit for sale and shipment.

"As a stone masonry building, the character is brought out clearly in the way and manner in which the stones, as the main construction material, were employed. You can see, for example (as in Fig 37), that in the wall fabric of both the single storey and double storey units of the house, stones of different sizes of random-coursed rubble have been used, in thicknesses ranging from forty centimeters to about forty-five centimeters, from the plinth level to the lintel level.

"Furthermore, there are the five afore-mentioned beautifully shaped stone arches found in this house. The first arch located just after the entrance portal connects the inner south masonry wall of the ground floor to the north-south aligned stairwell. Beyond this arch are found the gracefully formed arches rising from four stone masonry columns, which hold the outer south masonry wall of the ground floor, that rise to a height of about two meters to provide a balustrade for the upper verandah in front of the reception hall on the first floor.

"The other single standing stone arch is in the masonry wall of the west façade of the slave-holding long room. This arch defines the special space related to the function of the long room as a place for human cargo."

When Ataa Forkoyi makes reference to the long room as a place for human cargo, the impertinent student is stirred up again to voice the thoughts that have been going on in his mind all this while. He slowly formulates his words and as if he is in the design studio back in the university he says, "I think this building is schizophrenic. It has a split personality. I see the Vitruvius triad playing out so well in its form and function. At the same time, in contrast to the Miesian assertion that God is in the details, I see the Devil manifested in its details."

His wrinkled face beaming with amusement, Ataa Forkoyi turns to the student and says, "My good friend, I do not understand your theory but I can assure you that this historic building possesses a number of interesting and charming details. Let us for instance look closely at the following observable ones." Ataa Forkoyi raises his right hand and, pointing his finger, directs the students' attention to the main entrance, saying: "The two-leaf wooden door enclosing the one and a half meter-wide entrance doorway here has been crafted with wooden battens that have been arranged in a diamond shape. This gives special significance to the public entrance of the house. The cast-iron butt-hinges which hang the door leaves, by the way, were brought from Denmark."

He turns in another direction now and continues to speak: "At the feet of two of the three stone masonry columns carrying the three arches fronting the main yard from the north are located

Figure 37: Picture of the masonry wall on the north side of the Nii Okantey Shikatse We. *Photograph courtesy of author*

square rainwater stone boxes which link rain-water spouts from the roof to the underground channels running under the stone pavement. These once carried water into the underground cistern positioned on the south side of the main courtyard. As I have earlier explained, the outer cistern cover, constructed in stone, is a replica of the polygonal structure built over Christiansborg's underground cistern by Governor Engmann in the outer courtyard, in 1750. Note that careful attention was given to the points on the shafts of the stone columns where the arches radiate to give the space created by the arches, a key-hole effect."

Now Ataa Forkoyi, speaking with exhilaration and excitement, swings around to face the west wall of the long room and continues with his lecture on the details. "The molded horizontal lines in a bas-relief, found on the façade of the west wall of the long room fronting the main courtyard on the east, make the otherwise plain surface of the wall subtly interesting and attractive. These molded lines contrast effectively with the three arches on the north wall, fronting the courtyard on the ground floor."

The students, standing in awe, quite overwhelmed by Ataa Forkoyi's stimulating presentation, just keep quiet and listen. So, without any questions coming from them, he continues enthusiastically. "The straight stone staircase from the ground floor to the first floor stands out distinctly in the courtyard, to highlight the significant difference between the dignified private

Figure 38: Picture of Osu Salem with Old Boys of 1958 Year Group.
Photograph by courtesy of author

Figure 39: Contemporary photograph of Osu Salem from the west, showing some students of the school. *Photograph by courtesy of author*

residence of the owner on the first floor and the common ground of the courtyard on the ground floor, where all daily and mundane activities were conducted."

Ataa Forkoyi now runs out of breath and asks for some water. After drinking a whole bottle, he is refreshed and resumes his tour, asking the students to follow him upstairs. "Now I would like to show you some more details," he says as they arrive upstairs in the reception hall of the house. "The ceiling in this reception hall consists of two wooden jack rafters, which support traveler's palm tree joists. These carry wooden ceiling planks laid parallel to the north and south walls that lend a sense of spaciousness to the rather long and narrow room.

"Finally, I would like you to pay attention to the details on the two doors in this room. Each leads to the rooms Nii Okantey and his sister, Naa Okailey, respectively occupied. The doors have been crafted with moldings on the door leaves and jambs on the door frame, thus giving a dignified character to the front of the doorways."

Ataa Forkoyi now brings his tour of the Nii Okantey Shikatse We to an end, and the students gratefully and joyfully applaud him with shouts of various appellations. He nods in appreciation and, leading them out of the house, heads northwards towards the famous Osu Salem.

More than an Alma Mater

They walk up the old, tamarind tree-lined Danish slave route, now known as Salem Street. Reading the inscription "Salem" on the street signboard gives the architecture student an indescribable sense of anticipation and excitement. He is so exhilarated because he is on his way to actually experience this site of great significance in the Danish-Osu community. He has been wondering since the Heroes Day Durbar how Osu Salem served as the physical environment that provided living and learning space for the heroes mentioned in Ataa Forkoyi's Heroes Day narration. They arrive on the premises and before them looms a seemingly shabby and grey two-storey structure. Ataa Forkoyi announces to the students with the voice of a best-man introducing a newly wedded couple to their wedding guests: "Behold, Osu Salem, the Presbyterian Boys' Boarding School of Osu, born in 1865 and still going strong!

"We shall walk around and talk about this heritage site, which is a concept and a construct, a symbol and a system, a belief and a building, all at the same time." The students realize that Ataa Forkoyi is in the mood for poetry today and get ready for the emotive metaphors that will flow from his aged and experienced repertoire.

"As an educational facility, the mission school later called Osu Salem was birthed in 1843, when the Basel Missionaries realized that there was the need to provide an alternative to the Castle School in Christiansborg, which had been trudging along since the mid-eighteenth century. The Castle School was attended only by children with Danish blood, and the other Danish-Osu children had no formal educational program to guide their development, apart from what they received from their fathers, mothers, and the customary initiating societies. The missionaries found the traditional education children received from family and community, inadequate. So, in their hired premises on the edge of the old town next to the Danish watchtower, Provesten, they began a mission school with the medium of instruction English rather than the Danish used in the Castle School.

"The mission school progressed gradually, and with time notable mulatto children who were attending the Castle School, such as Carl Christian Reindorf, were attracted to join their local kith and kin in the new school. As the missionaries, including Rev J. Zimmerman, developed competence in Gã and were able to produce teaching materials in the language, the medium of instruction changed from English to Gã. With the bombardment of Danish-Osu in 1854, the school experienced a setback as it lost its premises and school furniture, including the property the old Danish administration had donated as left-overs from Christiansborg. To continue with its program nonetheless, the missionaries relocated the school to Abokobi village, and continued with the few pupils they were able to bring along as they sought refuge there.

"Upon the rebuilding of Danish-Osu after the bombardment, the Basel Mission, with the assistance of Carl Christian Reindorf, then about twenty-one years old, was able to acquire an expansive plot of land from the Osu-Ashinte-Blohum neighbourhood to develop what came to be christened 'Salem,' a Christian residential enclave and the fifth traditional quarter or community within the Danish-Osu community. This residential enclave was intended as a settlement where the missionaries and their local converts could be insulated and isolated from the non-Christian activities and practices of Christiansborg and Danish-Osu.

"So, with land having been made available at Danish-Osu, the missionaries and their pupils came back from Abokobi around 1857, to continue the school in makeshift structures on this acquired land. By 1865, an impressive building had been constructed on the grounds of Osu Salem. Boys were admitted from both the traditional quarters and the Christian quarter as well as from the Gã- Dangme areas covered by the Basel Mission's work.

"These boys enrolled in the first-ever boarding school in Ghana, under the headship of a Basel Missionary called Rev. Weiss, assisted by a local trained teacher by the name of David Kotei. The ensuing decades and centuries saw other dedicated heads and teachers such as Rev. C. C. Reindorf, Teacher Cornelius Malm, Master William T. Evans, Rev. E. Max Dodu, Rev C. H. Clerk, Rev. P. C. Richter, Rev. G. N. Kumah, Teacher Anim, Teacher E. K. Anum, Master Lamptey, Master A. M. O. Ayettey, Teacher T. T. Apo, Rev. B. Kwapong Lokko, Master Akpey, Rev. G. A. Adom, Teacher Vincent Okunor, Rev. Mate-Kodjo and many others.

"Being the first permanent public structure erected in this Christian quarter known as Osu Salem, the school adopted the quarter's name and thereafter came to be known as Osu Salem. Later, when the Basel Mission was taken over by the Presbyterian Church, Osu Salem came also to be known officially as the Presbyterian Boys' Boarding School."

Before Ataa Forkoyi can continue with the story of Osu Salem as a boarding school, one of the students, who has keen interest in ecclesiastical architecture, raises his hand to indicate that he has a question and, with the old man's permission, says: "Sir, you have just stated that Osu Salem became the first permanent public building on the land of the Osu Salem quarter. But on our way here, I saw a beautiful stone church building. It appears to have been built during the time of the Danish administration, which preceded the year 1865, when Osu Salem was completed. How do you explain this?"

With a chuckle, Ataa Forkoyi responds to the question: "Yes, it is a beautiful example of stone masonry architecture, characteristic of the period of the Danes on the Guinea Coast. But no, it was not built in that period. That piece of ecclesiastical architecture is the Ebenezer Presbyterian Church and it was completed in 1902. Is that clear? Well then, let us continue.

"According to the Stones, Osu Salem, as a boarding school, was an educational experience that derived its component parts from a number of sources. The Basel missionaries who were its initiators, had in mind an English school for boys to be kept away from their homes and community enclaves for a specific period, in order to be trained in accordance with a certain philosophy. The boarding concept was also derived from the old Castle School that took the children away from the community into Christiansborg, to be raised and cultured as Danes, and was also influenced by the missionaries' observations of traditional rites of passage that took boys of a certain age group away from the community for a period, into a grove, to have them initiated."

One of the students interjects with a question. "So, the boarding school idea of Osu Salem was not a totally strange phenomenon after all?" she says.

"Not at all," responds Ataa Forkoyi. He continues: "Osu Salem was a culturally sensitive response to the challenge of introducing a school system into a community which needed a life changing educational program. As you will see later when we examine the history and significance of this site, it was a system that had a phenomenally positive impact on the community, with far reaching consequences for the Osu people and Ghana in general.

"The training given to the boys was holistic. Their heads, hearts, hands and feet were given an education that would make them realize their God-given potential, to enable them to become agents of change in their community of origin. To achieve this goal, the founding fathers created an appropriate physical and pedagogical environment within which the boarders were kept for four years, with intermittent breaks to go home during the vacation. The school was laid out in the roughly five-hectare land parcel, consisting of classrooms, dormitories and teachers' accommodations plus recreational grounds, vegetable and flower gardens, and craft workshops including pottery, carpentry, joinery, bookbinding, shoemaking, blacksmithing and lock-smithing. The school had a capacity of 120 to 160 pupils with a maximum class size of 40.

"As an educational facility, it was made available to pupils of other senior secondary schools in the Gã-Adangme mission area, who had to be coached for the competitive examination to enter Achimota College and other similar institutions. Later, when other boys' schools were established, boys seeking admission to Osu Salem had to sit for a competitive entrance examination. Prior to this, entrance had been open to whoever wanted to attend the school. Boys came from near and far to enter this unique pedagogical environment.

"The environment at Osu Salem was underpinned by a strong pietistic religious ethic through Christian worship and mandatory church attendance. Within this framework was anchored an academic program that covered subjects such as English and Gã languages, arithmetic, handwriting as an art and a functional learning tool, geography, history, religious knowledge, nature study, hygiene and music, especially organ playing and choral singing. Emphasis was placed on assiduousness in learning for achievement of excellence in all fields of endeavor. The ultimate aim of the training program was to form not only the pupils' minds, but also their spirits so that they could go into the community as witnesses of the transforming power of the gospel of Jesus Christ.

"The bedrock of the school environment was discipline. To remind the pupils of the military traditions associated with discipline, they were made to wear a school uniform designed in military style. For classes, they wore a pair of khaki shorts and a white drill shirt with a white belt in the middle. For Sundays, everyone wore long white trousers, an open white shirt and a navy blue blazer, without shoes, since everybody had to go barefooted.

"Discipline was the watchword in all the undertakings of the school and the quadrangle around which the learning and living spaces were configured epitomized the practice of discipline. Any pupil who infringed on any school law was disciplined in the quadrangle in the presence of the school assembly. The disciplinary measures meted out invariably included undertaking of hard labour as in the military, and when the infringement was very serious, a certain amount of flogging was added. Notwithstanding this regimented atmosphere, boys remained boys and miscreant behaviour now and then showed up, which managed to escape the eagle eyes of the teachers."

When one of the female students hears the account of the school's culture of discipline, she exclaims: "My goodness! How did those boys survive such an environment?"

Ataa Forkoyi smiles and says with a sigh: "A few could not survive but most did. Those who survived went through the harsh but healthy training each day with the psychological attitude that eventually they would make it. To help them withstand the daily discipline, the boys coined the slogan, *'Salem dzee naanɔ'* meaning 'The tough times at Salem will not last forever.'"

He continues: "Until the end of the last century when the proverbial Osu Salem educational program was abandoned, most of the graduates of the school went on to occupy prominent positions in almost all spheres including the civil service, commerce and banking, artisanal trading and other areas of endeavor in Ghana."

With this, he pulls out a scroll with a long list of names and reads:

"A list of Old Boys that survived the Osu Salem environment includes Very Rev. L. L. Richter, a former Moderator of the Presbyterian Church of Ghana; Very Rev. E. Max Dodu, also a former Moderator of the Presbyterian Church of Ghana; Mr. H. H. Malm, the first African Assistant Colonial Secretary; Dr. C. E. Reindorf, an eminent medical officer and historian; Sir Charles Emmanuel Quist, the first Speaker of the Legislative Council; Justice Nii Amaa Ollennu, once the President of Ghana during the Second Republic, a former Speaker and a distinguished Judge and Jurist; Professor C. O. Easmon, the first Dean of the University of Ghana Medical School; Mr. Joe Ayettey, a renowned Civil Servant; Rear Admiral David Animle Hansen, the first Ghanaian Chief of Naval Staff and Naval Commander of the Ghana Armed Forces; Mr. S. Amate Akuetteh, a former deputy Managing Director of the Ghana Commercial Bank; Mr. Chris Hesse, former Chairman of the National Commission on Civic Education; Mr. L. Fifi Hesse, a former Director of the Ghana Broadcasting Corporation; Mr. Dowuona, a renowned teacher and Minister of State in the Convention People's Party Government; Dr. Modjaben Dowouna, a renowned Civil Servant; Professor Nii Lomote Engmann, a reputable Anatomist and Scholar, Mr. Harry Sawyerr, an elder Statesman and former Minister of State and Rev. Dr. N. T. Clerk, a former Director of Ghana Institute of Management and Public Administration.

Ataa Forkoyi pauses to drink some water and then continues:

"This list has the names of those who have joined the ancestors. But there is also a list of Old Boys who are still alive."

"And they are ..." one of the female students cuts in expectantly, but he continues without acknowledging. "They include names such as Dr. Emmanuel Evans-Anfom, a renowned Surgeon and former Vice Chancellor of the Kwame Nkrumah University of Science and Technology; Professor F. T. Sai, an international consultant and renowned authority on population and family planning; Professor G. A. Ashittey, a notable Professor of Public Health; Samuel Isaac Kofi Odotei, a United Nations appointed librarian who worked in the UN Regional Office in Dakar for several years; Professor George Clerk, an Emeritus Professor of Botanical Science at the University of Ghana; Vincent Richter, a world class pianist;

Rev. A. L. N. Annor, a former prominent banker; Dr. Nii Gbobilor Fleischer, a successful medical practitioner and political activist; Hon. Dr. N. Nyaho-Tamakloe, a medical practitioner and ambassador; Hon. Mr. Solomon Ofei-Darko, a former Mayor of the City of Accra; Rev. Prof. Andrew Seth Ayettey, former Provost, School of Medical Sciences, Legon, Ghana; Christian Charles Quist, successful public auctioneer; Nii Dzata, aka Lartey Laryea, Chief of a Youth of Osu; Edmund Abdo, a successful international banker; Elias Ablorh Odjidja, an international publisher and multi-media owner; Dr. Robert R. A. Bannerman, a prominent international medical practitioner; Dr. E. E. Amoonu Graham, a top-brass medical practitioner and anesthetic consultant; Dr. Sidney Torgbor Botwe, an international gynecological specialist; Professor Dr. Ing. H. N. A. Wellington, a one time Acting Pro-Vice Chancellor of the Kwame Nkrumah University of Science and Technology, Kumasi, and an iconic architectural scholar."

When the students hear the last name, they all express delighted surprise because they are familiar with him but never knew that he was an Old Boy of Osu Salem. Ataa Forkoyi then explains that there

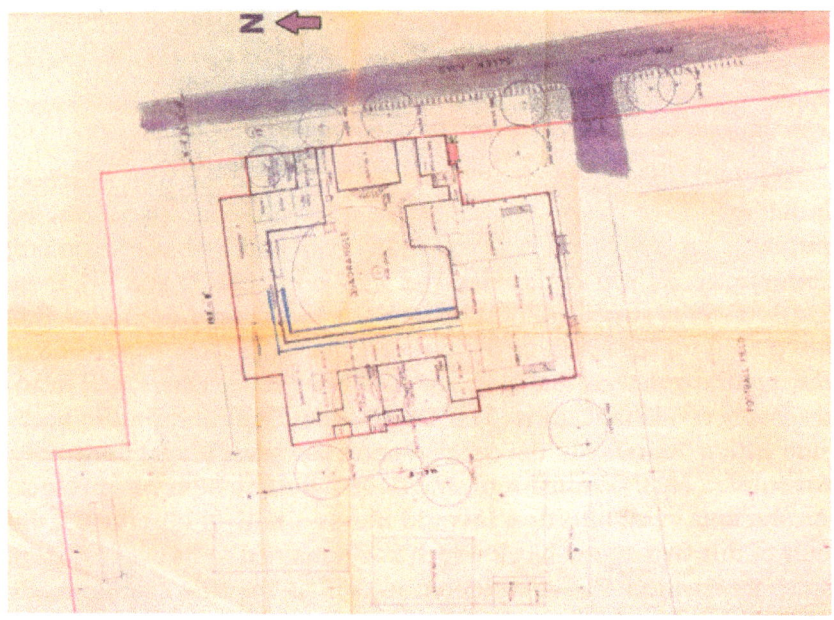

Figure 40: Architectural drawing of the ground floor plan of the school complex, showing the main block on the south, staff residential units on the east and west with another dormitory block on the north.
Illustration courtesy of Architectural Design Partnership, Accra

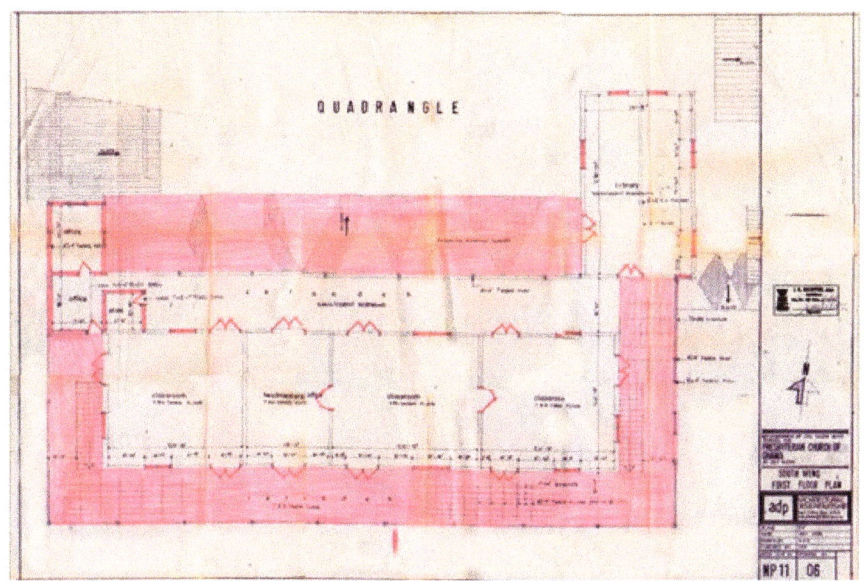

Figure 41: Osu Salem Building - Detailed drawing of first floor plan showing classrooms and the headmaster's office.
Illustration courtesy of Architectural Design Partners, Accra

Figure 42: Showing timber floor on timber-framed and adobe-infilled wall construction of Osu Salem building. *Photograph courtesy of author*

Figure 43: Showing various details of timber-framed and adobe infilled wall construction of Osu Salem building
Photographs by courtesy of author

are still many Old Boys who are associated with their University, but time will not allow all the names on the list to be mentioned. He then turns the students' attention to the various sections of the building they have been inspecting and continues with his lecture.

"Now, I would like to explain the architecture of this historic school building to you. The design clearly expresses the concept of bringing pupils and teachers together to teach, learn, and live in a close-knit community. As you can see (and as shown in Figs. 40 and 41), there is a two-storey structure comprising classrooms and dormitories, which are placed on the south of the central quadrangle. On either side of the quadrangle, west and east, are positioned the teachers' and headteacher's residential units.

"The single-storey building on the north side with a doorway in the centre, serves as an additional dormitory, to complement those on the ground floor of the two-storey main block. As students of architecture I would like you now to observe the details of this two-storey block which has remained in its original form since its erection and completion in 1865 as the first custom-made school building in Ghana."

The students now begin to take copious notes with annotated sketches as they follow Ataa Forkoyi. "According to the Stones, under the guidance of a southern-German master-builder, local craftsmen and builders were employed to erect and complete the two-storey building, which was symmetrically laid out with a large hall in the centre and two similar size dormitories on either side. Above this floor, which was based on a stone masonry plinth in the old Danish stone building style, is the first floor with a wide timber balustrade verandah which goes around to give cover to the ground floor below and provide circulation to link the other three classrooms and the Head-teacher's office.

"As the Stones recollect, the construction technology employed was the typical southern-German style of timber-framed and adobe in-filled structure, which as you may know from your lectures, is termed 'Fachwerk Konstruktion' in German.

"The horizontal section of the building has supporting posts and bearing girders. The dimensions of the tie-beams have reference to the width of the building. This is in accordance with the then north European building construction code of practice in timber works, which required that the width of a building should relate to the sectional dimensions of the beam to be used for the construction. In this regard, each of the beams used in this main building has a cross sectional dimension of nine inches deep and four to five inches wide, to correspond to the appropriate building span of five and a half meters.

"All the structural timber used is pinewood (Pinus sylvestris). According to the Stones, the pine trees from which this pinewood was obtained grew in the forests of northern Germany close to the Baltic Sea. The area was called Pomerania and therefore the pine obtained from the region was known as Pomeranian Pine. The Pomeranian pine hardwoods have a high resin content with large knots in their fabric. These properties make such timber very resilient and termite resistant. This explains why the integrity of the structural system of the Osu Salem building is unquestionable to date.

"The Pomeranian timber in this building arrived already shaped as pre-fabricated pieces, shipped possibly from Copenhagen. For ease of assembly in construction, all the shaped pieces had inscribed numbers in roman numerals and identification marks to indicate where each piece should be placed and fixed in the overall framework of the building. The identification marks on the timber pieces guided the builders to know precisely where the pieces would fit in the structure with respect to the solar axis and at every level of the structure, from the ground floor through to the first floor and the roof.

"The structural pieces were held together by means of mortise and tenon secured with wooden pegs. The resulting timber framework was in-filled with adobe to constitute the walling system, which was finished with sand/lime plastering. In order for the timber surfaces in the wall to receive and bond well with the sand/lime plastering, the timber work was finished rough. In between the timber planks that constituted the ceiling of the ground floor and the slab of the first floor and the roofing system, flat bags of sand were inserted to function as sound and heat insulating materials.

"To conclude, let me inform you that this building, which contains so many interesting construction details with historical significance, has stood the test of time. In 1939, when Osu and Accra were hit by a disastrous earthquake, Osu Salem, although seventy-four years old at that time, stood firm as other structures collapsed around it. Architectural conservators who have come to study it in its present state, are of the opinion that this structure can stand for the next hundred years."

A Monument and an Alma Mater

Overwhelmed by Ataa Forkoyi's concluding remark, one of the female students, whose grandfather and great-grandfather were Old Boys of Osu Salem, becomes ecstatic and shouts: "Osu Salem stood firm because it is a monument."

Now, as if charged by a spirit of poetry, with her broad-rimmed straw hat in her hand, she starts to hail her ancestors' Alma Mater in her own musical fashion:

> Osu Salem!
> A monastic edifice to develop spirituality of pupils
> To develop souls from Anahor, Alata,
> Souls from Ashinte Blohum, Kinkawe, Gã-Mashie...
> Osu Salem! A juvenile military academy
> The place to shape the mind, body and soul

The place to discipline all and sundry
And yet not all,
Osu Salem, a living academy,
An academy that produces quality men
An academy that produces professional minds
An academy that produces dexterous hands
An academy that produces agile feet.
Oo! Osu Saalem!
A Monument of Wisdom,
A Monument of Danish-Osu,
A Monument of Ghana,
You are the cherished
Alma Mater of my ancestors
You deserve conservation
You deserve consecration
You deserve preservation
By your offspring, the Old Boys,
For generations to come.
Osu Salem, You are the School!
A great Monument
An Alma Mater indeed
The source of great pupils and peoples!

Ataa Forkoyi, beaming with delight, turns around and looks at the young lady with admiration. With a nod, he says, "Well said and well done," and with a bow, adds, "That is it."

With this statement and with a sense of finality, he brings down the curtain on his fascinating presentation and the students give him tumultuous applause and a standing ovation.

An Incredible Community History

One of the female students then steps out, walks to Ataa Forkoyi and gives him a prolonged bear hug. When she releases her embrace, she takes his hand into hers and, looking tearful and emotional, begins a little speech:

"Colleagues, you will agree with me that this man whose hand I am holding not only in my hand, but also in my heart deserves to be honoured. It is now my responsibility as the class spokesperson to give the vote of thanks on your behalf and on my own behalf for this fantastic and fabulous session we have had with Ataa throughout this whole tour of these sites of significance at Danish-Osu. But I am lost for words to do so. May I therefore call upon our senior colleague who arranged the tour, to give the final vote of thanks?

Amidst shouts of *"Woyɛ buei, woyɛ buei,"* the familiar, impertinent architecture student, who has been part of Ataa Forkoyi's audience during the tour of Danish-Osu, steps forward to join his female colleague, who continues to hold Ataa Forkoyi's hand as they stand together in front of their colleagues.

"My friends," he begins, "My lady colleague claims she is lost for words. I am lost for thoughts to formulate what has been going on in my mind into comprehensible words. It has been many months since I have been in the company of this exceptionally great man; no, I mean great mind.

"He has shared with us what the Stones of Osu have been saying all these centuries. It has been most rewarding to listen to the story of how Osu came into existence. He has told us how Osu became tarnished with the transatlantic slave trade and 'Danish-ed,' through the Danish administration into Danish-Osu. He has shared with us the experiences of the mulattoes and how they became ancestors from which family trees grew, to develop the Danish-Osu cultural landscape. His profiling of the sung and unsung heroes of Danish-Osu has been illuminating and inspiring. And his ending today with Danish-Osu sites of significance has been most fascinating and educational."

"As these stories are re-played and re-hashed in my head, I must say that the learning experience I have gained during the years I have been studying at the university, cannot measure up to the information and insights I have acquired listening to the stories of the Stones through Ataa Forkoyi. I am most grateful to be acquainted with this incredible community history. My friends, this noble man has shown power, profundity and a prolific knowledge of history. He deserves a 'dry-ponding' for our respect, appreciation and gratitude."

At the insistence on the "dry-ponding" of Ataa Forkoyi, the students, as they do to a cherished colleague who is having a wedding or receiving the last respects before burial, respectfully grab the feet and shoulders of the old man, lift him up in a horizontal position, push his horizontally-aligned body high and then lower him gently on his back, to the ground. They do this three times.

When it is all over, they will not let him go. Instead, amid shouts of joy and merriment, they carry Ataa Forkoyi shoulder-high as if he were a national football hero victoriously returning from a World Cup tournament. As they bear him shoulder-high and cheer him enthusiastically, he begins to wonder if the people who hear the stories of the Stones will go beyond this youthful enthusiasm and learn the lessons of the stories. Do people learn at all from history? Will they ever learn from history? The thoughts keep cropping up in his now agitated and exhausted mind as he is carried aloft in his human palanquin.

Not aware of these troubling thoughts going on in Ataa Forkoyi's mind, the students keep him joyfully high on their shoulders as they march down the Salem Street towards Osu-Anahor, singing cheerfully into the fast approaching twilight.

Figure 44: Ruins of the Danish Country House at Osu Kuku Hill
Courtesy of author

Figure 45: A wall of ruins at Osu Amangfong bombarded by the British in 1854.
Courtesy of author

Epilogue

Epilogue

Looking Beyond Danish-Osu

ATAA FORKOYI, THE PROTAGONIST OF THIS BOOK, HAS FINISHED WITH his factual and absolutely fascinating narrations set within a fictional framework, as interpreted from the Stones of Osu. His listeners, the students, have returned to their homes and wherever they came from to listen to the stories of Danish-Osu.

What stories will the Stones continue to tell after this? One may wonder, and as one wonders, the mind goes back to appreciate how the community history and heritage of Osu dramatically mark the common history and heritage that belongs to Ghana, Denmark and Norway, the chief players in the transatlantic slave trade that was organized and managed from Christiansborg in the seventeenth and eighteenth centuries.

One hundred and sixty years ago, the Danish national flag was lowered from its flag mast in front of Christiansborg by the officiating military staff of the Danish administration. It was neatly folded and formally handed over to Edward Carstensen, the last Danish Governor of Christiansborg, to mark the end of nearly 200 years of Danish-Norwegian presence on the Guinea Coast. This was all done after Christiansborg, together with all the other Danish properties in the Gold Coast, had been sold to the British Government.

As Edward Carstensen ceremonially sealed the end of the Danish period and administration in the Guinea Coast by receiving the folded flag to be taken back to Denmark, one of the old, officiating military staff might have began to muse. Somewhere in the deep recesses of his mind and heart might have lurked a vague conviction that taking away the Danish flag would never sever the relationship between his homeland, Denmark, and the Gold Coast of Ghana, the country in which he discovered the true nature of his own heart. In the mind of this nameless soldier, there emerged a kind of foreknowledge, a vague hope that the Danes and Norwegians would return to the Guinea Coast. Thinking with passion about the number of Danish and Norwegian governors, administrators, merchants, and soldiers lying in graves inside and outside Christiansborg, Augustaborg, Fredensborg and Fort Prinsensten, he knew that one day, the Danes and Norwegians would come back to this place of muffled memories.

He believed they would come back because of the unbroken ancestral connections that had been established between the people of Denmark and Norway through the numerous mulattoes that had been fathered at Osu and the other Danish settlements on the Guinea Coast. He knew his compatriots would one day return to look for the African families that provided homes and hearths for their sojourning countrymen. He had a strong inclination to believe that, one day, generations beyond him would also come back to make amends for the evils of the transatlantic slave trade.

Since then, as this nameless old Danish soldier might have wished and foreseen, representatives of the former occupants of Christiansborg have, in official and unofficial capacities, returned and kept returning to Ghana. With the establishment of a permanent diplomatic base in Accra, the Government of the Royal Kingdom of Denmark has been operating in Ghana for several years to promote bi-lateral trade and inter-governmental co-operation in economic and social development for the mutual benefit of the two countries. The activities of DANIDA in Ghana have, for example, enhanced this co-operation for decades.

Non-governmental organizations as well as individual Danes have been collaborating with Ghanaian organizations and personalities to undertake development projects and social activities in both Ghana and Denmark. The recently restored and commissioned Fredericksgave, a slave museum at Seseme, located on the old Danish plantations in the Accra plains, helps to substantiate the common history and heritage of Ghana and Denmark.

Besides the Danish collaborative work, a Norwegian research team has also undertaken a number of projects in Ghana to demonstrate the reality of their return to this historic space that links the Nordic centre of the transatlantic slave trade to the history of Ghana, Denmark and Norway. The 1998 Fredensborg Slave Ship Project that was supported by UNESCO in Norway gave dramatic credence to the nameless Danish soldier's 1850 prescience.

Conscious of the common history and heritage of Ghana and the Nordic countries, Denmark has not been shy to confront the evils associated with the unequal trade relationship that existed in the past and which was very much associated with the transatlantic slave trade. It is believed that the sad and dark story of the inhuman slave trade and the concomitant slavery and all that it engendered at that time, with related activities such as the inter-tribal wars, 'panyerring,' pawning and selling and buying of people as human cargo perpetuated by the local chiefs and merchants, their Danish and other European counterparts, should not be swept under the carpet.

Similarly, the proverbial Ghanaian practice of avoiding talking about the history of slavery in the community, as alluded to by Ataa Forkoyi's reference to the *"Atsii mɔta"*— 'You do not mention it' attitude in his narration, must give way to an honest and unabashed discussion of the trade in human cargo and the slavery that formerly existed in Ghanaian communities. In the same vein, the horrors of the transatlantic slave trade, as organized and managed by the Danes and the Europeans, must not, out of embarrassment and guilt, be glossed over in international literature and trivialized by Western scholars who deal with the history of the period.

Adopting a position of honest confrontation of the horrors of the past will make the lessons to be learnt from this dark period in our common history authentic and proactive. By doing so, we will gain the moral strength to deal faithfully and decisively with any similar current or future inhuman activities that may rear their ugly heads, whether related to discrimination, child labour, human trafficking, racism, ethnic and religious intolerance, xenophobia or any form of injustice in the world.

Maintaining this stand may help us all to realize the strength of our common history and heritage that prevents the repetition of the evils and horrors of the past and reinforces and promotes the good in humanity. This is what may afford us a healthy and sound platform from which to look beyond Danish-Osu with its painful and pitiful past, to see good, hopefully, emerging from the future.

Acknowledgments

The second edition of *Stones Tell Stories at Osu* constitutes a narrative of memories of a community stretching four hundred years from 1607 to 2007 and cannot be told without acknowledging the contributions of many others.

First and foremost, I acknowledge Almighty God for giving me both the opportunity and the passion to undertake the research on Danish-Osu, and for sustaining me with the energy to undertake the arduous task of writing this book.

The process of researching to gain information and insights into Danish-Osu in locum, as well as other places outside Osu has not been easy. However, in the process, a number of milestones, marking exciting and depressing experiences have been reached.

Encounters and association with both collective entities and individuals along the way have been rewarding. Indeed, their support has eased the burden of being on the rugged road of extracting information from undefined nooks and curious crevices.

Throughout the research, vast amounts of information, both graphic and descriptive, were unearthed. The question arose of how to make the information available to those who might be interested in what the research findings might have to say, sing or shout about. For a long while, this question lay heavy, because the means to realize the goal of publishing the findings in the form of a book were not forthcoming. Then suddenly, one day, an advertisement appeared in a daily newspaper about grants obtainable from the Ghana Cultural Fund.

The problem of publication of the first edition was eventually settled when I applied for and received a grant from the same Ghana Cultural Fund to prepare the manuscript. The Fund, under the auspices of the Royal Danish Embassy in Accra, therefore, was the first organization that lent much appreciated support to ease the burden of writing the book.

In the same way, when printing and shipping the second edition from China became a challenge, the Royal Danish Embassy in Accra, came to the rescue through facilitated support from the Royal Danish, Queen Margretha II Fund.

Standing proudly beside the Ghana Cultural Fund are a number of other supportive organisations to which I owe unending gratitude. In 2005, the Ministry of Tourism and Diasporan Relations and the company APSTAR Ltd. offered me free return tickets to Germany to conduct research in the Moravian Archives, in Herrnhut, Germany. The donation of the free travel was an expression of the keen interest of the Ministry and of APSTAR in the outcome of the research on Danish-Osu, seen by them as beneficial to the newly conceived "Joseph Project," since the history of Osu was an essential part of the transatlantic slave trade narrative.

The Kwame Nkrumah University of Science and Technology (KNUST), Kumasi, with its usual practice of supporting laudable academic research, graciously provided a small research grant which helped to offset the cost of my travel and research in Germany.

The UNESCO-Accra Cluster Offices expressed interest in the research and extended initial encouragement and goodwill, firing my enthusiasm further at the prospect that the outcome might attract international recognition. Part of the cost of the publication of the book was also supported by the Accra Cluster Offices.

The Moravian Archives in Germany offered their guest accommodation in Herrnhut and also gave me permission to use copies of the original portraits of Christian Protten and his family, obtained from the well-maintained and resource-rich archives of the Moravian Brethren.

While working with the archival materials on Protten in Herrnhut, I was able to join Dr. Peter Sebald at his base in Niesky, some 60 kilometers from Herrnhut. Having previously introduced me to Protten as a historical figure in a lecture he gave at the Goethe Institut in Accra, he graciously sent me a copy of his transcribed version of Protten's Diarium in German.

On my research trip to Germany, I enjoyed the company of four families whose warm hospitality I wish to acknowledge here. First, my appreciation goes to my old classmate Dr. Sidney Botwe and his wife Mary, who hosted me for four days and gave me a home in Germany; next, I express my thanks to Rainer and Kornelia Bernhardt, who, in the company of my daughter Naa Lamile (Maa), drove over 200 kilometers from Bergneustadt in their camping minibus, to visit me at Herrnhut to offer me moral support in Schlesien, a place unfamiliar to me; third, my profound gratitude goes to Herr Udo Reip and his wife Monika, who provided me comfortable accommodation in their beautiful home in Bad Gandersee, and further protected my digitally recorded findings in Herrnhut by providentially making a copy of my originals, which were accidentally deleted after the research trip to Germany; and finally, my friends Wolfgang Brunssen and his wife Angelika, deserve my deep appreciation, for not only did they welcome me into their beautifully landscaped house in northern Germany for afternoon tea, but also provided me with important archival record of the geography of middle Europe in the eighteenth century.

I wish also to thank Messrs Darko Ltd, UK, whose company, directed by my former student Kwadjo Owusu Darko, generously provided financial support enabling me to reside at the Guest House of the Moravian Brethren to work in the Moravian Archives for 21 days.

Key figures among my deeply appreciated supporters are many Danish and Ghanaian friends and colleagues, especially Prof. Irene Odotei who gave me 1,000 cedis to pay my student field assistants, my field-assistants, final year students of the Department of History, KNUST, Ms. Audrey Ankrah, Ms. Sakyibia Tetteh and Mr. Laud Adjiri Nyantakyi, the collaborators who assisted in preparing the manuscript for publication; Ms. Margretta Morgan, my personal assistant, Mr. Kwesi Buami, my technical consultant; Mrs. Zenia Ossei, my editor and Mr. Elias Ablorh-Odjidja, my editorial and publishing consultant. Last, but by no means least, is my young friend Ruben Atekpe whose donation (2500 cedis) helped offset the cost of publication. They all deserve my profound gratitude.

The immense support I received for the preparation of the second edition of this book can never be forgotten nor taken for granted. I therefore wholeheartedly acknowledge my indefatigable new publisher, Amerley Treb Books, my capable and creative technical assistant, and dramatist, Victoria Ofei-Gyamera, and Edmund Nyarko, my ICT special assistant. They all became the kingpin around which the successful completion of the process of producing the second edition hinged.

Finally, my profound gratitude goes to the Osu chiefs, elders and citizens for their patience in responding to my incessant questions as I researched oral traditions; to the Centre for African Art and Civilization for sponsoring the exhibition of my research findings, and to Mr. Kweimonie Nerquaye Tetteh and Nii-Lante Wellington, who helped to mount the exhibition.

To crown these acknowledgements, I wish to thank my wife and children for the patience they showed in supporting me throughout, even when I became so thoroughly engrossed in my work that I had, unwillingly and unwittingly, to neglect them.

H. Nii-Adziri Wellington, November 2017

Appendix I

A brief write-up on the first exhibition organised to share the research findings with the Osu community: July, 2007

The theme for the Exhibition was *"Awusai Atso, Awusai Atsu, Awusai Atsemei Awe ... "* This theme, expressed in the Gã language, was both poetic and pivotal in the presentation of the essence of the Exhibition, which was meant to popularize the findings so that all and sundry would take interest in Osu as an important Ghanaian cultural heritage site.

This Exhibition is being mounted in the context of the Ghana @ 50 Panafest/Emancipation/Joseph Project. Consequently, the history of the slavery and slave trade must be featured. Hence, the main theme expressed in Gã, refers to the sense of the tragedy of slavery and the slave trade as epitomized in the place name of the Old Danish slave market at Osu, known as *"Awusai Atso"*:

> *'Awusãi'* is a corruption of the Akan word *'Ewusia.'* In the Akan worldview if one loses one's father, one becomes an *"Egyanka,"* to wit, "fatherless." If one loses one's mother, one becomes an *"Ewusia,"* to wit, "One who has lost everything."

Oral tradition has it that Osu people referred to the Old Danish Slave Market as "Awusai Atso." Under this tree those who had lost everything were sold! This was the tragedy of slavery and the slave trade.

The message of the Exhibition should remind all and sundry in Ghana, Africa and the world never to allow such a human tragedy to be repeated:

• not in child-trafficking

- not in domestic servitude
- not in forced marriage of under-age girls

The sub-theme, expressed in English, indicates the length and breadth of the perspective of the Exhibition. Osu history is so dense that we can only see it glimpses. This is because, to a large extent, Osu was influenced metaphorically by the beautiful but colossal architectural "monster" known as "Christiansborg." The Exhibition therefore concretizes the "shadow," this monster, this colossal architectural piece cast over the years. The shadows, both negative and positive have emanated from the European presence on our shores, beginning with the arrival of the Portuguese, followed by the Swedes and then again the Danes together with the Norwegians and finally the British!

Appendix II

Translations of a Gã Poem on Slavery (Ŋshɔ Naa) and Osu Salem School Anthem

Ŋshɔ Naa
(Translated by Rev. Dr. Philip Laryea)

On the beach, and at sea,
The sea is beautiful!
But many lie in it,
Africans, too many!
Africans who take life too lightly
Captors and captives
Profligates and perfidious
Disobedient and drunkards,
Many were captured and sold.
"I'll be back, I'll be back!"
"You can't come back anymore!
You are chained in a boat,
You will not see your country again!"
Many lie there,
Who have done no wrong.
The land of the African people,
Don't sell your children anymore!

Osu Salem School Anthem
(Translation by author)

Aren't you an Old Boy of the Salem School?
If indeed, you are an Old Boy,
You've got to arise, step out, and join us,
As we celebrate the day,
As we celebrate the day
In honour of our Alma Mater, Salem!
Come join us, so that all and sundry shall know
That you are a Salem Old Boy!
Come join us, so that all and sundry shall know
That you are a Salem Old Boy!

Appendix III

Glossary of Words and Phrases

Preface and Introduction
Adzoateh: a place name of a section of Osu-Kinkawe. Historically associated with a place where ammunition was distributed to community warriors in time of war.
Ajumanko: a place name of a section of Osu-Ashinte Blohum.
Agbadza Dzoohe: a place name at Osu Alata. Historically the place is associated with the drumming and dancing grounds of the Ewe sojourners from Keta.
Agblanshie: a place name of a section at Osu-Ashinte. The place could have been a grove, named "Agbla." Hence, the name literally means, under the "Agbla grove."
Amaganaa: cult place of a deity.
Amangfong: literally means "ruins." It is a place name for the old Danish-Osu that was bombarded in 1854 by the British administration.
Amantra: place name of a section of Osu-Kinkawe, which borders onto Osu-Ashinte Blohum Quarter.
Anumansa: place name of a section of Osu-Kinkawe.
Anyεmimεi: brethren
Ashinte-Blohum: name of the Osu Traditional Quarter associated with the place of sojourn by the Asante slave traders who brought slaves for sale at Christiansborg.
Ataa Forkoyi: name of a legendary old Osu man.
Ataa Forkoyi, enyiε atswa?: Ataa Forkoyi, what is the time? Literally, "How many have been struck?"
Atuwe: place name of a section of Osu-Ashinte Blohum. The name might have derived from the ancestral home of an Akwamu migrant by the name of Atu.

Blogodo: place name of a section of Osu-Ashinte-Blohum. It is a corrupted Ewe word for a place of ablution.
Dade We: place name of a section of Osu-Kinkawe.
Dadebu: name of the deity of Osu-Kinkawe.
Hei: an exclamation uttered either to draw attention to a discourtesy or to express surprise.
Karselieh: a Gã rendering of the word "Castle," i.e. Christiansborg.
Klottey: name of a Gã male. It is also the name given to the local Osu Lagoon. The Lagoon has this name because it is the male equivalent of the Lagoon Korle, located at Gã-Mashie. It is believed that the parts of the lagoon have both genders.
Mowule: place name of a section of Osu-Ashinte-Blohum and part of Kinkanwe, historically associated with migrants from Moree in the Central Region, where the first Dutch Fort was built in the seventeenth century. The Fante migrants introduced the Gã to sea fishing. Thus, this is most probably an adaptation of the Fante word "Moree."
Nuumo: old man. When the word is used in conjunction with the name of an old person, it signifies respect as a title.
Ofori Ayi: a typical male Gã name.
Ogbaamenaa: place name of a section of Osu Alata. Ogbaame is the name of one of the deities of Osu Alata.
Pioto: local name for underwear worn by both males and females. Children usually are seen in this underwear without anything on top as they play around.
Songme Naa: place name of a section of Osu-Alata an area of public gathering, historically used as a communication smithery and associated with postal functions for the early colonial masters.

Chapter One
Tolon: a female name originating from a woman called Tolon in Danish-Osu, a concubine of the then Governor Schionning in the nineteenth century, who built a house for her. The place where she lived has since been associated with that name.
Abentia: indigenous name given to the Danish cemetery located on the west of Christiansborg.
Adjangote: place name for the hills located on the north-west of the Accra Plains
Blofonyo bi: offspring of a Caucasian, ie. a mulatto or a mixed breed of African and European descent.
Dangme: place name of the ethnic enclave of the Adangme.

Den Blɔfo: Gã word for a Dane.

Harmattan: name of the dry and dust-laden weather caused by north-south winds blowing from the Sahel Zone.

Kadi gbɔi: guests of Kadi. The word is used as a sobriquet for the Osu community.

Kple: an ancient indigenous form of dance associated with the original settlers of the Gã cultural domain. Scholars of the Gã culture are able to gain insight into some of the Gã religious philosophy and practice through analysis of the Kple songs.

Kinka Blɔfo: Gã word for a Dutch.

Kpeshi: place name of the lagoon located between La and Teshie, on the east side of Osu.

Labadey: place name of present day La as found in Danish archival sources.

Ngleshie Blɔfo: Gã word for the English.

Noete Doku: name of a male of the Osu-Kinkawe and Osu-Ashinte Blohum quarters. This is the name born by the original Osudoku migrants.

Obodai Nyonmo: literally means, Obodai the almighty. This was the name of the leader who brought the returning Gã community from Anecho. He became the first Chief of the Osu-Anahor quarter.

Odoi Atsem: name of a king of La as found in Danish archival sources.

Remidors: Portuguese name for rowers and boatmen who manned the canoes that linked the shores with the slave ships which anchored in the roads on the Guinea Coast.

Chapter Two

Travados: Portuguese name of the stormy and rainy weather from May to July as found in archival sources.

Makaranta: a local Koranic school where the children are taught to learn by rote, especially lines from the Koran.

Naa Nyɔŋmɔ: Gã word for the Supreme Creator. The word "Ataa" is used to prefix "Naa Nyɔŋmɔ," connoting the notion that the Supreme Creator is both masculine and feminine or Father and Mother spontaneously.

Wulɔmɔ: title of the Gã traditional priest of the Supreme Creator

Chapter Three

Adinkra: name of Akan iconography associated chiefly with a mourning cloth that bears that name. The icons/symbols that constitute the Adinkra iconography are also employed in jewellery, graphic design and architecture.

Akan: the cultural term used to describe the ethnicity of the group of people in Ghana that speak the Twi language. The Akan ethnic group includes the Asantes, Akyems, Akwamus, Akwapims, Denkyeras and Fantes. Mostly of the central and southern parts of Ghana.

Ayekoo: Gã for "Well done."

Ataamɛi, Awomɛi, nyɛ bakwɛ aeii: Fathers and mothers, come around to behold! This is a typical Gã exclamation to draw the attention of the public to something unusual.

Gã Poem titled "Ŋshɔ Naa:" An English version is found in Appendix II.

Hii amli, Yei amli: men's quarters, women's quarters. The words describe a peculiar Gã cultural practice that keeps the residential enclave of men separated from that of women and children. Literally as amongst men, amongst women.

Obroni waa wu: an Akan expression that literally means "the white man is dead." It is used colloquially to refer to second-hand goods sold in the market, mostly clothing.

Yesah, saah: Ghanaian pidgin-English for, "Yes Sir," with emphasis on extreme courtesy or politeness.

Teshie, Nungua, Tema, Kpone: names of other Gã settlements found eastwards of Osu, beyond La.

Chapter Four

Ashiokai: name of a third-born female of Osu-Kinkawe and Osu-Ashinte-Blohum.

Awofio Dedei: a clan-specific name for an elderly female. The "Awofio" is a title of respect and identifies a person to be a junior grandmother in the family.

Aooo: an expression or sound of sorrow.

Gottesacker: the cemetery of the Moravian Brethren in Herrnhut, Germany. It literally means "Acre of God."

Hmmm: An expression or sound signifying wonder or reflection.

Inuits: an ethnic group of Eskimos in Iceland.

Korkoi: a Gã name of a second-born female.

Little Popo: a place name of a settlement in eastern Togo, known today as Anecho. Archival records indicate that it was established by the Portuguese after Elmina, and was the place where some of the Gã clans sought refuge after the sacking of Ayawaso. The Osu-Anahor community migrated from Anecho.

La Mantsɛ/Mantse: king of La. Literal meaning of "Mantsɛ" is 'Father of the town."
Maaan: Rastafarian styling of the word "man."
Mamaa: Rastafarian styling of the word "Madam."
Mblakoo: the forest of the place name Mbla, located north-west of Danish-Osu.
Mantse Oto Brafo: name of Chief or King of Kinka. The name Oto Brafo suggests origins of an Akwamu extraction.
Milo drink: a popular chocolate base beverage made by Nestle, Ghana Limited.
Neem tree: an exotic tree with the botanical name, Azadirachta Indica, introduced into Ghana by Governor, Sir Gordon Guggisberg from India in the 1920s and very medicinal.
Nii Maale: name of a La King.
Nkɛlɛ baaya ei, nkɛlɛ baaya ei: an expression of sorrow meaning, "I will accompany the deceased."
Ningo/Nungo: name of a Dangme settlement lying east of Osu along the coast, where the Danes built Fort Fredensborg.
Noye: name of a male of Osu-Kinkawe Quarter.
Onyankopong: Akan for 'the Supreme God." Literally, Magnificent or Great Friend.
Rixdaler: a currency used by the Danes in both Denmark and the Guinea Coast in the 17th and eighteenth centuries.
Sodza: name of a male from the Osu-Anahor Quarter.
Teshie: name of a Gã settlement lying east of Osu where the Danes built Fort Augustaborg. The Danish records refer to Tessing as the name of this community.
Teianshi: place name meaning "Under the rocks." Identified from Danish records as one of the major quarries from which stones were obtained to build at Danish-Osu. The location is between Osu and La on the north-east. As a result of the stone-winning from this place, it became what is known in Gã as "Tebu" meaning: "a stone quarry".
Teiko Sacki, Blofonyo Bi: a title Christian Protten adopted for himself; the first part is a name of a male of the Gã of Gã-Mashie. The second part means "Child of a Caucasian."
Wanna: Rastafarian styling for "want to."

Chapter Five
Aharabata: Gã pronunciation of the Portuguese word "Harmatao" for "Harmattan."
Aharabata Wɔŋ: the harmattan deity.

Atsii mɔta: a Gã phrase meaning "you don't mention a person's name," used when an allusion has to be made to a person, whose name may not be mentioned.
Adote Shelenkome: name of a Gã male, who has "Shelenkome" as an appellation, literally meaning "One shilling."
Akua Basua: an Akan female name. Akua is a day name for Wednesday and Basua literally means "Come and carry."
Akoto We: name of one of the royal gates of Osu Alata. Akoto suggests an Akwamu connection.
Asere, Gã-Mashie: a traditional Quarter in Gã-Mashie.
Akwetey: a typical Gã male name used to refer to a senior twin.
Dodowah: a place name of a historic town in the Greater Accra Region, where the war between the Ashantis and the Gã and their allies took place.
Gbonyo Party: a modern phrase used to describe the inordinate celebration of the dead in form of eating, drinking and dancing at a funeral reception.
Kweiki Quaynor: a typical name for a female of Ningo extraction, with Quaynor being the family name.
Kotsa gbamɔ: a Gã cultural funerary practice denoting the symbolic last bath given to a deceased relative.
Lomo, Lomote, Lomotetteh, Lomomensah: Gã names of males belonging to a particular clan. The suffix attached to "Lomo" is in accordance with the order of seniority - Lomo is most senior and Lomomensah is the youngest.
La Abese: a traditional quarter or community of La.
Nii Yull: Nii Julius - an adaptation of Julius
Nkulenu: an Ewe name meaning "Eyes that can recognize or notice."
Odoi Din, Legon Mantsɛ: Name of a chief or king of Legon. The name "Din" attached to Odoi stands for "Black." Legon is the place name for the hill, Le, where the University of Ghana is located. Oral tradition has it that Legon is a hill of knowledge.
Oware: Name of an Akan traditional marble game. Its play requires strategic thinking and it can last for a long time. The word "oware" means "of long duration."
Peki Dzake: place name of a settlement in the Volta region.
Shiatso: Gã word for "the household."
Shia Wulu: a Gã phrase referring to a main Family House. It literally means "the large house."
Sei Asafoatsɛ: head of the "Stool company" of Osu-Ashinte-Blohum.

Tolon Mɔɔ: the Fort of the Tolon neighbourhood.
Wekutso: Gã word for an extended family or clan, literally meaning 'Family Tree.'
Wolɛinyo: a fisherman.

Chapter Six
WOW: an acronym that stands for an expression of excitement and appreciation culled from the phrase "Wonders of wonders."
Agoo tsɛmɛi ke nyɛmɛi: a customary call for attention in a public Gã gathering at the head of proceedings. The "tsɛmei" and "nyɛmei" are the "fathers" and "mothers" of the community.
Alata Ntɛn: the pride of Alata. The red and black striped uniform of the Osu-Alata Youth group symbolises the pride of the community.
Asafo: a socio-military group existing in all the communities.
Asona: a clan of the Akan ethnic group.
Amanorkrom: a place name of a settlement in Akwapim, literally meaning, "Town of the man called Amanor."
Anii dzee Salem Skul otee lo?: Is it Salem School you attended or not? The English Version of the song is under Appendix II.
Amɛɛ: The customary positive response given to the call for attention by the audience. In other words: "We are ready," or literally, "Come inside," as in response to a knock announcing one's entrance.
Boycotthene: a sobriquet given to Nii Kwabena Bonne II for his successful national campaign to boycott the purchase of goods imported by Asian merchants in the country in 1948.
Colo, colo: a colloquial name tag given to what appears to be colonial or unprogressive – literally, an abbreviation of the word 'colonial.'
Duadetsean: a place name for a Gã farming community known for cultivating cassava.
Duadetsei lɛ amli: among the cassava trees.
Ei hiiabii, nyɛkabagbei awɔ eei: "Young men, make sure, you do not inflict harm on us." Literally, "Sons of men, don't come to kill us, we pray ohh."
Haadzi anyɛ: the mother of twins.
Hei Nii oo, Hei Nii oo. Boni oo Boni: "Hail Nii (the Chief), Hail Nii (Chief). You are the one. You are the one."
Kafugben: Local name of old Danish flintlock gun. The word is onomatopoeic, mimicking the sound the flintlock makes when it is shot.

Kente: a national woven textile of high heritage value of Akan or Ewe origin.
Kinkawe Mantsɛ/Mantse: chief of the Osu-Kinkawe Quarter.
Kinkawe osee yei, hee yei ee: a hailing appellation for the Osu-Kinkawe community.
Mantsɛ/Mantse Fetreke: a sobriquet given to Frederick Noi Dowuona when he eventually became the King of Osu and who consistently eschewed traditional practices.
Maa Sanku: a sobriquet for Mrs. Holm, literally meaning "Mother Organ."
Manfe: a place name of a settlement in Akwapim.
Ŋoo Wala: a Gã expression literally meaning, "Receive life." It is intended to extend blessings to the recipient.
Niimɛi naamɛi: respectful address title of the adult and respected males and females in the community.
Nyɔŋma saa nɔ wɔɔ: sleeping on the mat of ten.
Nyɔŋma Too: customary gift of a goat, given by a husband to his wife on the occasion of celebrating the woman for bearing ten surviving children.
Prampram: place name for an Adangme settlement on the east of Osu along the Coast. It is also known locally as Gbugbla.
Santse: place name of the village which was established by Frederick Noi Dowuona. The original name could have been 'Seitsɛ" that means "Stool owner." It is probable since Noi Dowuona was an heir apparent to the Osu Stool.
Sumsum: Akan for "Spirit."
Suhum: a place name of a town in the Eastern Region of Ghana.
Way Hearts: a clarion call used by the supporters of the Accra Hearts of Oak Football Club.

Chapter Seven
Atofotse: An expression referring to a man of wealth or substance. "Atofo" was a dress form to add size and shape to the back waistline of a woman. Hence, metaphorically, an "Atofo tse" is supposed to be of good size and shape due to his wealth.
Okaileytse We: the name of the ancestral home established by the father of Okailey.
Salem: an abbreviation of the word "Jerusalem."
Wuyɛ buei: an Akan expression to indicate that somebody is highly regarded. It literally means "You are great/marvellous."

Notes and Bibliography

Primary Sources

(I) Archival Materials -Unpublished

Jenkins, Paul (Compiler). *Abstracts of Basel Mission Gold Coast Correspondence available in the Institute of African Studies, Ghana Historical Society Collections,* University of Ghana

Protten, Jakob Christian 'Africanus. *Prottensdiarium, dated 1756-1761,* found in the Unitaet Archiv in Hernnhut, transcribed by Dr. Peter Sebald.

Archival materials Published

Bosman, William, *A New and Accurate Description of the Coast of Guinea,* London: 1705.

Justensen, Ole. *Danish Sources for the History of Ghana 16571754,* Vols I & II, Copenhagen: 2005.

Tilleman, Erick. *A short and simple account of the country Guinea and its nature'* (Trsl. by Selena Axelrod Winsnes), African Studies Program, University of Wisconsin, Madison: 1994.

(II) Oral Sources

Interviews with Traditional and Community Leaders of Osu with several Osu families with and without Danish ancestry.

Reflections on childhood memories and information received from parents, family members and former middle school-teachers at Osu Salem.

(III) Heritage Sites

Visits to historic sites and places at Osu, Herrnhut and Grosshennendorf in Germany, Christianshavn and Copenhagen in Denmark: Volkermuseum and Moravian Archives in Herrnhut, Museums in Grosshennesdorf and Copenhagen and the Ghana National Archives, Accra.

(IV) Exhibition

Visitors to three different Exhibition stands mounted at Osu and the Goethe Institut in Accra on the research fi ndings were interviewed.

(V)Newspapers: Readings of feature articles in the Ghanaian Daily

Graphic, Ghana.

Secondary Sources

Acquah, Ione. *Accra Survey,* University of London Press, London: 1958.
Anquandah, James Kwesi (ed). *The Transatlantic Slave Trade, Landmarks, Legacies, Expectations.* Proceedings of the International Conference on Historic Slave Routes Held at Accra, Ghana on 30 August – 2 September, 2004, Sub-Saharan Publishers 2007.
Ashitey, Gilford Amarh. *Frederick T. Sai: A Distinguished Advocate,* Compufin, Accra: 2005.
Ashitey, Gilford Armah: *Charles Odamtten Easmon: The Beacon,* Fredico Press, Accra: 2001.
Christaller, J. G. & Schopf J. (ed). *Gã Kanemɔ Wolo III (Gã Primer),* Basel Evangelical Missionary Society, 1895.
Decorse, Christopher R. *An Archaeology of Elmina-Africans and Europeans on the Gold Coast, 1400-1900,* Smithsonian Institution Press, Washington and London: 2001.
Evans-Anfom, E. *To the thirsty Land (autobiography of a patriot),* Africa Christian Press, Accra: 2003.
Field, M. J. *Social Organisation of the Gã People,* Crown agencies for the Colonies, 1940.
Field M. J. *Religion and Medicine of the Gã People,* Oxford University Press, London: 1937.
Hansen, Thorkild. *Coast of Slaves,* (Trsl. by Kari Dako) Sub-Saharan Publishers Legon, Ghana: 2002.
Henningsen, Henning. *Fjernt Fra Denmark- Billeder fra vore Tropekolonier, Sklavehandel og Kinfart,* Lademanns Forlagsaktieselskab, Copenhagen 1974
Isert, Erdmann Paul. *Letters on West Africa and the Slave Trade: Journey to Guinea and the Caribbean Islands in Columbia (1788).* The British Academy, Oxford University Press.
Japin, Arthur. *The Two Hearts of Kwasi Boachi: A Novel;* Chatto and Windus, London: 2000.
Jenkins, Paul ed., Reindolf, C. C and Samuel Johnson. *The Recovery of the West African Past: African Pastors and African History in the Nineteenth Century; C. C. Reindorf and Samuel Johnson,* Basler Afrika Bibliographien Postfach 2037, CH 4001 Basel, Switzerland: 2000
Kilson, Marion. *African Urban kinsmen: The Gã Urban Accra,* St Martins Press, New York: 1974.
Kropp, Dakubu, M. E. *Korle Meets the Sea - A Sociolinguistic History of Accra,* New York, Oxford: Oxford University Press, 1997.
Kropp, Dakubu, M. E. *One Voice - The Linguistic Culture of an Accra Lineage,* African Studies Centre, Leiden, the Netherlands: 1981.
Laryea, Philip Tetteh. *Yesu, Homowo Nuntsɔ: Nikasemɔ Nikɔɔ Bɔni Kristofoi naa Yesu yɛ Gamɛi Akusumfeemɔ kɛ Blema Saji Amli,* Akro-

pong: Regnum, 2004.

Lauring, Kare. *Merchant, Sailor and Supercargo - A Guide to the Copenhagen of the Palmy Days of Overseas Trade,* Handles & Sofartmueet pa Kronborg, Helsingor: 1998.

Lawrence, A. W. *Trade Castles and Forts of West Africa,* The Trinity Press, Worcester: Gt. Britain, 1963.

Monrad, H. C. (Trsl. By Selena Axelrod Winsnes). *Two views from Christiansborg Castle,* Vol. 2. Sub-Saharan Publishers, Legon, Ghana 2009.

Norregard, G. *Danish settlements in West Africa 1658-1850,* Boston: 1966.

Parker, John. *Making The Town-Gã State and Society in Early Colonial Accra,* Heinemann Portsmouth, NH; James Currey, Oxford; David Philip, Cape Town: 2000.

Perbi, Akosua Adoma. *A History of Indigenous Slavery in Ghana-From the 15th century to the nineteenth century,* Accra, Ghana: 2008.

Peuker, Paul ed. *Graf Ohne Grenzen-Leben und Werk von Nicholas Ludwig Graf von Zinzendorf,* Verlag der Comeniusbuchhandlung, Herrnhut: 2000.

Rask, Johannes. (Trsl. by Selena Axelrod Winsnes), *Two views from Christiansborg Castle,* Vol 1. Sub-Saharan Publishers, Legon, Ghana: 2009.

Reindorf, Carl Christian (Rev). *The History of the Gold Coast and Asante,* Ghana Universities Press, Accra: 1966

Romer, Ferdinand Ludewig (Trsl. by Selina Axelrod Winsnes, 2000). *A Reliable Account of the Coast of Guinea (1760);* The British Academy, Oxford University Press.

Schweizer, Peter A. *Survivors On The Gold Coast: The Basel Missionaries In Colonial Ghana,* Smartline Publishing, Accra: 2001.

Sensbach, Jon. *Rebecca's revival: Creating Black Christianity in the Atlantic World,* Cambridge, Massachusetts: Harvard Press 2005.

Svalesen, Leif (Trsl. by Pat Shaw and Selena Winsnes). *The Slave Ship Fredensborg,* Sub Saharan Publishers, Accra: 2000.

Van der Heyden, Ulrich, ed. *Unbekannte Biographien-Afrikaner im deutschsprachigen Raum vom 18. Jahrhundert bis zum Ende des Zweiten Weltkrieges,* Kai Hmilius Verlag, 2008

Wulff, Joseph Wulff. *A Danish Jew in West Africa,* Department of History, Norwegian University of Science and Technology, N- 7491 Trondheim, Norway: 2004.

Zimmerman, J. A. *Grammatical Sketch and Vocabulary of the Akra or Gã-Language,* Gregg International Publishers Limited, 1972

(VII) Articles

Hyllestad, Nikolas. "Old Basel Mission School, Salem Road: Building Technology and Materials, A Technical Report on the Conservation of the Osu Salem Building submitted to the OSABA, Legon, November 2008."

Priddy, Barbara. *Christiansborg Castle-Osu,* A publication of the Ghana Museums and Monuments Board, Accra: 1969.

Schilke, Iris & August, Ursula, eds. "Rebecca Protten, Verwitwete Freundlich, Geborene Schelli(?)" in Frauen in der Kirchengeschichte Sachsens, Ein Lesebuch, Dresden, 1997.

Wellington, H. Nii-Adziri. "In the Shadow of Christiansborg Architectural History and genealogical profiles of the Okantey Trading House at Danish Osu in Accra Before Colonial Times: Proceedings of a Colloquium on Early Accra," Research Review Supplement 17, Institute of African Studies, University of Ghana, 2006.

Wellington, H. Nii-Adziri. "Matse Sliki Tekle – A Cultural History of the Gã Funerary Loin-Cloth in Accra Before Colonial Times: Proceedings of a Colloquium on Early Accra," Research Review Supplement 17, Institute of African Studies, University of Ghana, 2006.

(VIII) Periodicals

Antwi, Daniel J. "The African Factor in Christian Mission to Africa: A study of Moravian and Basel Mission initiatives in Ghana" in Mission Miscellanea: International Review of mission Vol. LXXXVII No. 344, January 1998.

Bech, Neils. Christiansborg I Ghana 1800-1850 Det tropiske hus af europaeisk oprindelse, ARCHITEKTURA 11, Arkisteturhistorisk Arsskrift, Kobenhavn 1989.

Debrunner, Hans. "Notable Danish Chaplains on the Gold Coast," Transactions of the Historical Society of Ghana, 2 (1957).

Hauser-Renner, Heinz. "Examining Text Sediments: Commending a Pioneer Historian as an 'African Herodotus': On the Making of the New Annotated Edition of C. C. Reindorf's History of the Gold Coast and Asante, History in Africa 35(2008), 231-299

Justensen, Ole. "The Negotiation for Peace in the Gold Coast 1826 to 1831," Transactions of the Historical Society of Ghana, New Series No. 4&5, Legon, 2000-2001.

Justensen, Ole. "Henrich Richter 1785-1849: Trader and Politician in the Danish Settlements on the Gold Coast," Transactions of the Historical Society of Ghana, new Series No. 7, 2003

Kropp Dakubu, M. E. ed. "Accra Before Colonial Times: Proceedings of a Colloquium on Early Accra," Institute of African Studies Review Supplement 17, 2006

Osei-Tutu, J. K. "The Asafoi (socio-military groups) in the History and Politics of Accra (Ghana) from the 17th to the mid 20th Century, " Trondheim: NUST, Transactions of the Historical Society of Ghana, New Series No. 4 & 5, Legon, 2000-2001

Sebald, Peter. "Christian Jacob Protten Africanus (1715-1769)–Erster Missionaer Einer Deutschen Missionsgesllschaft in Schwarzafrika," in Wilfried Wagner, ed, Kolonien und Missionen: Referate des 3. Internationalen Kolonialgeschichlichen Symposiums 1993 in Bremen (Hamburg, 1994)

Dissertations and Theses

Ipsen, Pernille. (2008). *Koko's Daughters – Danish men marrying Gã women in an Atlantic slave trading port in the eighteenth century* (Doctoral Dissertation). Det Humanistiske Fakultet Kobenhavns Universitet,
Lamptey, T.L. (1971/2). *History of Osu- from the earliest times to 1854* (BA Dessertation). Department of History, University of Ghana.
Ankrah, Audrey Megan. (2005). *Genealogical Study of Danish Osu: A Case Study of the Richter Family* (B.A. Dissertation). KNUST, Kumasi.
Nyantakyi, Awere Agyiri Laud. (2005). *Genealogical Study of Nii Okantey Shikatse We (Lineage) and History of their Trading House,* (B.A. Dissertation). KNUST, Kumasi.
Tetteh, Esther Sakyibea. (2005). *A Genealogical Study of the Engmann Family of Osu - An Example of Danish Osu Relations* (B. A. Dissertation) KNUST, Kumasi.
Yankholmes, Aaron Kofi Badu. (2008). *Residents' Perceptions towards the Use of Transatlantic Slave Trade Resources for Tourism Development in Danish Osu, Ghana* (M.Phil Dissertation) University of Cape Coast, Cape Coast.

Internet Sources

http://grad.usask.ca/gateway/archive10.html
The Black Death in the Gold Coast: African and British Responses to the Bubonic Plague Epidemic of 1908, Jonathan Roberts

http://www.tidsskrift.dk
Danish Plantations on the Gold Coast 1788-1850, Henrik Jeppessen

In addition to the above, a number of other Internet sources were consulted which websites could not be traced because the related notes got lost. All these are gratefully acknowledged in cognito.

Index

References to figures are indicated by italics.

A

Aadza tuntɛ, 21
Aafio Dedei, 29
Aban ka ba, 67
abandonment, 19, 21, 38, 49, 56, 57, 231, 234, 276
Abdo, Edmund, 278
Abentia, 16
Abladzei, 97
Ablorh-Odjidja, Elias, ii, 278, 296
ablutions, xxviii, 26, 303
Abokobi, 97, 193, 194, 232, 273, 274
Abokobi Salem Boys' Boarding School, 194
abused, 72, 73, 84
Accra, xxxiv, 8, 113, 137, 151, 197, 235, 244, 246, 253, 278, 282, 292, 294
Accra Academy, 238, 244
Accra Hearts of Oak, 246
Accra lineage, *186, 203*
Accra plains, 4, 81–82, 89, 90, 95, 97, 98, 104, 193, 229, 292
achievers, xix, 185, 216, 247
Achimota College, 113, 236, 247, 249, 275, 287
Achimota School, 198, 236
Acraisch, *144, 148*
Ada, 92, 260
Adangme, xxxv, 5, 8, 17, 21, 22, 192, 229. *see also* Dangme
Adawso, 236
Addington, xxxv
Adinkra, 67
Adjangote Hills, 4
Adja Torgbor, 153
Adjovi, 182, 188
Adjumako, xxxiv, 18
Adom, G. A., Rev., 274
Adote Shelenkome, 197
Adoui, 188
Adu, Kwasi, 76
Adu, Nortei, 22
Adum, 84
Adum Tokori, 83, 84, 86
Adzei, Holm, 253
Adzoate, xxxiv, 21
Adzoateh, 21
Adzovi, Ashiokai, *190*
Adzovi, Ashiorkor, *190*
Adzovi, Manaa Adzovi, *190*
Adzovi, Shomeh, *190*
Adzuateh, 244
Afi, 75
African Art. See Centre for African Art
African Moravians, 170
African Romans, 36
African Studies, 245
Agbadza, 26, 287
Agbadza Dzoohe, xvii, xxxii, 26, 71, 258
Agblanshie, xviii, xxxiii, 243, 259
Agboogba, 74, 97
agent provocateur, 104, 105
  agents, 106;
  of change, 47, 275;
  Danish, 48;
  mulatto, 85;
  slave-trading, 69, 72, 84
Aharabata Wɔŋ, 175–76
Ahey, Mike, 243
Akan, xxxiv, 8, 69, 78, 79, 100, 298
Akatamasu, Battle of, 288
Akatanwiah, 79
Akonnor (king), 77, 80
Akoto, Theodora Benedicta, 208
Akoto We, 25, 215
Akromanus, 36
Akromas, 36
Akropong Akwapim, 83, 112, 233
Akuetteh, S. Amate, 277
Akuffo, F. O., 240
Akwamu(s), xviii, 22, 24, 25, 27, 34

35, 36, 37, 38, 92;
    culture, 79–80;
    deception and intrigue, 38;
    driven across Volta River, 287;
    ethnicity, 78;
    ills, 76;
    king, 123;
    lineage, 18;
    slave trading, 69, 71, 77;
    uncircumcised, 78, 94;
    vanquishment, 81;
    war, 76, 77–78, 80, 82, 252;
    warriors, 27, 69
Akwamufie, 80
Akwapim Hills, 89, 90, 104, 105, 113, 244
Akwapim(s), 83, 84, 170, 211, 233, 244
Akwei, Warren Gamaliel Kpakpo, 197
Akwetey. *See Briandt*, William Douglass Akwetey
Akyem(s), 27, 76, 78, 81, 92, 133, 252
Akyem, Owusu, 83–84
Alata, xxvii, xxxiii, xxxiv, 12, 23–26, 28, 47, 68, 73, 96, 98, 122, 129, 204, 215, 224, 226, 227, 230, 234–35, 236, 236, 238, 247, 282;
    Richter Fort, 212
    Alata Asafo Company, 238
    Alata Mantse, 234
    Alata Stool House, 258
    Alata Ntɛn, 226, 234, 236
Albrecht, Henning, 38
Allada, 12, 27, 28, 34, 69;
    becomes Alata 23–26
Almighty God, 133, 238
Amaganaa, xxxiv, 86
Amangfong, xxxiv, 8, 81, 96
Amanorkrom: chief, 244, 246
Amantra, xxxiv, 18, 184, 217, 258
ambivalent, 67
Amɛɛ, 227
American Virgin Islands, 226
Americas, 71, 83
Amerley Treb Books, xxiii–xxiv, 296
Amoonu Graham, E. E., 278
Ampem, Nana Wereko, II, 244, 245, 246
Amsterdam, 141, 159
    Anahor, xxvii, xxxiii, 26–30, 47, 68, 96, 98, 113, 131, 153, 156, 163, 167, 172, 181, 182, 227, 230, 243, 246, 247, 258, 282, 285;
    chief's house, 218
ancestors, 27, 40, 41, 98, 100, 101,107, 121, 163, 171, 177, 178, 182, 183, 185, 193, 199, 206, 211, 213, 214, 226, 234, 246, 259, 261, 277, 282, 284;
    Danish-Osu, 122–47;
    Osu, xxviii, 58

Anecho, 27, 28, 29, 137. *See also* Little Popo
Angermuende, 104
Anglican, 196
animals: domestic, 72, 77;
    protein, 7;
    wild, 5, 72
Ankrah, Audrey, 296
Ankrah, J. A., 114
Ankrah, T. C., 237
Ankrah-Badu, G., 237
Anlo(s), 25, 76
Anna Maria, 157
Anna Sophia, 133, 153, 155
Annor, A. L. N., 278–79
Anomabu, 37, 38
Anum, Alice, 253
Anumansa, xxxiv
Apalee, 260
APSTAR Ltd. 295
Arden-Clarke, Charles Noble, 113–14, 233
Armah, 200, *202*
Armed Forces Revolutionary Council, 240, 242
asafo, 79
Asafo, 224, 245
Asafo Company, 231, 232, 238
Asante, David, 112
Asante Brass Works Heritage Collections, 245
Asante Brono, 22
Asante Brono, xxxiv
Asante King, 235
Asante(s), 22–23, 24, 69, 71, 81–82, 83, 133, 208, 211–12, 215, 235, 252;
    war, 288
Ashangmor (king), 27
Ashinte Blohum, xviii, xxvii, xxxiv, 6, 17, 21, 22–23, 25, 47, 198, 200, 205, 231, 232, 260, 261, 273
Ashiokai, 128, 182, 188, 189
Ashiokai Adzovi, *190*
Ashiorkor, 189
Ashitey, George, 248
Ashitey, Gilford Amarh, 248, 249
Ashitey, Victoria, 248
Asomani, 80, 81
Asonas, 244
aspatre, 35
assembly hall, 160
Assistant Colonial Secretary, 194, 195, 277
Association of West African Merchants, 235
'Ataamɛi, awomɛi, nyɛ baakwɛ aeiiii!,' 85
Ataa Naa Nyɔŋmɔ, 41, 43
Atlantic Coast, 7, 222
Atlantic Ocean, xxxiii, 6, 42, 69, 70, 222

Atlantic slave trade. See transatlantic slave trade
Atofotsɛ, 261
Atsem, Sabah, 84–86
Atuwe, xxxiv
Augustaborg, 125, 292
Augustensborg, 92
August Street Carnival, xxvii
Augustts, 215
Auntie Dedee "Happy Corner," 253
Australia, 243
Avenor, 235
AWAM, 235
Awo Ashiokai, 182
Awo Ashong Fio, 113
Awuku, Mary Opeibia, 244
Awuley Nfeni We, 25
Awusai, 73, 298
Awusai Atso, xviii, xxiii, xxxv, 68, 74, 261, 298
Awusai Atso Street, xxxiv, 179, 180, 258
Axim, 7
Ayawaso, 27, 36, 39, 40, 43
Ayettey, A. M. O. 249, 274
Ayettey, Andrew Seth, 278
Ayettey, Joe, 277
Ayetteys, xxxv
Ayi, Ataa Ado, 188, 189
Ayi, Ataa Ofori, xxviii, 188, 189. *See also* Forkoyi, Ataa
Azambudja, 35
Azambuja, 25
Azus, xxxv

B

Bacchus, 159
Bad Gandersee, 296
Badger, 53, 199
Badsch, Catharina Maria, 126
Bagge, 53, 118, 199
Baltic Sea, 281
banku, 25
Bannerman, C. J., 248
Bannerman, James, 92
Bannerman, Robert R. A. 278
Bannermans, xxxiv
Barbara House, 210, 211
Basel, 214
    Basel Mission, xviii, xix, 74, 96, 97, 107, 109, 110, 169, 185, 196, 201, 204, 228, 232, 273, 274;
    Church, 112, 204, 232;
    School, 97, 231;
    Training Centre, 113
Basel missionaries xix, xxxv, 6, 97, 98, 107, 109, 110, 111, 112, 113, 193, 230, 231, 232, 273, 274, 275
Basel Mission Trading Company, 112

Bashiru, Bukari, 243
Basua, Akua, 207, *208*
Battle of Akatamasu, 288
Bebiase, 90
Bech, Johann, *144,* 159
beliefs, xxxv, 16, 19, 128, 138, 164;
    Moravian, 151
benda of gold, 41, 42
Bengali, 23
Bentzen, Djagble (Jamine), 80
Bentzen, Thomas, 80
Bergessens, xxxiv, 52
Bergneustadt, 296
Bernhardt, Kornelia, 295–96
Bible, xix, 6, 17, 58, 110, 112, 141, 192, 230
Billsen, Juergen, 133
Birthe, 260
Bishop, Anna, 189, 190, 192
blacksmithing, 62, 113, 125, 137, 261
Black Stars, 203, 204
Blass, Hans Hansen, 127
blessings, xxiii, 15, 43, 95, 99, 109, 159, 248, 252
Blofonyo Bi, 135, 142, *146,* 168
Blogodo, xviii, xxxiii, 26
Boakye-Gyan, Major, 242
Boi, 74, 97
Boi, Ataa Mleku, 113
Bolten, Peter, 79
bombardments, 81, 82, 86, 91, 96–97, 98, 112, 193, 201, 213, 230, 232, 273
Bonne, Nii Kwabena, III, 234, 235, 236
Bono Manso, 235
Bonte, Koikoi, 182
Boris, Governor, 129
Botwe, Katherine Ellenora Ayele, 213–14
Botwe, Mary, 295
Botwe, Sidney, 295
Botwe, Sidney Torgbor , 278
Boycotthene, 234, 236
Brandenburg, 104
branding, xviii–xix
Brandt, Ambiorn Christensen, 198–99, 200, *202*
Brandts, 53;
    Brandt becomes Briandt, 199, 200
Briandt, Adolf, 201, *203,* 204
Briandt, Ago, 204
Briandt, A. Hannah, *203*
Briandt, Akweley Aki, *203*
Briandt, Ambiorn Christiansen, 202
Briandt, Christian, *202, 203*
Briandt, Dede Bow, *203*
Briandt, Edgar Christian, *203*
Briandt, Emmanuel Christian, *203,* 204
Briandt, Evelina, *203*
Briandt, Frederich Richard, 204
Briandt, Evelina, *203*

Briandt, Francis, *203*
Briandt, Fredrick, *202*
Briandt, Juliana Emma Dede, 200
Briandt, Julius Caesar, *203*
Briandt, Mercy, 201
Briandt, Merya, 200
Briandt, Naa Meya, *202*
Briandt, Patience, *203*
Briandt, Richard, 204
Briandt, Victor Ago, *203,* 204
Briandt, William Douglass, 200, *203*
Briandts, 53, 96, 118, 182, 198, 199–205, 202–3, 213;
 house, *218*
British, 38, 40, 81, 86, 87, 91, 92, 93–94, 95, 201;
 administration, xviii–xix, 82, 98, 112, 193, 194, 195, 196, 213, 230;
 army, 239;
 bombardment, 230, 286;
 cocoa brokers, 204;
 colonialism, 197, 231, 233, 235;
 Danish forts, 288;
 Danish properties sold to, 291;
 Empire, 194, 195, 233;
 governor, 113, 211;
 lifestyle, 196;
 nobles, 239;
 Protectorate, 83;
 Union Jack, 111;
 warship, 96
British Accra, 39, 77, 86, 93
Brock, Neils, 260
Brock, Severine, 82, 91, 107, 260
Brocks, xxxiv, 52, 96, 206
Brong Ahafo, 235
Brother Jah, 210
Brunssen, Wolfgang, 296
brutalities, 53, 57
bubonic plague, 112
Builder Cornelissen, 44
Burma Camp, 240;
 Post Office, 239
Burns, Alan, 237

C

caboceer, 35, 47
cabuceer, 188
Cadbury, Messr, 204
Cameroon, 261
camisa, 35
Canada, xxiii, 184, 222, 243
cannons, 16, 19, 38, 58, 74, 78, 82, 86, 91, 94, 153, 193, 224, 231
canoes, 7, 8, 10, 11, 121, 167
Cantonments Road, 197
Cantonments Street, xxvii

Cape Coast Castle, 83, 91, 92, 238, 288
Caribbean, 11, 42, 45, 53, 55, 60, 62, 70, 73, 83, 86, 87, 99, 100, 105, 107, 111, 112, 119, 121, 124, 136, 138, 141, 142, 156, 170, 171–72, 183, 226, 228
Carstensen, Edward, xxxvi, 82, 83, 86–87, 89, 91, 106, 260, 291
Cassare, 35, 50
Castle School, 14, 55, 56, 57, 58, 59, 62, 103, 111, 158, 200, 204, 229, 231, 273, 275
catechism, 58, 157
Centre for African Art 296
chaplains, 14, 54, 111, 125, 136, 152, 154, 164, 168, 214
chiefdoms, 235, 246
chieftaincy, 83, 98, 185, 205
Christaller, J. G., 112–13
Christiansborg xxxiv, 3, 11, 12, 13, 14, 15–16, 19, 21, 28, 50, 69, 70, 71, 83–84, 98, 99, 118, 120, 121, 126, 129, 130–33, 135, 136, 141, 147, 155, 156, 185, 189, 192, 195, 200, 207, 211, 212, 226, 227, 242, 257, 275, 292, 299;
 cannons, 74, 78;
 castle, xxxiii, 9, 46, *46,* 47, 102, 112, 114, 119, 120, 151, 152, 235;
 chapel, 128, 153;
 cistern, 270;
 clothing trade, 102;
 coming of Christiansborg to Osu, 37–42;
 Danes, xxviii, xxxvi, 3, 12, 14, 15–16,19, 21, 48, *49,* 50, 68, 69, 72–73, 78–81, 82, 84–87, 89, 90–94, 96–97, 101, 102, 106, 107, 118, 123, 124–25, 126, 128, 131, 132, 147, 153,157–59, 181, 182–83, 196, 200, 258, 260, 274, 288, 291;
 dungeons xxxv, 10, 72, 73, 74, 110;
 emergence of a cosmopolitan community, 99–114;
 gardens, 264;
 governors, 53, 106, 127, 182, 198, 210;
 Governor's parlour, *49;*
 mortgage, 53;
 School, 109, 111, 124, 125, 163, 168, 204, 205, 229, 231, 236, 273;
 Secret Council, 182;
 settling down, 163–72;
 in the shadow of, 53–63, 68;
 slave trade, 103, 104, 123, 128, 129, 166, 198–99;
 sold, 79, 82, 91, 107;
 walls, 48, 49, 73, 109, 165

Christiansborg (ship), 161
Christiansdatter, Dorothea, 62
Christianshaven, 88
Christian V, 3, 12, 46
circumcision, 27, 78, 94
cisterns, *15*, 44, 45, 100, 170, 183, 211, 257, 258, 263, 265, 266, 270
citadels, 44, 46, 89, 100, 128
clanships, xxxv, 19, 54, 177, 183, 184, 185, 201, 204, 215
Clarke, A., *209*
Clelands, xxxv
Clerk, C. H., 274
Clerk, George, 277
Clerk, N. T., 277
Clerks, xxxv
Coleman, Mary, *209*
Colemans, xxxv, 215
Colonial Secretary, 195
Columbia, *326*
Commey, J. Oliver, 237
Community-Heroes Day, 222, 223, 226, 227, 236, 240, 252, 253, 254, 257, 272
concubines, 52, 77, 90, 91, 219
conflicts, 18, 34, 38, 69, 71, 81, 145, 229, 251
Congo, 261
Convention Peoples' Party, 253, 277
converts, 69, 97, 232, 273
Copenhagen, 44, 45, 62, 69, 83, 88, 134, 137, 138, 140, 147, 150, 158, 160, 161, 165, 228, 281
Cornelissen, Christen, 44
courts, 40, 41, 42, 77, 85, 109, 123, 137, 188, 229
Cramer, Jost, 41, 42, 43–44
custodianship, 40, 62

D

Dadebu, xxxiv
Dadewe, xxxiv
Dahomey, 23
Daily watchwords, 139–40
Dakar, 277
Dako, Chief, 18
Dako, Kari, xxiv, 18
Danes, xviii, xxvii, xxxii, xxxiii, xxxvi, 6, 10, 14, 22, 24, 25, 29, 35, 38–47, 51, 52, 56, 57, 62, 70, 71, 75, 77, 83, 98, 99, 103, 108, 120, 164, 165, 171, 188, 205, 212, 223, 224, 227, 252, 292, 293, 293;
Christiansborg, xxviii, xxxvi, 3, 12, 14, 15–16, 19, 21, 48, 49, 50, 68, 69, 72–73, 78–81, 82, 84–87, 89, 90–94, 96–97, 101, 102, 106, 107, 118, 123, 124–25, 126, 128, 131, 132, 147, 153, 157–59, 181, 182–83, 196, 200, 258, 260, 274, 288, 291
Danes-Norwegians, xxviii, 3, 10, 12, 14, 35, 38, 39, 40–41, 45, 48, 53, 68
Dangme, 4, 5, 6, 20, 21, 24
Dangmeland, 5
Danish-Osu: emergence of cosmopolitan community 99–114;
family trees 175–218;
high tides, 67–114;
low tide 97–99;
turbulence, turmoil and travails at high tide, 81–97
d'Azambuja, Don Diego, 25
Dedei, Aafio/Awofio, 29, 135, 136
Den Blofo, 16
Denkyeras, 69, 287
Denmark, xxviii, 3, 12, 29, 43–44, 45, 46, 48, 50, 54, 58, 60, 70, 72, 86, 90, 92, 103, 105, 106, 107, 109, 111, 121, 123, 125, 126, 127, 128, 132, 134, 136, 138, 140, 156, 157, 161, 163, 166, 170, 183, 205, 210, 227, 228, 258, 259, 268, 269, 291–93;
King of, 62, 69, 87, 140–41. *See also* Christianshaven; Copenhagen
Densu River, 152
Diaspora, 114, 227, 295
Dictorle, 89
Djagble (Jamenie), 53, 80
Djamlodja We, 25, 35
Djan, Ohene, 243
DNA, 213
Dodowah, 89, 212
Dodu, E. Max, 274, 277
Doku, xviii, xxxiv; becomes Kinkawe and Ashinte, 17–23
Doku, Noete, 4, 17, 53
Dokua (queen), 211
Dokutso, 90
domestic slavery, 73, 264
Dorph, Christian, 127
Dowouna, Modjaben, 277
Dowouna, Noi, 229, 230
Dresden, 223
drums, 26, 85, 86, 88, 123, 167, 232, 245–46
Dubois, W. E. B., 114
Duchess of Kent, 234
dungeons 45, 53, 57;
Christiansborg, xxxv, 10, 11, 14, 59, 72–73, 74, 86, 110, 121, 257
Dutch Accra, 16, 18, 19, 21, 71, 77, 165, 168, 198
Dwaben, 90
Dzake, Peki, 198
Dzani, Lily Kuorkor, *191*

E

earthquakes, 266, 282
Easmon, Charles (Charlie) Odamtten, 236–37, 277
Easmon, Victor Farrell, 236
Ebenezer Presbyterian Church, 231, 274
Edumegya, 28
elitism, 197
Elmina, 7, 27, 147, *326,* 305;
    Castle, 34, 141
Empire Day, 195
emporiums, 45, 46, 69
enclaves, xxxiii, xxxiv, xxxv, 8, 273, 275
English language, xxvi, 70, 231
Engmann, Ann, *187*
Engmann, Anna, *187*
Engmann, Augustus, *186*
Engmann, Augustus, II, *187*
Engmann, Carl, II, *186*
Engmann, Carl Gustav, 14–15, 15, 44, 163, 182–83, 185, *186*
Engmann, Caroline, *186, 187*
Engmann, Charles, *186, 187*
Engmann, Christian, *186, 187*
Engmann, Christiana, *186*
Engmann, Cynthia, *187*
Engmann, E. Augustus Wilkens, 185
Engmann, Edward, *186, 187*
Engmann, Edwin Oko, *186*
Engmann, Emmanuel, *187*
Engmann, Erich, 163, 183, *186*
Engmann, Erick, *186, 187*
Engmann, Eva, *187*
Engmann, Fred, *186, 187*
Engmann, Fredrick, *186, 187*
Engmann, Frederick Nii-Lomote, 185
Engmann, Friederich, 163, 183
Engmann, Gabriel Nii-Lomole, *186*
Engmann, George, *186*
Engmann, Gladys Naakai, *186*
Engmann, Gustav, 188
Engmann, Jeremias, 185, *186, 187,* 208
Engmann, Jeremias Carl, *186*
Engmann, Jonas, *186, 187*
Engmann, Kate, *186, 187*
Engmann, Kipans, *187*
Engmann, Lomotetteh, *186*
Engmann, Mary Ann, *186, 187*
Engmann, Naa Lomole, *186*
Engmann, Nii Lomole, *186*
Engmann, Patience, *187*
Engmann, Priscilla Naa Lomole, *186*
Engmann, Regina, *187*
Engmann, Sarah, *187*
Engmann, Sophia, *187*
Engmann, Theodosia, *187*
Engmann, Virginia Akweley, 186
Engmann, Wilken, *187*
Engmann, Wilkings Mensah, *186*
Engmann, Yorgen, 185, *187*
Engmanns, 182–87, *186–87*
Equatorial Guinea, 113
Eskimos, *144*
Europeans, iii, xxxii, xxxv, 3, 4, 6, 8, 10, 11, 12, 14, 16, 17, 24, 25, 34, 35, 36, 37, 39, 46, 47, *49,* 55, 56, 58, 71,75, 77, 78, 79, 86, 100, 107, 108, 109, 119, 126, 137, 157, 182, 212, 229, 293
Evans-Anfom, Emmanuel, 248, 277
Ewes, 25, 26, 27, 29, 109, 260
Ewusia, 298
Expatriate Quarters, xxxv
expeditions, 4, 153, 159, 201

F

family trees 175–218
Fanteland, 24, 38, 207–8
Fante(s), xxxiv, xxxv, 7, 8–10, 24, 25, 69;
    Chiefs 83;
    confederation, 288;
    language, 141;
    migrants, 303;
    religion, 157
Festival of Homowo, 95
Fetreke (king), 98, 99
fishing, xxxiv, 7–9, 75, 151
Fleischer, Nii Gbobilor, 278
Fleischer Lane, 117
Fleischers, 52, 70, 119, 127, 206, 258
Flindt, Governor, 82, 89, 107
Forkoyi, Ataa, iii, xvii, xviii, xxvii–xxviii, xxi–xxxvi, 3–12, 14–29, 33–63, 67–70, 72–87, 89–103, 105–11, 113–14, 117–27, 129–36, 138–40, 142–43, 145, 147, 149, 151–52, 154–57, 159–63, 165–72, 176–85, 188–89, 192–94, 196–97, 199–201, 205–7, 210, 212–13, 215–17, 221–24, 227–32, 234–35, 236, 238, 240, 242, 244, 246, 248–53, 257–61, 263–64, 266, 269–70, 272–77, 280–85, 291, 293
Fort Augustaborg, 125, 292
Fort Fredensborg, 92, 127, 132, 210, 292
Fort Prindzensten, 90
"Fredensborg," *13*
Fredensborg Slave Ship Project, 292–93
Frederick, Noi, 228, 229
Fredericksberg, xxxv, xxxvi, 89, 106
Fredericksgave, xxxiv, 90, 292
Fredericksknople, 105
Frederick V (king), 158
Frederick VI (king), 89
Frempong, 76

Freundlich, Martin, 166
Freundlich (Protten), Rebecca, 62, 142–43, *143*, 145, 147, 154, 156–57, 158, 159, 160–61, 162, 163, 164, 166, 167–68, 170, 171
Fry, Messr, 204
funerals, 67, 153, 154, 178, 179, 180, 181, 184, 185, 193, 194, 205, 215, 217, 246, 264

G

Gã, xvii, xxxv, 10, 17, 24, 28, 29, 41, 77, 85, 100, 110, 119, 121, 137, 180, 215, 223, 229, 235, 253;
    circumcision, 78;
    culture, 50, 54, 71, 78–79, 101, 103, 118, 162, 163, 181, 182, 199;
    language, xix, xxvii, 4, 5, 6, 9, 16, 21, 27, 33, 35–36, 57, 58, 70, 71, 79, 95, 97, 110, 113, 126, 128, 142, *144*, 145, 148, 152, 154, 157, 159, 164, 168, 177, 178, 184, 185, 197, 199, 204, 228, 230, 231, 232, 244, 252, 273, 276, 298;
    names, xxxiv; society, xvii, 78, 120;
    soldiers, 19
Gã-Adangme, 76, 83, 84, 97, 110, 212, 275. *See also* Gã-Dangme
Gã-Dangme, 7, 78, 95, 244, 274
Gã-Portuguese lingua france, 37
Gakk, Sanyek, 166
Gã-Mashie, xviii, 7, 16, 18, 27, 36, 38, 39, 40, 41, 42, 43, 76, 77, 82, 86, 92, 93, 111, 137, 182, 198, 200, 261;
    James Fort, 16, 91, 288
Garrison Church, 137
GBC. *See* Ghana Broadcasting House
Gbonyo Party, 179
Ghana, xvii, xx, xxxiv, 33–34, 182, 183, 216, 236, 275, 277–78, 292, 293, 298;
    agriculture, 113;
    Armed Forces, 240;
    Army, 239, 241, 243;
    boarding schools, 274;
    British rule, 114;
    Christian Church, xviii;
    economics, 245;
    fabrics, 226;
    football, 204, 205;
    Golden Jubilee of National Independence, xxvi, xxvii–xxviii;
    history, 7, 185, 231, 291;
    language, 252;
    medicine, 236–37, 238, 247, 249;
    National Archives, xxv;
    Parliamentary Institution, 233;
    population, 245;
    Presbyterian Church, xix, 185, 204, 214;
    school buildings, 281; slavery, 293
Ghanaba, Kofi, 197
Ghana Broadcasting House (GBC), 240, 241
Ghana Cultural Fund, 294, 295
Ghana Postal Service, 238
Ghana Post and Communication Training School, 239
Ghanaian Public Works Department, 185
Ghana Medical School, 237
Gold Coast, xix, 112, 228, 231–34, 291, 292;
    agriculture, 194;
    British Protectorate, 83, 231;
    ceremonial occasions, 195;
    development, 113;
    European forts, *64*;
    historical chart, *326–7*;
    name change from Guinea Coast, 93, 112;
    politics, 197
Gottesacker, *143*, 148, 157, 166
Great Assembly Hall, 157
Greats of the community, 252, 253
Gross Hennersdorf, 145, 147, 149, *150*, 156
Guggisberg, Gordon, 113

H

Hackenburg, August Frederich, 127, 153
Hagerup, Chaplain, 62
Hallestad, Nik, *218*
Hansen, David, Animle, 277
Hansen, Thorkild, xvii;
    Coast of Slaves, xviii, xxiv;
    Islands of Slaves, xviii;
    Ships of Slaves, xviii
Hansen-Norteys, xxxv
Hansens, xxxiv, 52, 70, 96, 119, 206;
    Anahor, 258
"Happy Corner," 253
harmattan, 5, 63, 175–76, 251
Hein, Amalie Wilhelmine Nicholine, 207, 208, 210–11
Heins, 206
Herrn, David, 55
Heroes Day, 222, 223, 226, 227, 236, 240, 252, 253, 254, 257, 272
Herrnhut, 138, 139, 140, 141, 142, *143*, 143, 145, 147, 149, *149*, *150*, 151, 155, 156, 157, 158, 160, 161–62, 164–65, 166, 167, 170, 295, 296
Hesse, Adeline Christian, *208*, 209
Hesses, xxxiv, 70, 206, 215, 258
HMS Scourge, 96
Hofman, Peder, 80
Holm, Adzei, 253
Holm, Mina, 253
Holms, 52, 96
Holmes, xxxiv, xxxv
Holt, John, 204

Homowo festival, 79, 95, 153, 178, 215, 221, 264, 266
Huckoff, Heinrich, 141, 159, 160, 163

I

International Planned Parenthood Federation, 247
Isert, Paul Erdman, 103, 104, 105, 108

J

Jamaica, 169, 170, 243
James Fort, 16, 91, 288
Jantuah, 74
Jenssen, Christian, 151
Jessen, Anna-Sophia, 155
Jessen, Governor, 153–54, 155
Jesus Christ, xxxv, 98, 107, 110, 111, 128, 138, 139, 140, 141, 152, 156, 157, 162, 164, 169, 171, 204, 214, 217, 228, 276
Johnson, Anyeley, *209*
Johnson, Catherine (Kate), *209*
Johnson, Edward Adjei Mensah, *209*
Johnson, George Lawrence Richter, *209*
Johnson, John Peter, *209*
Joint Theological College, 214
Joseph Project, xxvi, 295, 298
Juergensen, Governor, 127, 128, 132, 133

K

Kadi, xviii, 4–5, 17
Kadigbɔi, 3–30
Kadi Gbɔi, 99, 100
Karslieh, 12
Kasky, *207, 208*
Katamanso war, 82, 211
Keta, 25, 90, 92, 153, 192, 287
King Addo Dankwa, 211
King Adum, 84
King Akonnor, 77, 80
King Ashangmor, 27
Kingdom Bookshop, xxiv
King Fetreke, 98, 99
King Frederick V, 158
King Frederick VI, 89
King Odoi Atsem, 4, 39, 40
King Okai Koi, 39–40, 41, 42, 43
King Okpoti, 153
King Teinor, 21
Kinkawe, xviii, xxvii, xxxiv, 6, 16, 24, 25, 26, 47, 68, 84, 85, 86, 91, 96, 98, 99, 123, 129, 179, 182, 183, 184, 188, 192, 193, 205, 224, 227, 228, 230, 231, 232, 244, 248;
    Mantse, 229;
    Osu-Doku becomes Kinkawe and Ashinte, 17–23;
    Royal house, 109;
    Ruling House, 128
Kioge, J. A. 103, 108
Kleffel, Sigmund, 166
Klottey Lagoon, xviii, xxviii, xxxi, xxxiii, 6–8, 20, 23, 34, 37, 54, 84, 170
Klufio, Edward, *190*
Klufio, Enoch Joseph, *190;*
    Adote Shelenkome, 197;
    Odoi Din, Legon Mantse, 197
Klufios, 197
Klyn, 127
Koi, Okai (king), 39–40, 41, 42, 43
Korletey, 6, 7
Korley, 7
Korle-Bu Hospital, 237, 238
Kotey, Felicia Kutorkor, *191*
Kpeshi, 4, 5, 17, 20, 40, 170
Kple, 20
Kpone, 82
Kponkpo, 90
Kreppe land, 108–9
Krobo, xxxv, 72, 197
'Kronprinsens Oenske,' 134
Kuehberg, Anna Barbara, 207, *208*
Kuehberg, Frantz, 205–6
Kuehberg, Helena, 133
Kuehberg, Lene, 101–2, 205, 206, 207
Kuku Hill, xxxv, xxxvi, 89, 92, 106, 286
Kumasi, xxiv, 82, 113, 149, 257, 278, 295
Kumasi College of Technology, 214, 239
Kushi, Ayi, *326-7*
Kwame Nkrumah University, vii, xxiv, 214, 238, 277, 278
Kweifio-Okai, 'Chez Julie,' 253

L

La, xviii, xxxiii, xxxiv, 82, 129, 153, 197
La Abese, 200
La Anahor, 29, 113
Labadey, 4, 5, 20, 24, 28–29, 45, 77, 94, 95, 96, 126;
    King, 39, 40
Labadeye, 12, 17, 18, 25, 36
La Kpa, 28
La Mantse/ɛ, 153
Larsens, 53, 70, 96, 215
Lathbridges, xxxv
Lee, J. R., 114
Legislative Council, 233, 277
Legon, 90, 237, 248, 278
Legon Mantse, 197
Lemke, Daniel, 166
Linekensdorf, Miss, 102
Listowel, Lord, 114
Little Popo, 27, 137. *See also* Anecho
Lochau, Christian, 129–30
Loesungen, 139–40

Lokko, Betty, 236
Lokko, B. Kwapong, 274
Lokko, Patience, *186*
Lokko Road, 117
Lokko(s), xxxv, 53, 118, 182, 199
Lomotey, Catherine Nmai, *191*
Lord's Prayer, 58, 145, *148,* 163
Luecke, Hans, 53
Lutterodt Loop, 117
Lutterodts, xxxiv, 52, 70, 206
Lutterodt, Messr, 89
Lygaard, Erich, 100
Lykke, Hans, 53, 80
Lykkes, 118, 199

M

Maale, Nii, 153
Maclean, Governor, 211, *326*
Magnusen, Friedrich, 154, 155
Magnussen, 53
Malm, Abraham, 189, *190,* 192
Malm, Andreas, 192
Malm, Andrew, *190, 191,* 192
Malm, Andrews, *191*
Malm, Betty, *190,* 192, 197
Malm, Catherine, *191*
Malm, Cornelius, *191*, 194, 197, 274
Malm, Diana, *191*
Malm, Elizabeth, *190*
Malm, Elizabeth Virginia, *191*
Malm, Esther Kweiki, *191*
Malm, Eva Barbara, *191,* 197
Malm, Felicia, *191*
Malm, Henry, *190*
Malm, Henry Herbert, *191,* 194, 195, 195, 196, 197, 198, 277
Malm, Henry Herbert Papa Nii, *191*
Malm, Joana Zonia, *191*
Malm, Johannes Benedict, 189, *190,* 192
Malm, Jonas, *190, 191*
Malm, Kweikor, *191*
Malm, Mary, *190*
Malm, Meyer, *191*
Malm, Richard Otto, *191,* 194
Malm, Riemer, 191
Malm, Sarah, 189, *190, 191,* 192
Malm, Sophia, *190, 191*
Malm, Vincent, *191,* 198
Malm, William, *191*
Malms, 52, 96, 182, 185, 188–89, *190–91,* 192, 193–94, 196, 197, 198
Mampong, 113
Mampong, Akwapim, 113
Mandela Park, 223, 226
Mantse/ɛ, 23, 79, 153, 165, 168, 171, 226, 230, 232, 234, 240;
    Fetreke, 231;

Kinkawe, 229
Margretha II (queen), 295
Marienborn, 141, 142, 159
Martey, Cynthia, 204
Mate-Kodjo, Rev., 274
Mat of the Tenth, 252–53
Meder, Jacob, 166
Meyer, Peter, 188
Meyer, Sophia, *191,* 192
Meyers, 53, 70, 89, 182
Moellers, Charlotte, 62
Monrad, H. C. 108–9
Moravian Archives, 139, 142, 145, *150,* 295, 296
Moravian Brethren, 138, 140, 142, *146, 148,* 151, 162, 167, 169–70, 171, 228, 295, 296 AU: pp. 167, 171, 228
Moravian cemetery, 143, *143,* 157
Moravian Christians, 169
Moravian Church, 170
Moravian missionaries, 141–42, *144,* 145, 159, 161, 166, 171
Moravians, 141–43, 147, 152, 153, 154, 158–71, 228
Moravian Watchword, 161
Morch, F. S., 212–13
Moree, 7–8
mulattoes, xxxiii, 10, 29, 49, 52, 53, 57, 62, 68, 89, 92, 97, 132, 152, 180, 181, 199, 205, 231, 292;
    agents, 85;
    children, 54, 55, 56, 58, 59, 60, 89, 94, 111, 118, 119, 121, 122, 127, 136, 141, 147, 158, 162, 165, 169, 258, 273, 284;
    employees, 104;
    families, 96;
    fatherless, 55;
    girls, 56;
    merchants, 107;
    offspring, 94, 119–20, 122;
    pupils, 109, 111;
    relatives, 58, 109;
    school, 59;
    school children, 61, 151;
    soldiers, 86, 192;
    women, 101, 102, 103, 119, 153, 169, 205;
    youth, 54. *See also* Poor Mulatto Children's Chest

N

Nadu, 4
naming, xviii, xxxiv, xxxv, 3–4, 5–6, 7, 8, 12, 15, 16, 17, 18, 19, 20, 21, 22, 23, 24, 25–26, 28, 29, 34–35, 42, 50, 51, 52–53, 58, 59, 62, 73, 89, 90, 103–4, 106, 107, 111, 112, 117, 118–19, 121–22, 124, 125,

126, 127, 128, 135, 137, 138, 142, 177, 179, 180, 182, 183, 184, 189, 192, 196, 197, 198, 199–200, 204, 207, 215, 216, 229, 232, 235, 249, 251, 261, 277
Nartey, 71
National Central Organisation of Sport, 243
Negro-Portuguese, 35
New World, xxvii, 11 AU: p. 11: Add caps
Ngleshi Blofo, 16
Ŋoo Wala, 221, 254
Niagara Falls, 222
Nii Adza Tetteh Quarshie, 113
Nii Okantey Shikatse We, 243, 259, 261, *262, 265, 267, 268, 270,* 272
Ningo, 45, 92, 127, 128, 132, 153, 192
Nissen, Miss, 102
Nkrumah, Kwame, 114, 237, 243, 253
Nkulenu, Esther, *191,* 198
Nkulenu Food Industries, 114, 197
Noble Chartered Danish African Company, 42, 45–46
Noete Doku, 4, 17, 53
Nougodo, 26
Nsawam, 248
Nungua, 82
Nsawam, 248
Nyarko, Edmund, 296
Nyɔŋmɔ, Ataa Naa, 41, 43
Nyonmo, Obodai, 28–29

O

Ocansey, A. J., 197
Ocloo, Esther, 114, 197–98
Odartey-Wellington, Neville Alexander, 238, 240, 242
Odjidja, Philipa A., 249
Odjono, Naa Odoley, 200, *202, 203*
Odoi Atsem (king), 4, 39, 40
Odoley, Naa, 201
Odonkor, Josephine Dedei, 253
Odumase, Krobo, 197
Ogadjo, Ayi, 202
Ogbaame Naa, xviii, xxxiii
Okantey, Michael Francis, 243
Okantey-Ayettey, Beatrice Adubea, *191*
Okarsto (Ogadjo), Ayi, *202*
Okpoti (king), 153
Omaboe, Emmanuel Noi, 244, 245
Omaboe, Peter Nortey, 244
Osagyefo, 114, 237, 243
Osu: settlement, xviii, 3–30
Osu-Cantonments Road, 197
Osu Castle, xxxi, xxxii, 106, 135, 235
Osudoku, 5, 6, 16, 24, 50;
    becomes Kinkawe and Ashinte, 17–23
Osu Kadigbɔi, 3–17
Otumfuor Nana Asantehene Prempeh II, 235

P

Palm, Kate Awura Akua, *186*
Palms, 52, 182
PANAFEST/Emancipation/Joseph Project, xxvi, 298
Papao, 74, 229
Pedersen, Cornelius, 133
Pedersen, Christian Friederich, 136, 137
Pedersen, Frederick, 59, 61, 62, 118, 125. *See also* Svane, Christian Friederich
Pedersen, Hendrik, 125
Pedersens, 52
Perigino-Peters, George J., 197
Petersen, Cornelius, 124
Petersens, 119, 124
PMCC. *See* 'Poor Mulatto Children's Chest'
Po, Fernando, 113
'Poor Mulatto Children's Chest' (PMCC) 56–57
Portuguese lingua franca 33–63, 71, 84, 119, 120;
    coming of Christiansborg to Osu, 37–42;
    shadow of Christiansborg, 53–63;
    tarnishing of Osu with Danish markings, 42–53
Power of Adansi, 287
Prempeh, Otumfuor Nana Asantehene, II, 235, 288
Presbyterian Boys' Boarding School, 272, 274; Assembly Hall, 248
Presbyterian Boys' Day School, 239, 243, 247
Presbyterian Church Education Unit, 55
Presbyterian Church of Ghana, xix, 185, 204, 214, 277
Presbyterian Hymn Book, 253
Presbyterianism, 215, 244. 284. *See also* Ebenezer Presbyterian Church
Presbyterian Junior School, 244
Presbyterian Primary School, 234
Presbyterian Secondary School, 185, 197
Presbyterian Senior School, 244
Protten, Anna, 59, *148,* 157
Protten, Christian Jakobus Africanus, 29, 58, 59, 62, 122, 124, 125, 134–47, *148, 149, 150,* 151, 152, 153–54, 155–72, 183, 198, 205, 228, 295;
    'Protten's Diarium,' 149, 295. *See also* Protten, Uldrich
Protten, Jacob, 59, 61, 135, 137
Protten (Freundlich), Rebecca, 62, 142–43, 143, 145, 147, 154, 156–57, 158, 159, 160–61, 162, 163, 164, 166, 167–68, 170, 171
Protten, Uldrich, 59, 135. *See also* Protten, Christian Jakobus Africanus
Protten, Wilhelm Frederick, 59, 61, 136
Provesten, xxxiv, 16, 19;
    Watchtower, 60, 86, 91, 94, 109, 257, 273

Q

Quakye, B., 76
Quarshie, Nii Adza Tetteh, 113
Quaynor, Cynthia, 204
Quaynor, Eva Vida Narki, *191*
Quaynor, Kweki, *190, 191,* 192
Queen Dokua, 211
Queen Margretha II Fund, 295
Quist, Charles Emmanuel, 232, 233, 234, 277
Quist, Christian, 110, 278
Quist, Esau Christensen, 153, 236
Quist, Jacob, 163
Quist, Johann, 163
Quist, Karl, *208*
Quists, xxxiv, 52, 72, 96, 182, 194, 206, 215, 258

R

Rask, Rasmus, xix, 228
Rastafarian, 97, 102, 107–8, 109, 119, 120, 126, 129, 133, 135, 142, 152, 155, 159, 160, 166, 169, 170, 180, 189, 192, 210, 217
Rawlings, J. J., 114
Reimers, 52
Reindorf, Carl Christian, xix, 110, 231–33, 273, 274;
    History of the Gold Coast and Ashanti, 232
Reindorf, C. E., 233, 277
Reindorfs, 52, 72, 127
Reinholdts, xxxv
Resch, Governor, 62
Rheinholdts, 52
Richter, Adeline, *209*
Richter, Anna Barbara, 207
Richter, Benedicta, *209*
Richter, Christian, 207, *208, 209*
Richter, Ernest, *209,* 214
Richter, Eva, *208, 209,* 215
Richter, Gilbert, *209,* 214
Richter, Gladys, *209*
Richter, Henrich, 207, *208,* 210, 211–12, 213, 216, 260
Richter, Henrich, II, 207, *208*
Richter, Henry, *209*
Richter, Henry Austin, 216
Richter, Herbert, *209*
Richter, Irene, *209*
Richter, Johann, *209,* 210
Richter, Johann Emmanuel, 24–25, 206, 206, 207, *208,* 213, 260
Richter, Johann Emmanuel, II, 207, *208,* 213
Richter, Julius, *209*
Richter, Lawrence, *208, 209*
Richter, Lawrence Ludwig, *208, 209,* 213, 214
Richter, Ludwig Lawrence, *209,* 213, 214, 215, 277
Richter, Ludwig Lawrence, II, *209*
Richter, Ludwig (Red), *209*
Richter, Mary, *209*
Richter, Messr, 89, 90
Richter, Paulina, *208, 209*
Richter, Philip, *209*
Richter, Philip Christian, *209,* 214, 216, 274
Richter, Regina, *208, 209*
Richter, Robert, 207
Richter, Robert, Wilhelm, 207, *208*
Richter, Sophia, *209*
Richter, Vincent, *209,* 214, 216, 277
Richter, Wilhemina, *208, 209*
Richter, William, *209*
Richter, William Albert, 214, 216
Richter Fort, 212, *212,* 216, *217,* 258, 266–67
Richter Road, 117
Richters, xxxiv, xxxv, 52, 70, 96, 106, 201, 205– 17, *208*–9, 236
Riemers, xxxiv, xxxv, 96, 119, 182
Roemer, Ferdinand, 153
Roemers, 119, 127
Rottmann, H. C. 110
Rottmann, Hermann L., 112
Royal Danish Africa Company, 125, 130, 136, 166
Royal Danish Embassy, 294, 295
Royal Military Academy, 239
Ruhberg, Governor, 165

S

Sai, 29
Sai, Frederick Torgbor, 246–47, 248, 249, 277
Saki, Teiko, 29, 137
Salem, xviii, xxxv, 237, 247, 257, 258, *271,* 272
Salem Boys' Boarding School, 194, 214, 233, 236, 238, 247, 272–73, 274–77, *279, 280,* 281, 282
Salem Old Boys' Association, 250, *271*
Salem Road, 117
Salem School, 248;
    Assembly Hall, 247;
    Honour List, 247
Salem Street, 272, 285
Sandhurst, 239, 240
Santse, 98, 229–230
Schandorfs, 52, 70, 206
Schiedlerup, Governor, 126
Schonnings, 89
Schultze, Gottfried, 166
Sei Asafoatse, 200
Sekyi, Kobina, 197; The Blinkards, 196
Sensbach, Jon: Rebecca's Revival, 171
Sesemi, 90, 92
Shakespeare, William: As You Like It, xxvii
Shama, 7

Shelenkome, Adote, 197
Shormeh, 188
silk, 102, 223, 224, 228
slave market, 68, 74, 76, 260, 298
SMC. *See* Supreme Military Council
Sodring, Miss, 102
Sodza, 29, 131, 181–82
Songme Naa, xxxiii, 84, 101-2, 226, 247, 300
Sonne, Ann, 186
Sonne, Joergen, 153, 181, 182
Sonne Close, 117
Sonne-Engmann, 184
Sonnes, xxxiv, 52, 96, 119, 181, 182
Sorterup, 125–26, 137
Steffens, Governor, 106
Steiner, Clara, *209*
St. Croix, 45, 55, 62
St. Francis Xavier, 34
St. Thomas, 45, 55, 62, 171
Suhm, H. V. 60, 123, 136
Supreme Military Council (SMC), 239, 240, 241
Svane, Elias, 55, 56, 58, 59, 60, 61, 62, 108, 125–26, 127, 128, 129, 130–31, 132–33, 134, 136–37
Svane, Frederik Petersen, 122, 124–35, 137, 155. See also Pedersen, Frederick
Svanekjaer, 53, 106, 199
Swaniker, Adeline, *209*
Swanikers, 199
Swedes, xviii, xxxii, 6, 12, 37–39, 69, 299

T

Tagoe-Darko, Dedei, xxiv
Takoradi Harbour, 113
Tamarindus Indica, 90
Taylor, Theodore, 234
Teiko Sacki, Blofonyo Bi, 135, 142, *146*, 168
Teinor (king), 21
Telfers, xxxv
Tema, 82
Teshie, 82, 92, 94, 113, 125, 126, 133; House, *203;* Military Academy, 239
Tetteh, Kweimonie Nerquaye, 297
Thionning, Governor, 106
Tilleman, Erich, 80
Tokori, Adum, 83, 84, 86
Tolon, xviii, xxxiii
Tolon, Naa, 90, 210
Tolon Mɔɔ, 211
Touchstone, xxxiv, 16
transatlantic slave trade, *ii,* xviii, xxiv, xx vii, xxviii, xxxiii, 46, 69, 70, 83, 87, 100, 103, 104, 106, 108, 129, 140, 172, 184, 216, 226, 227, 261, 284, 291, 293, 295
Trebi-Ollennu, Flora, iii, xxiii

Trounischek, Jessie, *209*
Truelsen, Birthe, 260
Truelsen, Caroline, 260
Truelsen, Charlotte, 260
Truelsen, Hans Christian, 89, 260
Truelsen, Johanne, 260
Truelsens, 89
Tsuro/u, Naa Tsua, 198, 200, *202*
Tunma Ayi, 19, 21
Twi, 37, 84, 112

U

Underground Railroad, xxviii, 222
UNESCO-Accra Cluster Offices, 295
Union Jack, 111, 114
United Nations, 34, 247, 277
University Bookshop, xxiv
University of Copenhagen, 62, 125, 137, 154
University of Ghana Medical School, 249

V

Volta River, 5, 23, 27, 36, 39, 109, 260, 287, 307
von, Richelieu, Governor, 106, 107

W

Wallace-Johnson, I. T. A. 197
Warren, Guy, 197
We, Nii Tetteh, 258
We, Okaileytse, 261
We, Sanshi, 231
Weiss, Jonas, 160, 274
Wellington, Archibald Mensah, 238
Wellington, H. Nii-Adziri, xxviii, 278, 297
Wellington, Nii-Lante, 297
Wert, Jakob Wilhelm, 113
West Indies, 100
Wikstrand, Miss, 102
Wilkens, Governor, xxxvi, 89, 106
Wilson, John, *208*
Winsnes, Selena, xxv
Witt, Anna Sophia, 133, 143
Witt, Christian Petersen, xxviii, 122–24, 125, 133, 189
Wolenyo, Kojo, 200, 202
woye buei, 259, 284
Wrisberg, Johan P. D., 89, 106, 227
Wrisbergs, 106
Wulff, Frantz, *190*
Wulff, Joseph Wulff, 189, *190,* 192, 258, 259
Wulff, Sarah, 197
Wulff, Theodore, *190*
Wulff, Wilhemina, *190*
Wulff, Wilhelmine Josephine, 259
Wulff, W. J., 258–59
Wulffs, xxxiv, 52, 206
Wulomo, 78

Wutta-Offei, Robert Benjamin, 197
Wutta-Offeis, 197

X
X'Borg, 112, 114

Y
Yei Amii, 100

Z
Zeist, 159, 160, 228
Zimmerman, J. G., 230, 231, 273
Zimmerman, Johannes, xix, 97, 110
Zinzendorf, Ludwig Nicholas von, 138, 139, 140–41, 145, 148, 149, 155, 157, 160, 162, 166, 171

Year	World Events	Gold Coast Events	
1950	War of 1939	1946 constitution	
		Ashanti confederacy restored	
	War of 1914	Achimota College founded	
	Aeroplane invented		
1900	Motor-cars invented		
	Bicycles invented		
	Suez Canal made	Battle of Datsutagba	
		Battle of Gyadam	
1850	Darwin		
	Telegraph invented		
	Beethoven	Adinkera	
1800	Napoleon	Atta Wusu	
	French Revolution		
		Sagbadre war	
	War of American Independence		
		Gariba	
1750			
	Handel	Ofori Kuma	
	Bach	Akwamus driven across river Volta	
		Ofori Panyin	
		Kumpati	
1700			
		Zangina	
	Milton		
	Cromwell		
1650	Galileo		
		Power of Denkyera	
	First English in America	Building of Keta	
		Wenya	
1600		Fall of Songhai Empire	
	Queen Elizabeth	Ewurade Basa	
		Power of Adansi	
		Jakpa	
1550			
	Martin Luther		
	Henry VIII		
		Songhai conquers Melle	
1500	Columbia discovers America		
		Nyagsi	
		Moshis take Walata	
	Printing invented		
		Sonni Ali	

Figure 46: Historical Chart of the Gold Coast © 1955 W. E. Ward

		University College opened	1950
	Yaa Asantewa war	Lands Bill	1900
Prempeh			
		The Sagrenti War	
Kofi Karikari		Dutch leave the Coast	
Kwaku Dua I		Fante Confederation	
		Poll Tax Ordinance	1850
		British buy Danish forts: Danes go	
Battle of Akatamasu		Bond of 1844 - Maclean	
Battle of Nsamankow		Freeman Basel Mission	
		MacCarthy	
		Rowdich and Dupuis	
Osei Bonsu – First Ashanti war - Torrane			1800
		Danes build Fort Prinzenstein	
		Kotoku-Twerebo war	
Wetshe Kodso		Phillip Quacoe	
Osei Kojo			
Teiko Tsuru			1750
Okaidja			
Ahantan war			
Opoku Ware			
Osei Tutu			
Okomfo Anokye		Asameni at Christiansborg	1700
		English build James Fort, Accra	
Ashangmo		English take Cape Coast	
Obiri Yeboa		Danes take Christiansborg	
Okai Koi			
			1650
Twum and Antwi			
Dede Akai		Dutch take Elmina	
		First Dutch attack on Elmina	
Owura Mankpon Okai?			1600
		First English voyage to Gold Coast	1550
Ayi Kushi?			1500
		Portuguese build Elmina	

H. Nii-Adziri Wellington, a professor emeritus of the Department of Architecture, Kwame Nkrumah University of Science and Technology, is a Fellow of the Ghana Academy of Arts and Sciences and a cultural heritage activist.

As a scholar, he has published extensively in the disciplines of architecture, urban design, housing and cultural heritage. To date, he has to his credit over 100 published papers, journal articles, mimeographs, technical reports and exhibition brochures, including recent publications.

Since 2009, he has been on post-retirement contract in the Department of Archaeology and Heritage Studies, University of Ghana, where, as a part-time lecturer, he is currently teaching and researching in Heritage Issues and Monuments Conservation as well as Architecture in Autism.

Outside of academic work, he is an avid Bible Teacher. Wellington is a happily married man with three adult children.

www.ingramcontent.com/pod-product-compliance
Ingram Content Group UK Ltd.
Pitfield, Milton Keynes, MK11 3LW, UK
UKHW021252180426
11946UKWH00004B/98